EARLY JEWISH WRITINGS

THE BIBLE AND WOMEN

An Encyclopaedia of Exegesis and Cultural History

Edited by Christiana de Groot, Irmtraud Fischer,
Mercedes Navarro Puerto, and Adriana Valerio

Volume 3.1: Early Jewish Writings

EARLY JEWISH WRITINGS

Edited by

Eileen Schuller and Marie-Theres Wacker

Atlanta

Library of Congress Cataloging-in-Publication Data

Names: Schuller, Eileen M., 1946- editor. | Wacker, Marie-Theres, editor.
Title: Early Jewish writings / edited by Eileen Schuller and Marie-Theres Wacker.
Description: Atlanta : SBL Press, [2017] | Series: The Bible and women
Number 3.1 | Includes bibliographical references and index. | Description based on print version record and CIP data provided by publisher; resource not viewed.
Identifiers: LCCN 2017019564 (print) | LCCN 2017020850 (ebook) | ISBN 9780884142324 (ebook) | ISBN 9781628371833 (pbk. : alk. paper) | ISBN 9780884142331 (hardcover : alk. paper)
Subjects: LCSH: Bible. Old Testament—Feminist criticism. | Women in the Bible. | Women in rabbinical literature.
Classification: LCC BS521.4 (ebook) | LCC BS521.4 .E27 2017 (print) | DDC 296.1082—dc23
LC record available at https://lccn.loc.gov/2017019564

Printed on acid-free paper.

Contents

Abbreviations

Primary Sources

1 En.	1 Enoch
1QS	Community Rule
1QSa	Rule of the Congregation
2 Bar.	2 Baruch
2 En.	2 Enoch
3 Bar.	3 Baruch
4QD	Cave 4 Damascus Document
A.J.	Josephus, *Antiquitates judicae*
Abr.	Philo, *On the Life of Abraham*
Abst.	Porphyry, *De abstinentia*
ALD	Aramaic Levi Document
Amat.	Plutarch, *Amatorius*
Ann.	Tacitus, *Annales*
Ant.	Josephus, *Jewish Antiquities*
Apoc. Ab.	Apocalypse of Abraham
Apoc. Sedr.	Apocalypse of Sedrach
Aug.	Suetonius, *Divus Augustus*
b.	Babylonian Talmud
Bib. hist.	Diodorus Siculus, *Bibliotheca historica*
C. Ap.	Josephus, *Contra Apion*
Cal.	Suetonius, *Gaius Caligula*
CD	Damascus Document
Cher.	Philo, *On the Cherubim*
Chr. Ps.-Zech. Rhet.	Chronicle of Pseudo-Zacharias Rhetor
Claud.	Suetonius, *Divus Claudius*
Cod. Theod.	Theodosian Code
Congr.	Philo, *On the Preliminary Studies*
Conj. praec.	Plutarch, *Coniugalia praecepta*

Contempl.	Philo, *On the Contemplative Life*
Decal.	Philo, *On the Decalogue*
Deipn.	Athenaeus, *Deipnosophistae*
Det.	Philo, *That the Worse Attacks the Better*
Deus	Philo, *That God Is Unchangeable*
Diatr.	Musonius Rufus, *Diatribai* (*Discourses*)
Ebr.	Philo, *On Drunkenness*
Ep.	*Epistle*
Ep.	Seneca, *Epistulae morales*
Eth. nic.	Aristotle, *Ethica nicomachea*
Exod. Rab.	Exodus Rabbah
Fin.	Cicero, *De finibus*
Flacc.	Philo, *In Flaccum*
Fug.	Philo, *On Flight and Finding*
G^a	Codex Panopolitanus
G^s	MS of Byzantine Chronographer Georgios Synkellos
Gen. Rab.	Genesis Rabbah
Geogr.	Strabo, *Geographica*
Gig.	Philo, *On Giants*
GLAE	Greek Life of Adam and Eve, or Apocalypse of Moses
Helv.	Seneca, *Ad Helviam*
Her.	Philo, *Who Is the Heir?*
Hist.	Herodotus, *Histories*
Hist.	Polybius, *Histories*
Hist. rom.	Dio Cassius, *Historiae romanae*
Hypoth.	Philo, *Hypothetica*
Id.	Theocritus, *Idylls*
Inst.	Quintilian, *Institutio oratoria*
Ios.	Philo, *De Iosepho*
Itin.	Egeria, *Itinerarium*
Jos. Asen.	Joseph and Aseneth
Jub.	Jubilees
J.W.	Josephus, *Jewish War*
LAB	Liber antiquitatum biblicarum
LAE	Life of Adam and Eve
Leg.	Philo, *Allegorical Interpretation*
Leg.	Plato, *Leges*
Legat.	Philo, *On the Embassy to Gaius*
Lives	Diogenes Laertius, *Lives of Eminent Philosophers*
LXX	Septuagint
Marc.	Seneca, *Ad Marciam de consolatione*

Marc.	Tertullian, *Adversus Marcionem*
Meg.	Megillah
Migr.	Philo, *On the Migration of Abraham*
Mor.	Plutarch, *Moralia*
Mos.	Philo, *De vita Mosis*
MT	Masoretic Text
Mulier. virt.	Plutarch, *Mulierum Virtutes*
Mut.	Philo, *On the Change of Names*
Nat. Hist.	Pliny, *Natural History*
Opif.	Philo, *On the Creation of the World*
Or.	Tertullian, *De oratione*
Praem.	Philo, *On Rewards and Punishments*
Praep. ev.	Eusebius, *Praeparatio evangelica*
Prot.	Plato, *Protagoras*
QG	Philo, *Questions and Answers on Genesis*
Qoh. Rab.	Qoheleth Rabbah
Rhet.	Aristotle, *Rhetorica*
Sacr.	Philo, *On the Sacrifices of Cain and Abel*
Sib. Or.	Sibylline Oracles
Sifre Num.	Sifre Numbers
Somn.	Philo, *On Dreams*
Sot.	Sotah
Spec.	Philo, *De specialibus legibus*
Symp.	Plato, *Symposium*
Syr. d.	Lucian, *De syria dea*
T. Reu.	Testament of Reuben
Tanh. Exod.	Tanhuma Exodus
Tib.	Seutonius, *Tiberius*
Virg.	Tertullian, *De virginibus velandis*
Virt.	Philo, *De virtutibus*
Vulg.	Vulgate

Secondary Sources

AAev	*Aedium Aevum*
AB	Anchor Bible
AcBib	Academia Biblica
ADPV	Abhandlungen des Deutschen Palästina-Vereins
AGJU	Arbeiten zur Geschichte des antiken Judentums und des Urchristentums
AIL	Ancient Israel and Its Literature

ALGHJ	Arbeiten zur Literatur und Geschichte des hellenistischen Judentums
ANRW	Temporini, Hildegard, and Wolfgang Haase, eds. *Aufstieg und Niedergang der römischen Welt: Geschichte und Kultur Roms im Spiegel der neueren Forschung*. Part 2, *Principat*. Berlin: de Gruyter, 1972–.
AOAT	Alter Orient und Altes Testament
ATANT	Abhandlungen zur Theologie des Alten und Neuen Testaments
ATID	Das Alt Testament im Dialog
BA	La Bible d'Alexandrie
BCAW	Blackwell Companion to the Ancient World
BEATAJ	Beiträge zur Erforschung des Alten Testaments und des antiken antiken Judentums
BETL	Bibliotheca Ephemeridum Theologicarum Lovaniensium
BGU	*Aegyptische Urkunden aus den Königlichen Staatlichen Museen zu Berlin, Griechische Urkunden*. 15 vols. Berlin: Weidmann, 1895–1937.
BibInt	*Biblical Interpretation*
BibInt	Biblical Interpretation Series
BJP	Brill Jewish Project
BJS	Brown Judaic Studies
BKV	Bibliothek der Kirchenväter
BLS	Bible and Literature Series
BM	British Museum
BP	Bibliothèque de la Pléiade
BR	*Biblical Research*
BThS	Biblisch-Theologische Studien
BW	Bible and Women: An Encyclopedia of Exegesis and Cultural History
BWANT	Beiträge zur Wissenschaft vom Alten und Neuen Testament
BZAW	Beihefte zur Zeitschrift für die alttestamentliche Wissenschaft
CBET	Contributions to Biblical Exegesis and Theology
CBQ	*Catholic Biblical Quarterly*
CBQMS	Catholic Biblical Quarterly Monograph Series
CCSA	Corpus Christianorum: Series apocryphorum
CEJL	Commentaries on Early Jewish Literature
CJA	Christianity and Judaism in Antiquity

COS	Hallo, William W., ed. *The Context of Scripture*. 3 vols. Leiden: Brill, 1997–2002.
CSCO	Corpus Scriptorum Christianorum Orientalium. Edited by Jean Baptiste Chabot et al. Paris, 1903.
CSEL	Corpus Scriptorum Ecclesiasticorum Latinorum
CurBR	*Currents in Biblical Research*
CWS	Classics of Western Spirituality
DCLS	Deuterocanonical and Cognate Literature Studies
DCLY	*Deuterocanonical and Cognate Literature Yearbook*
DDD	Toorn, Karel van der, Bob Becking, and Pieter van der Horst, eds. *Dictionary of Deities and Demons in the Bible*. Leiden: Brill, 1995.
DJD	Discoveries in the Judaean Desert
DSD	*Dead Sea Discoveries*
EJL	Early Judaism and Its Literature
Euphrosyne	*Euphrosyne: Revista de Filologia Classica*
FAT	Forschungen zum Alten Testament
FB	Forschung zur Bibel
FCB	Feminist Companion to the Bible
FJTC	Flavius Josephus: Translation and Commentary
FSBP	Fontes et Subsidia ad Bibliam Pertinentes
FTh	Film und Theologie
GAP	Guides to Apocrypha and Pseudepigrapha
GOI	Göttinger Orientforschungen Iranica
GSR	Geschlecht-Symbol-Religion
HABES	Heidelberger althistorische Beiträge und epigraphische Studien
HBM	Hebrew Bible Monographs
HBS	History of Biblical Studies
HCS	Hellenistic Culture and Society
Historia	*Historia: Zeitschrift für alte Geschichte*
Hen	*Henoch*
HThKAT	Herders Theologischer Kommentar zum Alten Testament
HTR	*Harvard Theological Review*
IFTh	Introductions in Feminist Theology
IG	*Inscriptiones Graecae. Editio Minor*. Berlin: de Gruyter, 1924–.
IJSStud	IJS Studies in Judaica
ISACR	Interdisciplinary Studies in Ancient Culture and Religion

JAOS	*Journal of the American Oriental Society*
JBL	*Journal of Biblical Literature*
JBQ	*Jewish Bible Quarterly*
JCP	Jewish and Christian Perspectives
JJS	*Journal of Jewish Studies*
JPS	Jewish Publication Society
JQR	*Jewish Quarterly Review*
JSem	*Journal of Semitics*
JSHRZ	Jüdische Schriften aus hellenistisch-römischer Zeit
JSJ	*Journal for the Study of Judaism in the Persian, Hellenistic, and Roman Periods*
JSJSup	Supplements to the Journal for the Study of Judaism
JSOTSup	Journal for the Study of the Old Testament Supplement Series
JSP	*Journal for the Study of the Pseudepigrapha*
JSPSup	Journal for the Study of the Pseudepigrapha Supplement Series
LCL	Loeb Classical Library
LISup	Literatura Intertestamentària Supplementa
LLS	Los Libros Sagrados
LSAM	*Lois sacrées d'Asie Mineure*. École Française d'Athènes. Travaux et mémoirs des anciens membres étrangers de l'École 9. Paris: De Boccard, 1995.
LSJ	Liddell, Henry George, Robert Scott, Henry Stuart Jones. *A Greek-English Lexicon*. 9th ed. with revised supplement. Oxford: Clarendon, 1996.
LSTS	The Library of Second Temple Studies
LthB	Lüneburger theologische Beiträge
Marginalia	*Marginalia Review of Books*
Mosaic	*Mosaic: A Journal for the Interdisciplinary Study of Literature*
MSU	Mitteilungen des Septuaginta-Unternehmens
Neot	*Neotestamentica*
NETS	Pietersma, Albert, and Benjamin G. Wright, eds. *A New English Translation of the Septuagint and Other Greek Translations Traditionally Included under That Title*. Oxford: Oxford University Press, 2007.
NIB	Keck, Leander E., ed. *The New Interpreter's Bible*. 12 vols. Nashville: Abingdon, 1994–2004.
NovTSup	Supplements to Novum Testamentum
NRSV	New Revised Standard Version

NTOA	Novum Testamentum et Orbis Antiquus
OBO	Orbis Biblicus et Orientalis
OGIS	Dittenberger, Wilhelm, ed. *Orientis Graeci Inscriptiones Selectae*. 2 vols. Leipzig: Hirzel, 1903–1905.
OTP	Charlesworth, James H., ed., *The Old Testament Pseudepigrapha*. New York: Doubleday, 1983–1985.
OTS	Oudtestamentische Studiën
PAAJR	*Proceedings of the American Academy of Jewish Research*
PACS	Philo of Alexandria Commentary Series
PMS	Publications in Medieval Studies
P.Flor.	Vitelli, G. *Papiri greco-egizii, Papiri Fiorentini*. 3 vols. Supplementi Filologico-Storici ai Monumenti Antichi. Milan: Hoepli, 1906–1915.
P.Köln	Kramer, Bärbel, et al., eds. *Kölner Papyri*. Wiesbaden: VS Verlag für Sozialwissenschaften, 1976–.
P.Lond.	Kenyon, F. G., H. I. Bell, and W. E. Crum. *Greek Papyri in the British Museum*. 7 vols. London: British Museum, 1893–1974.
P.Oxy.	Grenfell, Bernard P., et al., eds. *The Oxyrhynchus Papyri*. London: Egypt Exploration Fund, 1898–.
P.Ross.Georg.	Zereteli, G., O. Krüger, and P. Jernstedt. *Papyri russischer und georgischer Sammlungen*. 5 vols. Tiflis: Universitätslithographie, 1925–1935.
Proof	*Prooftexts: A Journal of Jewish Literary History*
PTSDSSP	Princeton Theological Seminary Dead Sea Scrolls Project
PVTG	Pseudepigrapha Veteris Testamenti Graece
PW	Wissowa, Georg, and Wilhelm Kroll, eds. *Paulys Real-Encyclopädie der classischen Alterumswissenschaft*. New ed. 50 vols. in 84 parts. Stuttgart: Metzler and Druckenmüller, 1894–1980.
RAC	Theodor Klauser et al., eds. *Reallexikon für Antike und Christentum*. Stuttgart: Hiersemann, 1950–.
RelSoc	Religion and Society
RevQ	*Revue de Qumran*
RIL	*Religion and Intellectual Life*
RMCS	Routledge Monographs in Classical Studies
SAeth	Scriptores Aethiopici
SAPERE	Scripta Antiquitatis Posterioris ad Ethicam Religionemque pertinentia
SBLCP	Society of Biblical Literature Centennial Publications

SBLDS	Society of Biblical Literature Dissertation Series
SBLSP	Society of Biblical Literature Seminar Papers
SBLTT	Society of Biblical Literature Texts and Translations
SC	Sources chrétiennes
SCS	Septuagint and Cognate Studies
ScrHier	*Scripta Hierosolymitana*
Semeia	*Semeia*
SeptCS	Septuagint Commentary Series
SDEK	Septuaginta deutsch, Erläuterungen und Kommentare
SFFT	*Science Fiction Film and Television*
SFSHJ	South Florida Studies in the History of Judaism
Signs	*Signs: Journal of Women in Culture and Society*
Spec	*Speculum*
SPhA	Studies in Philo of Alexandria
SPhilo	*Studia Philonica*
SPhiloA	*Studia Philonica Annual*
SSN	Studia Semitica Neerlandica
SSP	Scriptores sacri et profane
STDJ	Studies on the Texts of the Desert of Judah
StPB	Studia Post-biblica
StudJ	Studia Judaeoslavica
SVF	August, Hans Friedrich von Arnim. *Stoicorum Veterum Fragmenta*. 4 vols. Leipzig: Teubner, 1903–1924.
SVTG	Septuaginta: Vetus Testamentum Graecum
SVTP	Studia in Veteris Testamenti Pseudepigraphica
SymS	Symposium Series
Tarbiz	*Tarbiz*
TANZ	Texte und Arbeiten zum neutestamentlichen Zeitalter
TAPA	*Transactions of the American Philological Association*
TBN	Themes in Biblical Narrative
Th	Theodotion
ThSt	Theologische Studien
TS	Texts and Studies
TSAJ	Texte und Studien zum antiken Judentum
TUAT	Kaiser, Otto, et al., eds. *Texte aus der Umwelt des Alten Testaments*. Gütersloh: Mohn, 1984–.
UCLF	*The University of Chicago Legal Forum*
VTSup	Supplements to Vetus Testamentum
WCS	Wisdom Commentary Series
WUNT	Wissenschaftliche Untersuchungen zum Neuen Testament

YCS	*Yale Classical Studies*
ZABR	*Zeitschrift für altorientalische und biblische Rechtgeschichte*
ZAW	*Zeitschrift für die alttestamentliche Wissenschaft*
ZDMG	*Zeitschrift der deutschen morgenländischen Gesellschaft*
ZNW	*Zeitschrift für die neutestamentliche Wissenschaft und die Kunde der älteren Kirche*

Introduction

Eileen Schuller and Marie-Theres Wacker

This volume in the international encyclopedia The Bible and Women[1] treats early Jewish writings. In our introduction, we want to discuss this phrase, its extent, and its implications before we explain the scope and goal of our project and describe its structure and approaches.

1. Terminology

The phrase *early Jewish writings* will be used in our volume to designate books/scriptures sharing three characteristics: they originate from the period after the arrival of Alexander the Great in Palestine (ca. 330 BCE) until the decades following the destruction of the Second Temple in Jerusalem (70 CE); they are, in modern research, considered as Jewish; and they were not included in the emerging canon of sacred Scriptures of Judaism.

Early Jewish writings cover a wide variety of literary genres, such as stories, novels, historiographies, testaments, apocalypses, sapiential admonitions, fictitious letters, early commentaries on biblical books, philosophical tractates, and hymns and prayers.[2] Their place of provenance is not only

1. The Bible and Women: An Encyclopedia of Exegesis and Cultural History, ed. Christiana de Groot, Irmtraud Fischer, Mercedes Navarro Puerto, and Adriana Valerio, 20 vols. (Stuttgart: Kohlhammer; Atlanta: SBL Press; Estella: Editorial Verbo Divino; Trapani: Il pozzo di Iacobbe, 2010–). For the scope and goals of the project, see Irmtraud Fischer, Jorunn Økland, Mercedes Navarro Puerto, and Adriana Valerio, “Introduction—Women, Bible and Reception History: An International Project in Theology and Gender Research,” in *Torah*, ed. Irmtraud Fischer and Mercedes Navarro Puerto with Andrea Taschl-Erber, BW 1.1 (Atlanta: Society of Biblical Literature, 2011), 1–30; see http://bibleandwomen.org/download/Introduction_Torah.pdf. The website, in the four languages of the project, shows the volumes which have appeared already.

2. Not to mention documents concerning inheritance, marriage or divorce, purchase, and other administrative or economic issues. Usually, these are dealt with separately in modern research.

Jerusalem or the province of Judaea but also Egypt, notably Alexandria. Hellenistic Alexandria is known as a site of Hellenistic-Jewish erudition where numerous Hebrew books were translated into Greek and not a few of them were adapted to new challenges, where in particular the Septuagint is supposed to have its origin, and where Jewish philosophy developed in productive encounter with its non-Jewish Hellenistic context. Moreover, in the period at issue there is evidence for Jewish communities in different regions of Mesopotamia and in Asia Minor, although it is disputed if any of the preserved texts has its origins from there.

The number and extent of existing early Jewish writings outside the canon cannot be given exactly, as some of them are preserved only as fragmentary quotations in other ancient works and others were transmitted in different versions. Not many authors are known by name; notable exceptions are Philo in Alexandria and Flavius Josephus in Rome. The canonical status of some of the early Jewish works is somewhat fluid: for example, the book of Sirach, originally written in Hebrew, became, in a Greek translation, part of the Septuagint and the Latin Vulgate, but not part of the Hebrew Bible; the so-called Ethiopic book of Enoch, a complex composition from which Aramaic fragments were discovered at Qumran, owes its preservation to the fact that it was accepted into the canon of the Christian Ethiopian church. In general, not a few of these texts are preserved in translations, or even translations of translations, into languages like Ethiopic, Syriac, Georgian, Armenian, and Slavonic as well as Latin, Greek, or Aramaic, and a distinction between Jewish and Christian elements in a text is not always obvious.

Finally, the designation of all these texts as early Jewish writings is not the only one in use. Classical collections bear titles such as *The Apocrypha and Pseudepigrapha of the Old Testament*,[3] where the term *Apocrypha* reflects the Protestant tradition of designating the seven deuterocanonical books in the larger Catholic canon (Sirach, Wisdom of Solomon, Tobit, Judith, 1 and 2 Maccabees, and Baruch), and *Pseudepigrapha* alludes to the fact that many of the extracanonical writings are in circulation under the name of biblical pseudonyms. In older research literature until the 1960s the term *late Jewish writings* is used, grounded in the nineteenth and early twentieth century Christian scholarly construction of prophetic religion replaced, after the exile, by Judaism, which finds its end in 70 CE, leaving little room for Judaism after

3. Robert Henry Charles, ed., *The Apocrypha and Pseudepigrapha of the Old Testament in English*, 2 vols. (Oxford: Clarendon, 1913); James H. Charlesworth, ed., *The Old Testament Pseudepigrapha*, 2 vols. (New York: Doubleday, 1983–1985); in German: Emil Kautzsch, ed., *Die Apokryphen und Pseudepigraphen des Alten Testaments*, 2 vols. (Tübingen: Mohr Siebeck, 1900).

the rise of Christianity. In view of these biased and, in the latter case, even anti-Jewish terms, our decision to title this volume *Early Jewish Writings* hopes to be inclusive as regards to different religious options as well as to the range of texts taken into consideration.

2. Structure

The encyclopedia of The Bible and Women as a whole aims to develop a history of biblical interpretation with special emphasis on those texts and traditions that became important for the structure of gender relations in cultures informed by the Bible. De facto, the writings summed up under the heading of early Jewish writings came into being in the context of an already growing corpus of normative (biblical) literature, and most of them can be considered as an early form of biblical reception. On the other hand, motifs, traditions, and concepts from these writings that exist alongside the Bible found their reception in Judaism, Christianity, and also in Islam. This is true especially with regard to images of women and men and more generally to concepts of gender and gender relations. Our volume places itself at the cutting edge of literary or textual analysis (including historical perspectives) and reception history with a gender-specific focus on both.

The first part of our volume, with four essays, will focus on selected single books; the second part, with three contributions, on specific subjects in a more cross-sectional approach through different writings; and the third part, again with four essays, on a broader textual corpus. The topics and subjects chosen are each informative for gender relations as represented in a text and for their reception of biblical figures or a constellation of problems.

Because the two deuterocanonical wisdom texts Sirach and Wisdom of Solomon are already analyzed in volume 1.3 of the encyclopedia of The Bible and Women, we did not include them; the same applies to the story of Susannah (Dan 14 in Catholic Bibles).[4] In volume 1.3 the Hebrew book of Esther receives attention as part of the five scrolls read out at Jewish holy days; in our volume we deal with the book of Esther in its Greek (Septuagint) shape with the distinctive additions that are part of the Catholic version (Adele Reinhartz). In addition, we include another deuterocanonical book, the book of Judith with its strong female hero (Barbara Schmitz and Lydia Lange). The third contribution analyzes the Letter of Jeremiah (in the Vulgate part of the deuterocanonical book of Baruch), a pseudepigraphon

4. See Christl Maier and Nuria Calduch-Benages, eds., *The Writings and Later Wisdom Books*, BW 1.3 (Atlanta: SBL Press, 2014).

in terms of its presumed author, a letter according to its superscription, a polemical speech in its content, that uses prophetical traditions and weaves them together with descriptions of women's activities to denigrate the idol worship of the "Babylonians" (Marie-Theres Wacker and Sonja Ammann). The fourth essay in part one takes up a "classical" pseudepigraphic writing, Joseph and Aseneth, an expansive narrative about the relation between the Egyptian daughter of a priest and the son of Jacob (Angela Standhartinger).

In the second part, three foundational stories from Genesis and Exodus come into focus: the paradise story (Gen 2–3); the mythical constellation of the sons of heaven and the daughters of men (Gen 6:1–4); and the birth story of Moses (Exod 2:1–10). Magdalena Diaz Araujo surveys a range of early Jewish writings with their different images of Eve (Sirach; the book of Parables [1 En. 37–71]; the Slavonic book of Enoch; and the first Sibylline Oracle) and then turns to the Life of Adam and Eve in its Greek version of supposedly Jewish origin. Similarly, Hanna Tervanotko deals with the women in Exod 2:1–10 and gives special attention to the daughter of Pharaoh, Moses's adoptive mother who in the writings she analyzes (the book of Jubilees; the Exagoge; Philo's Life of Moses; the Pseudo-Philonic Liber antiquititatum biblicarum) becomes responsible for Moses's Hellenistic education. Veronika Bachmann not only considers 1 En. 1–36, the so-called Book of Watchers, in her survey of expanded retellings of Gen 6:1–4 but also includes the Animal Apocalypse, 1 En. 85–90, the book of Jubilees, the second book of Baruch, and the Testament of Ruben.

In the third part, Tal Ilan analyzes renarrations of biblical figures of women in Flavius Josephus's *Jewish Antiquities*. She sees Josephus as a historian and attributes the modifications he makes mainly to the sources he uses, not to an alleged wish to soften or to Hellenize these figures. In contrast, Maren R. Niehoff considers Philo's encounter with Roman culture during his diplomatic journey to Rome to be essential for his view of biblical women figures: it is only after his visit to Rome that he writes Roman virtues into his images of biblical women. Joan E. Taylor focuses on the Therapeutae, a group of men and women living a contemplative life near Alexandria. She insists that Philo's description can be used as a document illustrative of Jewish women's religion in Hellenistic Egypt. Maxine L. Grossman introduces the world of Qumran texts. She examines the so-called sectarian writings from Qumran and pays particular attention to the treatments of gender, sexuality, and norms of group order in these texts. The hypothesis emerges that at least some women in the community represented by these scrolls must have had some authority in their group and that the sectarian texts reveal tensions around such authoritative roles of women.

3. Approaches

The scholars who contributed to the volume come from different academic disciplines (including Christian theology, Jewish studies, and religious studies), from different religious/denominational backgrounds (Christian and Jewish), and from different geographical regions (Canada, United States, Argentina, Israel, Germany, Switzerland, England, and Finland). They represent the scholarly traditions of their academic contexts and their specific expertise documented by their research activities and publications. Reinhartz uses literary criticism, including film, to elucidate the dynamics of the Esther narrative of the Septuagint. Schmitz and Lange compare the Greek book of Judith with Jerome's Latin version to sharpen the profile of the figure of Judith. Standhartinger unfolds relations of gender, class, status, ethnos, religion, and their intersections in Joseph and Aseneth; Wacker and Ammann see the dynamics of othering in the Letter of Jeremiah. Araujo describes the fluid concept of sin in the Greek Life of Adam and Eve by a careful linguistic analysis with focus on semantic aspects. Bachmann's perspective could be characterized as ideological critical, aiming at a critical reception history of the motif complex she analyzes; Tervanotko proceeds by close reading of her texts and sets her results against the Hellenistic context in which her texts originate. Ilan's focus is on reception history, using a specific form of source criticism; Niehoff reckons with new experiences as crucial for an author's perspectives. Taylor's interest is to show Philo's historical reliability as regards the Therapeutae, and Grossman's concern is to describe the hermeneutical complexities of seeking to recover historical circumstances through highly ideological texts. Indeed, optimism about deducing historical information from literary or prescriptive texts has shrunk in the last decades in favor of greater reluctance in stating historical facts.

In particular, the authors of our volume bring in different approaches to questions of gender. Some of the contributions work from a clear women-centered perspective without reflecting specifically on the category of gender; others focus on gender relations with emphasis on women's roles; several authors explore a wider range of gender perspectives by including aspects of sexuality, embodiment, female agency, or intersectionality. We hope that such a variety of approaches and methods will stimulate further research.

4. Acknowledgments

In preparation for the volume, a research colloquium gathering most of the contributors was held in Münster, June 5–7, 2015. Through its provision of opportunities for fruitful discussions and personal contacts, it was crucial to the development of this project. Three of the principal editors of the series The Bible and Women joined us: Irmtraud Fischer, Christiana de Groot, and Adriana Valerio. We are very grateful to Simone Bomholt, Verena Suchhart, and Ludger Hiepel in Münster who were a great help in the organization before and during the colloquium. We received financial assistance from Deutsche Forschungsgemeinschaft, Bonn; McMaster University, Hamilton; University of Graz; International Office of WWU, Münster; Equal Opportunity Commissioner of the WWU Münster; and the Ursuline Sisters of Chatham, Canada. Their support helped us to organize and hold the symposium and to pay for some translations in the preparation of the German and English volumes to appear simultaneously.

We had wonderful translators who struggled successfully with the often very complex and technical material. Sincere thanks go to Martha M. Matesich and Richard Ratzlaff for translations from German to English and to Gerlinde Baumann and Peter Porzig for translations from English to German. Special thanks also to our assistants in Hamilton and Münster, Nicholas Meyer and Katharina Fockenbrock, who worked on the manuscripts and their formatting, who adapted bibliography and footnotes to bring them into a coherent system, and who never lost courage in the thicket of thousands of formalia.

We are grateful to Irmtraud Fischer and Christiana de Groot for advice as German and English editor of other volumes in the series and as principal editors. Last but not least we want to say thank you for the support and guidance of the publishers: at SBL Press, Nicole Tilford and Heather McMurray; and at Kohlhammer (Stuttgart), Sebastian Weigelt, Florian Specker, and Janine Schüle.

As editors, we have learned so much from this project—we hope it will be but the beginning of continued discussions both among the contributors and more widely among all our readers.

Part 1
Early Jewish Works

LXX Esther: A Hellenistic Jewish Revenge Fantasy

Adele Reinhartz

1. Introduction

The Greek Book of Esther is one of several early Jewish novels that feature female protagonists who prevail over the machinations of men to save themselves and their people.[1] In contrast to Judith and other early Jewish writings, Greek Esther has a counterpart in the Masoretic text of the Hebrew Bible (MT) and has two major versions, generally known as LXX Esther and the Alpha Text. The present discussion will be based on the LXX version of Greek Esther on the grounds that it is this version that became more widespread and influential due to its inclusion in the Septuagint.[2]

LXX Esther follows the same general narrative as MT Esther. The Persian King Artaxerxes banishes his wife Vashti after she refused his command to join him at his lengthy feast. On the advice of his advisors, he holds a "beauty" contest in which the female contestants not only must look their best but also please him overnight (2:14). The winner is Esther, an orphan raised by her close relative Mordecai, a courtier who had been forced from Jerusalem at the time of the Babylonian conquest (2:6–7). Haman, the king's vizier, bears a grudge against Mordecai, who, citing his Jewish identity, had refused to bow down to him (3:4). Haman manipulates the king into issuing a decree of destruction against the Jews in his empire (3:8–11). Mordecai, in turn, persuades Esther to intercede (4:13–14). She thwarts Haman's dastardly plan and the tables are turned: on the day destined for their destruction, the Jews kill

1. On Esther as a novel, see Lawrence M. Wills, *The Jewish Novel in the Ancient World* (Ithaca, NY: Cornell University Press, 1995).

2. See Karen Jobes, *The Alpha-Text of Esther*, SBLDS 153 (Atlanta: Scholars Press, 1996); Kristin De Troyer, *The End of the Alpha-Text of Esther*, SCS 48 (Atlanta: Society of Biblical Literature, 2000); Aaron J. Koller, *Esther in Ancient Jewish Thought* (Cambridge: Cambridge University Press, 2014), 120; and Elias J. Bickerman, "Notes on the Greek Book of Esther," *PAAJR* 20 (1951): 102.

their enemies (9:1–2). The celebration of Purim is instituted by Mordecai and Esther as an annual memorial of the Jews' salvation (9:19–23).

The LXX version of Esther differs from MT Esther in two significant ways. First, in contrast to MT Esther, from which God's name is entirely absent, LXX Esther contains numerous direct references to God. In doing so, the LXX version explicitly attributes the Jews' salvation to divine agency, rather than simply to the cleverness of Mordecai and Esther themselves.

Second, LXX Esther contains six major sections, known as the Additions, that are not present in the MT.

- Addition A: Mordecai's dream and the plot of the two eunuchs against the king (11:2–12:6);[3] this addition introduces the Greek version and appears prior to chapter 1 in the MT.
- Addition B: The text of the king's edict authorizing the destruction of Persian Jewry (13:1–7), which appears between MT Esth 3:13 and 14.
- Addition C: The prayers of Mordecai and Esther for averting the tragedy (13:8–14:19).
- Addition D: Esther's unauthorized approach to the king, which puts in motion Esther and Mordecai's plan to save the Jews (15:1–16); C and D are inserted sequentially between MT Esther chapters 4 and 5.
- Addition E: The edict reversing the decree of destruction (16:1–24), which appears after MT Esth 8:12.
- Addition F: The interpretation of Mordecai's dream, followed by the scribe's concluding note (or colophon), about the origin of the manuscript (10:4–11:1). This addition is the conclusion of LXX Esther and follows the ending of MT Esther.

These additions do not significantly alter the overall storyline, but they do expand the narrative in four ways.

1. Additions A and F provide an overarching framework for the story, via the inclusio of Mordecai's dream in Addition A and the interpretation of the dream in Addition F.
2. In providing the ostensible text for the edicts referred to in MT Esther, Additions B and E add pathos and verisimilitude to the drama and accentuate the potential danger to the Jews.
3. Addition C amplifies the theme of piety by adding the prayers of Mordecai and Esther.

---

3. The chapter numbering follows the chapter divisions in the New Revised Standard Version except as noted.

4. In dramatizing the account of Esther's approach to the king, Addition D focuses attention on the risk that Esther is taking and adds drama and tension to the narrative.

On literary grounds, it is generally agreed that Additions A, D, and F may have been composed in Hebrew, and Addition C in Aramaic. The Edicts (Additions B and E) were probably written originally in Greek, perhaps by the translator of the body of the book. The additions were gathered at the end of the canonical portion of Jerome's Latin translation (ca. 404 CE); their chapter and verse designations in the NRSV and other translations therefore reflect this placement. The additions are considered to be "deuterocanonical" by the Roman Catholic Church and "apocryphal" by Protestant churches.[4]

Because Additions B, C, D, and E are included in Josephus's account of the Esther story, their latest possible dating is ca. 93–94 CE. Further precision in dating is usually attempted on the basis of the colophon in Addition F, which states that the Greek translation of Esther was brought to Egypt by a priest and Levite named Dositheus in the fourth year of the reign of Ptolemy and Cleopatra. If the colophon is authentic, the question of date rests on an identification of the specific Ptolemy and Cleopatra couples that are known from the Second Temple period and that reigned for at least four years. The candidates are Ptolemy IX (his fourth year would be around 114 BCE), Ptolemy XII (ca. 77 BCE), and Ptolemy XIV (ca. 48 BCE). Scholars disagree on which of these Ptolemies is intended but agree that the colophon would place the composition of the additions in the late-second to mid-first centuries BCE.[5]

Provenance is difficult to discern. The colophon implies that the book was translated in Palestine and delivered to Egypt, perhaps Alexandria. If so, it reflects a Palestinian perspective on the situation of the Jews in the diaspora. On the other hand, it is also possible that the book was translated in a major diaspora center such as Alexandria and then attributed to a Palestinian origin by means of the colophon.

It is generally assumed that the LXX version of Esther is based on a Hebrew *Vorlage* that was similar if not identical to MT Esther. For this reason,

4. Some printed editions group the additions at the end of the body of the story that parallels MT Esther. For online versions that place the additions in their appropriate narrative contexts, see BibleGateway at http://tinyurl.com/SBL066006e and the electronic edition of the NETS at http://tinyurl.com/SBL066006f.

5. Elias J. Bickerman, "The Colophon of the Greek Book of Esther," *JBL* 63 (1944): 339–62. He opts for the middle dating (see also n. 29 below). Carey Moore opts for the earliest dating. See Carey A. Moore, "On the Origins of the LXX Additions to the Book of Esther," *JBL* 92 (1973): 383.

many discussions of LXX Esther engage in a detailed comparison of the MT and Greek versions.[6] Others focus on the Additions alone in order to pin down a more precise provenance and process of composition and translation.[7] Approaches that consider LXX Esther as a literary whole have been developed in recent years,[8] although most of them describe its overall profile again in comparison to or at least with side glances to MT Esther. Important as such studies are, the present discussion will take a decisively reader-oriented approach that considers LXX Esther as a literary whole by treating the additions in their contexts within the overall narrative. The aim is to consider the ways in which LXX Esther, as a whole, might have been read or heard by its early Greek-speaking Jewish audiences. While it is theoretically possible that these audiences would have known or known of Hebrew Esther, the very existence of Greek versions suggests that the Hebrew book was not regularly heard and read among them. They were therefore unlikely to have compared the Greek version with the Hebrew but, on the contrary, would have viewed the Greek version as the "real" story.

2. Hypothesis and Approach

My hypothesis is that audiences in the Greek-speaking diaspora would have read or heard LXX Esther as a "revenge fantasy" that allowed them to experience vicariously the power absent from their own lives as part of a minority group. Instrumental in this reading is the portrayal of Esther, who, though herself a marginalized (if well-positioned) diaspora person, engages in an empowered act of vengeance that provided both entertainment and solace to a disempowered community.

LXX Esther makes use of Hellenistic literary forms, characterization, and narrative conventions.[9] To consider LXX Esther as a revenge fantasy is by no means to deny the book's affinities with other genres that were common in

6. For example, see David Creech, "Now Where's the Fun in That? The Humourless Narrator in the Greek Translation of Esther," *BR* 52 (2007): 17–40.

7. For example, Moore, "On the Origins of the LXX Additions to the Book of Esther."

8. See Linda Day, *Three Faces of a Queen: Characterization in the Books of Esther*, JSOTSup 186 (Sheffield: Sheffield Academic, 1995). More recent examples are: Marie-Theres Wacker, "Mit Toratreue und Todesmut dem einen Gott anhangen: Zum Esther-Bild der Septuaginta," in *Dem Tod nicht glauben: Sozialgeschichte der Bibel; Festschrift für Luise Schottroff zum 70. Gebertstag*, ed. Frank Crüsemann et al. (Gütersloh: Gütersloher Verlagshaus, 2004), 312–32; and Cathérine Vialle, *Une analyse comparée d'Esther TM et LXX: Regard sur deux récits d'une même histoire*, BETL 233 (Leuven: Peeters, 2012).

9. See Sara R. Johnson, "Novelistic Elements in Esther: Persian or Hellenistic, Jewish or Greek?," *CBQ* 67 (2005): 572–89.

the context of classical or Hellenistic Greek literature. Many literary works participate in multiple genres; analyzing the text through the lens of one genre does not preclude other types of genre analyses.[10]

Nor am I the only one to detect the theme of revenge in this book. Indeed, many modern commentators view revenge as central to this book's narrative and to its reception on the part of ancient readers.[11] The motif of revenge is well-represented in stories from the ancient world to the present, in all narrative forms including poetry, drama, fiction, and film. Literary examples include the Greek myth of Medea, Shakespeare's *Hamlet* and *Othello*, and Alexandre Dumas's novel *The Count of Monte Cristo*.[12] Revenge narratives share a number of common plot elements, including an act or threat of violence and retribution for violence. In addition, there is often supernatural involvement in that the "agents of the revenge" are either divine or somehow associated with the divine.[13]

In this essay I will argue that viewing LXX Esther as a revenge fantasy allows for insights into its female hero as well as the possible social context in which the book was produced and/or received. To do so I will compare LXX Esther with a modern and very overt example of the revenge fantasy: Quentin Tarantino's 2009 film, *Inglourious Basterds*. To be clear: I am not claiming that Tarantino's film was influenced in any way by the book of Esther in any of its forms, nor am I arguing that LXX Esther has parallels to all elements of the film. I also do not ignore their obvious differences in subject matter, medium, and historical context. I do hope to show, however, that despite these differences, the comparison between these narratives highlights the central role of the female protagonist as the one who avenges not only herself but her entire people against the murderous machinations of a male antagonist.

---

10. Anne H. Stevens, *Literary Theory and Criticism: An Introduction* (Peterborough, ON: Broadview, 2015), 28.

11. See, for one example of many, Judy Fentress-Williams, "Esther," in *Fortress Commentary on the Bible*, ed. Gale A. Yee, Hugh R. Page, and Matthew J. M. Coomber (Minneapolis: Fortress, 2014), 493. For an attempt to discern historical events behind the revenge motif in MT Esther, see Stephanie Dalley, *Esther's Revenge at Susa from Sennacherib to Ahasuerus* (Oxford: Oxford University Press, 2007).

12. For discussion of literature and film, see Lesel Dawson, "Revenge and the Family Romance in Tarantino's Kill Bill," *Mosaic* 47 (2014): 121–34; John Rieder, "Race and Revenge Fantasies in Avatar, District 9 and Inglourious Basterds," *SFFT* 4 (2011): 41–56; Christopher James Crosbie, "Philosophies of Retribution: Kyd, Shakespeare, Webster and the Revenge Tragedy Genre" (PhD Diss., Rutgers, The State University of New Jersey, 2007).

13. Patrick Colm Hogan, *Affective Narratology: The Emotional Structure of Stories* (Lincoln: University of Nebraska Press, 2011), 231.

3. Revenge in LXX Esther

While popular representations of Esther focus on her demure beauty, the narrative itself portrays her as an agent of revenge.[14] After Esther finally reveals to the king that she is Jewish and therefore personally threatened by Haman's anti-Semitic decree, she asks him immediately to rescind the decree: "If it pleases you and if I have found favor, let an order be dispatched to revoke the letters sent by Haman, which were written to destroy the Jews who are in your kingdom" (8:5).[15] The king then gives Esther carte blanche: "What more do you seek? You also write in my name as it pleases you, and seal it with my ring" (8:7–8). This subsequent edict "ordered them to live in accordance with their laws in every city, both to help themselves and to deal with their adversaries and their enemies as they wished" (8:11). As a result, many non-Jews "were circumcised and became Jews out of fear of the Jews" (8:17) and their enemies perished; "no one resisted, because they feared them" (9:2). Jews killed five hundred people in Susa (9:12). Then Esther asked the king for permission to hang the bodies of Haman's ten sons and to continue the rampage the next day (9:13–14). Permission was granted; fifteen thousand Persians were killed, and a joyous Jewish celebration—Purim—was instituted.

Esther's boldness secured revenge for a murder—a massacre—that had in fact been preempted thanks to her timely intervention. Yet revenge seems appropriate within the narrative as retaliation for the planned massacre and the fear that Haman's edict had aroused in the Jewish population. Whereas Haman's death may be seen as justice, from our twenty-first century perspective the murder of his sons and fifteen thousand others seems excessive under the circumstances. The narrator's delight at the turn of events, however, does not allow room for compassion for the dead. Exultation rules, not only in the story, but also in the rituals associated with Purim: feasting, drinking, gifts of food to friends and the Jewish poor so that all might partake in the celebration of sweet revenge.

Of course, Esther does not bear sole responsibility for the turnaround in Jewish fortunes. Whereas MT Esther does not refer explicitly to the divine, LXX Esther portrays God as the one who oversees the entire chain of events. God's involvement is emphasized particularly in the prayers of Mordecai

---

14. The conclusion to this paper will address the ethical aspects of considering Esther as a revenge story.

15. The translations of Greek Esther are based on NETS with one modification: the replacement of "Judeans" by "Jews." See Karen Jobes, "Esther," in *A New English Translation of the Septuagint*, ed. Albert Pietersma and Benjamin G. Wright, 2nd ed. (Oxford: Oxford University Press, 2009), 424–40.

and Esther in Addition C. Their appeal to God for help and protection suggests that readers interpret the subsequent success of their plot as the result of divine intervention. This interpretation is further supported by God's role in softening the king's heart towards Esther when she comes to him unbidden (see Addition D). In this regard, LXX Esther conforms to the revenge fantasy genre, in which supernatural or divine intervention can play an important role.

4. Revenge in Tarantino's *Inglourious Basterds*

Quentin Tarantino's 2009 film *Inglourious Basterds* glories in a gory but highly satisfying revenge scenario: the counterfactual 1944 murder of Adolf Hitler and the entire Nazi leadership. The plot has two narrative threads that merge in one spectacular revenge scene. In 1941, the Apaches, an American Jewish commando group led by Aldo Raine, lands behind enemy lines in France. Their mission: to kill as many Nazis as possible. Later on, having struck fear in the heart of Hitler and the entire Nazi establishment, they are recruited by the British government to carry out Operation Kino, a plan to assassinate Hitler, his henchmen, and numerous Nazi officials at the premiere of a Nazi propaganda movie called *Nation's Pride*.

Unbeknownst to Aldo Raine, a young French woman named Shosanna Dreyfus too is plotting revenge. Shosanna is the sole survivor of a Jewish family brutally shot by Colonel Hans Landa and his men in 1941. She flees the farmhouse where she had been hiding with her family, as Landa watches in amusement, and ends up in Paris, living under a false name and identity. By 1944 she has come into possession of a Parisian movie theater, where she meets, and charms, a young German soldier named Fredrick Zoller. Zoller was a Nazi war hero, and his exploits are the subject matter of *Nation's Pride*, in which Zoller stars as himself. Zoller persuades Goebbels, Hitler's minister of propaganda, to hold the high-profile film premiere at Shoshana's theater.[16]

The two story lines converge on the night of the premiere. Numerous complications prevent the two plots from proceeding as planned, but in the end, the movie theater explodes in spectacular fashion and thereby ends the war in 1944, a year earlier than it did in reality.[17]

---

16. For detailed analysis, see Heidi Schlipphacke, "Inglourious Basterds and the Gender of Revenge," in *Quentin Tarantino's Inglourious Basterds: A Manipulation of Metacinema*, ed. Robert Dassanowsky (New York: Continuum, 2012), 113–33.

17. On alternative histories involving Hitler and World War II, see Gavriel David Rosenfeld, *The World Hitler Never Made: Alternate History and the Memory of Nazism* (Cambridge: Cambridge University Press, 2005).

5. Comparing the Revenge Plots

The main theme of both LXX Esther and *Inglourious Basterds* is anti-Semitism. Both stories are propelled by an intense desire to avenge the violence or threat of violence against a minority Jewish population that is well-established and relatively comfortable in its diaspora setting. In LXX Esther, the anti-Semitic threat is neutralized before it can be acted upon. Not so in *Inglourious Basterds*, where the Holocaust is evoked in the very first scene depicting the massacre of Shosanna's family. While LXX Esther is a comedy—the villain dies and a raucous new festival is created—*Inglourious Basterds* is both tragedy and comedy. The film ends with the death of the heroine, Shosanna, but the survival and, indeed, the triumph, of the hero, Aldo Raine. The psychopath Hans Landa lives, but the primary villains Hitler, Goebbels, and their friends die.

Three elements of the revenge plot come to the fore in this comparison: the reversal of fortunes, the double-cross, and the upending of social hierarchies.

5.1. Reversal of Fortune

In *Inglourious Basterds*, the reversal of fortunes is enacted most explicitly in the relationship between Aldo Raine and Hans Landa. Raine is captured by Landa at the movie theater in the moments before the film premiere begins, but then, through a truly unbelievable turn of events, Landa surrenders, and Raine prevails.

In LXX Esther, the reversal of fortunes is twofold and is illustrated most dramatically through the fate of the villain, Haman. Haman is King Artaxerxes's right hand man; he not only persuades the king to issue the decree against the Jews but convinces himself that the king is about to bestow on him great honors. How else, he tells himself, could he explain why the king asked him: "What shall I do for the person whom I wish to honour?" (6:6). But to Haman's surprise, it is not he that is to be honored, but rather the despised Mordecai! The second, and more, shall we say, life-altering reversal, occurs when Haman is hanged on the very gallows that he had prepared for Mordecai (7:10). An even more significant reversal in LXX Esther occurs on the collective level: the Jews whom Haman had condemned are not only saved but also carry out their revenge. Through the actions of Esther, Mordecai, and, of course, God, they are transformed from victims to perpetrators, an ethically problematic transformation perhaps from the point of view of twenty-first century readers, but fully in keeping with the revenge genre as such.

5.2. The Double-Cross

A double-cross can be defined as a dramatic and sudden betrayal of allegiances. At the climax of the film, Landa, the epitome of anti-Semitism and brutality, and Hitler's right-hand man, suddenly offers to let Project Kino—and the deaths of Hitler and the entire Nazi leadership—go ahead on condition that he be allowed to emigrate to America without any repercussions. In doing so he has betrayed his leaders. This act of betrayal would have been commendable had it been prompted by an ethical change of heart rather than purely selfish reasons. Haman too engages in a double-cross. As the king's minister, he should have the king's best interests at heart, yet he was secretly planning to deceive him out of his kingdom, at least according to the king's edict in Addition E:

> For Haman son of Hammedatha, a Macedonian (really an alien to the Persian blood, and quite devoid of our kindliness), ... undertook to deprive us of our kingdom and our life, and with intricate craft and deceit asked for the destruction of Mordecai, our saviour and perpetual benefactor, and of Esther, the blameless partner of our kingdom, together with their whole nation. He thought that by these methods he would catch us undefended and would transfer the kingdom of the Persians to the Macedonians. (E, 16:12–14)

5.3. Upending of Social Hierarchies

In both *Inglourious Basterds* and LXX Esther the administrative and military power is concentrated in the hands of non-Jewish, even anti-Jewish men: Hitler and Artaxerxes, Goebbels and Haman, plus their aides, administrators, advisors, and soldiers. These powerful masculine forces are outwitted and undone by the weakest of the weakest: Jewish women. These women are doubly marginal, on account of their ethnicity and their gender. But they make up for what they lack in political and military power with cunning and strategic thinking. In the film, the crucial moment comes when the festive Nazi audience realizes that they have been trapped in a fiery furnace by their seemingly charming hostess. In LXX Esther, the crucial moment is Esther's unbidden approach to the king. It is at this point that she is transformed from a passive beauty queen to a proactive savior of her people.

6. Comparing Vengeful Women

6.1. Hiding and Revealing Jewish Identity

While the heroic role in their respective revenge stories cannot be attributed solely to Shosanna and Esther, it is these women who are the most complex, interesting, and alluring figures. These women are at the emotional core of the film and the book, and for this reason, the audience identifies most strongly with them.[18] Both are young and beautiful; both outsmart older and more powerful men, against tremendous odds, and both contribute to the salvation of their compatriots, if not always to their own.

Important to both stories is the element of deception. Both women conceal their identities until an opportune moment. Shosanna is known in Paris as Emmanuelle Mimeux; she does not reveal her Jewishness until the climax of the film. Only her lover Marcel knows her true identity. Esther hides her Jewish identity, as per Mordecai's strict instructions, from the moment she enters the king's household as a matrimonial candidate: "Now Esther had not disclosed her people or country, for Mordecai had commanded her not to make it known" (2:10). She kept the secret even when chosen as queen: "Esther had not disclosed her country—such were the instructions of Mordecai; but she was to fear God and keep his laws, just as she had done when she was with him. So Esther did not change her mode of life" (2:20). Both Esther and Shosanna teeter on the brink of discovery. Shosanna's identity may not have been questioned by the smitten Frederick but she is visibly shaken when Landa unexpectedly entered the restaurant where she is being questioned by Goebbels about her movie theater. She knew that he would recognize her and feared that he would blow her cover.

Similarly, Esther's secrecy may seem futile. How indeed was she to live in the king's harem—hardly a private living arrangement—and nevertheless "fear God and keep his laws" without changing her way of life? Certainly Mordecai's own Jewish identity was well-known. Haman's plot to "destroy all the Jews under Artaxerxes' rule" (3:6) is attributed to Mordecai's refusal to do obeisance on the grounds that he is Jewish (3:4–5). Given that Esther's relationship to Mordecai was known by at least some members of the king's household—such as her eunuch Hachratheus who carried messages and objects between her and Mordecai (4:5–16)—is it plausible that her Jewish identity remained a secret? Perhaps not, but the narrative does not explore this potential contradiction, perhaps because the success of the narrative—and the revenge plot

18. This is true also of the MT version. See Koller, *Esther in Ancient Jewish Thought*, 77.

around which it is structured—requires that Esther, like Shosanna, maintain control of the secret.

6.2. Sexuality and Guile

Many of the biblical and apocryphal stories involving women focus on the interwoven motifs of sexuality and guile. A prime biblical example is the story of Judah and Tamar (Gen 38) in which Tamar takes her revenge on her father-in-law Judah by disguising herself as a prostitute, sleeping with him, and becoming pregnant.[19] Of the apocryphal novels, it is the book of Judith that stresses this theme the most. Judith sets out to seduce an enemy general, Holofernes, and then cuts off his head, thereby saving her people from destruction and exile.

In contrast to Tamar and Judith, Shosanna and Esther do not engage in overt sexual seduction. Yet the undercurrent of sexuality cannot be ignored, for neither woman hesitates to use her beauty to achieve her goals. The element of sexuality is signified by the role of clothing, and, more specifically, the changing of clothing in preparation for the narrative climax.[20] Shosanna prepares herself as carefully for the night of the Nazi film premiere as she might for a night at the opera. Already possessed of a haunting beauty, her red, tightly fitted dress and her carefully applied make-up were appropriate to the role of a woman hosting a major film premiere for a house full of dignitaries; the viewer, however, recognizes her careful attention to her appearance as a means of disguising her true intention and a signal that she was about to take charge of her fate and claim her place in world history on behalf of her people.

Esther too changes her clothing to suit the occasion. In preparation for her audacious approach to the king, Esther engages in prayer. In approaching God in this way, she sheds her royal garments and dresses in a humble manner befitting her role as a supplicant. According to Addition C, Esther removed

---

19. See also the story of Yael and Sisera, in which Yael invites the general into her tent, ostensibly to offer him a glass of milk—and hints at other sorts of comforts—and then kills him by driving a tent peg into his head (Judg 4:17–22); Nehama Aschkenasy, *Woman at the Window: Biblical Tales of Oppression and Escape* (Detroit: Wayne State University Press, 1998), 28. Tikva Frymer-Kensky, *Reading the Women of the Bible* (New York: Schocken Books, 2002), 52, disputes this interpretation, however, viewing Yael instead as a "mother" who delivers Sisera to death.

20. On the role of clothing in apocryphal novels, see Adele Reinhartz, "Better Homes and Gardens: Women and Domestic Space in the Books of Judith and Susanna," in *Text and Artifact in the Religions of Mediterranean Antiquity: Essays in Honour of Peter Richardson*, ed. Michel Robert Desjardins and Stephen G. Wilson (Waterloo, ON: Wilfrid Laurier University Press, 2000), 325–39.

"the garments of her glory, she put on the garments of distress and mourning, and instead of costly perfumes she covered her head with ashes and dung, and she utterly humbled her body; every part that she loved to adorn she covered with her tangled hair" (14:2; C, 13).[21] After three days of fasting, she resumes her disguise: "And it happened on the third day, as she ceased praying, she took off the garments of service and put on her glory" (15:1; D, 1) and became "majestic" again (see 15:2; D, 2).

Although she does not overtly engage in sexual overtures, as does Judith, it may be inferred that Esther's appearance was intended to beguile the king, in more ways than one, and to remind him of the reasons he chose her as his queen. After her prayer, Esther enters the presence of the king supported by two maids. When the king gazes at her in anger, Esther falters, pales, and faints upon one of her maids. But a miracle occurs! God intervenes and changes the king's spirit to one of gentleness (15:8; D, 8). (If God could harden Pharaoh's heart against Moses, surely God can also soften Artaxerxes's heart toward Esther.) Taking her in his arms, Artaxerxes reassures Esther that she will not die for her bold act (15:10; D, 10). Esther revives, expresses her awe of his glory and splendor and promptly faints again, inspiring further attempts to revive and comfort her.

Esther's weakness may just have been the result of three days of fasting, combined with extreme fear. But it also raises some questions. Does her faintness signify that her prayers to God for strength have been denied? Or, on the contrary, is it precisely by inducing her to faint that God helped her disarm the king's anger and make him receptive to her plan?

6.3. Beauty

Shosanna's beauty charms the Nazis she is forced to deal with, despite her cool manner. Esther's beauty too worked wonders, on the king and perhaps also on Haman. Indeed, the king's decision to execute Haman was prompted not only, or perhaps not even primarily, by a desire to protect his queen and her people as by jealous anger. After Esther reveals Haman as the villain, the king exits to the garden, "and Haman began to beg for his life from the queen, for he saw that he was in serious trouble. When the king returned from the garden, Haman had thrown himself on the couch, pleading with the queen. The king said, 'Will he dare even assault my wife in my own house?' Haman, when he heard, turned away his face" (7:7–9).

21. The numbering in parentheses is according to the NRSV, followed by the NETS numbering.

6.4. Corporate Responsibility

Both Esther and Shoshanna are concerned not only with their personal safety but also with the survival of the Jewish people. As she declares in the movie clip that plays during the conflagration in her cinema, Shosanna's is the face of Jewish revenge—not just for herself and her family, but for all who faced Nazi persecution.

It takes Esther more time to embrace the role she can play on behalf of her people. Initially she is cautious: when Hachratheus reports Mordecai's concerns and his plan, she tells him: "Go to Mordecai and say, 'All nations of the empire know that if any man or woman goes to the king inside the inner court without being called, there is no escape for that person. Only the one to whom the king stretches out the golden scepter is safe—and it is now thirty days since I was called to go to the king' " (4:10–11). But Mordecai persists by appealing to her self-interest. He warns Esther through Hachratheus that despite her exalted position she too is vulnerable: "Esther, do not say to yourself that you alone among all the Jews will escape alive. For if you keep quiet at such a time as this, help and protection will come to the Jews from another quarter, but you and your father's family will perish" (4:13–14).

In this way, Esther not only takes on corporate responsibility on behalf of her people but also, for the reader, comes to symbolize a diaspora community that despite its relative comfort must still see itself as marginal, and therefore vulnerable to the political winds of politics. As Aaron Koller notes, "The female may be taken as a symbol of the less powerful and less confrontational, but potentially more subversive and more effective in resisting."[22]

6.5. Relationships with Men

6.5.1. Enemies

In many revenge fantasies, the male villains—the most powerful men—are portrayed as ridiculous buffoons. Certainly Tarantino's depiction of Hitler fits the bill: he is vicious and vindictive, but also oafish, particularly in the scene immediately prior to the conflagration in the cinema in which he is depicted laughing uproariously at an image on the screen. Similarly, LXX Esther, like its Hebrew counterpart, portrays the king as a buffoon who is easily manipulated

22. Koller, *Esther in Ancient Jewish Thought*, 77. See also Rebecca S. Hancock, *Esther and the Politics of Negotiation: Public and Private Spaces and the Figure of the Female Royal Counselor* (Minneapolis: Fortress, 2013).

and who spends much of his time feasting and drinking.[23] This type of portrayal may have no connection whatsoever to history, but within the revenge genre it serves to widen the gap in intelligence and craftiness between the lowly female protagonists—for even a queen is lowly in the world created by LXX Esther—and the powerful male ruler.

But Hitler, though evil, and the Persian king, though ridiculous, are not the only villains. Shosanna and Esther also have more immediate targets for their subversive acts: the Nazi Landa and the minister Haman. Both Landa and Haman are portrayed not only as filled with hate but also as crafty and manipulative and yet more concerned for their own honor and safety than for the ideals of the regimes which they claim to serve. Interestingly enough, neither acts directly against the women who hate them. Landa has the knowledge and power both to expose Shosanna and arrange for her swift demise, yet he does not do so. Haman is too preoccupied with hating Mordecai to realize that his actions affect the queen and therefore jeopardize his own position and life. Yet both women realize that it is these men who must be neutralized in order for their larger plans to be effective.

6.5.2. Allies

Shosanna and Esther have not only male enemies but also male allies. Shosanna's ally is Marcel, who is persuaded to help her out of love. Without Marcel, Shosanna's plan would have failed, for it was he who was tasked with setting fire to the highly flammable reels of film that literally brought the house down.

Esther's ally is Mordecai. Mordecai had raised Esther after the death of her parents; he had encouraged her to enter the king's beauty pageant and watched over her, if from a distance, since her entrance into the king's harem. Technically, Mordecai is Esther's cousin, but the wording of the LXX implies that he was also her husband, as it indicates that "this man had a foster child, a daughter of Aminadab, his father's brother, and her name was Esther. And when her parents died, he trained her for himself as a wife [εἰς γυναῖκα]" (2:7). This introduces the interesting and somewhat uncomfortable notion that Esther was not only married to a non-Jew, but also guilty of bigamy. This motif is not developed further in the book, though it is in midrash and later Jewish exegesis.[24] Like Marcel in Tarantino's film, Mordecai has an integral role to

---

23. See, for example, Jo Carruthers, *Esther through the Centuries* (Malden, MA: Blackwell, 2008), 53.

24. On Esther as Mordecai's wife, see Barry Dov Walfish, "Kosher Adultery? The Mordecai-Esther-Ahasuerus Triangle in Midrash and Exegesis," *Proof* 22 (2002): 305–33, esp.

play in the success of Esther's plan. Indeed, as we have noted, he is the one who initiates the plan and convinces her to undertake it.

7. The Vengeance Motif

The defining characteristic of the revenge genre is a spectacular, over-the-top vengeance scene. The degree of revenge may or may not outstrip the degree of suffering that prompted the vengeful retaliation in the first place, but the act of vengeance is always memorable. In *Inglourious Basterds*, as already noted, the vengeful climax takes place in Shosanna's movie theater, where her plan and the allies' Operation Kino, though not intentionally coordinated, coalesce in a magnificent conflagration killing Hitler and all of his attendants. Esther's vengeance is less fiery but perhaps even more destructive. On the day appointed for their destruction, the Jews in Susa killed five hundred people; on the next, they kill three hundred more in Susa, and fifteen thousand altogether. It is a small mercy that no plunder was taken (9:16).

Both film and book stress the vulnerability of Jews in the diaspora. In fictional Persia and historical Germany, Jews had lived in relative safety and security, with some access to positions of authority. Their fortune could turn on a dime, however, as they remained subject to the whims and ideologies of political leaders. This notion of vulnerability is accentuated by the female gender of the protagonists in each case.

Revenge fantasies encourage audiences to identify with their protagonists to the point that the violence they depict seems well-deserved rather than excessive. In doing so, they provide not only escapism and narrative satisfaction, but also catharsis and wish fulfillment. This impact is particularly strong for audiences that identify with the protagonists' cause not simply due to the effects of the narrative but because of their identities and situations. The impact of *Inglourious Basterds*, for example, depends on the audience's knowledge about the holocaust. The film arouses a "what if?" wistfulness: How many lives would have been saved had Operation Kino or a similar plot succeeded in cutting even a year off the length of the war? Viewers can laugh wholeheartedly at Hitler and cheer for Shosanna and Aldo in their respective quests for vengeance.

Revenge is made sweeter by the inversion of hierarchies in which weak women speak truth to male power. In the authoritarian regimes of Nazi

307. The wording of Esth 2:7 LXX is not unambiguous, however, and could also refer to Esther having reached marriageable age when the king's servants came and brought her into the harem.

Germany and ancient Persia, these two works suggest, it is men who dominate, while women, and particularly, Jewish women, represent the lowest of the low, even if they happen to please the king. By succeeding in their often devious schemes to reverse their own situations and that of their people, the women protagonists enact the hopes and aspirations of all powerless peoples.

8. Revenge and the Audience of LXX Esther

Presumably the revenge motif was satisfying to the Greek-speaking audiences who heard or read the story annually at the festival of Purim. On the basis of its popularity,[25] we may assume that Greek Esther (like its Hebrew version) was particularly meaningful to diaspora Jews, in the same way that *Inglourious Basterds* is both satisfying and meaningful to twenty-first century viewers, both Jews and non-Jews.

LXX Esther acknowledges the particular situation of diaspora Jews, who struggle to maintain a balance between accommodation and particularity. The book stresses the importance of maintaining Jewish identity in the diaspora. Esther's prayer expresses solidarity with her people and the history of Israel: "I have heard from my birth in the tribe of my family that you, O Lord, took Israel out of all the nations and our fathers from among all their forebears, to be an everlasting inheritance, and you did for them all that you said" (14:5; C, 16).

On a concrete level, maintaining Jewish identity requires abstaining from gentile food and gentile beds—at least, not enjoying them. As Esther reminds God in Addition C:

> You have knowledge of everything, and you know that I hate the glory of the lawless and abhor the bed of the uncircumcised and of any foreigner. You know my predicament—that I abhor the sign of my proud position that is upon my head on days when I appear in public. I abhor it like a menstrual cloth, and I do not wear it on the days when I am in private. And your slave has not eaten at Haman's table, and I have not honored the king's banquet nor drunk the wine of libations. (14:14–18; C, 25–28)

Indeed,

> Your slave has not rejoiced since the day of my change until now, except in you, O Lord, God of Abraam. O God who has power over all things, hear the

25. Joshua Ezra Burns, "The Special Purim and the Reception of the Book of Esther in the Hellenistic and Early Roman Eras," *JSJ* 37 (2006): 4.

voice of those who despair, and save us from the hand of evildoers. And save me from my fear! (14:18–19; C, 29–30)[26]

More subtly, LXX Esther not only stresses the importance of endogamy and the dietary laws, but also provides a nuanced view of the situation of diaspora Jews vis-à-vis their host cultures. Like MT Esther, the LXX demonstrates the virtues of Esther's strategy by implying a contrast with her royal predecessor Vashti. Strictly speaking, both women defy the law of the land: Vashti in her refusal to come before the king when ordered, and Esther in her insistence on coming before the king though she was not summoned. Even in her defiance, however, Esther exemplifies the overawed and submissive woman who faints at the sight of royal splendor; in doing so, she disarms the king and ultimately gets her way.

Exactly what message the audience would have drawn, however, depends on how we view the colophon in relation to the book's aim and provenance. Some scholars, such as Charles Torrey, situate LXX Esther in the Hellenistic diaspora, among the Greek-speaking Jews of Egypt, and perhaps in Alexandria.[27] If so, then, the message of the book is: obey the torah, venerate the temple, speak Greek, put your hopes in the Ptolemaic dynasty,[28] and, of course, celebrate Purim with joy. Diaspora Jewish audiences may therefore have read LXX Esther's tale of vengeance not as an indictment of the regime under which they lived but rather as a strategy manual for how to make the diaspora work for them. The book encourages its audience to insert themselves in the political structures as appropriate and possible; not to flaunt their Jewish identity but to be judicious about when, why, and to whom to reveal it; to use whatever means at their disposal to survive and thrive; and to take advantage of their position to seek revenge against their enemies. This is not to say that in promoting the lively and joyful celebration of the Purim holiday LXX Esther is also advocating violence as a course of action. Ancient audiences would, I believe, have recognized that there is an element of whimsy and fantasy in the book, in keeping with its genre, just as modern

---

26. This statement throws into relief Esther's own silence at the beginning of the book. One can assume that she was in agreement with Mordecai in the idea of presenting her as a candidate for queen, in the process of which she had to join the harem. But one wonders how she managed to please the king if she abhorred his bed so much, and, on a more prosaic note, how she managed to abstain from gentile food without divulging her ethnic identity, especially since, as specified in 2:9, the eunuch Gai provided Esther with a packet of food when she entered the harem.

27. See Koller, *Esther in Ancient Jewish Thought*, 122.

28. Ibid.

movie goers would not take Tarantino's *Inglourious Basterds* as license to burn down movie theaters.

This perspective is based on the assumption that LXX Esther was composed in and for the diaspora. But those who attribute historicity to the colophon in Addition F view the book differently: as a translation from Hebrew to Greek done by a Jerusalemite named Lysimachus son of Ptolemy and brought to Alexandria by Dositheus and Ptolemy in the late first or early second century BCE.[29] On the basis of this signature, it may be argued that LXX Esther was intended to persuade Egyptian Jews to celebrate the festival of Purim. Elias Bickerman, for example, argues "that Dositheus and his backers in Jerusalem were eager for the diffusion of Purim and of the pamphlet designated to explain to the Diaspora the anti-alien meaning of the new festival."[30]

If so, LXX Esther may have had a rhetorical purpose. Rather than reflecting the existing and complex social situation of diaspora Jews vis-à-vis the local population and its government, it may have been intended to create suspicion, dislike, perhaps even animosity of the diaspora Jews towards their neighbors.[31] If so, the book may have been read as a warning not to trust the local powers unreservedly. These messages would have been reinforced by the annual celebration of Purim, of which the reading of Esther was a central ritual.

Perhaps the most reasonable is the "both-and" position held by Joshua Ezra Burns, who suggests that the Hellenized agenda present in LXX Esther "was … designed for audiences in Jerusalem and Egypt alike, appealing to the common issues facing the Jews both in Judaea, where the Hasmonaean court was engaged in its ongoing struggles with the Greek *poleis* of the province, and in the Mediterranean Diaspora, offering Jewish readers 'moral support in their efforts to rise in the service of the kingdom.' "[32]

Above all, LXX Esther teaches that even when the chips are down, reading or hearing about the vengeful exploits of a smart and brave woman can provide temporary catharsis and relief and the hope that a reversal of fortunes may yet occur.

---

29. Bickerman, "Colophon," 347, prefers a dating of 78–77, based on the identification of Ptolemy XII Auletes and Cleopatra V (see n. 5 above).

30. Ibid., 361. The NRSV translation suggests that there were only two envoys: Dositheus (who was a priest and a Levite) and his son Ptolemy. But Bickerman reads "a Levite" as a proper name and therefore sees three envoys: Dosithetus, who was a priest, Levitas, and his son Ptolemy.

31. Ibid., 362.

32. Burns, "Special Purim," 18. The quoted phrase is from John J. Collins, *Between Athens and Jerusalem: Jewish Identity in the Hellenistic Diaspora* (New York: Crossroad, 1983), 112.

9. Conclusion: Reading Revenge in the Twenty-First Century

Lawrence Wills has noted that Greek Esther—and its Hebrew version—"caused great discomfort to many later readers because of its 'nationalist' spirit and bloodthirsty revenge" and may therefore have been problematic for Christians who "see its spirit of revenge as a violation of the Christian ethic of love and nonretaliation."[33] The revenge theme is also difficult for some modern Jewish readers. In a 1993 article, Haim Gevaryahu insisted that (Hebrew) Esther simply depicts a successful and praiseworthy act of self-defense that "never degenerated into *revenge*."[34] Gevaryahu also discusses modern Christian dislike for this book, which he attributes largely to Martin Luther who, in his anti-Semitic work *About the Jews and Their Lies* "accuses the Jews of yearning to treat the Gentiles of his time in just the same way that they treated the Gentiles in the time of Esther."[35] In 1938 Shalom Ben-Chorin referred to the actions in Esther as a pogrom committed by the Jews and advocated that the reading of the book and the celebration of Purim be cancelled. In his view, the model of diaspora behavior exemplified by Esther's actions, that is, deference to an autocratic regime, was not an appropriate model in the context of the modern Zionist movement and Jewish settlement in Palestine.[36]

Exegesis alone cannot counteract the destructive ways in which biblical texts are used. Nor does denying the obvious revenge theme that is present in LXX Esther as well as the MT and other versions solve the problem of the book's problematic reception history. It can be helpful, however, to consider Esther, in any of its versions, as a literary—and fictional—text that was written within a diaspora context and preserved because it empowered, at least vicariously, a vulnerable Jewish minority community. Furthermore, considering the book within the context of "revenge fantasy" works, whatever their form (literature, film, drama), can help us to discern certain elements of LXX Esther, such as the portrayal of women, more clearly. Finally, insofar as such genre criticism insists on the transcultural nature of these sorts of stories, a

33. Wills, *Jewish Novel in the Ancient World*, 96. For a detailed discussion of morality in all versions of Esther, see Charles D. Harvey, *Finding Morality in the Diaspora? Moral Ambiguity and Transformed Morality in the Books of Esther*, BZAW 328 (Berlin: de Gruyter, 2003).

34. Haim M. Gevaryahu, "Esther Is a Story of Jewish Defense, Not a Story of Jewish Revenge," *JBQ* 21 (1993): 3, emphasis original.

35. Ibid., 6.

36. Shalom Ben-Chorin, *Kritik des Estherbuches: Eine theologische Streitschrift* (Jerusalem: Salingre, 1938). For detailed discussion of Christian views on Esther, see Tricia Miller, *Jews and Anti-Judaism in Esther and the Church* (Cambridge: James Clarke, 2015).

study of LXX Esther as a revenge fantasy may also help to disarm its potential for further damage in the present-day relationship between diaspora Jews and the majority cultures within which they live.

Judith: Beautiful Wisdom Teacher or Pious Woman? Reflections on the Book of Judith

Barbara Schmitz and Lydia Lange
Translated by Richard Ratzlaff

1. Introduction

"No other woman from one end of the earth to the other looks so beautiful or speaks so wisely!" (Jdt 11:21 NRSV)—such is how the soldiers in the Assyrian camp marvel as they look at Judith. They marvel above all at her beauty.

The focus in the following contribution will be on the portrait of Judith as presented in the Septuagint; one of the central concerns of this version is the beauty of Judith. In order to describe the portrait of Judith, the Septuagint (LXX), the Greek version of approximately 100 BCE, will first be analyzed and then compared with the Latin Vulgate version, which was made between 398 and 407 CE. Comparing the two versions will not only reveal more fully the contours of the LXX version, but will also stimulate new insights into the question of the original version of the book of Judith. The present contribution is one in a long list of feminist studies on and gender-sensitive analyses of the book of Judith and the figure of Judith,[1] but it also adds its own, new accents.

1. The following list is representative only: one of the early commentators was Toni Craven, *Artistry and Faith in the Book of Judith*, SBLDS 70 (Chico, CA: Scholars Press, 1983); followed by Linda Bennett Elder, "Judith," in *A Feminist Commentary*, vol. 2 of *Searching the Scriptures*, ed. Elisabeth Schüssler-Fiorenza (New York: Crossroad, 1994), 455–69; Athalya Brenner, *A Feminist Companion to Esther, Judith, and Susanna*, FCB 7 (Sheffield: Sheffield Academic, 1995; London: T&T Clark, 2005); Claudia Rakel, "Judith: About a Beauty Who Is Not What She Pretends to Be," in *Feminist Interpretation: A Compendium of Critical Commentary on the Books of the Bible and Related Literature*, ed. Luise Schottroff and Marie-Theres Wacker (Grand Rapids: Eerdmans, 2012), 515–30. To these can be added numerous studies of the reception history of the Judith story, for example: Margarita Stocker, *Judith: Sexual Warrior; Women and Power in Western Culture* (New

Compared with the story of Judith in the LXX, the Vulgate version is, on one hand, shorter by a fifth. On the other hand, it has been expanded in places, and so only half of it overlaps with the Greek texts.[2] A character named Judith appears in both, but there are significant differences between the two versions. There are fundamental differences not only in how they portray the figure of Judith but also in the rest of the narrative. In the reflections that follow, however, only the figure of Judith will be discussed, with the focus above all on how Judith is introduced in chapter 8. Moreover, it is not our prime concern to explore the differences from a text-critical and text-historical point of view; rather, the two versions will be treated as autonomous texts in order to address their distinct points of view and the social-historical presuppositions related to both. We will see that the figure of Judith in the LXX has a distinctly different character from the figure of Judith in the Vulgate.[3]

2. Text Transmission and Narrative Structure

Represented by the uncials B, S, A, and V as well as more than forty minuscules, the LXX version is well attested.[4] The LXX serves as the base for the ancient translations (Vetus Latina, translations into Syriac, Sahidic, Ethiopic, and Armenian). These need to be distinguished from the Vulgate translation of Judith made in Bethlehem by the church father Jerome.[5] The longer versions represented by the medieval Hebrew texts from the tenth century CE on are related above all to the Vulgate; the shorter Hebrew versions that also begin to appear in the tenth century are rather free reworkings.[6]

Haven: Yale University Press, 1998); Marion Kobelt-Groch, *Judith macht Geschichte: Zur Rezeption einer mythischen Gestalt vom 16. bis 19. Jahrhundert* (Munich: Fink, 2005); Kevin R. Brine, Elena Ciletti, and Henrike Lähnemann, eds., *The Sword of Judith: Judith Studies across the Disciplines* (Cambridge: OpenBook, 2010).

2. See Helmut Engel, "Das Buch Judit," in *Einleitung in das Alte Testament*, ed. Erich Zenger et al., 8th ed. (Stuttgart: Kohlhammer, 2012), 363.

3. When figures or places from the Vulgate version of the book of Judith are intended, the spelling will follow the Latin version: "Judith" refers to the LXX version and "Iudith" to the Vulgate version. When a text is cited according to the LXX version, the abbreviation used is "Jdt"; when according to the Vulgate version, "Idt."

4. Critical edition of the LXX version: R. Hanhart, *Iudith*, SVTG 8.4 (Göttingen: Vandenhoeck & Ruprecht, 1979).

5. Critical edition of the Vulgate version: Robert Weber and Roger Gryson, eds., *Biblia Sacra: Iuxta Vulgatam Versionem*, Editio Quinta (Stuttgart: Deutsche Bibelgesellschaft, 2007).

6. See Debora Levine Gera, "The Jewish Textual Traditions," in Brine, Ciletti, and Lähnemann, *Sword of Judith*, 23–39; Gera, "Shorter Medieval Hebrew Tales of Judith," in

Jerome's version begins, as do all of his translations, with a foreword in which he describes, among other topics, his approach to the translation.[7] Jerome writes that he has based his translation of Judith on a "Chaldean" source, probably referring to a Syriac or Aramaic version. The Jews, he writes, include it only among the Apocrypha (*hagiographa*) but the Christians among the historical writings; it can contribute little to settling theological disagreements (ll. 1–3, *praefatio* to the book Iudith).

Jerome goes on to assert that he prepared the translation in a single night (*unam lucubratiuculam*). Moreover, he has undertaken to shorten the text because of variations caused by errors in transmission (*varietatem vitiosissimam*) among the many manuscripts (he probably means the Vetus Latina) and translated only what he has found fully comprehensible in "Chaldean words" (*in verbis chaldaeis*) (ll. 6–7, *praefatio* to the book of Judith). Because Jerome writes in his *praefatio* of a textual source, scholars of the book of Judith have long assumed that the LXX text of Judith was a translation from Hebrew or Aramaic.[8] They found confirmation of this thesis in the text, as it contains frequent instances of parataxis, Hebraizing syntax, putative translation errors, or word choices that could be explained by a Hebrew original. There are, however, no manuscript witnesses for such a presumed original. A "Chaldean" text, as reported by Jerome, has not been transmitted.

In the last few years, much attention has been paid to the question of the original language of the Judith narrative.[9] Helmut Engel was one of the first to propose that the present LXX version was originally composed in Greek.[10]

Brine, Ciletti, and Lähnemann, *Sword of Judith*, 81–95. A Hebrew-German text edition: Dagmar Börner-Klein, *Gefährdete Braut und schöne Witwe: Hebräische Judit-Geschichten* (Wiesbaden: Marix-Verlag, 2007).

7. See Barbara Schmitz, "Ιουδιθ und *Iudith*: Überlegungen zum Verhältnis der Judit-Erzählung in der LXX und der Vulgata," in *Text-Critical and Hermeneutical Studies in the Septuagint*, ed. Johann Cook and Hermann-Josef Stipp, VTSup 157 (Leiden: Brill, 2012), 359–79; Philipp Thielmann, *Beiträge zur Textkritik der Vulgata insbesondere des Buches Judit*, Beigabe zum Jahresbericht 1882/1883 der Kgl. Studienanstalt Speier (Speier: Gilardone, 1883).

8. Hanhart concludes, "Der griechische Text des Buches Iudith ist ein Übersetzungstext. Seine Vorlage war entweder hebräisch oder aramäisch." See Robert Hanhart, *Text und Textgeschichte des Buches Judith*, MSU 14 (Göttingen: Vandenhoeck & Ruprecht, 1979), 8.

9. See, in more depth, Barbara Schmitz and Helmut Engel, *Judit*, HThKAT (Freiburg: Herder, 2014), 42–43. See also Debora Levine Gera, *Judith*, CEJL (Berlin: de Gruyter, 2014), 79–97.

10. Helmut Engel, "'Der HERR ist ein Gott, der Kriege zerschlägt': Zur Frage der griechischen Originalsprache und der Struktur des Buches Judit," in *Goldene Äpfel in silbernen Schalen*, ed. Klaus-Dietrich Schunck and Matthias Augustin, BEATAJ 20 (Frankfurt: Lang, 1992), 155–68.

In particular, he highlighted the verses in which the Judith story quotes or alludes to texts from the LXX that are very different from the Hebrew version of the same text.[11] The Greek text of the book of Judith is not, therefore, a translation of a lost semitic original but rather—and this is Engel's new thesis—was composed originally in Greek. Jan Joosten has provided some additional arguments in favor of this thesis, pointing to an array of instances in which the Greek text displays elevated vocabulary and syntax.[12] Jeremy Corley examined the peculiarities of the Greek narrative that sound Hebraic and came to the conclusion "that the proposed instances of Hebraic phraseology and style in the Greek text of Judith do not necessarily indicate a Hebrew origin of the book, since they can easily be evidence of either mimetic appreciation of Septuagintal style or Semitic interference.... [A] Hebrew *Vorlage* cannot be presumed, while a Greek origin can be suggested as very possible."[13]

A closer examination of the structure of the book of Judith—of its inclusions, temporal indications, introduction of new figures at various points in the narrative, the alteration of location and scenes, its speeches and prayers, the way the latter are introduced and what effects they have—reveals a two-part composition consisting of the sections Jdt 1–7 and Jdt 8–16.[14]

While the first part (Jdt 1–7) narrates how the whole world is threatened by the overwhelming power of the army of the Assyrian king, who wishes to rule the world and be worshiped as a god by all, the first appearance of Judith (Jdt 8) constitutes a new beginning. This new beginning is marked not only by a new indication of time and the introduction of a new character, but also by the structural parallel between the new beginning of the second part and the beginning of the first part of the narrative.[15]

---

11. One example of this is the citation of Exod 15:3 in Jdt 9:7–8 and in Jdt 16:2, which is cited according to the LXX, not the Hebrew text; other examples are Num 23:19 LXX in Jdt 8:16 or Gen 34:7 LXX in Jdt 9:2.

12. Jan Joosten, "The Original Language and Historical Milieu of the Book of Judith," in *Meghillot: Studies in the Dead Sea Scrolls V–VI; A Festschrift for Devorah Dimant*, ed. Moshe Bar-Asher and Emanuel Tov (Jerusalem: Bialik Institute, 2007), 159–76.

13. Jeremy Corley, "Septuagintalisms, Semitic Interference, and the Original Language of the Book of Judith," in *Studies in the Greek Bible: Essays in Honour of Francis T. Gignac*, ed Jeremy Corley, CBQMS 44 (Washington, DC: Catholic Biblical Association, 2008), 65–96.

14. On the structure, see Schmitz and Engel, *Judit*, 45–50. The first part (Jdt 1–7) can be further divided into the sections Jdt 1–3 and Jdt 4–7. See, for more on this issue, Barbara Schmitz, "The Function of the Speeches and Prayers in the Book of Judith," in *A Feminist Companion to Tobit and Judith*, ed. Athalya Brenner-Idan and Helen Efthimiades-Keith (London: Bloomsbury T&T Clark, 2015), 164–74.

15. As in Jdt 1:1 (with a new indication of time and the introduction of a new figure,

The speeches and prayers, which comprise almost a third of the book, have a special function in the narrative. The story reaches its low point in the description of the misery in Bethulia (Jdt 7) and its high point in the execution of Holofernes (Jdt 13), but the concentrically arranged speeches and prayers form another narrative arc,[16] which reaches its high point in Judith's theological discourse and prayer (Jdt 8–9). This section is framed by two dialogues, between Achior and Holofernes (Jdt 5:1–6:6) and Holofernes and Judith (Jdt 11), which take place at and in Holofernes's tent respectively and refer to each other textually. These two dialogues are in turn framed by the anticipatory speech of Nebuchadnezzar (Jdt 2) and Judith's retrospective hymn of thanks (Jdt 16).

The book of Judith, as a whole, does not tell the story of a historical event but is rather conceptualized as a fictional narrative. Already in the first sentence of the book it is clear that figures, places, and events spanning approximately six hundred years, from the eighth or seventh century BCE to the second century BCE, have been brought together into one narrative. Historical events, characters, geographic locations, and so on from different eras are reused and brought into new fictional constellations. To give only one example, in the book of Judith, Nebuchadnezzar[17] is portrayed as the king of the Assyrians, whereas he was in fact the king of the Neo-Babylonian Empire (605–562 BCE).

3. The Portrait of Judith in the LXX Version

In the LXX version Judith does not make her appearance until chapter 8.[18] The name Judith, or Ιουδιθ,[19] is the Greek transcription of the Hebrew יהודית ("Judahite"). In the context of the Judith narrative the choice of name could

Nabuchodonosor) the sentence in Jdt 8:1 has a beginning but does not end. It is rather interrupted in order that a long parenthetical explanatory passage can be inserted. Only in Jdt 8:9 (and Jdt 1:5) does the author return again to his sentence in order to finish it.

16. See here Barbara Schmitz, *Gedeutete Geschichte: Die Funktion der Reden und Gebete im Buch Judit*, HBS 40 (Freiburg: Herder, 2004).

17. In the LXX Nebuchadnezzar is named "Nabuchodonosor."

18. For what follows, see Schmitz and Engel, *Judit*.

19. In the Hebrew Bible the name יהודית is used only in Gen 26:34 for the daughter of the Hittite Beeri; the LXX uses here the accusative form Ιουδιν. It is also possible that the name Judith was chosen as the feminine counterpart of the historical figure Judas (Ιουδας ὁ καλούμενος Μακκαβαῖος, 1 Macc 2:4); see Lawrence M. Wills, "The Book of Judith: Introduction, Commentary, and Reflections," in *Esther, Additions to Esther, Tobit, Judith, 1 and 2 Maccabees, Wisdom of Solomon, Sirach, Introduction to Apocalyptic Literature, Daniel, Additions to D*, ed. Leander E. Keck, NIB 3 (Nashville: Abingdon, 1999), 1131.

be a way of referring to the fact that the fictional figure of Judith is not only an individual character. This Judith is also a Judahite; that is, she represents every woman in Israel.

Judith is introduced via sixteen generations of her genealogy (Jdt 8:1). This is an unusually long family tree; it is the longest genealogy of any woman in the Bible. Judith is presented as a descendent of the patriarch Jacob, who is referred to by his honorary title "Israel" (see Gen 32:29; cf. Jdt 9:2). Through this genealogy the time of the narrative is connected to the origins of Israel, and Judith is portrayed as a woman of noble and authentic, "old Israelite" stock. The need to give an account of one's origins was especially strong in the postexilic period (see Ezra 2:62; Neh 7:64).

In the presentation of Judith following the genealogy, the fate of Judith's husband Manasseh and part of her own biography is described (Jdt 8:2–3). It it noteworthy that Judith is not included among the people of Israel through her husband Manasseh but rather that Manasseh is included through his wife Judith. He belongs to *her* tribe and *her* family (τῆς φυλῆς αὐτῆς καὶ τῆς πατριᾶς αὐτῆς, Jdt 8:2). That Judith has married someone from the same tribe should be understood within the context of the issue of *mixed marriages* (see Ezra 9) and the laws of inheritance (Num 36) and is also an indication of her faithfulness to a life lived in accordance with torah (so also in Tob 1:9; 4:12–13 B; cf. Gen 24). Even though Manasseh is at the center of Jdt 8:2–3, this section functions to introduce Judith: she was exemplary in her choice of husband and became a widow soon thereafter, apparently before having children. In other words, important prerequisites for Judith's unusual situation in life that will be described in the next section (Jdt 8:4–6, 7–8) are introduced here: Judith is a torah-faithful, young, beautiful, rich widow.

Judith's situation in life is at the center of the third section (Jdt 8:4–6, 7–8). Judith has been a widow for three years and four months (Jdt 8:4). Throughout that time she has lived in a tent on the roof of her house (Jdt 8:5). Whereas the interior of the house is private space (see also Jdt 10:2–5), the roof and therefore also the tent on top are publicly visible.[20] In this way, Judith lives openly, as an honorable widow. In her tent, visible to all, she also receives the elders of the town she has summoned and delivers her teaching to them (Jdt 8:36). In this tent she dresses in sackcloth, wears her widow's clothing, fasts (Jdt 8:5–6), and prays (Jdt 9). Judith practices her own way of life: she wears sackcloth around her waist as well as widow's clothing (Jdt 8:5) and fasts every day, except on the Sabbath and the day before the Sabbath, the feast of the new moon and the day before, and generally on the "festivals

20. See Schmitz and Engel, *Judit*, 244–45.

and days of rejoicing of the House of Israel," which are here not identified by name. This is very unusual, since it was common to fast and wear sackcloth in times of disaster (see Jdt 4:10, 13, 14; 1 Kgs 21:31, 32; 2 Macc 10:25) or mourning (see Gen 37:34), but in both cases only for a limited period of time. Judith can apparently afford to practice her lifestyle whereas other widows who are also young and childless have to marry as quickly as possible after a period of mourning in order to be secure legally and economically. Judith in contrast remains a widow for the rest of her life (Jdt 16:22).

Four features of the presentation of Judith are especially highlighted: her beauty, the way she treats her body, her wealth, and her education.

3.1. Judith's Beauty

According to Jdt 8:7 Judith "was beautiful in appearance, and was very lovely to behold" (καλὴ τῷ εἴδει καὶ ὡραία τῇ ὄψει σφόδρα).[21] The beauty of Judith, described here with two terms, is a theme that runs through the entire Judith narrative.[22]

The first expression in Jdt 8:7 for Judith's beauty is "beautiful in appearance" (καλὴ / -ὀς τῷ εἴδει). This expression is used in the Bible to describe men and women, but also animals and objects: for example, Rachel in comparison to Leah (Gen 29:17), Joseph (Gen 39:6), the seven sleek and fat cows out of the Nile (Gen 41:2, 4, 19), a beautiful woman among the prisoners of war (Deut 21:11), Abigail (1 Sam 25:3), Bathsheba (2 Sam 11:2), and Susannah (Sus 31 Th). In the LXX "beautiful" (καλός / καλή) and "beauty" (τὸ κάλλος) appear frequently. These words are used especially to refer to the *physical beauty* of men and above all of women.

The second expression in Jdt 8:7 is "very lovely to behold" (ὡραία τῇ ὄψει σφόδρα). "Lovely" (ὡραῖος) is derived from ἡ ὥρα, "hour," and literally means "ideal for harvesting, ripe, at full bloom, in the bloom of youth." In the LXX the expression is used infrequently: in 1 Kgs 1:6 Adonijah is described as "resplendent in appearance" (ὡραῖος τῇ ὄψει σφόδρα) but so are Rebecca (Gen

---

21. This two-part expression is used in the LXX, besides here of Judith, only to describe Rachel (Gen 29:17, without σφόδρα) and Joseph the son of Jacob (καλὸς τῷ εἴδει καὶ ὡραῖος τῇ ὄψει σφόδρα, Gen 39:6).

22. Jdt 10:7 (admiration by the town elders), Jdt 10:14 (admiration by the Assyrian patrol), Jdt 10:19 (admiration by the Assyrian soldiers in the camp), Jdt 10:23 (admiration by Holofernes and his attendants), Jdt 11:21 (renewed admiration by Holofernes and his attendants), Jdt 12:13 (Bagoas addresses Judith as "pretty girl"), and finally in the closing hymn in Jdt 16:6, 9. See Claudia Rakel, *Judit—Über Schönheit, Macht und Widerstand im Krieg: Eine feministisch-intertextuelle Lektüre*, BZAW 334 (Berlin: de Gruyter, 2003), 202–8.

26:7), Rachel (Gen 29:17), and Joseph (Gen 39:6). The beloved in Cant 2:14 says to his "dove": "your face is lovely" (ἡ ὄψις σου ὡραία).

In Jdt 11:23 there is a third expression for Judith's beauty: "graceful in appearance" (ἀστεία ἐν τῷ εἴδει). Besides Judith, only Susannah in Sus 7 LXX is described as "graceful in appearance" (ἀστεία εἶ σὺ ἐν τῷ εἴδει). ἀστεῖος/ἀστεία is derived from τὸ ἄστυ "city"; it means therefore "urbanely elegant in appearance" and is also an expression of respect. The term "graceful in appearance" (ἀστεία εἶ σὺ ἐν τῷ εἴδει) gives a distinct accent to Jdt 11:23: Holofernes admires not only Judith's beauty, but even more her refined appearance *and* her culture. As soon as Judith is introduced in the story the narrator elaborates on her beauty by describing her as God-fearing (Jdt 8:8). The fear of God, an attitude of respect, reverence, trust, and connection, describes Judith's relationship to God. At the end of her introduction, the attitude "fear of God" serves as a summation of the fact that the purpose of the introduction is not to focus on Judith's appearance but on how her beauty and fear of God are reciprocally constitutive: her beauty is an expression of her fear of God and her fear of God is an expression of her beauty. Later the town elders will call her εὐσεβής, "god-fearing, pious" (Jdt 8:31) and in the presence of Holofernes she refers to herself as θεοσεβής, "god worshipper, god-fearer" (Jdt 11:17).

3.2. Judith Stages Her Body

Twice in the narrative Judith, the God-fearing and beautiful woman, changes her outer appearance and thereby draws special attention to her body. The first occasion is in Jdt 9:1. After a conversation with the elders and her theological discourse, Judith prostrates herself for prayer. Two gestures are described, which serve as a purposeful staging of her body. Judith first covers her head with ashes. To strew ashes on one's head is a customary act of mourning (see Jdt 4:11, 15). Tamar, for example, does the same after she is raped: Tamar takes ashes, strews them on her head, and tears her clothing (2 Sam 13:19). Similary Esther, before she goes to the king—without being summoned, thereby risking death—in order to rescue her people, removes her costly clothing, puts on garments of distress and mourning, and covers her head with ashes and dung (Esth C 13 [= Esth 4:17k], see also Esth 4:1–2 and Esth 4:3). Then Judith "uncovers" (ἐγύμνωσεν) the sackcloth (σάκκος) that she has worn around her hips, that is, under her widow's garments, since she became a widow (see Jdt 8:5). The words can be understood to mean that Judith has now made this sackcloth public/visible. By strewing ashes on her head and uncovering her sackcloth Judith displays her body in a situation in which she appears to be alone. In this scene Judith turns in intense prayer to God, so her staging of her body is intended to be viewed by God. God is supposed to see the sackcloth of the widow Judith; God is intended to see that Judith has prostrated herself in supplication; and it is God who is intended to see that Judith has displayed herself with ashes on her head. In doing so, Judith deliberately models her prayer on that of Tamar: she, a woman who is still untouched, prays herself into the situation in which she will place herself beginning in Jdt 10; in the Assyrian camp she is a woman in danger who will have to confront the real possibility that she will be sexually assaulted. She proleptically stages with her body the danger threatening her and by this performance asks for God's saving and helping support. She not only calls on God as God of the oppressed, helper of the lowly, upholder of the weak, protector of the despised and savior of those without hope (see Jdt 9:11), but also evokes the dishonoured Dinah and pleads for the sword of Simeon (Jdt 9:2–4).

The staging of her body is repeated in the following scene in Jdt 10:2–4. After her prayer Judith comes down from the roof of her house and makes her way inside. There now follows a long account of her change of clothing:[23] In Jdt 10:3–4 there is a detailed description of how the beautiful Judith (see Jdt 8:5) makes herself beautiful (ἐκαλλωπίσατο Jdt 10:4). Judith takes off the sackcloth and her widow's clothing (see Jdt 8:5; 9:1), thereby setting aside the symbols of the lifestyle she herself has chosen. Next she takes a bath and anoints herself with myrrh. She combs her hair and puts on a head-band and dresses herself in the "festive attire"[24] that she still has from her previous life with Manasseh. Readers are not told what exactly these clothes look like; not until Jdt 16:8 is there mention of a linen gown. Finally, she puts on her jewelry.

Whereas Judith *is* a beautiful and god-fearing woman (Jdt 8:5–9), she *makes* herself beautiful for a specific reason, "to entice the eyes of all the men who might see her" (Jdt 10:4). Unlike the situation in Jdt 9:1, where God is the implicit addressee of the staging, in Jdt 10:4 it is stated explicitly who is intended to see Judith: the soldiers in the Assyrian camp, especially Holofernes himself. It is clear that with her new appearance and her outward change Judith has taken on and is playing a role: She is staging herself in order to mislead the men who see her. The ambiguity of the lexeme, ἀπάτ-, which can mean "deceive" but also "seduce" is taken up in the narrative that follows: Judith wants to deceive Holofernes through her beauty put on display, while Holofernes wants to seduce Judith (Jdt 12:16; see also 12:12).

23. Deliberately staged and effective changes of clothing can be found also in the cases of Ruth (Ruth 3:3, 7), Esther (Esth D 1–16 [= Esth 5:1a–2b LXX]), or Tamar (Gen 38:14 LXX).

24. "Festive," i.e., "joyful," could have sexual overtones here and hints at the scene to come, in which Bagoas and then Holofernes invite Judith to "become joyful/merry" (Jdt 12:13, 17).

In order to do so Judith plays a role: she, the beautiful woman leading a withdrawn life, wearing garments of widowhood and mourning, stages herself in the manner of the women of the Jerusalem upper class, who are described in Isa 3:20 as living in splendor and luxury.[25] The role played by Judith in Jdt 10–14, which includes her staging herself for the men who will see her, has two components. For the men who will see her in the Assyrain camp, Judith transforms herself into a "strange woman," the women who is the object of warning in Prov 5:3–6 and 7:5–23 because she is a source of danger—from the male perspective, at any rate. Neither the men in the camp nor Holofernes himself recognize initially that Judith, who has made herself beautiful, can be a source of great danger. For Israel, on the other hand, and thus for the whole world, Judith's staging of herself is salvation. It is not surprising therefore that there are many and close verbal parallels between Jdt 10:3 and Isa 61:10 LXX, the song in which the saved and those who have been restored by their God praise God with the words "My soul rejoices in the Lord! For he has clothed me with the cloak of salvation, and the garments of joy; he put a garland on my head as on a bridegroom, and adorned me with jewelry as a bride." It cannot be a coincidence that in Jdt 10:3 there are numerous key words also found in Isa 61:10 LXX, since, after all, the staging of the body described here in the Judith narrative leads in the end to salvation and joy.

3.3. Judith's Wealth

In addition to her beauty, a second characteristic feature of Judith is her wealth. Her husband Manasseh has left her great wealth: gold and silver, servants, cattle, and land (Jdt 8:7). It is interesting that she, a widow, is the lawful owner of this wealth (καὶ ἔμενεν ἐπ' αὐτῶν, "she maintained this estate," Jdt 8:7) and can freely dispose of it as she pleases (see Jdt 16:23, 24).

In the biblical literature widows are usually portrayed as needy, threatened, and weak, as without economic security and as those whose rights are often ignored (Isa 1:17, 23; 5:28); because of their situation they are commonly named together with other groups on the margins of society.[26] They are owed the special solidarity of the community (see Exod 22:21; Deut 24:17, 19) or the King (Ps 71[72 MT]:4) and are under the special protection of God (Exod 22:22–23; Deut 10:17–18; Ps 67[68 MT]:6).[27] Judith appears to appeal

25. See here also Rakel, *Judit*, 202–8.

26. They are named together with orphans, the so-called *personae miserae* (Job 24:3; Ps 93[94 MT]:6; Mal 3:5, etc.), the foreigners (Exod 22:21–23; Deut 10:18; Zech 7:10), the day laborers (Mal 3:5), or the poor, i.e., the "powerless" (Isa 10:2; Job 24:3–4; 31:16).

27. See Gera, *Judith*, 261–62.

to this biblical tradition in her prayer in Jdt 9:4, 9, even though she in fact has little in common with the precarious situation of the poor widow. Judith is much more the exception: she is a rich widow who has inherited a large estate from her husband.

She is independent as well. That she intends to remain single until she dies, despite numerous offers to marry (Jdt 16:22), shows that she herself has consciously chosen her way of life. That way of life, in turn, is possible because Judith is able to dispose of her property by herself. With her gold and silver, servants, cattle, and land (Jdt 8:7), Judith has everything that belongs to a traditional "house" (בית, οἶκος). The head of such a household is customarily a man, but in this story it is a woman. Moreover, Judith has put a woman in charge of her estate (Jdt 8:10). This woman is designated in the narrative as an ἅβρα. Usually this Greek word is translated as "servant" or "favorite slave,"[28] which, in light of the position occupied by this ἅβρα, would not be accurate. She is described as having the same responsibilities as Bagoas, Holofernes's personal assistant (Jdt 12:11), but unlike him she has no name of her own[29] and never appears in a speaking role. The word ἅβρα, which is rare in the LXX (see Exod 2:5), refers to a female person who is in a position of dependence but who is nevertheless entrusted with special responsibilities and duties. Judith's ἅβρα is responsible for overseeing her entire estate (τὴν ἐφεστῶσαν πᾶσιν τοῖς ὑπάρχουσιν αὐτῆς, Jdt 8:10). The verb ἐφίσταμαι, "oversee, supervise," is a *terminus technicus* for the functions of overseers and supervisors, as, for example, in Exod 1:11; Num 1:50; and Ruth 2:5, 6. Although the ἅβρα is a bondservant, we should not see her as a "maid," but much rather as the

28. So, for example, Cameron Boyd-Taylor, "Ioudith," in *A New English Translation of the Septuagint and other Greek Translations Traditionally Included under That Title*, ed. Albert Pietersma and Benjamin G. Wright (Oxford: Oxford University Press, 2007), 441–55.

29. In the reception history of the story, the unnamed ἅβρα is often given the *name* "Abra," as in Sixt Birck's drama *Judit* (1534), in Samuel Hebel, *Spiel von der Belagerung der Stadt Bethulia* (1566), the Jesuit drama from Ingolstädt, "Tragoedia von Holoferne" (1642), the Benedictine Judith "Holofernes" (1640) from Salzburg, or in Martin Opitz, *Judit* (1635). In Hebbel and Nestroy the maid is named "Mirza." The shift from a functional term to a personal name may be due to the Latin translation: La^C = Hs 151 and the Vulgate take over the word "*abra*," which is not in fact a Latin word (used only in Jdt 8:32 Vulg. = 8:33 Hs151; 10:10 Vul+Hs151). In the medieval Hebrew Judith versions, which are verbally very close to the Vulgate version, the figure is designated only by her function, translated into Hebrew as "servant," שפחה (e.g., in Jdt 10:5 HebrText D as well as in Jdt 16:28 HebrText B), whereas Text C understands the term as a name and adds the functional term ("Abra, my servant," אברה שפחתי, in Jdt 8:32 HebrText C); see the edition of these texts: Börner-Klein, *Gefährdete Braut und schöne Witwe*.

"manager" of her mistress. She has taken on the work for which Judith's husband had formerly been responsible (see ἐπέστη in Jdt 8:3).

Even though Judith is free and the ἅβρα is not, in the context of the lower social, economic, and legal status of women in biblical literature, the question arises how it is possible that two such women, acting independently and autonomously, can be portrayed here in this way.

Law codes, for example, the one from Gortyn on the island of Crete from the fifth century BCE,[30] show that there were social systems that gave women a very high and relatively independent position; at least, they reflect the theoretical possibility.[31] In the papyrus from Elephantine in Upper Egypt, from the sixth century BCE, there are similar references to independent women with business acumen. In her analysis of the documents from Elephantine relating to the three women Tamut, Mibtahiah, and Yehoyišma, Annalisa Azzoni concludes "that after a spouse's death, a woman had possession of her deceased husband's property."[32] This conclusion is especially interesting for the Judith narrative: the documents from Elephantine attest to the fact that the situation described in the Judith narrative is imaginable. It is clear, therefore, that the legal status of women began to improve in the Persian and Hellenistic periods. Precisely in Egypt in the Persian and Hellenistic periods more

30. Ronald F. Willetts, *The Law Code of Gortyn, Edited with Introduction, Translation and a Commentary* (Berlin: de Gruyter, 1967). See also Linda-Marie Günther, "Witwen in der griechischen Antike: Zwischen Oikos und Polis," *Historia* 42 (1993): 308–25.

31. See Carol Meyers, "Archaeology: A Window to the lives of Israelite Women," in *Torah*, ed. Irmtraud Fischer, Mercedes Navarro Puerto, and Andreas Taschl-Erber, BW 1.1 (Atlanta: Society of Biblical Literature, 2011), 61–108. See, on Prov 8 and 31, Christine Roy Yoder, *Wisdom as a Woman of Substance: A Socio-economic Reading of Proverbs 1–9 and 31:10–31*, BZAW 304 (Berlin: de Gruyter, 2001).

32. Annalisa Azzoni, *The Private Lives of Women in Persian Egypt* (Winona Lake, IN: Eisenbrauns, 2013), 39. See also Annalisa Azzoni, "Women of Elephantine and Women in the Land of Israel," in *In the Shadow of Bezalel: Aramaic, Biblical, and Ancient Near Eastern Studies in Honor of Bezalel Porten*, ed. Alejandro F. Botta, LSTS 64 (Leiden: Brill, 2013), 3–12; Bezalel Porten and H. Z. Szubin, "Exchange of Inherited Property at Elephantine," *JAOS* 102 (1982): 651–54; Anke Joisten-Pruschke, *Das religiöse Leben der Juden von Elephantine in der Achämenidenzeit*, GOI 2 (Wiesbaden: Harrassowitz, 2008); Ulrike Türck, "Die Stellung der Frau in Elephantine als Ergebnis persisch-babylonischen Rechtseinflusses," *ZAW* 5 (1928): 166–69. See also Eberhard Bons, "Konnte eine Witwe die *naḥalah* ihres verstorbenen Mannes erben? Überlegungen zum Ostrakon 2 aus der Sammlung Moussaïeff," *ZABR* 4 (1998): 197–208; and Arndt Meinhold, "Scheidungsrecht bei Frauen im Kontext der jüdischen Militärkolonie von Elephantine im 5. Jh. v. Chr.," in *"Sieben Augen auf einem Stein" (Sach 3,9): Studien zur Literatur des Zweiten Tempels; Festschrift für Ina Willi-Plein zum 65. Geburtstag*, ed. Friedhelm Hartenstein and Michael Pietsch (Neukirchen-Vluyn: Neukirchener, 2007), 247–59.

and more women are named as sellers and purchasers, as renting or leasing, providing credit or borrowing. The women were able on their own to petition local authorities or the government itself about their interests and to demand help by referring to their poverty and lack of protection.[33] Women were able to grant loans, to donate generously and to own slaves. In this context the freeing of the ἄβρα (Jdt 16:23) can be seen as a literary example of the changed economic and legal situation.[34]

In other words, as a rich, childless widow Judith is able to lead an independent life. That she is portrayed as a widow is not intended to imply that she is poor and in need of protection; rather it is this particular situation in life that gives her the freedom to sharply rebuke the elders (Jdt 8) and to carry out her saving act. Conversely, her wealth also makes it possible for her to withdraw to a pious life of prayer and fasting, since she does not need to be concerned about economic necessity but can delegate the work and management of her estate to others.

3.4. Judith, the Cultured Woman

Although our analysis focuses especially on the introduction of Judith, above all on her beauty and wealth, a comprehensive look at how Judith is characterized naturally means that the entire story needs to be taken into account. Two aspects from the chapters that follow will be mentioned at least briefly. In the course of the entire story Judith gives four long speeches.[35] In her first speech (Jdt 8), she rebukes the elders of the town of Bethulia and opposes their political decision, which in her eyes is wrong for theological reasons. In her great prayer that follows (Jdt 9), she takes the position of a violated woman in order to beseech God for the strength and sword of her ancestor Simeon. In her speech before Holofernes (Jdt 11) she is presented as a beautiful but defenceless foreign woman in the massive Assyrian military camp. Her speech here is ambiguous: Holofernes believes that she is promising him victory, but in fact she is speaking of the victory of her κύριος. Finally, in the great concluding hymn (Jdt 16), Judith summarizes the events that have taken place, interprets what has happened, and gives thanks to God. In these speeches and prayers,

33. See Sarah B. Pomeroy, *Frauenleben im klassischen Altertum* (Stuttgart: Kröner, 1985), 191–92; Tamara Cohn Ezkenazi, "The Lives of Women in the Postexilic Era," in *The Writings and Later Wisdom Books*, ed. Christl M. Maier and Nuria Calduch-Benages, BW 1.3 (Atlanta: SBL Press, 2014), 11–32; Tal Ilan, *Integrating Women into Second Temple History*, TSAJ 76 (Tübingen: Mohr Siebeck, 2001).

34. For example, Aseneth in Jos. Asen. 26:2 speaks to Joseph of "our inheritance."

35. Schmitz, *Gedeutete Geschichte*.

Judith reveals herself as a woman who is theologically well-educated, proficient in the scriptures and tradition, able to act with political astuteness.

Another aspect of her presentation is revealed in the death scene, which is central to the plot of the story. Judith's act to save Israel and the world is not an action guided by emotions;[36] rather it is much better understood within the context of ancient discourse on the killing of tyrants.[37] Judith, unlike the elders, does not wait for God to act, but rather she acts so to speak proleptically, understanding that salvation will come from humans who are prepared to take responsibility.

Two factors make possible the freedom that the figure of Judith in the LXX version has to act: her wealth and her status as a widow. As a rich widow she is economically independent and not subservient to any man. This status makes it possible for Judith to intervene and to undertake her saving acts. The figure of Judith in the LXX as well as the figure of her ἄβρα are therefore literary examples for the changed social, legal, and economic situation of women in the Persian period. Increasingly, women were able to control property, manage estates, engage in trade, buy and sell, et cetera. It appears that in the Judith narrative, new opportunities for women to act are explored and announced in the form of a fictional account.

4. Excursus: The Figure of Iudith in the Vulgate (by Lydia Lange)

In the Vulgate version the portrayal of Iudith is different. This changed portrait is evident not only in the narrative translated by Jerome but also, interestingly, already in his *praefatio* placed at the beginning of the book of Iudith:[38] "Behold the widow Judith, an example of chastity, and proclaim her with triumphant praise in unceasing acclamations! She was given not only to women but also to men as an example by the one who, rewarding her for her chastity, accorded her such strength that she was able to conquer the one whom no human had ever conquered before, to vanquish the unvanquished one" (ll. 9–12, *praefatio* to Iudith).[39]

36. Barbara Schmitz, "Judith and Holofernes: An Analysis of the Emotions in the Killing Scene (Jdt 12:10–13:9)," in *Ancient Jewish Prayers and Emotions*, ed. Stefan Reif and Renate Egger-Wenzel, DCLS 26 (Berlin: de Gruyter, 2015), 177–91.

37. Barbara Schmitz, "War, Violence and Tyrannicide in the Book of Judith," *DCLY* 2010:103–19.

38. For a more thorough analysis, see Lydia Lange, *Die Juditfigur in der Vulgata: Eine theologische Studie zur lateinischen Bibel*, DCLS 36 (Berlin: de Gruyter, 2016).

39. The English is translated from the German translations of the book of Iudith (*Liber Judith*) and its *praefatio* (*Prologus Judit*) prepared by Helmut Engel for the project Vul-

Two important aspects are highlighted already in the *praefatio*: that she is a widow and that she is an example of chastity. It is interesting that whereas in the LXX version Judith is also portrayed as a widow (see Jdt 8:4, 5, 6; 9:4, 9; 10:3; 16:7), the motif of chastity appears in the Vulgate version only[40] and is found in no other Greek or Latin version. At the same time, the two motifs, widowhood and chastity, play a central role in the story as translated by Jerome but are developed with their own distinct dynamic in comparison with the LXX version. The introduction of Iudith in Idt 8 is a good example of this difference. In the Vulgate, the text reads as follows:

> Judith however had been left as his widow for three years and six months already, and in the upper portion of her house she had prepared for herself a secluded room in which she was cloistered together with her maidservants. About her loins she wore sackcloth and fasted all the days of her life, except on the Sabbaths and the New Moons and the Feasts of the House of Israel. She however was very refined in appearance. Her husband had left her great wealth, countless servants and extensive possessions in cattle and sheep. She was regarded by all with great reverence, therefore, because she greatly feared the Lord, and there was no one who spoke ill of her. (Idt 8:4–8)

Many differences compared with the LXX could be discussed. In what follows the focus of the analysis will be on the terms *cubiculum*, *cilicium* (Idt 8:5, 6), and the motif of Iudith's beauty. According to Idt 8:5 Iudith spends most of her time in a "room" (*cubiculum*), which is located in the upper part of the house.[41] In the Greek *Vorlage* there is no such room in the house, but only a tent on the roof. This room is moreover described in the Vulgate version as a "secluded room" (*secretum cubiculum*). This is a noteworthy semantic alteration. A tent on the roof is a public space in which Judith lives, whereas the secluded room in the upper part of the house portrays the private life made possible by typical Greco-Roman gabled roofs. The Iudith of the Vulgate remains in her house, protected from the eyes of the public in a secluded room, in which she is surrounded exclusively by female servants (*in quo cum puellis suis clausa morabatur*, Idt 8:5b) and in which she will also receive the town elders (Idt 8:9d–10b). Her way of life reflects that of the wealthy female

gata deutsch, ed. Andreas Beriger, Widu-Wolfgang Ehlers and Michael Fieger (Berlin: de Gruyter, forthcoming).

40. In the Vulgate version the theme of "chastity" appears in two additions found only in the Vulgate (in Idt 15:11 and 16:26) and is placed there in the context of Iudith's election by God and the resulting salvation of Israel.

41. The same word is also used for the sleeping chamber, the inner tent in the tent of Holofernis, in which he will find death (Idt 13:1, 3, 5; 14:9, 10, 11, 13).

ascetics of Jerome's time. Numerous rich Roman widows and virgins were part of a moderate ascetic movement beginning in 350 CE.[42] Representing the nonactive part of the Christian communities, they withdrew, often in groups, into private ascetical practices of prayer and Bible study.[43] Although these women were not the majority of the Roman widows, they were able by their financial contributions to the church to gain in their time a certain degree of recognition. When readers among Jerome's contemporaries heard that Iudith had withdrawn into a community in her house, they would be prompted to connect her story with the examples with which they were familiar from their own experience. There are also many letters in which Jerome recommends to women life in a "room" (*cubiculum*), surrounded by like-minded woman. For example, he writes to Pacatula in 410 CE: "Females should only mix with their own sex.… She should not appear in public too freely nor always seek a crowded church. Let her find all her pleasure in her own room (*in cubiculo*)."[44]

Iudith is also described as wearing a "sackcloth" (*cilicium*) around her hips (Idt 8:6a). Such a *cilicium* was worn in Christian times first in periods of mourning but became over time the customary clothing of monks and persons who lived a religious live on their own.[45] Whereas in the LXX *σάκκος* (sackcloth) and widow's clothing are an outer symbol of mourning (Jdt 8:5), in the Roman world of late antiquity the *cilicium* was the symbol of a private religious way of life; that is, it was no longer restricted to an extraordinary situation such as mourning but became a way for men and women publicly to display their piety.[46] Through this clothing, monks as well as Christian widows and virgins signaled to their immediate surroundings that they were living in chastity; they made visible to everyone that they belonged to this state of life.[47]

---

42. See Jens-Uwe Krause, *Witwen und Waisen im römischen Reich IV: Witwen und Waisen im frühen Christentum*, HABES 19 (Stuttgart: Steiner, 1995), 74–80; Christine Steininger, *Die ideale christliche Frau: Virgo—Vidua—Nupta; Eine Studie zum Bild der idealen christlichen Frau bei Hieronymus und Pelagius* (St. Ottilien: EOS-Verlag, 1997), 61.

43. See Steininger, *Die ideale christliche Frau*, 61–62.

44. Jerome, *Ep.* 128,4: "sexus femineus suo iungatur sexui … nec liberius procedat ad publicum nec semper ecclesiarum quaerat celebritatem. in cubiculo suo totas delicias habeat." See Jerome, *Select Letters of St. Jerome*, transl. F. A. Wright, LCL (London: Heinemann, 1933).

45. See H. Emonds and B. Poschmann, "Bußkleid," *RAC* 2:814.

46. Differently from Jdt 8:5 LXX, the widow's clothing that Judith wears over top of her sackcloth is first mentioned in Idt 10:2 as Iudith's clothing: "abstulit a se cilicium et exuit se vestimentis viduitatis suae."

47. In Jerome's epistolary writings there is the added interpretation that Iudith's clothing was also "dirty"; see, on this point, Lange, *Die Juditfigur in der Vulgata*.

The two versions are also different in their description of Iudith's beauty (Idt 8:7 Vulg./LXX). Whereas the LXX maintains that Judith was "beautiful in appearance and very lovely to behold," the Vulgate stresses that Iudith was "very refined in appearance" (*eleganti aspectu*).

To mark Judith's beauty the LXX uses the words "beautiful" (καλός) and "lovely" (ὡραῖος); the Vulgate on the other hand speaks only of *elegans* instead of the expected *pulchra*.[48] Although *pulchra* would have been the obvious translation for "beautiful" in Greek, Jerome translates as *elegans*. When this word is used to refer to a person's appearance, it means "choice, nice, neat, tasteful, elegant."[49] The Iudith of the Vulgate version is presented therefore less as "beautiful" than as "elegantly refined." The description of Iudith as *elegans* distinctly changes the characterization of Judith in the LXX. The connection that the LXX brings out between outer beauty, inner integrity, and God's blessing[50] is no longer present. Instead of giving information about Iudith's beauty, the Vulgate characterizes her as morally good.

In the Vulgate version the beauty of Iudith is mentioned for the first time in Idt 10:4:[51] "The Lord also gave her a radiant appearance [*splendor*], because her outer appearance did not originate in desire, but rather in virtue; the Lord therefore increased her beauty [*pulchritudo*] so much, that in the eyes of all she appeared to have incomparable beauty [*decor*]." The difference is immediately apparent: whereas in Jdt 10:4 LXX it is mentioned only that Judith herself enhances her beauty ("she made herself very beautiful, to entice the eyes of all the men who might see her"), in the Vulgate version God is the one who make this happen. God's beautifying of Iudith is the culmination of Iudith's personal toilet; she has already washed, changed her clothing, and put on all of her jewelry (Idt 10:2–3). For the first time the attributes *splendor*, *pulchritude*, and *decor* are ascribed to Iudith, but only *after* God has intervened (Idt 10:4).[52]

48. See Lydia Hilt [Lange], "Dominus contulit splendorem (Idt 10,4): Das Motiv der Schönheit im Buch Iudith," in *Kongressakten vom 14. bis 17. November 2013 in Bukarest*, vol. 1 of *Vulgata Studies*, ed. Andreas Beriger, Stefan Maria Bolli, Widu-Wolfgang Ehlers, and Michael Fieger, ATID 8 (Bern: Lang, 2014), 91–108.

49. Charlton T. Lewis and Charles Short, "elegans," in *A Latin Dictionary* (Oxford: Clarendon, 1966), 636.

50. See Margareta Gruber and Andreas Michel, "Schönheit," in *Sozialgeschichtliches Wörterbuch zur Bibel*, ed. Frank Crüsemann (Gütersloh: Gütersloher Verlagshaus, 2009), 503; Rakel, *Judit*, 202–8.

51. This means that only beginning in Idt 10:4 are the words *pulchra* "beautiful" and *pulchritudo* "beauty" used to describe Iudith's outer appearance (in Idt 10:4, 7, 14; 11:19; 16:11).

52. *Incomparabilis* is used in the Vulgate only to describe the unparalleled scream of the headless Assyrians in Idt 14:18.

Her beauty is only now characterized as exceptional. Whereas in Jdt 10:4 LXX Judith enhances her beauty in order to entice the eyes of all of the men who might see her, the Vulgate wants to explain why God has only now given Iudith a radiant appearance: God enhances Iudith's beauty because she has put on her jewelry and cosmetics not out of "lust" (*libido*) but out of "virtue" (*virtus*) (Idt 10,4). An opposition between the words *libido* and *virtus* is thereby established:[53] *Libido*, "pleasure, desire, eagerness, longing, fancy, inclination, … unlawful or indorinate desire, passion, caprice, willfulness, wantonness, … sexual desire, lust, especially unnatural lust"[54] is used in the Vulgate for sexual desire with negative connotations (Judg 19:4; 20:5; Ezek 23:9, 11, 20; Tob 3:18; 6:17, 22; Idt 10:4; Col 3:5). In the Vulgate version, therefore, Iudith is depicted as a woman who does not make herself beautiful in order to fulfill some personal sexual desire but rather as doing so motivated solely by virtue. In the Vulgate God makes Iudith radiantly beautiful on the basis of her moral integrity (*elegans*, Idt 8:7) and her chastity (l. 11, *praefatio* to Iudith; see also Idt 15:11), so that she can accomplish her saving act.

In the Vulgate version readers encounter in Iudith a wealthy and virtuous woman. Even more so than in the Hellenistic period, women in the Roman Imperial period from the first century CE on increasingly gained legal status and economic possibilities[55] through the growing acknowledgment of widowhood, thereby opening up new freedoms for them.[56]

At the same time, it is clear that efforts were made in Christian theological reflection to "channel" these freedoms. Beauty was no longer regarded as a value in itself; rather women were now expected to live in seclusion in freely chosen asceticism and give away their wealth. This new ideal is found not only in Jerome's writings but also in the biblical texts translated by him. Are the differences really due only to a different *Vorlage* used by Jerome, as scholars have

---

53. On *virtus* see Lange, *Die Juditfigur in der Vulgata*, 238.

54. Lewis and Short, *A Latin Dictionary*, 1060.

55. In 9 CE, under Augustus, widows between the ages of twenty-five and fifty had to remarry within two years or face financial penalties. Under Theodosius II (439) they could lose guardianship over their children when they remarried (Cod. Theod. 3,17,4,1; 160). See Christine Steininger, *Die ideale christliche Frau*, 38, 47–48 as well as *lex Iulia de maritandis ordinibus* and *lex Papia Poppaea* in Dio Cassius, *Hist. rom.* 4.51–60 (Cary, LCL); Theo Mayer-Maly, "Vidua," *PW* 2.15:2104.

56. Similarly, Siquans, in her reflections on marriage and asceticism in Greco-Roman antiquity, comes to the conclusion that in the fourth century CE there was a change in the area of marriage and family law ("Im 4. Jahrhundert ist ein Wandel im Bereich des Ehe- und Familienrechts festzustellen"). See Agnethe Siquans, *Die alttestamentlichen Prophetinnen in der patristischen Rezeption: Texte—Kontexte—Hermeneutik*, HBS 65 (Freiburg: Herder, 2011), 487.

usually assumed on the basis of the *praefatio* to the book of Judith? The statements in the Iudith narrative specific to the Vulgate could just as well be seen as evidence that Jerome in his "little night shifts" did after all translate the book of Judith, a book he did not like very much, more carefully than he allows.

5. A Summing Up

In the LXX Judith is beautiful and wealthy and appears as a personally, socially, and economically independent woman, autonomous and competent. She argues persuasively as a wisdom teacher and encourages others as a theologian, with outstanding knowledge of the scriptures and traditions of Israel. Judith's beauty as well as her godliness are expressions of her attitude towards God. It does not serve merely to reveal her appearance. It is this difference that is characteristic of the LXX's portrayal of Judith and that makes this text exemplary of the early Jewish view that beauty and the fear of God go together.

The Vulgate version, on the other hand, has a different point of view: Iudith is made beautiful by God only in order that she can fulfill her plan; otherwise, beauty is even regarded as harmful to a life of godliness. Such a view of beauty, like the motif of chastity that also appears only in the Vulgate version, is better explained by reference to Jerome's social context than by a "Chaldean" *Vorlage*. Such an explanation enhances the unique profile of the LXX version and supports the thesis that the book of Judith is not a translation but that it was originally written in Greek.

Besides her "natural" beauty, Judith in the LXX stages herself as a beautiful and beautified woman for the Assyrian camp, where she will appear as the "foreign woman." That her plan succeeds means the redemption not only of Israel but also of the whole world.

The Holy and the Women: Gender Constructions in the Letter of Jeremiah

Marie-Theres Wacker and Sonja Ammann
Translated by Martha M. Matesich

1. Introduction

1.1. Literary and Historical Contour of the Letter of Jeremiah

In the Septuagint four writings altogether are compiled into a corpus under the authority of the prophet Jeremiah and his scribe Baruch: the book of Jeremiah itself and Lamentations, ascribed to him, both of which are to be found in the Hebrew Bible, and then the book of Baruch as well as the so-called Letter of Jeremiah (*Epistula Jeremiae*).[1] The latter pertains to a small, originally self-contained writing that was attached to the book of Baruch in the Vulgate as a sixth chapter and thus found its way into the Catholic canon.[2]

This contribution is based on our commentaries on the Letter of Jeremiah in Marie-Theres Wacker, *The Book of Baruch and the Letter of Jeremiah*, WCS 31 (Collegeville, MN: Liturgical Press, 2016), 97–131; and Sonja Ammann, *Götter für die Toren: Die Verbindung von Götterpolemik und Weisheit im Alten Testament*, BZAW 466 (Berlin: de Gruyter, 2015), 147–88. The present text has been expanded to include new issues, perspectives, and materials.

1. For Greek editions of the text, see Joseph Ziegler, ed., "Epistula Ieremiae," in *Ieremias; Baruch; Threni; Epistula Ieremiae*, SVTG 15, 4th ed. (Göttingen: Vandenhoeck & Ruprecht, 2013), 494–504; and Alfred Rahlfs and Robert Hanhart, eds., "Epistula Ieremiae," in *Septuaginta: Id est Vetus Testamentum Graece iuxta LXX interpretes; Editio altera*, 2 vols. in one (Stuttgart: Deutsche Bibelgesellschaft, 2006), 766–70. The Letter of Jeremiah is included in New Revised Standard Version editions that include apocryphal/deuterocanonical books. See also Benjamin G. Wright, "The Letter of Jeremiah," in *A New English Translation of the Septuagint and the Other Greek Translations Traditionally Included under That Title*, ed. Albert Pietersma and Benjamin G. Wright (New York: Oxford University Press, 2007), 942–45.

2. In Catholic translations (such as the Jerusalem Bible) it is customarily presented as the sixth chapter of the book of Baruch.

With respect to its genre, it is not a typical letter, even though it poses as a "copy of a letter" (ἀντίγραφον ἐπιστολῆς) in its initial verse. Its designation as a "letter" (ἐπιστολή), however, aptly relates to the assumed fictitious situation: with his communication Jeremiah addresses the inhabitants of Jerusalem who are facing their imminent deportation to Babylonia. He wrote a letter once before, namely, from Jerusalem to the community in Babylonia (see Jer 29 MT; 36 LXX), so that he can draw on an already known form of communication with his new epistle. The written medium serves the purpose of overcoming great geographical distances and of keeping the words of the prophet present in regions far apart from one another. What became a necessity narratively in the exilic period (i.e., the sending of a message) was historically a common mode of communication in the Hellenistic period when the Letter of Jeremiah was probably originally composed.[3]

1.2. Overall Structure

Judging by its content, the Letter of Jeremiah can best be characterized as a satirical speech on the impotence of idols. Its structure[4] emerges chiefly via refrain-like lines that time and again reach the conclusion: the cultic images venerated in Babylonia are not deities at all; thus, one should not fear them. Introductory verses in the style of an admonition (vv. 2–7) follow the title. The subsequent three sections (vv. 8–29) can be combined into a first part which has to do with the appearance of the idols (vv. 8–16), the sacred places where

3. All recent commentaries agree on a dating in the Hellenistic period; for instance: Sean Adams, *Baruch and the Epistle of Jeremiah: A Commentary Based on the Texts in Codex Vaticanus*, SeptCS (Leiden: Brill, 2014), 147–203; Luis Alonso Schökel, "Carta de Jeremias," in *Daniel; Baruc; Carta de Jeremias; Lamentaciones*, LLS 18 (Madrid: Ediciones Cristiandad, 1976), 167–78; Georg Gäbel and Wolfgang Kraus, "Epistole Jeremiu/Epistula Jeremiae/Der Brief des Jeremia," in *Psalmen bis Daniel*, ed. Martin Karrer and Wolfgang Kraus, SDEK 2 (Stuttgart: Deutsche Bibelgesellschaft, 2011), 2842–48; Reinhard G. Kratz, "Der Brief des Jeremia," in *ATD Apokryphen*, ed. Odil H. Steck, Ingo Kottsieper, and Reinhard G. Kratz (Göttingen: Vandenhoeck & Ruprecht, 1998), 5:69–108; Jacqueline Moatti-Fine, "Lettre de Jérémie," in *Baruch, Lamentations, Lettre de Jérémie*, ed. Isabelle Assan-Dhôte and Jacqueline Moatti-Fine, BA 25.2 (Paris: Cerf, 2005), 287–330; Carey A. Moore, "Epistle of Jeremiah," in *Daniel, Esther and Jeremiah: The Additions*, AB 44 (Garden City, NY: Doubleday, 1977), 317–58; Anthony J. Saldarini, "The Letter of Jeremiah: Introduction, Commentary, and Reflections," in *Introduction to Prophetic Literature, the Book of Isaiah, the Book of Jeremiah, the Book of Baruch, the Letter of Jeremiah, the Book of Lamentations, the Book of Ezekiel*, ed. Leander E. Keck, *NIB* 6 (Nashville: Abingdon, 2001), 983–1010.

4. The verse numbering used here follows the NRSV. The critical edition by Ziegler, "Epistula Ieremiae," has a different numbering in many details.

they are set up (vv. 17–23), and their alleged animate nature (vv. 24–29), thus dealing with the objects themselves, as it were. A second part covers verses 30–65 and revolves around the supposed power of the deities/divine images. Using the refrains, one can identify altogether seven subsections here. Verses 66–72 function like a double coda in which various motifs are taken up once again before the last verse draws a final conclusion (v. 73).

1.3. A Continuous Reception Process

The Letter of Jeremiah is a record of a continuous reception process. Its title already indicates this. The fiction of being a letter implies that the deported can take it with them to Babylonia and also read it (again) there, whereas the copy—which the epistle makes itself out to be in the title—remains in the kingdom of Judah and can be read there.[5] With that the text itself already opens several different reception contexts. Moreover, the medium of a letter is not only suited to bringing widely separated geographical areas into communication with one another or to making a message present simultaneously in different places, but also to allowing that message to cross time-spans, such that a message from the past becomes accessible not only to the present but to future generations as well.

The assumed text history of the epistle may also be interpreted in a reception-historical way. Although the Letter of Jeremiah has been handed down only in Greek, several textual peculiarities indicate a Semitic original.[6] At the same time, the Letter of Jeremiah contains formulations that are difficult to conceive of in a Semitic language or more likely belong to the linguistic usage of Greek philosophers.[7] The frequently used verbal adjectives ending in -τεον,

---

5. See Lutz Doering, "Jeremiah and the 'Diaspora Letters' in Ancient Judaism: Epistolary Communication with the Golah as Medium for Dealing with the Present," in *Reading the Present in the Qumran Library: The Perception of the Contemporary by Means of Scriptural Interpretation*, ed. Kristin De Troyer and Armin Lange (Atlanta: Society of Biblical Literature, 2005), 43–72, specifically 51 and 53.

6. See, for example, the formulation in v. 31 which can easily be explained as a translation of a Semitic text (with respect to this, see n. 29; see also n. 20, which refers to v. 10). Concerning the discussion about the language of the original, see Diether Kellermann, "Apokryphes Obst: Bemerkungen zur Epistula Jeremiae (Baruch Kap.6), insbesondere zu Vers 42," *ZDMG* 129 (1979): 25–28; Kratz, "Brief des Jeremia," 74; Weigand Naumann, *Untersuchungen über den apokryphen Jeremiasbrief*, BZAW 25 (Gießen: Alfred Töpelmann, 1913), 31–47.

7. See Benjamin G. Wright, "The Epistle of Jeremiah: Translation or Composition?," in *Deuterocanonical Additions of the Old Testament Books: Selected Studies*, ed. Géza G. Xeravits and József Zsengellér, DCLS 5 (Berlin: de Gruyter, 2010), 126–42, specifically 130–

for example, can hardly be explained on the basis of a Semitic prototype. This indicates that the Letter of Jeremiah is (at least in part) a more or less free adaptation or revision of a Semitic text.[8] For this reason, one will have to reckon with a reception situation for this pseudepigraphical writing which had already changed several times in the more immediate temporal setting of its origin.

With its guiding theme, the mockery of the idols, the writing stands in the context of the early Jewish polemic against idols as this is encountered beyond the Hebrew Bible in the Septuagint, in the very vivid narrative of Bel and the Dragon (in Catholic Bible editions Dan 14), as well as, with a rather more philosophical approach, in the Wisdom of Solomon (Wis 13–15). In certain motifs, the Letter of Jeremiah harks back to the criticism of images in chapters 40–48 of Isaiah and, in some word-for-word formulations, is faithful to chapter 10 of the book of Jeremiah with its criticism of idols,[9] thus emphasizing in this respect as well the Jeremian pseudepigraphy. But beneath these Jeremian (or Isaian) references, as it were, the text again stresses its own main points. In great attention to detail it talks about the appearance of the idols, about the temples in which they stand, about the cultic rites, as well as about the cultic personnel, and thus goes far beyond the rather more general polemic in Jer 10 or Isa 40–48. Other literary sources, for instance, the *Histories* of Herodotus, could be hovering in the background. As has often been suspected in the research literature,[10] however, one cannot rule out the possibility that the circle of authors draws on knowledge of concrete cultic customs.

1.4. Gender Perspectives

For the Letter of Jeremiah the presence of women in different situations and activities belongs to the context of the cult of idols. Sometimes women appear together with their male equivalents, sometimes independently. In that respect as well, this document has no model in the older biblical traditions

---

33; Adams, *Baruch and the Epistle of Jeremiah*, 150–55; Moatti-Fine, "Lettre de Jérémie," 306–7; Naumann, *Untersuchungen*, 32–44.

8. Wright ("Epistle of Jeremiah") doubts that the work derives from a Semitic original and thinks it is possible that Greek is the original language. We agree that the text wording here should not be downgraded as a flawed imitation of a lost original, but should rather be taken seriously in its current linguistic form. Nevertheless, it still seems to us that the linguistic findings more likely support a translation, so that the Greek version at hand can be understood as a productive reception of its (Hebrew/Aramaic) prototype.

9. Regarding this, see Reinhard G. Kratz, "Die Rezeption von Jeremia 10 und 29 im pseudepigraphen Brief des Jeremia," *JSJ* 26 (1995): 1–31.

10. See, first of all, Naumann, *Untersuchungen*; among the more recent literature, see, above all, Kratz, "Brief des Jeremia."

of Isa 40–48 or Jer 10. The craftsmen who play a central role in the criticism of idols found in the older texts (and also in the Wisdom of Solomon) retreat into the background in the Letter of Jeremiah. Instead, one encounters primarily priests and women in addition to other figures like robbers and kings. A similar repertoire of figures can be found in the polemical narrative Bel and the Dragon. In this narrative Daniel discovers that it is not the cult image of Bel, but the priests together with their wives and children who are eating the sacrificial offerings. But whereas women only appear as family members in Bel and the Dragon, they are present in the Letter of Jeremiah as autonomous figures who act independently of a male entourage. The prominent portrayal of women in the cult of idols is remarkable and cannot be explained from a dependence on older biblical traditions.[11]

In the following discussion an overall interpretation of the Letter of Jeremiah is sketched. In the process, special attention is paid to those situations and circumstances in which women are taken into consideration.[12] This will make it clearly discernible that the reference to women has a rhetorical function: looking at their lived reality or actions serves the purpose of the Letter of Jeremiah as a whole, namely, to deprive the idols of their mystique and to break their power. Consequently, this writing purposefully utilizes the gender perspective for its rhetorical strategies and goals. Women appear here in different roles and are not always an object of the polemic themselves. They are, however, attacked polemically wherever they actively perform cultic actions and come into contact with sacrifices to the gods.

2. Sharp Differentiations (vv. 2–7)

Verses 2–7 constitute an initial cohesive section of the letter. On account of the sins of Israel, which are recalled here, exile is looming. The exilic period, however, is also conceptualized as a time of probation, in which those deported to Babylon will be confronted with a particular challenge. They will experience

11. The other biblical texts, few in number, in which women are encountered as subjects in the worship of gods (see Jer 44; Ezek 8:14; 1 Kgs 15:13) bear only a slight resemblance to the Letter of Jeremiah. Literary connections are apparent to a greater degree to biblical texts in which (apart from the priests' wives in Bel and the Dragon) no female figures are encountered, such as Jer 10:1–16; Isa 40:18–20; 41:6–7; 44:9–20; 45:20, 46:5–7; see Kratz, "Rezeption," 8–17.

12. A woman-centered short commentary, though with different specifics than ours, is the commentary of Patricia Tull, "The Letter of Jeremiah," in *Women's Bible Commentary*, ed. Carol A. Newsom and Sharon H. Ringe, expanded ed. (Louisville: Westminster John Knox, 1998), 309–10.

magnificent processions with idols before which the population of Babylon performs *proskynesis*, expressing in this way their fear of the divine. Those addressed in the letter, however, are urged not to let themselves be "infected" by this fear, but to realize instead, with a kind of brief, interior prayer, that: "It befits you, Lord and Master, that one prostrates oneself" (v. 6).[13] Their difference from the "others," who are called "those of a different tribe" (ἀλλόφυλοι), the "peoples" (τὰ ἔθνη), and, in general, the "multitude" (ὄχλος), is to be denoted therein. The God of Israel is invoked here with δέσποτα ("lord and master"), a designation sometimes used to translate the Tetragrammaton YHWH in the LXX and which underlines absolute power even more convincingly than the more frequent κύριος ("Lord"), thereby stressing the contrast to the gods of the "others."

A gender-specific differentiation does not occur in these introductory exhortations. Since the impending deportation to Babylon is named as the (fictitious) situation, however, one should certainly also imagine women (and children) alongside the men among the addressees:[14] all are being called on to profess the one God alone. On the basis of the "brief prayer," it is possible to deduce that this should be expressed in a refusal to perform *proskynesis* before the gods of the others, although this is not explicitly demanded.[15]

The Letter of Jeremiah does not differentiate with respect to the idols either since all of them have to be rejected. This becomes apparent in a linguistic characteristic which is only possible in Greek and which also runs through the entire address that follows: the images are denoted with a pronoun in the neuter plural form (αὐτά) and are thus (dis)qualified as mere "stuff." The foundation for the sharp opposition which "Jeremiah" demands in the name of God between those whom he addresses and the majority culture that surrounds them is therefore already laid in the introductory verses of the letter.

3. Appearances Are Deceptive: Demystification of the Gods (vv. 8–29)

The following verses, 8–29, are divided into three subsections, each concluding with the almost identically formulated sentence: "From this you know that

13. All translations are by the authors.

14. See, for instance, Jer 52:14 or Bar 1:4 where there is talk of "all the people" or the "rest of the people" who are carried into exile. A relief from the Palace of Sennacherib also shows women and children among those deported from the Judean city of Lachish by the Assyrians (BM WA 124908–10; Richard D. Barnett et al., *Sculptures from the Southwest Palace of Sennacherib at Nineveh* [London: British Museum Press, 1998], no. 432–34).

15. In contrast to this, see Dan 3 or Esth 3–4 LXX as examples of early Jewish texts which explicitly reject a *proskynesis* before idols or representatives of the ruler.

they are not gods. Do not fear them" (v. 23; see also v. 16 and v. 29b). This refrain takes up the motif of fear (φόβος) from the beginning of the address and makes clear that the statements preceding the refrain seek to quell such fear, and this in two senses: to dispel the fear and to render it superfluous, indeed, meaningless. The remarks in the three subsections count on their listeners not to let themselves be dazzled by the staging of the images, their magnificent appearance, the temples in which they are placed, and the associated suggestion of their animateness; instead, they trust the ability of their listeners to go behind the appearances. In the first and the third section, women from the group of the "others" come into view.

3.1. The Jewelry-Loving Woman

Verses 8–15 survey the outward appearance of the idols, the gold and silver overlay of their carved wooden core, their precious garments, and their insignia. Right at the beginning, a catchword is mentioned that runs through the entire text of the epistle: the gods are ψευδῆ (v. 8), they are only pretending; the appearances are deceptive; they themselves are deceitful or mendacious. This is the case because, in spite of their splendid coating which makes them appear powerful, and in spite of an ornately made tongue, they cannot speak. The reference to the "tongue smoothed by a craftsman" (v. 8) leads one to assume that there was knowledge of the great importance in Babylon of the region of the mouth when idols were made and ceremoniously put into service through a distinct mouth-washing ritual.[16]

One's gaze wanders upwards from the tongue to the headdress of the idols:

> And, as if for a young woman who loves ornaments, they take gold and from it make wreaths/crowns[17] on the heads of their gods. (v. 9)

Here, by way of comparison, the gods/idols are placed close to a παρθένος, an unmarried, probably young woman who loves ornaments. The comparison with verse 18, which is construed in a parallel manner, shows that the

16. Regarding this, see Angelika Berlejung, "Washing the Mouth: The Consecration of Divine Images in Mesopotamia," in *The Image and the Book: Iconic Cults, Aniconism, and the Rise of Book Religion in Israel and the Ancient Near East*, ed. Karel van der Toorn, CBET 21 (Leuven: Peeters, 1997), 45–72; on the complexity of Babylonian theology of gods/images, see Berlejung, *Die Theologie der Bilder: Herstellung und Einweihung von Kultbildern in Mesopotamien und die alttestamentliche Bilderpolemik*, OBO 162 (Fribourg: Universitäts-Verlag, 1998).

17. The Greek noun στέφανος has both meanings.

text refers to a figure with negative connotations: according to verse 18, when they bolt their temples like a prison, the priests are treating the gods like (καὶ ὥσπερ) a criminal who has been condemned to death; according to verse 9, when the idols receive wreaths or crowns as votive offerings from their worshipers, they are being treated like (καὶ ὥσπερ) a woman who loves ornaments. Here it is probably not the comparison with a female figure per se that disparages the idols. It is rather the infatuation with ornaments—the authors create the adjective φιλόκοσμος for this—as a negative characterization that is more likely the center of attention, even though this characterization could well be applied to the "object of comparison," the παρθένος, since various Greek and Roman authors depict it as unseemly when women who are not hetaerae wear gold ornaments.[18] Such ornaments do not befit a παρθένος, that is, an unmarried woman who should live chastely in the house of her father. Here the "woman infatuated with ornaments" represents "unseemly behavior" that discredits the gods and, moreover, possibly retrieves a gender-typical stereotype.

3.2. "Prostitutes on the Roof"?

The precious material with which the gods are decorated serves at the same time purposes that are frowned upon, inasmuch as the priests grow rich on it and put it to other questionable use:

> But the priests sometimes steal gold and silver from their gods and use it for themselves. They also give some of it to the prostitutes in the brothel/on the roof [ταῖς ἐπὶ τοῦ τέγους πόρναις]. (v. 10)

The meaning of the Greek wording that describes the women who are receiving gold and silver from the priests cannot be unequivocally determined. If one assumes that πόρναι describes professional prostitutes and that the location ἐπὶ τοῦ τέγους is to be understood as a synonym for a brothel,[19] then this could simply be the accusation that the priests of the deities get involved with whores and pay them with temple property for their sexual services.[20]

---

18. Here the reference is to purported old laws in Greek cities. See Diodorus Siculus, *Bib. hist.* 12.21; Athenaeus, *Deipn.* 12.521b (as a quotation from Phylarcus).

19. Thus, for example, Gäbel and Kraus, "Epistula Jeremiou," 1359; this meaning of τέγος has been verified from the second century BCE on (see LSJ, s.v. "τέγος III").

20. Charles C. Torrey, *The Apocryphal Literature: A Brief Introduction* (New Haven: Yale University Press 1945), 66, and Diether Kellermann, "Apokryphes Obst," 23–42, specifically 27–28, point out that the Aramaic עַל־אַגְרָא "as a wage" may form the basis, which could also be read as עַל־אִגָּרָא "on the roof."

This could possibly be an allusion, in a modified form, to a prescription from the book of Deuteronomy. Deuteronomy 23:18 states that a prostitute's wage should not come into the temple and thus that a boundary drawn between the sacred place and the prostitutes must not be crossed from the outside to the inside. The Babylonian priests, however, take temple property to the prostitutes. As a result, they cross this boundary in the opposite direction, as it were, from the inside to the outside.

The Greek text with its indication of location ἐπὶ τοῦ τέγους can, however, also be applied to a flat roof, then suggesting that the women labeled πόρναι are on the roof of the priests' dwellings or the temple. In this case, the assessment as to what degree the evoked image is based on knowledge of real circumstances at Babylonian temples is particularly difficult to make. In principle, one must certainly reckon that the term *whores* is a component of the rhetorical disparagement in which the text is obviously engaged. The term could thus refer to women who are involved in one way or another in temple service or the cult of the temple, who have their living quarters or workspaces "on the roof" of the temple, and who are remunerated by the priests. The reconstruction of the nature of their service depends in particular on the following: which rites with women's participation does one consider possible in the Babylonian region during the Hellenistic period and how completely does one yield to the suggestion that these rites have to be connected with sexuality in some form or another. In the older literature one frequently finds the assumption that the πόρναι mentioned in verse 10 are, indeed, "cult prostitutes" or "sacred prostitutes." Although this designation itself could in turn connote different perceptions, the main concern was always that sexual intercourse was performed as a ritual act. More recent research discusses the problematic nature of the entire field of assumptions and hypotheses connected to "cult prostitution,"[21] and scarcely anything remains of the sexual rites that were formerly presumed. It is thus entirely possible that verse 10 represents a polemically tinged imagination that relies perhaps on literary witnesses, but that cannot be enlisted for the historical reality of "cult prostitution."

In any case, it is clear that the circle of authors brings into contrast with the settled order in one's own group circumstances that one perceives

21. Concerning this discussion, see Tanja S. Scheer and Martin Lindner, eds., *Tempelprostitution im Altertum: Fakten und Fiktionen* (Berlin: Verlag Antike e.K., 2009); Christine Stark, "*Kultprostitution*" *im Alten Testament? Die Qedeschen der Hebräischen Bibel und das Motiv der Hurerei*, OBO 221 (Göttingen: Vandenhoeck & Ruprecht, 2006); Marie-Theres Wacker, "'Kultprostitution' im Alten Israel? Forschungsmythen, Spuren, Thesen," in Scheer and Lindner, *Tempelprostitution im Altertum*, 55–84. Also, see below the explanations with respect to vv. 42–43.

as different, thereby wishing to prove that one's own group is superior to the others. The argumentation works because the envisaged reality involving women has negative connotations for the authors themselves, and they evidently assume that their play with the clichés or with their own external perception of this reality resonates with their listeners or readers. At the same time, the male priests are also discredited by the way they associate with these women in the temple area; the cultic personnel of the "others" is thereby radically delegitimized.

3.3. Reality of Women and "Semiotic Unmasking"

The rhetorical strategy of the entire section is, to put it succinctly, one of semiotic unmasking or of unmasking by semiotic means, more precisely, of separating a sign, the signifier, from that which is signified. The assumption is that gold, silver, a scepter, crown, and weapons (see vv. 14–15) are signs that point to divine dignity and power. Furnishing idols with materials and insignia that are precious or promise an effect suggests that the sculptures concerned are deities. To circumvent this suggestion, to undermine this plausibility, the Letter of Jeremiah attempts to separate the sign and the signified in two different ways. The first approach looks at the substrate of the signs, the precious material, and shows that this material at the same time finds a much less noble use as well, and hence acquires completely different meanings. The precious material, specifically the gold as a sign, possibly refers to the remuneration of prostitutes or points to young, unmarried women's unseemly craving for ornaments (see vv. 9–11a). A second approach (vv. 11b–15) directs attention to the fact that the signs themselves, the plating made from valuable material and the paraphernalia of the images, point to nothing at all. The valuable clothes only conceal the woodworm and the rust; they do not indicate divine power, but only feign it. Analogously, a dagger or a sword on the image does not protect it from robbery at all, cannot develop divine power, and thus remains an empty sign. In summary, it can be noted that this section relies on a kind of deconstruction—the destabilization of all that is taken for granted and the delegitimization of prevailing plausibilities through the multiplication of meaning. Women, as well, turn into objects or scenes of such deconstruction and represent the counter-world to the realm of the divine.

3.4. The Place of the Gods and Its Desacralization through Reevaluation

The second section, verses 17–23, attends to the idols inasmuch as they stand in a temple. The text mercilessly takes aim at the nimbus of the holiness of the images' place. It gathers a whole range of topoi, and among these one specific image stands out in particular: the temple is constructed like a tomb, like a place of death and, as such, of impurity, an antipole to holiness. The idols are locked up in the temple like prisoners awaiting the death penalty (v. 18), there is soot and dust everywhere as in tombs (vv. 18 and 21), and the robes and the wooden core of the idols are eaten away by worms, as are corpses (v. 20).[22] Thus, the text once again names, in part, the same phenomena as in the first section, but these are now placed in a different argumentative context; they illustrate the tomblike atmosphere of the temple and thus its impurity. The intended effect of this construction becomes comprehensible when one consults the Levitical laws for priests. If one assumes that a priest is not permitted to come into contact with the dead or with places of death (see Lev 21:1), then it becomes clear that the interpretation of Babylonian temples as burial caves denotes an extreme form of rhetorical desacralization.

3.5. Women Put Their Hands on Food for the Gods

The theme of the inanimateness of the idols can be designated as the common thread that runs through the next section, which includes verses 24 to 29. The idols do not shine without human assistance (v. 24a); their radiance, though, would be a sign of their divine life. They have no feeling; instead they have been made from inanimate material (v. 24b). It is then explicitly stated that they have no breath; they lack the element that, along with the blood, is considered to be a vital element per se (v. 25; also see Jer 10:14; Ps 135:17; Hab 2:19). They have to be carried because they themselves cannot use their feet (v. 26). The image is constantly in danger of toppling over (v. 27)—this, too, is not exactly an indication of animateness and is moreover a motif of crude mockery that recalls Deutero-Isaian texts.[23] One places food before these images just as one does before the dead (v. 27b), thus treating them like the dead. Finally, these gods do not prevent others from misusing their food (vv. 28–29a). If they were alive they would do something about this.

The second argument that is mentioned once again includes the everyday reality of women:

22. The presence of birds could be seen to emphasize the aspect of impurity in another way when one bears in mind that the birds sully the temple with their excrement (see Eupolemos, frag. 2.34,11, who in this way justifies the claim that birds have to be kept out of the Jerusalem temple).

23. Isa 40:20; 41:7, as well as Jer 10:4. See 1 Sam 5:3–4 regarding a cultic image falling down.

> Their priests use their sacrifices by selling them, just as their wives also bring some and give neither the poor nor the weak any of it. Menstruating women and women who have just given birth touch their sacrifices. (vv. 28–29)

Women from the families of the priests are presumably the focus here.[24] They are being charged with a twofold transgression. First, they prepare the sacrificial meat only for themselves instead of giving some of it to the needy, and in this they behave no better than their husbands who sell the sacrificial meat and put the proceeds from the sale into their own pockets. The self-preservation of the families of the priests is envisaged in a precise, gender-specific assignment of roles and branded as selfish.

The second transgression of the women concerns them in a specific way: they approach the sacrifices even during menstruation or too soon after the birth of a child. The corresponding Levitical prescriptions in Lev 12 and 15 can be heard here; according to them, what is touched by women during these periods becomes impure. The circle of authors of the Letter of Jeremiah posits the acceptance of these regulations, insinuates that the sacrifices for the idols in Babylon are impure, and reckons with a reaction of revulsion on the part of its listeners, male and surely female as well.[25] It is conspicuous that the regulations valid for men and their discharges in Lev 15 are not used to disparage the male members of the priests' families. As a result, the function of women as a negative foil for the plausibilities presupposed in the group of addressees is all the clearer. Otherwise, the juxtaposition of the evocation of care for the poor and of respect for regulations of cultic purity corresponds in turn to the Priestly-Levitical horizon of thought, which probably also forms the background for the construction of the temples as tombs.

---

24. The reading "their wives" is only verified in some of the manuscripts; Ziegler, "Epistula Ieremiae," considers αὐτῶν to be a later addition. It would thus also be possible to interpret the "women" in v. 28 as personnel of the temple.

25. In particular, the notion that a woman is impure after giving birth could be presumed to be generally known since this idea was widespread in Mesopotamia and in the Mediterranean area; see Susan Ackerman, "Women and the Religious Culture of the State Temples of the Ancient Levant, Or: Priestesses, Purity, and Parturition," in *Temple Building and Temple Cult: Architecture and Cultic Paraphernalia of Temples in the Levant (2.–1. Mill. B.C.E)*, ed. Jens Kamlah, ADPV 41 (Wiesbaden: Harrassowitz, 2012), 259–89, specifically 275–78. The situation is perhaps different with menstruating women for whom a biblical *terminus technicus* (ἀποκαθημένη, literally "a woman sitting apart or isolated") is used.

4. Power of the Gods/Idols: Not Credible (vv. 30–65/66–72)

For the second part of the letter it is possible, on the basis of the refrain, to detect an organization into seven subsections, but they are thematically less clearly set off from one another than in the first part. The leitmotifs of the respective sections can be summarized under the overall theme of the merely feigned or implausible power of the images. References to women only occur in the first two sections; accordingly, attention is focused on these sections in the following discussion.

4.1. Unworthy Cults: Women and Priests

In the first subsection of this second part, which closes with a rhetorical question and includes verses 30 to 40, two aspects are bound together: the first concerns, once again, what is strange or odd, indeed repulsive, about the cult of the "others," and the second pertains to demonstrating that these gods are incapable of asserting their power in the face of sacrilegious people or of acting beneficently towards needy people. Here the realms of the cult and of political and ethical action are once more seen on one level.[26]

Women also come into view in this section, and once again in a parallel to men that is gender-specifically structured:

> For how could they be called gods? For women serve (food) for (the) gods made of silver and gold and wood. And in their temples the priests drive[27] with torn garments and shaved heads and beards, their heads uncovered. They whine and shout before their gods like some do at the funeral banquet of a dead person. The priests take some of their clothing and outfit their wives and children with it. (vv. 30–33)

Once again this concerns ritual acts. It is obviously presumed that women on the Babylonian side have an active role in the sacrificial cult by providing the idols with food. If this is to be understood as disqualifying—and the lack of an official title for these women could already be an indication of this—then it must be presumed that the participation of women in the sacrificial cult was not regarded as acceptable either by the writers of the letter or by the addressees. In fact, it seems there were no females among the cultic personnel in the sacrificial area at the postexilic temple in Jerusalem, whereas female

26. This view also characterizes the book of Jeremiah. One need only recall the so-called temple speech in Jer 7–8.

27. See discussion below, esp. in n. 29.

personnel in the sacrificial cult is not ruled out for the preexilic period, at least for certain local holy places or local cults (see Hos 4:12–14).[28]

The men, referred to as priests (ἱερεῖς), stand beside the women who bring the food offerings. The former perform certain liturgies described as a lamentation of the dead, a description that is probably calculated to summon negative connotations on the part of the listeners or readers. The Greek translation perhaps expanded this image of a liturgy of lament by adding the element of a procession in the temple with an idol at which the priests "drive"[29] the processional chariots. In addition, a reproach appears again which focuses on the utilization of the materials donated to the gods for one's own use. As in Bel and the Dragon, the wives and children of the priests profit from the wrongfully purloined objects. Unlike that narrative, however, the women in the Letter of Jeremiah do not participate actively in the plundering of the gods; the reproach here is only directed at the priests. The garments, like gold and silver (see vv. 10–11), are probably votive offerings for the gods or their cultic images, which could be variously outfitted with them. Since there was probably no cultic image of the God of Israel in the temple in Jerusalem at the time of the Letter of Jeremiah,[30] this reproach also capitalizes on the notion, which is grotesque in the eyes of the authors as well as the recipients, that deities need garments at all.

The picture of unworthy female servants of the gods and the unworthy behavior of the designated male servants is designed to cause head-shaking on the part of the addressees. The second part of the subsection fits into this picture, where, almost like a litany, it maintains that those seeking consolation and help from the images are in fact forsaken. As in a negative of a photo, the significance of one's own relationship to God becomes clear here for people in existential difficulties of all kinds. Widows and their children are specifically named among those seeking help (v. 38). They who live without male pro-

28. Regarding this, see Wacker, "Kultprostitution," 77–79. In contrast, Stark, *Kultprostitution*, 165–82, sees no possibility at all that the use of the term *qedeshot* in Hos 4:12–14 can help solve the historical question concerning female cult attendants.

29. In this way one could glean meaning from the verb διφρεύω in v. 31. The Hebrew (or Aramaic) verb נהג could be the root here, which, in addition to "drive," also means "to cry, wail" and which, with this meaning, sustains the overall picture of mourning gestures (see Kellermann, "Apokryphes Obst," 26).

30. Regarding the state of the discussion, see Martin Leuenberger, "'Siehe, das sind deine Götter, Israel, die dich heraufgeführt haben aus dem Land Ägypten' (1 Kön 12,28): Materielle und symbolische Repräsentationen Jhwhs in der offiziell-staatlichen Religion Israels," in *Zwischen Zion und Zaphon: Studien in Gedenken an den Theologen Oswald Loretz (14.01.1928–12.04.2014)*, ed. Ludger Hiepel and Marie-Theres Wacker, AOAT 438 (Münster: Ugarit-Verlag, 2016), 288–311.

tection and who, according to the reproach, cannot count on the protection of their gods, form a sharp contrast to the wives and children of the priests' families who attire themselves in the precious garments of their gods, but who are without pity for the poor.

4.2. Speaking: The Inability of the Gods, The Spitefulness of the Women

The second subsection in the second part has clear opening and concluding signals. Verse 44 closes with a rhetorical question that also appears almost verbatim in verse 40, and it opens with an adverb that introduces an additional observation (ἔτι, v. 40b). Once again two quite different themes stand side by side; the motif of "speaking" seems to establish a connection between them. Verses 40 and 41 concern a mute who, as a person suffering from a disease, is brought before Bel, the Babylonian principal deity, in the hope that he might get him to speak. But how can a god who is mute himself, despite a carefully carved tongue (see v. 8), accomplish such a thing? The name Bel for the deity of the Chaldeans also recalls texts such as Isa 46:1–2 or Jer 50:2 and 51:44 in which the power of this Babylonian god is likewise doubted or mocked.

The scene spread out over verses 42 and 43 once again places women at the center:

> The women, however, with cords twined around them, sit along the paths and burn bran for incense. But when one of them, hauled off by someone passing by, has slept with him, she scoffs at the woman next to her for not having been similarly honored as she and that her cord had not been broken. (vv. 42–43)

Women entwined with cords sit along the roads and burn bran as incense. The cords are not specified in greater detail. The Greek formulation could refer to a headband,[31] but it is also conceivable that the cords are worn around the body. The burning of incense may be interpreted as a ritual for a deity. According to verse 43, one of the women is led away during the ritual by a passerby to sleep with him, whereby the cord is broken. The breaking of the cord probably indicates that this is a matter of a one-time act.

The text leaves open whether the sexual act described in verse 43 is an integral part of the ritual which the women perform. One can understand the text in such a way that the polemical reproach is directed against the behavior

31. The term περιτίθημι is frequently used for the wearing of wreaths or crowns. For the discussion with regard to v. 42, see Friedrich Jacobs, *Zerstreute Blätter*, vol. 6 of *Vermischte Schriften* (Leipzig: Dyck'sche Buchhandlung, 1837), 38.

of the woman who gets involved in sexual contact with a passerby during a ritual act (the presentation of an incense offering), and who is also proud of this.[32] If, however, one understands verse 43 to describe the intended goal of the ritual act, one could interpret the cords mentioned in both verses as a symbolic binding of feminine sexuality and fertility, bonds that are to be undone under the protection of the deity. It would then perhaps be about the first sexual intercourse a woman has with a stranger and not with her husband, a kind of initiation rite.[33] With respect to the addressed divinity, one would then think of the great Mesopotamian goddess Ishtar, who was worshiped as being responsible for the realm of sexuality.

To what degree the Letter of Jeremiah refers to historically verifiable rituals is quite uncertain. The rhetoric of verses 42 and 43 clearly aims at arousing negative reactions: whoever envisions this description gets the impression that the streets of Babylon are full of such women, which underscores the strange, disconcerting nature of such a practice. The image of women burning incense in the streets reminds one of the incense offerings for other gods in the streets of Jerusalem which Jeremiah deplores and criticizes (see Jer 44). But the use of bran in particular for the burning incense is only verified in Greek sources; the closest parallel is found in a work by Theocritus (*Id.* 2.33).[34] The ritual meaning of this burning of bran is unclear.[35] The alleged sexual availability of the women burning incense recalls Herodotus's description of Babylonian rituals. In section 1.199 of his *Histories* the Greek historian gives an account of a practice according to which every woman of Babylon had to submit to a ritual intercourse once in her life in honor of the goddess Ishtar-Mylitta. Herodotus's depiction is a polemical text formed in a literary fashion: 1.199 describes "the most infamous practice" (ὁ δὲ δὴ αἴσχιστος τῶν νόμων) as the reverse of the "wisest practice" (ὁ μὲν σοφώτατος [sc. τῶν νόμων]) of the Babylonians reported in 1.196, namely, the auctioning off of marriageable women.[36]

---

32. It could speak in favor of this interpretation that ὅταν ("when") introduces a situation in vv. 41, 48, and 54 in which the inability of the gods and the misconduct of their priests becomes apparent. Accordingly, v. 42 may also only constitute the lead-in for the really scandalous scene in v. 43.

33. Scholars discuss to what extent a rite of this kind was also practiced in preexilic Israel; the *locus classicus* is Hos 4:12–14.

34. The following authors refer to this passage: Naumann, *Untersuchungen*, 23; Moatti-Fine, "Lettre de Jérémie," 325; Kellermann, "Apokryphes Obst," 34–35.

35. See the discussion in Kellermann, "Apokryphes Obst," 34–35 and 42, who concludes that the burning of bran as incense is supposed to make the gods attentive and well-disposed. The sources, however, are sparse.

36. In both cases it is mentioned that the beautiful women are the first in line. Regard-

Such an "infamous" practice is not historically proven.[37] Other Greek authors, however, adopted Herodotus's polemical depiction and thus contributed to the dissemination of this image.[38] It is completely conceivable that the circle of the authors of the Letter of Jeremiah also knew Herodotus's account or at least drew from the tradition established by Herodotus.[39] In any case this image fits well into the mental framework that presupposes the incompatibility of sexuality and cult and must therefore reject the carrying out of sexual acts under the protection of or in honor of a deity. Such an action does not serve the glory of a god but only his degradation, as verse 40a notes at the beginning.

More precisely, as the section makes clear, the dishonoring of their deities by the Babylonians themselves does not occur so much through the rite as such, but through the behavior of the women: they scoff at those among them whose cord has not yet been broken. They talk disdainfully about each other; they strip each other of their honor. Gods who tolerate such things are false gods. Those listening to the Letter of Jeremiah could recall Hannah and Peninnah (1 Sam 1) and that their God had turned to the childless Hannah in the end and had silenced her mocker Peninnah. In this depiction of women, gender stereotypes might also be retrieved: as the quarrel between Rachel and Leah in Gen 30 shows, women do not fight each other with weapons, but with words. The Letter of Jeremiah would then be referring once again to a gender-specific cliché here, as perhaps it also does in the case of the ornament-loving girl (see v. 9), in order to convey its message.

---

ing the literary structure and function, see Stephanie L. Budin, *The Myth of Sacred Prostitution in Antiquity* (Cambridge: Cambridge University Press, 2008), 58–92.

37. See Naumann, *Untersuchungen*, 20–21, who already demonstrates this. Martha T. Roth, "Marriage, Divorce, and the Prostitute in Ancient Mesopotamia," in *Prostitutes and Courtesans in the Ancient World*, ed. Christopher A. Faraone and Laura K. McClure (Madison: University of Wisconsin Press, 2006), 21–39, specifically 22, points out that, interestingly enough, no other custom which Herodotus describes in this section is considered to be historical.

38. Strabo, *Geogr.* 16,1; Lucian, *Syr. d.* 6 (in addition, see Budin, *Myth*, 94–103).

39. Herodotus as well as the Letter of Jeremiah relate that women, clad with cords, sit along the paths (ὁδοί) on which men pass and take a woman with them for the purpose of sexual intercourse. Both texts portray this as an example of a disgraceful Babylonian custom; an implicit rivalry among the women—whoever gets chosen first can feel superior—is mentioned. In addition to these similarities there are also differences: in Herodotus the women sit in the temple area and are paid by the suitors; in the Letter of Jeremiah the women perform incense offerings. With respect to the similarities, see Stark, *Kultprostitution*, 20, who envisages a literary dependence on Herodotus; in contrast to this, with a view to the differences, see Moore, "Epistle of Jeremiah," 348; Naumann, *Untersuchungen*, 20.

4.3. The Gods of the "Others": Deceitful and Without Value and Usefulness

The motif of deception is a recurring theme that runs through the following four short sections (vv. 45–47a, 47b–49, 50–52, 53–56a), a collection that appears to be random: the deities of the others are deceitful, behind their appearances there is only false being. The section consisting of verses 57–64 brings up a new theme, the comparison of the idols with the forces of nature created by God and obeying his will, thereby adopting a motif from Jer 10 (which also recurs in Bar 3:33–35). It shows that the deities are without value or usefulness. In the final part, several other themes are brought into play. In verses 66–69, the impotence of the gods in the cosmos is shown, and in verses 70–72, the gods are ridiculed as inanimate material and their destruction is announced (see Jer 10:15; 50:2).

5. A Rereading of the "Letter" in Its Closing Appeal (v. 73)

The Letter of Jeremiah closes with a sentence that is formulated in the style of a sapiential rule of life: "Better, therefore, a just person who has no idols for he will be far from vilification." The sentence disambiguates the speech, since now the text speaks not about θεοί, deities, but about εἴδωλα, images or idols. As a result, this last sentence, which is the only one that reduces the gods terminologically to their images in an unequivocal way, brings in, at the very end of the speech, a demystifying or unmasking perspective for the overall context. Moreover, it individualizes the implications of what has been said and applies the set of issues discussed in the text to the area of the responsibility of each and every person: "better the person who has no idols." With that the text returns to the recommendation in the introduction to say a quick prayer in one's mind (v. 6). Although the form of address appears in the plural, it intends to speak to every single person as an individual.

But the concluding verse also entails an important shift or expansion of the set of issues. This is no longer just a matter of the temple and the processions, but of personal piety and the household cult. The listeners are urged quite categorically not to have images. This means not only that they should shun the cult of the gods in public, but also that they should avoid the veneration of images in private piety. Seen from this final exhortation, the entire Letter of Jeremiah, which clearly concerns "official religion" above all, the religion of processions and temples run by the official side and practiced publicly, could be reread with respect to its implications for personal piety and the household cult. In this respect this final verse of the letter already instructs one to remove the epistle from the situation sketched in the introduction and to apply it to new contexts.

6. In Conclusion: The Holy … and the Women

The primary message of the Letter of Jeremiah, however, is directed towards demonstrating the irrelevance of the divine images or imaged gods of Babylonia on the level of the "official religion." The theological or cultic-practical problem that the text seeks to address should therefore also be located here. Much like the negative of a photo, the text mirrors the great fascination of the processions of the deities and the cult of the gods, and it investigates the theological question of whether one must indeed fear the gods of the others as powerful and thus, just to be on the safe side, venerate them in a ritual fashion. The strategy of the Letter of Jeremiah in view of this question is to rudely mock the gods of Babylonia and in this sense to engage in "enlightenment" about the factual impotence of the gods of the "others." The Letter of Jeremiah has obviously already freed itself from fearing the impressive gods of Babylon. In the letter, the mockery of the images occurs on the basis of the certainty of one's own superiority.

Certainty of one's own superiority is one aspect—but the length and intensity of the analysis which the Letter of Jeremiah undertakes could also be an indication that the community of the addressees is uncertain and needs support for its position of distancing itself from the cult. This support is conveyed through the strategy of a clear degradation not only of the deities, but also of those responsible for their cult. The priests are accused of deceiving the people across the board. The Letter of Jeremiah thereby follows an approach that is similar to the story of Bel and the Dragon, which relates that the families of the priests get into the temple of Bel at night through a secret entrance and eat the sacrificial food so that even the king sees through the trickery only when Daniel, a Jewish confidant of the king, finds the priests guilty by means of a trick. In the Letter of Jeremiah, criticism of the women in the families of the priests is woven into this criticism of priests; but other women who are active in the cult of the deities are also woven into this criticism.

The depiction of women in the Letter of Jeremiah cannot be detached from the polemical character of this writing. In the older literature, the role of women in verses 11 and 42–43 is usually interpreted in connection with alleged Babylonian sexual rites. As was explained above, however, the newer research strongly doubts the historicity of "cult prostitution." Corresponding descriptions like, for instance, in the work of Herodotus, might therefore rather be considered as polemical attributions. Since the Letter of Jeremiah aims at a degradation of Babylonian cults, it would be conceivable that such polemical attributions are encountered here. Hence, with regard to the gender constructions in the Letter of Jeremiah, the questions can be posed as to what degree the sexualization of the women acting ritually is part of the design of the text itself, as part of its polemical rhetoric, and to what extent this only occurs through a sexist interpretation by scholars. In the end, a corresponding motif can only be explicitly found in verse 43. It seems likely that the Letter of Jeremiah uses women-specific stereotypes as part of its rhetorical strategy for the purpose of degrading the cult of the gods. Verse 29 targets the physical impurity of women—whereas the corporeality of men is not polemically exploited anywhere. The descriptions of the ornament-loving young woman in verse 9 and of the spiteful women in verse 43 possibly emphasize gender-specific clichés as well. The interpretation, however, always runs the risk of inserting one's own gender-clichés into the polemical depiction. For this reason, the connection between women, cult of the gods, and sexuality requires a deconstruction itself, akin to that which the Letter of Jeremiah practices so masterfully with regard to the idols.

It is therefore all the more important to view the female figures in the Letter of Jeremiah in a differentiated way. The letter does not accuse all women of actively participating in the cult of the gods. Some of the female figures are objects, not subjects of the actions (vv. 9, 11, 33, 38). Through them the idols are disparaged and the actions of the (male) priests criticized. The women in verses 28–30 and 42–43, however, are themselves subjects of actions. All these women are accused of taking an active part in the cult of the gods, in particular, in connection with sacrifices. They are depicted in a parallel role to the priests: both sections about the actions of women have an equivalent in which the priests act (vv. 28–30: vv. 31–33; vv. 42–43: vv. 40–41). The women, just like the priests, are negatively portrayed as active agents in the cult of the gods. In this sense the polemic does not specifically target women—even if the Letter of Jeremiah possibly uses gender-specific clichés in some places. In addition, it is conspicuous that the male staff of the cult are always designated as "priests" (ἱερεῖς, or in v. 40 Χαλδαῖοι, Chaldeans), whereas a corresponding designation of the female personnel is missing. The women performing sacrifices are simply called "women" (γυναῖκες). In contrast, the word "man" (ἀνήρ) cannot be found in the Letter of Jeremiah; male figures are always designated by their functions (besides "priests," also "king," "judge," etc.). Provided that it does not occur simply out of ignorance of their titles, the designation of the active female figures of the cult as "women" could thus have the rhetorical function of delegitimizing the active role of women in the cult.

By criticizing women for their active role in the cult of the gods, the Letter of Jeremiah ascribes to them a responsibility for the cult of the gods analogous to that of the priests. That the women in verses 28–30 and 42–43 become a target of the polemic shows that the circle of authors was aware of women as independent cultic agents. In this sense the Letter of Jeremiah ultimately testifies to the important role of women as subjects of ritual acts.

Intersections of Gender, Status, Ethnos, and Religion in Joseph and Aseneth

Angela Standhartinger

In Gen 41:45, Joseph receives from Pharaoh, in gratitude for interpreting Pharaoh's dreams, Aseneth (Ἀσενέθ; Hebrew: אסנת: Asenath/Osnath), daughter of Pentephres (Hebrew: Potiphera), priest of Heliopolis (Hebrew: On) as his wife. She gives birth to two sons, Ephraim and Manasseh, ancestors of two of the later tribes of Israel (Gen 42:50; 46:20). In the Bible this is only a marginal note. But postbiblical narrators expand on this scant information to create a romantic adventure story that today is called Joseph and Aseneth (Jos. Asen.).[1]

Based on the storyline of the ancient novel, this Jewish pseudepigraphon narrates how the Egyptian Aseneth and the biblical Joseph meet for the first time and fall in love at first sight; how the heart-sick Aseneth converts to Israel's God, is visited by a heavenly man in her isolated tower chamber, and finally marries Joseph.[2] Later she is integrated into Jacob's family but, while traveling through the country, is attacked by Pharaoh's son in conspiracy with some of Joseph's brothers. Yet with the help of God and some miracles, she

1. The modern title Joseph and Aseneth was generated by analogy to titles of the ancient Greek novels. Many feminist interpreters prefer the title Aseneth. See, e.g., Ross S. Kraemer, "The Book of Aseneth," in *A Feminist Commentary*, vol. 2 of *Searching the Scriptures*, ed. Elisabeth Schüssler Fiorenza (New York: Crossroad, 1994), 789–816. For various titles in the ancient manuscripts, see Christoph Burchard, *Joseph und Aseneth kritisch herausgegeben von Christoph Burchard mit Unterstützung von Carsten Burfeind und Uta Barbara Fink*, PVTG 5 (Leiden: Brill, 2003), 337–40.

2. For a comparison of Joseph and Aseneth and the ancient novel, see Angela Standhartinger, *Das Frauenbild im Judentum der hellenistischen Zeit: Ein Beitrag anhand von 'Joseph und Aseneth,'* AGJU 26 (Leiden: Brill, 1995), 20–26. Standhartinger, "Recent Scholarship on Joseph and Aseneth (1988–2013)," *CurBR* 12 (2014): 375–80. For a comparison of Joseph and Aseneth with Susanna, Esther, Tobit, and Judith, see Lawrence Wills, *The Jewish Novel in the Ancient World* (Ithaca, NY: Cornell University Press, 1995).

manages to escape and saves Jacob's hostile sons from the revenge of their brothers. In the end—and this is unique in ancient Jewish literature—Joseph becomes Pharaoh of Egypt and reigns for forty years. The story of Joseph and Aseneth draws heavily not only upon the biblical Joseph story but also upon various other texts from the Septuagint, including the story of Shechem's rape of Dinah (Gen 34) and that of David and Goliath (1 Sam 17). In addition, topics and motifs from the Psalms, the Song of Songs, Daniel, and the later prophets are interwoven into the story. Most likely, Joseph and Aseneth was composed by Jewish authors in Greek between 100 BCE and 200 CE.[3]

The plot of Joseph and Aseneth centers on a female figure. Therefore, it is hardly surprising that our novel has been the object of much feminist research. Yet the evaluation of Aseneth as a female figure has led to diverging conclusions. Some read Joseph and Aseneth as a story of liberation in which a woman frees herself from confinement in a tower and moves out into the world to establish a better ethic of loving one's enemy.[4] Others, however, read the text as a legitimatization of patriarchal role models and as viewing a woman's place as being in silence and subordination to her husband as well as other male relatives.[5] In this paper I will add to the discussion on the construction of gender in Joseph and Aseneth an intersectional analysis of the story.

The metaphor *intersectionality* was coined by professor of law Kimberlé Crenshaw in 1989. In a study of a lawsuit brought by seven black female workers against General Motors, Crenshaw concluded that the women lost their case because the court weighed discrimination based on race against

---

3. For the recent scholarly discussion of date and place of origin, see Standhartinger, "Recent Scholarship," 371–74. Some scholars argue for a later Christian provenance of the writing; see Ross S. Kraemer, *When Aseneth Met Joseph: A Late Antique Tale of the Biblical Patriarch and His Egyptian Wife, Reconsidered* (New York: Oxford University Press, 1998); Rivka Nir, *Joseph and Aseneth: A Christian Book*, HBM 42 (Sheffield: Sheffield Phoenix, 2012). Yet, their arguments are not convincing. For details, see Standhartinger, "Recent Scholarship," 371–75.

4. See Susan H. Doty, "From Ivory Tower to City of Refuge: The Role and Function of the Protagonist in 'Joseph and Aseneth' and Related Narratives" (PhD diss., Iliff School of Theology and University of Denver, 1989); Ross S. Kraemer, *Her Share of the Blessings: Women's Religions among Pagans, Jews, and Christians in the Greco-Roman World* (New York: Oxford University Press, 1992), 110–13.

5. Sally O. Langford, "On Being a Religious Woman: Women Proselytes in the Greco-Roman World," in *Recovering the Role of Women: Power and Authority in Rabbinic Jewish Society*, ed. Peter J. Haas, SFSHJ 59 (Atlanta: Scholars Press, 1992), 61–83; Sabrina Inowlocki, "Le roman d'Aseneth: Un roman feministe," in *La femme dans les civilisations orientales et Miscellanea Aegyptologica: Christiane Desroches Noblecourt in honorem*, ed. Christian Cannuyer (Louvain-la-Neuve: Centre d'Histoire des Religions, 2001), 111–18. For an overview, see Standhartinger, "Recent Scholarship," 380–83.

discrimination based on sex, effectively making both forms invisible.[6] To the contrary, Crenshaw argued, axes of discrimination do not act independently but rather intersect with each other and thereby become more intense. In social science, intersectional analysis studies the interactions and interconnections between manifold forms of discrimination, oppression, and domination, including on the basis of sex/gender, race/ethnicity, class/status, body, religion, et cetera.

In historical research, an analysis of the structural categories of gender, status, ethnos, and the like in a fictional narrative allows us to observe the complex discourse on identity that is at stake.[7] Identity—for example, the Jewish identity discussed in Joseph and Aseneth—is not an intrinsic essence or substance of a given people or group but is rather composed out of multifarious categories applying to the various characters in a story. Religious practice is one of numerous categories out of which an ancient people was constructed. A famous definition of "the Greeks" by the ancient historian Herodotus (fifth century BCE) lists the following identifying markers: "the kinship in blood and speech, and the shrines of gods and the sacrifices that we have in common, and the likeness of our way of life" (*Hist.* 8.144.2).[8] Religion functions here as one of numerous markers of Greekness, alongside blood kinship, a common ethos, and a shared language. Joseph and Aseneth originated at a time when, in a gradual process, religion went from being an exclusively ethnic marker to being a system of belief independent of ethnicity. It is currently under debate whether the term *Judaism* designates a religious belief or the people of the *ethnos* Judeans at the turn of the era.[9] Some scholars hold

6. Kimberlé Crenshaw, "Demarginalizing the Intersection of Race and Sex: A Black Feminist Critique of Antidiscrimination Doctrine," *UCLF* 139 (1989): 139–67.

7. For theory, methods, and history of research, see Ute E. Eisen, Christine Gerber, and Angela Standhartinger, "Doing Gender—Doing Religion: Zur Frage nach der Intersektionalität in den Bibelwissenschaften; Eine Einleitung," in *Doing Gender—Doing Religion: Fallstudien zur Intersektionalität im frühen Judentum, Christentum und Islam*, WUNT 302 (Tübingen: Mohr Siebeck, 2013), 1–33. See also Laura Nasrallah and Elisabeth Schüssler Fiorenza, eds., *Prejudice and Christian Beginnings: Investigating Race, Gender, and Ethnicity in Early Christian Studies* (Minneapolis: Fortress, 2009), as well as Birgitta L. Sjöberg, "More than Just Gender: The Classical Oikos as a Site of Intersectionality in Families in the Greco-Roman World," in *Families in the Greco-Roman World*, ed. Ray Laurence and Agneta Strömberg (London: Continuum, 2012), 48–59.

8. Translation by A. D. Godley, *Herodotus, with an English Translation*, LCL (Cambridge: Harvard University Press, 1920).

9. Shaye J. D. Cohen, *The Beginnings of Jewishness: Boundaries, Varieties, Uncertainties*, HCS 31 (Berkeley: University of California Press, 2000), 109–39, argues that Judaism became a religion in Hasmonean times (first century BCE), when conversion became

that it is more likely that the idea of religion as personal belief started with the rise of a non-Jewish Christian identity in the second century CE or even later. At any rate, it is obvious that Joseph and Aseneth formed part of a discourse on Jewish identity as a fictional story about the acceptance of an Egyptian lady into Jacob's family and the patriarch Joseph's ascent to the Egyptian throne.

Identity is built of independent yet intersecting categories such as gender, ethnicity, status, ethos, and religious practice. In Joseph and Aseneth all of the aforementioned categories are at work. In its main figure, the writing generates an elaborated model of womanhood. Constructions of masculinity can be observed in the characterizations of Joseph, his brothers, and Pharaoh's son. Status is at stake when some of Jacob's sons are referred to as having been born of slaves, in contrast to their freeborn brethren, including Joseph. The whole novel addresses the opposition between the Egyptians and Jacob's family, thereby persistently drawing as well as blurring borderlines between the two ethnic groups. In the following I shall analyze our story by focusing on gender, status, and ethnicity. Afterwards I will ask, whether and how religion transforms these categories. Finally, I will present some information on potential authors and actual female readers of this piece of writing.

Texts and Transmission of Joseph and Aseneth

In modern editions, the text of Joseph and Aseneth is arranged in twenty-nine chapters.[10] By number of words, it is longer than the Gospel of Mark but shorter than the Gospel of Matthew. Based on references to the "seven years of plenty" (Gen 41:47–52 = Jos. Asen. 1.1) and the "the seven years of famine" (Gen 41:43–47:27 = Jos. Asen. 22.1), the story divides into two sections. In the first part, Jos. Asen. 1–21, Joseph is traveling throughout Egypt, gathering the wheat harvest during the years of plenty, while Jos. Asen. 22–29 is set after Jacob and his family have followed Joseph to Egypt and settled down at Gosem.[11]

possible (see, beside Joseph and Aseneth, Jdt 14:1 and 2 Macc 9:11–17). Steve Mason, "Jews, Judaeans, Judaizing, Judaism: Problems of Categorization in Ancient History," *JSJ* 38 (2007): 457–512, argues that up to the third century CE Judeans thought of themselves and were seen as an ethnos. Christians who tried to distinguish themselves from Judeans and to establish a non-Judean identity of their own were the first to argue for a Jewish religion.

10. For texts and translations, see below nn. 11, 13, and 14.

11. Translations are taken from Lawrence M. Wills, "The Marriage and Conversion of Aseneth," in *Ancient Jewish Novels* (Oxford: Oxford University Press, 2002), 121–62; and Patricia Ahearne-Kroll, "Joseph and Aseneth," in *Outside the Bible: Ancient Jewish Writings Related to Scripture*, ed. Louis H. Feldman, James K. Kugel, and Lawrence H. Schiffman (Philadelphia: Jewish Publication Society of America, 2013), 3:2525–89. For the short

The narrator begins with a description of Aseneth and her home (Jos. Asen. 1–4). When Joseph arrives at the house of her father, Pentephres (Jos. Asen. 5–8), the two main characters, Aseneth and Joseph, meet for the first time. Yet because Joseph initially rejects her welcoming kiss, Aseneth mourns for seven days and turns to Joseph's God on the eight day with a long prayer (Jos. Asen. 9–13). A heavenly visitor appears to her in her tower chamber, telling her that that she has been accepted by God and sharing with her a mysterious honeycomb, before returning into heaven (Jos. Asen. 14–17). At the end of the first part of the story, Aseneth and Joseph meet again (Jos. Asen. 18–19), and their love is celebrated across the country with a wedding officiated by the Egyptian Pharaoh (Jos. Asen. 20–21). Later, during the seven years of famine, Joseph and his wife Aseneth visit Jacob at Gosem (Jos. Asen. 22). However, when Pharaoh's son sees her, he tries to abduct her and seeks help for his conspiracy among Joseph's brothers (Jos. Asen. 23–25). With God's help, the plan fails, and Joseph becomes the pharaoh of Egypt (Jos. Asen. 27–29).

Joseph and Aseneth has been passed down to us through more than ninety manuscripts and in seven ancient and medieval languages. This piece of writing is much better preserved than any other so-called Old Testament Pseudepigrapha. Manuscript versions written in ancient Greek go back to the eleventh century CE, those written in Syriac even to the sixth century CE. In the Armenian tradition the writing was included in the biblical canon in the medieval era.[12]

The manuscripts differ from one another sharply. Today four critical reconstructions of an ancient Greek *Urtext* (or original text) are available, all based on various manuscripts.[13] The most popular of these are a short version by Marc Philonenko and a longer (indeed, the longest) version by Christoph

---

version: D. Cook, "Joseph and Aseneth," in *The Apocryphal Old Testament*, ed. Hedley F. D. Sparks (Oxford: Clarendon, 1984), 465–503, accessible also at: http://tinyurl.com/SBL6006e. If not indicated, translations are mine.

12. On the history of individual manuscripts, see Standhartinger, "Recent Scholarship," 354–61.

13. Burchard, *Joseph und Aseneth*. Burchard based his text principally on versions, above all on Syriac, Armenian, and one of the Latin translations (L2), and reconstructs a Greek text with the help of the Greek manuscripts FW and G. His "vorläufiger Text" counts 13,403 words. Uta B. Fink, *Joseph und Aseneth: Revision des griechischen Textes und Edition der zweiten lateinischen Übersetzung*, FSBP 5 (Berlin: de Gruyter, 2008), revised Burchard's text. Her text counts 13,141 words. Unfortunately, her edition has no critical apparatus. A much shorter text of 8,256 words was edited by Marc Philonenko, *Joseph et Aséneth: Introduction, texte critique, traduction et notes*, StPB 13 (Leiden: Brill, 1968), from the Greek manuscripts B (eleventh century), D (fifteenth century) and the Slavonian translation. A fourth edition based exclusively on the sixteen Greek manuscripts was edited most recently

Buchard. Philonenko's text is five thousand words shorter than Buchchard's.[14] Since the early 1990s, feminist interpreters have observed that each version presents a different image of Aseneth.[15] More recently, Christine Thomas and Patricia Ahearne-Kroll have argued that the texts of the manuscripts, fixed on some points and fluid in others, might best be understood as snapshots of oral performances of our story throughout history.[16] In the following, I shall limit myself to calling attention to some major differences between the texts at a few select points. As many more translations (into English, German, French, Italian, and Spanish) are available for the longer version of the text than the shorter version, I will refer to the former when citing chapter and verse. At

by Pius-Ramon Tragan, *Josep i Àsenet: Introducció, text grec revisat i notes*, LISup 4 (Barcelona: Ed. Alpha, 2005).

14. Philonenko adds a French translation. A French translation of Philonenko's text is also available by Sabrina Inowlocki, *Des idoles mortes et muettes au dieu vivant: Joseph, Aséneth et le fils de Pharaon dans un roman du Judaïsme Hellénisé* (Turnhout: Brepols, 2002), 159–80. Burchard's text is translated into English in *OTP* 2:177–247, and into German in Christoph Burhard, *Joseph und Aseneth*, JSHRZ 2.4 (Güttersloh: Mohn, 1983), 631–720. Fink's text is translated into German by Eckart Reinmuth, ed., *Joseph und Aseneth*, SAPERE 15 (Tübingen: Mohr Siebeck, 2009), 56–137. Burchard's text is also translated by Lawrence M. Wills, "Marriage and Conversion of Aseneth," 121–62 and Ahearne-Kroll, "Joseph and Aseneth," 3:2525–89. For Italian, see D. Maggiorotti, "Giuseppe e Aseneth," in vol. 4 of *Apocrifi dell'Antico Testamento*, ed. Paolo Sacchi (Brescia: Paideia, 2000), 423–525. Tragan, *Josep i Àsenet*, translates his own text into Catalan.

15. Independently of each other, Kraemer (*Her Share of the Blessings*, 110–13) and Standhartinger (*Das Frauenbild*) observed that the image of Aseneth differs in the two textual reconstructions and that she appears as a more autonomous subject in the shorter version. See also Standhartinger, "Joseph and Aseneth: Perfect Bride or Heanvely Prophetess," in *Feminist Biblical Interpretation: A Compendium of Critical Commentary on the Books of the Bible and Related Literature*, ed. Luise Schottroff and Marie-Theres Wacker (Grand Rapids: Eerdmans, 2012), 578–86. Later Kraemer changed her mind, arguing that both texts reflect an androcentric revision. See Kraemer, *When Aseneth*, 50–88. Edith M. Humphrey, *Joseph and Aseneth*, GAP 8 (Sheffield: Sheffield Academic, 2000), 65–74, 71, concedes that "Aseneth appears to be placed more firmly at centre stage in the shorter version." However, missing from the short text (but present in the longer) are several elements that round out the character of Aseneth in other ways: a deeper inner character revealed by her twice aborted confession (ch. 11), constant reference to her spiritual sight, her use of wisdom language, and mystical descriptions of her physical presence.

16. Christine M. Thomas, *The Acts of Peter, Gospel Literature and the Ancient Novel: Rewriting the Past* (Oxford: Oxford University Press, 2003), 78–85; Patricia Ahearne-Kroll, "Joseph and Aseneth and Jewish Identity in Greco-Roman Egypt" (PhD diss., The University of Chicago, 2005), 73–85.

some points, I will point out some differences between the longest and shortest versions, referring to the former as "B" and to the latter as "Ph."[17]

Women in Joseph and Aseneth

Joseph and Aseneth centers on a female character. Aseneth is introduced as the supremely beautiful daughter of the Egyptian priest Pentephres (1.5). As with a fairytale princess, all of the high and mighty of the country, including Pharaoh's son, desire her as a wife and compete over her. But she despises all men and lives cloistered in a tower. Her room in the tower functions as a temple of the Egyptian gods (2.6). When her parents return home, she adorns herself as a "bride of God" (3.5–4.1). When her father suggests that she marry Joseph, "the mighty one of God," she indignantly rejects the notion. She is not prepared to marry the "shepherd's son from Canaan who was caught in the act of sleeping with his female master" (4.10, trans. Ahearne-Kroll; cf. Gen 39). However, observing Joseph standing on his splendid chariot while entering her father's courtyard, she realizes her mistake. Now, she perceives Joseph as the "son of God" (6.3) and wants to become his slave and to serve him (6.8). Joseph greets the "man-hating virgin" but rejects her kiss. Yet, he blesses her and asks God to renew her (8.9). When Joseph departs, Aseneth mourns for eight days. She exchanges her royal garments for sackcloth and ashes and throws her Egyptian gods out of the window (chs. 10–13). In some versions, a silent prayer in which she confesses her sins is added.[18] On the eighth day she sends up a prayer to God, imitating psalms of lament and those praising God as creator (12).[19] A human being from heaven appears in her tower chamber, dressed like Joseph but with a fiery head and body, resembling the archangel of Dan 10:5–13. This heavenly visitor tells her to throw off her black mourning tunic and put on a new, untouched linen robe (Jos. Asen. 14.13). She no longer needs a veil because, as a chaste virgin, her "head is like that of a young man" (15.1, trans. Wills). Then the heavenly visitor reveals to her that her prayers have been heard by God and that she has been given to Joseph as a bride. Furthermore, he renames her "City of Refuge" (15.2–6). The image of the City of Refuge is expounded upon to greater or lesser extent in

17. Unfortunately Philonenko added his own verse numbers, so that one has to apply a double numbering system when comparing Burchard's and Philonenko's texts side by side. In the following, I mark quotes from Philonenko's text with "Ph" and those from Burchard's text with "B."

18. Chapter 11 appears only in very few manuscripts and in none of them as presented in Burchard's text.

19. See Standhartinger, *Frauenbild*, 180–84.

the various manuscripts as a place of shelter for those who flee to God (15.6; 16.16B). The heavenly visitor adds that it is the heavenly figure Metanoia, like Lady Wisdom, daughter of God, who has entreated on her behalf in heaven as well as on behalf of those who return to God (15.7–8).[20] Furthermore, the heavenly visitor blesses Aseneth as the secret mysteries of the Most High have been revealed to her (16.14), and he shares with her a miraculous honeycomb. Undoubtedly, this scene has some symbolical meaning.[21] However, because nearly every single manuscript tells its own sequence of actions, the symbols remain hard to decipher. Finally, the heavenly visitor, like Elijah, rides back to heaven on a chariot of fire (17.7–8; cf. 2 Kgs 2:11).

Then Aseneth prepares herself to meet Joseph by reclothing herself and once again veiling her head (ch. 18). Again the manuscripts differ here and some include erotic metaphors to describe Aseneth's transcendent beauty.[22] Finally Joseph appears. Having, like her, been informed by heaven, he gathers her in his arms, and the loving couple merges into each other with a kiss (19.10). But for her wedding, Aseneth has to wait until her father leads her to Pharaoh (21.1–8). While the writing devotes three chapters to the reunion and marriage of the couple, it devotes only one sentence to the birth of Aseneth's sons, Ephraim and Manasse (21.9). Some manuscripts include a prayer of repentance—a confession featuring the formula "I sinned, O Lord, I sinned," outlining Aseneth's transgressions, her idol worship, her arrogance, her hatred of men, and how Joseph won his victory over her (21.10–21B).[23]

Eight years later, in the years of famine, Aseneth visits Jacob and his sons, who have meanwhile migrated to Egypt. She particularly makes friends with "the prophet" Levi (22.13; 23.8). While riding out to the fields she has inherited (26.1), Pharaoh's son, who has aligned himself with Dan, Gad, Naphtali, and Asher (Jacob's sons by his slaves Bilhah and Zilpah), tries to capture her with an army of 2,050 soldiers. God, however, protects her with the help of some miracles (ch. 27). Finally the slave-born sons flee to her and beg for protection from the revenge of their brothers. Aseneth calms them. In the short text she says: "Have courage … for your brothers are god-fearing men and do

---

20. Ibid., 192–97.

21. For representative interpretations, see Standhartinger, "Recent Scholarship," 384–85.

22. Diane B. Lipsett, *Desiring Conversion: Hermas, Thecla, Aseneth* (Oxford: Oxford University Press, 2011), 86–122, points to the eroticism of this imagery.

23. Helena Zlotnick, *Dinah's Daughters: Gender and Judaism from the Hebrew Bible to Late Antiquity* (Philadelphia: University of Pennsylvania Press, 2002), 95, is reminded by its form and place in the narrative of the genre of the *hymenaios*, the Hellenistic wedding song.

not repay evil for evil to anybody" (28.4Ph, trans. Cook).[24] When Simon does not stop seeking revenge against his brothers, she holds this against him: "the Lord will avenge this outrage" (28.14Ph, trans. Cook).[25] As a summary, this version of the text adds: "Thus Aseneth saved the men from their brothers' wrath, so that they did not kill them" (28.16Ph, trans. Cook).

The female protagonist undergoes several transformations: from a conscious virgin despising all men to a loving wife; from a proud daughter of a priest to a humble mourning woman clothed in sackcloth and ashes who wishes to become Joseph's slave (6.6; 13, 15); from one who worships innumerable Egyptian gods to one who allows herself to be renewed by "Joseph's God" (6.6).

Yet, this narrative pursues more than one concept of female gender. In a theological context, self-abasement can be read as a voluntary renunciation of one's former status. Thus a biblical narrative becomes apparent: Whoever humbles her or himself will be raised. Then, some crosscurrents of Aseneth's transformation emerge: from solitude in a tower to inclusion in Jacob's family; from exclusion to mobility in the world. Her virginity elevates Aseneth to the same level as Joseph (4.7; 7.7). In any event, it is only her hatred of all men that makes her acceptable to him in the first place (7.8). From the beginning, she is named the "bride of God" (4.1), and her beauty is, if anything, just a bit inferior to the attractiveness of Joseph.[26] In the end, the final focus is not her happy marriage and motherhood but her life-saving acts in favor of Jacob's sons. She is the only character whose visionary experience is expanded upon in the narrative (chs. 14–17). When the heavenly visitor calls her a "young man" (15.1), her gender-role finally becomes complex. In Joseph and Aseneth, the classical narrative pattern "woman finds a husband and a family" is at once reinforced and performatively blurred.

In contrast to Aseneth, minor female characters receive little attention. Her mother appears in the company of Aseneth's father.[27] Only once, however, when she takes Aseneth down from her tower to meet Joseph, does she

---

24. This ethical maxim is quoted also by Paul in Rom 12:17 and 1 Thess 5:15. In the longer text Aseneth does not argue with this maxim but argues that all sons of Jacob fear God.

25. "This outrage" could refer to the revenge or to what the sons have done. The longer text clarifies: "it is for the Lord to punish this crime" (28.14B).

26. See Meredith Warren, "A Robe like Lightning: Clothing Changes and Identification in Joseph and Aseneth," in *Dressing Judeans and Christians in Antiquity*, ed. Kristi Upson-Saia, Carly Daniel-Hughes, and Alicia J. Batten (Farnham, Surrey, UK: Ashgate, 2014), 137–54. This might explain the many versions of chapter 18 in the particular manuscripts.

27. Jos. Asen. 3.5; 4.1, 5; 5.2; 8.1, 6; 20.6. In Jos. Asen. 4.2; 5.3, 7 she is called "Missis Pentephres."

act alone (8.1).[28] Another group of female characters are the seven virgins who stay with Aseneth in her tower and share her ascetic life (2.6). Their role oscillates between that of friend and servant (2.6; 10.4–8). On the one hand, Aseneth asks the heavenly visitor to include them in his blessing (17.4). Some versions of the text refer to them as the seven pillars of the City of Refuge, an allusion to the seven pillars of the House of Wisdom (e.g., 17.6B; see Prov 9:1). On the other hand, however, both Aseneth and Joseph still treat them as servants (18.8; 20.3). Female solidarity is not a major theme in this story.

Men in Joseph and Aseneth

The image of masculinity presented in the figure of Joseph has been interpreted variously.[29] This character has two, not well-integrated sides. On the on hand, there is a divine figure that only selectively intervenes in the world. He is the "son of God,"[30] who, while relegated to only the second of Pharaoh's chariots, resembles a *triumphator* or the sun god Helios in that his quadriga is drawn by four white horses, he wears his golden *stola* and a crown with golden rays, and he holds a scepter (5.4–5).[31] His divine self is able to bless Aseneth effectively and initiate her transformation. The heavenly visitor is clothed like him (14:9). In some manuscripts, when he meets Aseneth again, he conveys to her the spirit of life, wisdom, and truth (19.11B). After his wedding, he has to safeguard all the people, so that "the earth shall not vanish from the sight of the Lord" (26.3, trans. Wills).

On the other hand, beyond this divine and sovereign aspect of the figure, there is another aspect that plays with the story of Potiphar's wife. Genesis

28. Zlotnick, *Dinah's Daughters*, 96–97, sees this as "a significant measure of spousal equality," yet she also observes that Aseneth's mother does not attend her wedding in chapter 21.

29. For Hanna Stenström, "Masculine or Feminine? Male Virgins in Joseph and Aseneth and the Book of Revelation," in *Identity Formation in the New Testament*, ed. Bengt Holmberg und Mikael Winninge, WUNT 227 (Tübingen: Mohr Siebeck, 2008), 199–222, "the story basically affirms the dominant discourse of masculinity, because through his sexual self-control he becomes a husband and a father in an active political life" (214). In contrast to this, Jessica Lyn Tinklenberg deVega, "'A Man Who Fears God': Constructions of Masculinity in Hellenistic Jewish Interpretations of the Story of Joseph" (PhD diss., Florida State University, 2006), argues that Joseph's self-mastery runs counter to ancient male role models, in opposition to the masculinity performed by Pharaoh's son (57–88).

30. Jos. Asen. 6.3, 5; 19.8; 21.4; 23.10.

31. Standhartinger, *Frauenbild*, 84, n. 158. Kraemer, *When Aseneth*, 99–109, sees the God Helios on his solar chariot, which is on display, among other places, at the ancient synagogue of Bet Alpha.

39 was frequently retold in Jewish-Hellenistic circles, and it is referred to no fewer than three times here.[32] The first time, Aseneth tells a persiflage of the story and mocks Joseph as an adulterer, a runaway slave, a shepherd's son, and a charlatan who made a career by interpreting dreams (4.10). Then the narrator multiplies Potiphar's wives: "For all the wives and daughters of the notable men and satraps of all the land of Egypt used to annoy him, desiring to sleep with him" (7.3, trans. Ahearne-Kroll). The appeal of Joseph "the virgin" attracts not only one but all the women of Egypt.[33] He, however, remains steadfast and obedient to his father's words: "Guard yourself against strange women" (7.5, trans. Ahearne-Kroll). Therefore, when Joseph enters, every male and female stranger has to remain outside Pentephres's courtyard (5.6). Only a virgin who hates all men, such as Aseneth, is acceptable to him (7.7). Alternating between closeness and distance, he slowly turns from a misogynist into a lover. After overcoming his fear of strange women, he greets Aseneth but rejects her sisterly kiss. Since, as he explains: "It is not fitting for a god-fearing man who praises the living God with his mouth … to kiss a strange woman who praises dead and dumb idols with her mouth…. But a god-fearing man will kiss his mother and his sister and women from his family" (8.5–6, trans. Ahearne-Kroll).[34] Coming from the mouth of Joseph, this ethical maxim expresses the greatest difference between the peoples of Israel and Egypt. Yet, Joseph asks God for a renewal of Aseneth and her acceptance into the people of God (8.9).

The reunion of the lovers, eight days later, is still shaped by the same tension between distance and closeness. Informed by heaven, Joseph is now ready to embrace Aseneth (19.2–3Ph).[35] But sexuality has to wait (21.1). The same man who refused any contact with strange women, based on the word of his father, is now adamant in requesting of his new father, the Egyptian Pharaoh, that she be given to him as his wife.

Despite divinity, the man Joseph has to change. He has to convert from a chaste and arrogant "virgin" into a loving husband by overcoming his xenophobia.

32. Philo, *Ios.* 40–53; Josephus, *Ant.* 2.39–59; Testament of Joseph. See Angela Standhartinger, "Humour in *Joseph and Aseneth*," *JSP* 23 (2015): 239–59.

33. Joseph is called a παρθένος (virgin) in Jos. Asen. 4.7; 8.1. This is the only reference to a male as a virgin beside Rev 14:4 in Greek literature.

34. The maxim continues inclusively: "Likewise, it is not fitting for a god-fearing woman to kiss a strange man because this is an abomination before the Lord God" (Jos. Asen. 8. 7, trans. Ahearne-Kroll).

35. In other manuscripts Joseph does not recognize her at first (19.4B). Only after Aseneth reports to him about the heavenly visitor does he summon her with a gesture of his eyes (19.10B) and kiss her and give to her spirit of life, spirit of wisdom, and spirit of truth (19.11B).

Pharaoh's son is another figure of discussion with regard to constructions of masculinity in Joseph and Aseneth. When he sees Aseneth for the first time, he is immediately driven to distraction and wants to have her for himself.[36] Thereby he becomes the male model of Potiphar's wife from Gen 39. In the role of a flatterer, he approaches Simeon and Levi and praises their strength, which they proved by killing thirty thousand men in the city of Shechem.[37] Meeting with no success, he turns to the other sons of Jacob, born of Leah's and Rachel's slaves, Bilhah and Zilpah. He flatters Gad, Dan, Asher, and Naphtali with the strongest gender stereotype articulated in the story: "I know … you are powerful men and you will not die like women, but act like men and defend yourself against your enemies" (24.7; cf. 25.7, trans. Ahearne-Kroll). Won over, the slave-born sons allow themselves, equipped with two thousand soldiers, to lie in wait for and capture Aseneth. Meanwhile, Pharaoh's son sets out to kill his father. However, as Pharaoh is suffering from a headache that night, his son is not admitted to his chamber (25.1–3) and so cannot carry out his plan. Unsurprisingly, the whole attack collapses. Benjamin, sitting on Aseneth's chariot, picks up a stone and, like David fighting Goliath, hurls it at Pharaoh's son, who falls to the ground, seriously wounded (27.3, cf. 1 Sam 17:49). The latter's army is defeated by Lea's sons, who appear on the scene, armed with the weapons of Goliath (25.7; cf. 1 Sam 17:45, 47). The manly Dan, Gad, Asher, and Naphtali have to seek shelter from the revenge of their brothers, of all places, at a woman's side (28.1–4).

His patricidal/tyrannicidal intentions, huge army, and expressed veneration of military might signify an exaggerated masculinity. However, his lack of sexual self-control feminizes the figure of Pharaoh's son. This gender confusion makes this tragic-comic character ridiculous. That through him, Potiphar's wife sneaks into the story as a male character can be seen as a critique of the antique stereotyping of women lacking sexual self-control. The fact that, of all the figures, it is Pharaoh's tragic-comic son who expresses the most explicit gender stereotype suggests that some caricature of this position might be implied.

Slaves in Joseph and Aseneth

Yet if ancient notions of masculinity are critiqued in the text, slavery is not. Female and male slaves remain mostly in the background. Minor slave roles

---

36. For features of comedy and mime, see Standhartinger, "Humour."

37. This is a reference to Gen 34. There is no other evidence for this seemingly exaggerated number.

are played by Aseneth's seven virginal companions, Pentephres's attendants (5.1–2; 18.1), a house steward (3.4; 18.2), the servants in charge of Joseph's chariot (9.3), and the servants of Pharaoh's sons (24.2). In this text, slaves fill the homes of the ruling class in order to elevate noble-born characters above the *hoi polloi*.[38] As a sign of her self-abasement, Aseneth declares that she wishes to become Joseph's slave (6.8; 13.15). Noble-born as she is, she never steps down from her role as a slave-mistress.[39] Nor does the designation "slave of God" (17.7; 23.10Ph) lead to a more general critique of the institution of slavery. To the contrary, the slaves of Pharaoh's sons initiate the fatal plot against Aseneth and Joseph by suggesting an alliance with the slave-born sons of Jacob. Slaves behave in a servile manner and unite against their masters. Only at one point in the story do these categories become slightly blurred. The rebellious and disloyal slave-born sons are reintegrated as brothers into Jacob's family (28.14–17). At the very least, the identity of these slaves is renewed and readjusted.

Egyptians and Hebrews in Joseph and Aseneth

The narrative of an Egyptian woman converting to Israel's God presupposes two opposing people or ethnicities. At the very beginning the two groups are confronted with each other: Aseneth "bore little resemblance at all to Egyptian woman but was in every way more like the women of the Hebrews" (1.5, trans. Wills).

Her gods, however, are Egyptian. Their idols decorate her bedroom (2.3; 10.12) and her jewelry (3.6), and she make sacrifice to them and eats from their table every day.[40] Hence Joseph rejects her as a foreign woman who does not belong to his family unit (8.5–6). Yet Aseneth refers to the Egyptians most negatively in her psalm when she laments being pursued by the "ancient wild lion … the father of the Egyptian gods" (12.9, trans. Ahearne-Kroll).[41] She feels hated by her father and mother for destroying their gods and idols.[42] This motif is taken from Ps 27:9–10 and reflects typical imagery of proselytes.[43]

38. Lawrence M. Wills, "The Depiction of Slavery in the Ancient Novel," *Semeia* 83/84 (1998): 113–32, 127–28.

39. Jos. Asen. 10.2; 18.11; 28.2, 11.

40. Jos. Asen. 2.3; see also 12.5; 11.16B.

41. For the image of a lion for the devil, see 1 Pet 5:8.

42. Jos. Asen. 12.12–13; see also 11.4B.

43. Ps 27:9–10: "Do not hide your face from me.… If my father and mother forsake me, the Lord will take me up" (NRSV). The experience is described as typical for proselytes; see Philo, *Virt.* 102–103; *Spec.* 1.52, 309.

Yet the narrative frame paints a different picture. Pentephres, the priest of Heliopolis, eulogizes at the very beginning of the story: "Blessed is the Lord, the God of Joseph, because my lord, Joseph, regarded me as worthy to come to us" (3.3, trans. Ahearne-Kroll). He introduces Joseph to his daughter not only as the "ruler of the entire land of Egypt and its "savior" (4.7) but also as the "mighty one of God"[44] and "rich in wisdom and knowledge" and filled with "the spirit of God" (4.7, trans. Ahearne-Kroll). When after eight days Aseneth's parents meet her again, they give "glory to God, who brings the dead back to life" (20.7, trans. Ahearne-Kroll). Even the Egyptian Pharaoh recognizes that "Joseph's God" has chosen Aseneth as a bride for his son (21.4). In this text, most Egyptians worship the God of Israel.

Jacob's family are referred to as Hebrews only once (1.5).[45] More frequently they are called Israel's children, this being Jacob's second name.[46] The God of Israel is the God of Joseph's father Jacob (7.4). His commandment is intended to maintain familial boundaries. A God-fearing woman who kisses a foreign man "is an abomination" before this God (8.7). Consequently, Joseph asks this "God of his father Jacob" to integrate Aseneth into his family (8.9).

Over the course of the narrative, borderlines between ethnic groups become increasingly fluid. By the time of his wedding, Joseph has accepted Pharaoh as his second father (20.9). Levi conveys the same impression when Benjamin is about to kill the wounded son of Pharaoh: "If he lives, he will be our friend. After this, his father, Pharaoh, will be like our father" (29.4, trans. Ahearne-Kroll). At the same time, the table fellowship also becomes inclusive. Joseph's extra table (7.1) is no longer necessary at his second visit to Pentephres' home (20.8; cf. 21.8). Joseph is now ready to celebrate his wedding with the whole land of Egypt (21.8). At the end, he inherits the throne from his (new) father, Pharaoh. Israel is transformed in(to) Egypt.

Here ethnos is defined by family as well as by religious practice. Both demarcation lines become increasingly blurred. Yet the body does not serve as an ethnic marker here. Both Egyptians and the sons and daughters of Israel are supremely beautiful. Beauty can, as Marianne Kartzow has shown, include another ethnic marker. In an extended figurative description of Jacob in some manuscripts, it is said: "the hairs of his head were all exceedingly close and thick like (those) of an Ethiopian" (22.7, trans. Wills).[47]

---

44. Jos. Asen. 3.4; 4.6; see also 11.6; 18.1–2; 21.20.

45. Some manuscripts mention also the "God of the Hebrews" in 11.10B.

46. Jos. Asen. 7.4; 8.9; 22.2–3, 6; 23.11, 14; 25.5; 28.11, 13.

47. See Marianne B. Kartzow, *Destabilizing the Margins: An Intersectional Approach to Early Christian Memory* (Eugene, OR: Pickwick, 2012), 67. The Syriac tradition compares

Intersections between Gender, Status, Ethnos, and Religion

For the Greek historian Herodotus, temples and sacrifices are two of several markers of an ethnos. In Joseph and Aseneth, veneration of Israel's God becomes a practice transcending family and ethnicity. God becomes universal. He is no longer merely a "God of my father Israel" (7.4; 10) and "Jacob's God" (3.3; 6.6; 20.4) but the "living God," the "Most High," and the "Creator of the World."[48]

Yet very few religious rites are mentioned. The Egyptian cult is only obliquely referred to by means of two catchwords: idols and offerings. Egyptian gods can easily be destroyed through defenestration (10.12–13; 13.11). What we learn elsewhere about Jewish practice is missing here. There is no mention of either Sabbath or circumcision. Joseph's extra table, which one might interpret as symbolizing the observation of Jewish dietary laws, or kashrut, is forgotten when it comes to the Egyptian wedding table. Levi is, here as elsewhere, the guardian of letters. However, it is not earthly laws that he reads and interprets but rather the celestial torah, which he, as a prophet, is able to read (22.13). God reveals himself through visions and acts of divine rescue. Religious practice becomes most visible in the text when it interprets the Bible. Weaved into the text of Joseph and Aseneth are not only motifs from the biblical Joseph story (Gen 37–50) but also many from Gen 34; Exod 34:6; 1 Sam 17:2; 2 Kgs 2; Prov 8, and Psalms. Does belief in the Living and Most High God transform categories like gender, status, and ethnos? As we have seen, one can equally affirm and deny this question with respect to each of these categories.

Most obviously, the category ethnos is transformed. Every Egyptian who accepts "Joseph's God" is applauded. All the characters with the exception of Pharaoh's son belong to this group in the end. Israel also undergoes a transformation from an exclusive family into an inclusive ethnos. Yet only Aseneth, Joseph's wife, and Pharaoh, his second father, are actually incorporated. Joseph and the slave-born sons of Bilhah and Zilpah require an extra revelation to arrive at this realization.

By contrast, the category of status remains relatively unchanged. Most slaves retain their role. However, Jacob's slave-born sons are not punished for their act of aggression. An Egyptian lady intervenes for them despite

---

Jacob to an Ethiopian, whereas manuscripts from the Armenian tradition liken him to an Indian. In most manuscript versions, no such comparisons are made.

48. Living God: Jos. Asen. 8.5–6; 11.19; 19.8; 20.7; Most High: in total thirty-eight times; Creator of the World: Jos. Asen. 8.3; 9.5; 12.1.

their rebellious behavior. The question of whether they will be emancipated remains unanswered.

Gender constructions are the most complex in their design. The last remaining Egyptian man in the narrative, Pharaoh's son, displays exaggerated masculine traits as well as feminine ones. Joseph fluctuates between being the "Son of God" and a man. As a divine figure, he remains the same; yet he makes only three brief appearances in the world. As a man, he has to be transformed from an abstinent into a lover. Only slowly is he able to overcome his ambivalence towards his beloved, thereby mirroring the approach of Israel to the Egyptians.

The main figure, Aseneth, is a paradigm for conversion or a shift in loyalty from the Egyptian gods to God, the Living and Most High. That she exchanges her freedom for self-abasement and transforms herself from a proud and autonomous virgin into a wife who declares herself a slave of her husband has been criticized by feminist scholars, and for good reason. Along these lines Joseph and Aseneth establishes certain female role models. However, as I have argued above, our narrative moves at some point in the opposite direction. To be sure, here a virgin is transformed into a loving wife, but it is not motherhood but rather emergence into the world that completes this role. Her self-abasement remains a transitional stage on the road to becoming the queen of Egypt and a savior of Israel's sons. A female goddess-like figure, Metanoia, paves the way for her (15.7).

Finally our story includes some queer features. Pharaoh's son bears female characteristics, not only in that he serves as a double for Potiphar's wife but also when his exaggerated military might is defeated through God's intervention. He is the only one in the story who has to "die like a woman" (24.7; 25.7). The visionary female Aseneth, on the other hand, is declared by the heavenly visitor to be "a man" (15.1). In this narrative, the stabilizing and blurring of gender roles lie close to each other.

Authors and Readers

I hope to have shown that such an intersectional analysis of gender, status, and ethnos/race opens up new perspectives on this ancient Jewish novel. It would likely be fruitful to interrelate this intersectional analysis to a social analysis of authors and readers. However, nothing more is known about their historical identity than that which can be deducted from the writing itself. One cannot even be sure that the authors lived and wrote in Egypt, as has been assumed my most scholars. The information that is provided about the Egyptian religion does not presuppose intimate knowledge of Egyptian gods, myths, or rituals. The Egyptian landscape is described in a very abstract manner: The city of

Heliopolis, for example, consists of one house with a tower, and the surrounding landscape is referred to as a *wadi* with a forest of reeds. Equally striking is the discrepancy between the social world of satraps, kings, and queens that provides the narrative of the story and the simple Greek in which it is told. The style and wording of the writing cause one to doubt that the authors actually belonged to the class of Hellenistic nobility within which their heroes and heroines circulate. Yet, while we can only speculate about the identity of the authors of the text, more information can be gleaned about its readers from the history of manuscripts, reception, and interpretation.

We do not know whether the author of Joseph and Aseneth was female or male. Both options have been put forward.[49] At any rate, some women have contributed to handing down the story. Ahearne-Kroll and Thomas suggest that women's narratives and texts entered into the more than ninety manuscripts of Joseph and Aseneth.[50] As far back as antiquity, wet nurses and elderly women were credited as originators of fairy tales and romances.[51] Despite the gender stereotype driving these theses, the influence of both genres is evident in our story. There is also evidence of the influence of female scribes. For example, in some versions, Aseneth's slim fingers are strikingly compared to the "delicate fingers of a skilled scribe" (Jos. Asen. 20.5B, trans. Wills).[52] From the beginning, Joseph and Aseneth was most likely disseminated in a manner quite similar to the books of Ezra and Jubilees, as is suggested in a papyrus-letter discovered in Oxyrhynchus: "To my dearest lady sister in the Lord, greetings. Lend the Ezra, since I lent you the little Genesis."[53]

We are aware of only a few early female readers of Joseph and Aseneth. The Christian pilgrim Egeria admired Aseneth's tower at Heliopolis on her pil-

---

49. For the discussion, see Ross S. Kraemer, "Women's Authorship of Jewish and Christian Literature in the Greco-Roman Period," in *"Women Like This": New Perspectives on Jewish Women in the Greco-Roman World*, ed. Amy-Jill Levine, EJL 1 (Atlanta: Scholars Press, 1991), 221–42; and Mary Lefkowitz, "Did Ancient Women Write Novels?," in Levine, *"Women Like This,"* 199–219. See also Standhartinger, *Frauenbild*, 225–29.

50. On the influence of oral tradition on the ancient novel, see Lawrence Kim, "Orality, Folktale and the Cross-Cultural Transmission of Narrative," in *The Romance between Greece and the East*, ed. Tim Whitmarsh and Stuart Thomson (Cambridge: Cambridge University Press, 2013), 300–21.

51. John Heath, "Women's Work: Female Transmission of Mythical Narrative," *TAPA* 141 (2011): 69–104.

52. See Humphrey, *Joseph and Aseneth*, 71.

53. P.Oxy. 4365 (fourth century CE). See Kim Haines-Eitzen, *The Gendered Palimpsest: Women, Writing, and Representation in Early Christianity* (Oxford: Oxford University Press, 2012).

grimage to the Holy Land in the fourth century CE (Egeria, *Itin.* 7.1 [9.1.6]).[54] The name Aseneth appears on some documentary papyri in Egypt from the fifth to the seventh centuries. More than once she is referred to as the daughter of Paul and Thecla.[55]

It is possible to reconstruct different readings of our story. The translator into Syriac, Moses of Ingila, added his interpretation in a cover letter, explaining the story as an allegory of Christ's marriage to the soul (Chr. Ps.-Zech. Rhet. 1.6).[56] Ruth Nisse points to problematic receptions. Most likely some monks in twelfth century England translated our story into Latin in order, with the help of a Jewish apocryphon, to convince Jewish women to convert to Christianity.[57] Original Jewish readings are likely as well.[58] Yet some midrash count Aseneth among the female Jewish proselytes, alongside Yael, Hagar, Shiphrah, Puah, the unnamed daughter of Pharaoh, Zipporah, Rahab, and Ruth (Qoh. Rab. 8.10.1).[59] A famous Kurdish-Jewish scholar who founded a Yeshiva in Mosul shares her name: Aseneth Bazarni (1590–1670).

There is clear evidence of female readers in early modern times. A noblewoman commissioned a poem, "The Storie of Asneth," in fifteenth-century England.[60] This version highlights Aseneth's spiritual practice and has her give her consent to the marriage; it furthermore adds to the tale that she celebrates her wedding anniversary with an annual public holiday. Here, Aseneth seems to provide a biblical role model for pious married women of noble birth. Two centuries later, Philipp von Zesen wrote his lengthy novel *Assenat*, which he

54. For the history of reception of Joseph and Aseneth, see Angela Standhartinger, "Zur Wirkungsgeschichte von *Joseph und Aseneth*," in *Joseph und Aseneth*, ed. Eckart Reinmuth, SAPERE 15 (Tübingen: Mohr Siebeck, 2009), 219–34; Standhartinger, "Recent Scholarship," 385–88.

55. P.Köln 2.102 (418 CE, Oxyrhynchus). The name appears on a tax list from Antiaopolis in Egypt: P.Flor. 3.297,62 (525 CE); P.Lond. 4.1419,99, 100, 671, 987 (716–717 CE); and in a loan agreement: P.Ross.Georg. 5.41 frag. 4–5 and *BGU* 3.972 (sixth–seventh century).

56. Geoffre Greatrex et al., eds., *The Chronicle of Pseudo-Zachariah Rhetor: Church and War in Late Antiquity* (Liverpool: Liverpool University Press, 2011).

57. Ruth Nisse, "'Your Name Will No Longer Be Aseneth': Apocrypha, Anti-Martyrdom, and Jewish Conversion in Thirteenth-Century England," *Spec* 81 (2006): 734–53.

58. Many point to a tradition in midrash according to which Aseneth is the daughter of Dinah and was recognized by Joseph by means of an amulet she was wearing. See Tamar Kadari, "Asenath: Midrash and Aggadah," in *Jewish Women: A Comprehensive Historical Encyclopedia*, Jewish Women's Archive, http://tinyurl.com/SBL066006b.

59. See also Moshe Reiss and David J. Zucker, "Co-opting the Secondary Matriarchs: Bilhah, Zilpah, Tamar, and Aseneth," *BibInt* 22 (2014): 307–24.

60. C. Hume, "The Storie of Asneth: A Fifteenth-Century Commission and the Mystery of Its Epilogue," *AAev 82* (2013): 44–65.

dedicated to a German duchess. In this retelling, special attention is paid to Aseneth's wedding, but also to the weddings of her seven maidens and to the couple's lengthy educational journey through Egypt. The latter section features banquets and other duties familiar to a seventeenth century duchess. Shocked by the attack of Pharaoh's son, Aseneth becomes depressed but finds some comfort by reading the book of Enoch and in serving the poor. In the end, she dies, much lamented. Zesen's novel is illustrated with copperplate prints, including an image of Aseneth's sarcophagus and mummy.[61]

It is plausible that changing concepts of gender, status, ethnos, and religion have left some traces in the textual transmission of our story. In recent years it has been shown that some manuscripts clearly bear the influence of Christian liturgy.[62] Also, Aseneth's African identity was rediscovered. Further research will undoubtedly deepen our understanding along these lines of interpretation.[63]

---

61. Philip von Zesen, *Assenat: Das ist Derselben/ und des Josefs Heilige Stahts- Lieb- und Lebens-geschicht* (Amsterdam: Kristian von Hagen, 1670), Aseneth as a mummy with a sarcophagus p. 310. The text is available on the internet: http://www.deutschestextarchiv.de/book/show/zesen_assenat_1670.

62. Ljubica Jovanovic, "Aseneth's Gaze Turns Swords into Dust," *JSP* 21 (2012): 83–97.

63. David Tuesday Adamo, "The African Wife of Joseph, Aseneth (GN 41:45, 41:50, 46:20)," *JSem* 22 (2013): 409–25.

Part 2
Interpretations of Biblical Women

The Sins of the First Woman: Eve Traditions in Second Temple Literature with Special Regard to the Life of Adam and Eve

Magdalena Díaz Araujo
Translated by Marie-Theres Wacker

1. Eve Traditions in Second Temple Literature

The figures of Adam and Eve both frequently appear in early Jewish writings from Hellenistic-Roman times but with different significance and characteristics. While Adam emerges in numerous passages (2 En. 30–32; 42; 58; 4 Ezra 3.4–27; 4.30–32; 7; 2 Bar. 4.17–19; 23; 48.42–50; 54; 56; 3 Bar. 9; Sib. Or. 3.24–28; Apoc. Sedr. 4–8), Eve appears mainly in association with her companion (Jub. 2–4; 1 En. 32; 2 En. 31; 2 Bar. 48.42–43; Apoc. Ab. 23–24; 3 Bar. 4; Apoc. Sedr. 7.6–7), or she comes on the scene to admit her implication in sin and death (Sir 25:24; 1 En. 69.6–7; 2 En. 30; Sib. Or. 1.39–45, and several passages from Philo's work). In most of these texts, it is Adam who seems charged with the responsibility for transgression and mortality,[1] and Eve is simply the other member of the protoplastic couple. However, in the few places where the first woman receives exclusive blame, she is indicted for dissimilar transgressions. It is this distinction in how Eve is portrayed that I would like to sketch briefly as a first step.

1.1. Eve in the Wisdom of Sira

The Wisdom of Ben Sira, also known as Sirach or Ecclesiasticus, belongs to the wisdom literature of the Second Temple period and originated as a book

I am deeply indebted to Marie-Theres Wacker for her dedication during the revision of my text.

1. John R. Levison, *Portraits of Adam in Early Judaism*, JSPSup 1 (Sheffield: Sheffield Academic, 1988), 155–61, 187–88.

written in Hebrew in the early second century BCE. In a Greek translation it has been included in the Septuagint, and therefore in the Latin Vulgate, as a canonical writing, and it appears as an apocryphal book in Protestant editions of the complete Bible. This instructional text shows, according to Warren C. Trenchard, and feminist scholars tend to agree,[2] a negative bias against women, probably nurtured by the author's personal perspective. Among the misogynistic instructions stands the affirmation of Sir 25:24:

> In a woman [ἀπο γυναικός] was sin's beginning: on her account we all die.[3]

This passage has generated a substantial debate given the context of this phrase, since it is inserted in a paragraph regarding the good and the evil wife (ch. 25–26). I cannot discuss here this controversy,[4] but I think that even if a scholar could prove that Ben Sira did not intend to establish Eve's guilt in this passage, as Jack Levison claims,[5] we have to consider that the readers of Sirach might have understood these lines differently, charging Eve with the responsibility for sin and death. We detect in this sentence a clear association between woman, sin, and death that became crucial for the representation of women in the following texts.

---

2. Warren C. Trenchard, *Ben Sira's View of Women: A Literary Analysis*, BJS 8 (Chico, CA: Scholars Press, 1982), 172–73; see Angelika Strotmann, "Sirach (Ecclesiasticus): On the Difficult Relation Between Divine Wisdom and Real Women in an Androcentric Document," in *Feminist Biblical Interpretation: A Compendium of Critical Commentary on the Books of the Bible and Related Literature*, ed. Luise Schottroff and Marie-Theres Wacker (Grand Rapids: Eerdmans, 2012), 539–54; Claudia Camp, "Understanding a Patriarchy: Women in Second Century Jerusalem through the Eyes of Ben Sira," in *"Women Like This": New Perspectives on Women in the Greco-Roman World*, ed. Amy-Jill Levine (Atlanta: Scholars Press 1991), 1–39; Silvia Schroer, "Der eine Herr und die Männerherrschaft im Buch Jesus Sirach: Frauenbild und Weisheitsbild in einer misogynen Schrift," in *Die Weisheit hat ihr Haus gebaut: Studien zur Gestalt der Sophia* (Mainz: Grünewald, 1996), 96–106; Pamela M. Eisenbaum, "Sirach," in *Women's Bible Commentary*, ed. Carol A. Newsom and Sharon H. Ringe, expanded ed. (Louisville: Westminster John Knox,1998), 298–304.

3. Translation of Patrick W. Skehan, in Alexander A. Di Lella and Patrick W. Skehan, *Wisdom of Ben Sira: A New Translation with Notes*, AB 39 (New York: Doubleday, 1987), 343.

4. Besides the authors quoted in n. 2, see Alexander A. Di Lella, "Women in the Wisdom of Ben Sira and the Book of Judith: A Study in Contrasts and Reversals," in *Congress Volume: Paris, 1992*, ed. John A. Emerton, VTSup 61 (Leiden: Brill, 1995), 39–52.

5. Jack Levison, "Is Eve to Blame? A Contextual Analysis of Sirach 25,24," *CBQ* 47 (1985): 617–23.

1.2. Eve in the Parables of the Ethiopic Book of Enoch

In the so-called Parables of Enoch (1 En. 37–71), a controversial text dated by many scholars to the first century CE,[6] a few verses postulate a connection between Eve and death:

> The third [angel] was named Gader'el; this one is he who showed the children of the people all the blows of death, who misled Eve, who showed the children of the people (how to make) the instruments of death (such as) the shield, the breastplate, and the sword for warfare, and all (the other) instruments of death to the children of the people. Through their agency (death) proceeds against the people who dwell upon the earth, from that day forevermore. (1 En. 69.6–7)[7]

This paragraph incorporates Eve among the women deceived by the fallen angels and, by this amalgamation, she acquires her involvement in her descendants' mortality. This is all the more striking as the first part of 1 Enoch (1–36), dated to the second century BCE,[8] evokes a rather different picture: the antediluvian sage, Enoch, is shown on his journey through cosmic spheres to the place of paradise with its beautiful tree of wisdom (1 En. 32). When Enoch admires that tree, Raphael, his companion angel explains to him:

> This very thing is the tree of wisdom from which your old father and aged mother, they who are your precursors, ate and came to know wisdom; and (consequently) their eyes were opened and they realized that they were naked and (so) they were expelled from the garden. (1 En. 32.6)

The fruit of the forbidden tree conveys wisdom, and the only consequence mentioned is nakedness and loss of the garden. No sin is mentioned, neither in relation to Adam nor to Eve. In 1 En. 1–36, the "fall" with its disastrous consequences comes from the watcher-angels who came down to earth to mingle with human women (1 En. 6–11).[9] The first couple's deed seems to have no specific relevance for that chaotic development between heaven and earth.

---

6. Ephraim Isaac, "1 (Ethiopic Apocalypse of) Enoch," *OTP* 1:7; Michael K. Knibb, "The Book of Enoch or Books of Enoch? The Textual Evidence for 1 Enoch," in *The Early Enoch Literature*, ed. Gabriele Boccaccini and John J. Collins, JSJSup 121 (Leiden: Brill, 2007), 28.

7. Translations of 1 Enoch taken from Isaac, "1 (Ethiopic Apocalypse of) Enoch," *OTP* 1:47–48.

8. Ibid., 1:7.

9. See Veronika Bachmann's contribution in this volume.

1.3. The Slavonic Book of Enoch

The text of 2 Enoch, also known as The Book of the Secrets of Enoch, is attested in Slavonic, in Greek, and more recently in Coptic. In this pseudepigraphic text, usually dated to the first century CE,[10] Enoch discloses instructions to his descendants, the account regarding his journey through the heavens, and the revelations he had received. The creation of Eve appears in a very specific connection here:

> And I [= God] gave him [= Adam] his free will; and I pointed out to him the two ways—light and darkness. And I said to him, "This is good for you, but that is bad"; so that I might come to know whether he has love toward me or abhorrence, and so that it might become plain who among his race loves me. Whereas I have come to know his nature, he does not know his own nature. That is why ignorance is more lamentable than the sin such as it is in him to sin. And I said, "After sin there is nothing for it but death." And I assigned a shade for him [MSS J, R; MSS P, P^2: from him]; and I imposed sleep upon him, and he fell asleep. And while he was sleeping, I took from him a rib. And I created for him a wife, so that death might come [MSS B, V: to him] by his wife. And I took his last word, and I called her name Mother, that is to say, Euva. (2 En. 30.10)[11]

According to 2 En. 30.10, the creation of Eve is intended by God to make Adam become aware of and exercise the free will with which he is invested and to involve him in a choice between two ways, light and darkness. Before Eve's creation, Adam received his free will from God but did not know his own nature which involved an option to choose sin ("Whereas I have come to know his nature, he does not know his own nature. That is why ignorance is more lamentable than the sin such as it is in him to sin"). To activate Adam's capacity to decide between good and bad, God created the woman. Furthermore, the creation of Eve implies the introduction of death ("And I created for him a wife, so that death might come by his wife"), which can only be thought of as the consequence of sin ("After sin there is nothing for it but death"). The logic, then, seems to be that Eve was created to stimulate the exercise of Adam's free will, but at the same time she acquires in this text an association with sin and death.

---

10. Andrei A. Orlov and Gabriele Boccaccini, eds., *New Perspectives on 2 Enoch: No Longer Slavonic Only*, StudJ 4 (Leiden: Brill, 2012).

11. Translation from F. I. Andersen, "2 (Slavonic Apocalypse of) Enoch," *OTP* 1:152.

1.4. Eve in the Sibylline Oracles

The Sibylline Oracles are considered to be composite texts, with diverse Jewish and Christian stages. This "apologetic literature" has been dated between the second century BCE and the seventh century CE, but for the passage concerning Eve, John J. Collins suggests a probable Jewish composition between 30 BCE and 250 CE.[12]

Eve becomes Adam's betrayer in a singular passage:

> But a very horrible snake craftily deceived them to go to the fate of death and receive knowledge of good and evil. But the woman first became a betrayer to him. She gave, and persuaded him to sin in his ignorance. He was persuaded by the woman's words, forgot about his immortal creator, and neglected clear commands. (Sib. Or. 1.39–45)[13]

Adam sins in his ignorance and, as a result of the woman's words, neglects God's commands. He is not responsible for his disobedience since he is in ignorance and is persuaded by Eve. Nonetheless, the snake appears behind the woman's deception that led the first couple to the "fate of death and the knowledge of good and evil."

1.5. A Brief Look at Philo of Alexandria

Philo's representations of Eve have motivated numerous studies that I cannot consider here.[14] However, I would like to point out the complexity of Philo's treatment of this matter, as we can observe in this passage, a commentary on Gen 2:21:

> The literal sense is clear. For by a certain symbolical use of "part" it is called a half of the whole, as both man and woman, being sections of Nature, become equal in one harmony of genus, which is called man. But in the figurative

12. John J. Collins, "Sibylline Oracles," *OTP* 1:331.

13. Ibid., 1:336.

14. See Annewies van den Hoek, "Endowed with Reason or Glued to the Senses: Philo's Thoughts on Adam and Eve," in *The Creation of Man and Woman: Interpretations of the Biblical Narratives in Jewish and Christian Traditions*, ed. Gerard P. Luttikhuizen, TBN 3 (Leiden: Brill, 2000), 63–75; Richard A. Baer, *Philo's Use of the Categories Male and Female*, ALGHJ 3 (Leiden: Brill, 1970); Dorothy Sly, *Philo's Perception of Women*, BJS 209 (Atlanta: Scholars Press, 1990); Genevieve Lloyd, *The Man of Reason: Male and Female in Western Philosophy* (Minneapolis: Methuen, 1984), 22–28; Colleen Conway, "Gender and Divine Relativity in Philo of Alexandria," *JSJ* 34 (2003): 471–91.

> sense, man is a symbol of mind, and his side is a single sense-faculty. And the sense-perception of a very changeable reason is symbolized by woman. (Philo, *QG* 1.25, Marcus, LCL)

The tension Philo introduces between the literal and the allegorical meaning of the biblical statement reflects the complexity of his conception of woman. Regarding the literal meaning of Gen 2:21 he finds an equality of two parts, man and woman, whereas in the allegorical meaning woman reveals her inferiority to man. Sense-perception, a faculty of the soul, is able to get in contact with sensible realities and to let the mind (or: reason) approach concrete material objects. Sense-perception is the "irrational" element of the soul and therefore its inferior part. The irrationality of woman/senses enables the serpent/pleasure to bring about the fall of man/mind.

This brief survey of distinctive mentions of Eve in Second Temple literature is intended to illustrate the diversity in these images and the complicated manner in which the protoplasts are seen to be involved in sin and death. The responsibilities diverge, according to different roles allotted to Adam, Eve, the serpent, and/or angelic beings, as well as to different constructions of the nature of sin and the consequences of transgression.

This complexity increases in the Greek Life of Adam and Eve, a Jewish text of this epoch that I will analyze further in this essay, with special attention to the particular indictment of Eve.

2. The Character of Eve in the (Greek) Life of Adam and Eve

The pseudepigraphic text known as the Greek Life of Adam and Eve (GLAE), or the Apocalypse of Moses, presents the story of Adam and Eve before and after their expulsion from paradise. The first four verses (1.1–4) recount Gen 4, the birth of Cain, Abel, and Seth, with some characteristic new traits. The story proper starts with Adam suffering enormous pains at the end of his life. When his children ask him the reason for that he refers to the forbidden fruit from which Eve took and gave him to eat. Eve then offers to go with Seth to the paradise garden and bring back remedial oil from there, but they do not succeed. Adam asks Eve to report about their transgressions in paradise, and Eve reveals in a long speech (GLAE 15–30) how she was deceived by the devil and how the devil had already seduced the snake to assist him. She then summarizes how God discovered what both of them, she and her husband, had done and how God drove them out of the garden (see Gen 3:8–24). The second part of the story (GLAE 31–43) revolves around Adam's death, the forgiveness given to him by God, the promise of resurrection he receives, and his burial in the garden of paradise (31–41). The story ends with a note about Eve's death and her burial at her husband's side (42–43).

2.1. The Life of Adam and Eve and Its Manuscript Traditions

The twenty-seven manuscripts of GLAE form part of a larger textual tradition usually referred to as the Life of Adam and Eve (LAE), preserved in eight different linguistic versions (Greek, Latin, Georgian, Armenian, Slavonic, Romanian,[15] Coptic, and Arabic).

The problem of the provenance and the date of the GLAE has sparked fierce debates among scholars. As a matter of fact, since the publication of Marinus de Jonge and Johannes Tromp's *The Life of Adam and Eve and Related Literature* in 1997, the Jewish origin of the text and its dating before the second century CE have been called into question, while a new theory about its Christian origin has started a controversy that is still ongoing.[16]

At the same time, the fundamental studies by Michael E. Stone and by Stone and Gary A. Anderson have questioned whether the Greek version is the original one.[17] Thereby they initiated a second controversy regarding the priority and place of the GLAE in the larger tradition of the LAE.[18] According

---

15. For the little-known Romanian version, see Émile Turdeanu, *Apocryphes slaves et roumains de l'Ancien Testament*, PVTG 5 (Leiden: Brill, 1981), 75–144, 437–38.

16. Marinus de Jonge and Johannes Tromp, *The Life of Adam and Eve and Related Literature* (Sheffield: Sheffield Academic, 1997). I cannot introduce here the extensive bibliography on the discussions after de Jonge and Tromp, which is presented in detail in Magdalena Díaz Araujo, "La représentation de la femme et l'invention de la notion du 'péché de la chair' d'après la *Vie grecque d'Adam et Ève*" (PhD diss., Université de Paris IV–Sorbonne, 2012), 22–119. See also, Albert-Marie Denis, ed., "La vie d'Adam et Ève," in *Introduction à la littérature religieuse judéo-hellénistique*, 2 vols. (Turnhout: Brepols, 2000), 1:7–13; George W. E. Nickelsburg, "Adam and Eve, Life of," in *Encyclopedia of Religious and Philosophical Writings in Late Antiquity: Pagan, Judaic, Christian*, ed. Jacob Neusner and Alan J. Avery-Peck (Leiden: Brill, 2007), 17–18; Jean-Pierre Pettorelli, "Adam and Eve, Life of," in *The Eerdmans Dictionary of Early Judaism*, ed. John J. Collins and Daniel C. Harlow (Grand Rapids: Eerdmans, 2010), 302–6.

17. Michael E. Stone, *A History of the Literature of Adam and Eve*, EJL 3 (Atlanta: Scholars Press, 1992); Gary A. Anderson and Michael E. Stone, *A Synopsis of the Books of Adam and Eve*, 2nd ed., EJL 5 (Atlanta: Scholars Press, 1999); Gary A. Anderson, Michael E. Stone, and Johannes Tromp, eds., *Literature on Adam and Eve: Collected Essays*, SVTP 15 (Leiden: Brill, 2000), esp. Stone, "The Angelic Prediction in the Primary Adam Books," 131; Anderson, "The Original Form of the *Life of Adam and Eve*: A Proposal," 215–31; and Anderson, "The Penitence Narrative in the *Life of Adam and Eve*," 3–42.

18. On this controversy, see Michael D. Eldridge, *Dying Adam with His Multiethnic Family: Understanding the Greek Life of Adam and Eve*, SVTP 16 (Leiden: Brill, 2001);

to Stone and Anderson, the more intelligible forms of some traditions attested in the Armenian and Georgian versions would demonstrate their priority and would suggest that the Greek version had truncated an essential part of the original story.[19]

Concerning the other versions, scholars agreed about the dependence of the Slavonic version on Greek manuscripts R and M and about the Latin version being the final step in textual evolution.[20] The discovery by Jean-Pierre Pettorelli of an unknown recension of the Latin version in two manuscripts renewed the hypothesis of Stone and Anderson.[21]

Nevertheless, in terms of the history of reception, it is the Latin version, identified in more than a hundred manuscripts,[22] that became the most significant in terms of the transmission of the Life of Adam and Eve. The Latin version is rightly at the center of discussions on the figures of Adam and Eve and on stories about them that circulated in the West in medieval times; it is mainly this source from which originated the dissemination of the Life of Adam and Eve in the vernacular languages.[23]

Thomas Knittel, *Das griechische "Leben Adams und Evas": Studien zu einer narrativen Anthropologie im frühen Judentum*, TSAJ 88 (Tübingen: Mohr Siebeck, 2002); Pettorelli, "Adam and Eve, Life of," and Pettorelli, "Essai sur la structure primitive de la *Vie d'Adam et Ève*," *Apocrypha* 14 (2003): 237–56; Jean-Daniel Kaestli, "La *Vie d'Adam et Ève*: Un enchaînement d'intrigues épisodiques au service d'une intrigue unifiante," in *La Bible en récits 2*, ed. Camille Focant and André Wénin, BETL 191 (Leiden: Peeters, 2005), 322–36, and Kaestli, "Se nourrir après l'expulsion du paradis: De la Bible hébraïque à la Vie d'Adam et Ève," in *La littérature apocryphe chrétienne et les Ècritures juives*, ed. Rémi Gounelle and Benoît Mounier (Prahins: Editions du Zèbre, 2015), 27–43; as well as his assessment published in Albert Frey et al., *Vita latina Adae et Evae: Synopsis Vitae Adae et Evae Latine, Graece, Armeniace et Iberice*, CCSA 19 (Turnhout: Brepols, 2012), 745–54; Albert Frey and Frédéric Amsler, eds., *Actes du Colloque International sur la Vie d'Adam et Ève et les traditions adamiques* (Prahins: Éditions du Zèbre, forthcoming).

19. Anderson, "Original Form of the *Life of Adam and Eve*," 216, 220.

20. See Marcel Nagel, "La Vie Grecque d'Adam et Ève: Apocalypse de Moïse," 3 vols. (PhD diss., Université de Strasbourg II, 1972), 3:90–112; Turdeanu, *Apocryphes slaves et roumains*, 81–82; de Jonge and Tromp, *Life of Adam and Eve*, 34–35; Johannes Tromp, *The Life of Adam and Eve in Greek: A Critical Edition*, PVTG 6 (Leiden: Brill, 2005), 105.

21. Jean-Pierre Pettorelli, "Deux témoins latins singuliers de la *Vie d'Adam et Ève* Paris, BNF, LAT. 3832 and Milan, B. Ambrosiana, O 35 SUP.," *JSJ* 33 (2002): 1–27, esp. 2.

22. Jean-Pierre Pettorelli et al., *Vita latina Adae et Evae*, CCSA 18–19 (Turnhout: Brepols, 2012–2013).

23. Brian Murdoch, *The Apocryphal Adam and Eve in Medieval Europe: Vernacular Translations and Adaptations of the Vita Adae et Evae* (Oxford: Oxford University Press, 2009).

It would be interesting to discuss more in depth that reception, but I prefer to focus on the context of the production of this pseudepigraphic text, in order to discuss a text that I consider to be at the source of many widespread normative representations, which are still significant nowadays. The GLAE provides, in my opinion and against the hypothesis of Stone and Anderson, the more ancient narrative of these representations. The Greek version of the LAE reflects a particular exegesis of biblical texts in a milieu that I situate in a Palestinian environment, between the first century BCE and the end of the first century CE or the beginning of the second century CE.[24]

I explore the representation of Eve, both her innocence and her guilt, in the GLAE. Indeed, previous research by John R. Levison, Marinus de Jonge and Johannes Tromp, Anne Marie Sweet, and more recently contributions by Daphna Arbel, J. R. C. Cousland, and Dietmar Neufeld already have offered a complex description of the figure of Eve in the GLAE that considers the ambiguous involvement of the first woman in the "fall of humankind."[25]

2.2. Eve's Culpability for Sin

The Greek Life of Adam and Eve contains very strong accusations of Eve's guilt. They are expressed, on the one hand, by Adam:

> Adam said to him [Seth], "When God made us, me and your mother—through whom also I die." (GLAE 7.1)[26]

---

24. This hypothesis is also supported by Otto Merk and Martin Meiser, *Das Leben Adams und Evas*, JSHRZ 2.5 (Gütersloh: Mohn, 1998), 769.

25. John R. Levison, "The Exoneration of Eve in the *Apocalypse of Moses* 15–30," *JSJ* 20 (1989): 135–50; and Levison, "The Exoneration and Denigration of Eve in the *Greek Life of Adam and Eve*," in Anderson, Stone, and Tromp, *Literature on Adam and Eve*, 251–75; De Jonge and Tromp, *Life of Adam and Eve*, 53; Anne Marie Sweet, "A Religio-historical Study of the *Greek Life of Adam and Eve*" (PhD diss., University of Notre Dame, 1992); Daphna Arbel, J. R. C. Cousland, and Dietmar Neufeld, *And So They Went Out: The Lives of Adam and Eve as Cultural Transformative Story* (London: T&T Clark, 2010), 3–40, 67–85; Vita Daphna Arbel, *Forming Femininity in Antiquity: Eve, Gender, and Ideologies in the Greek Life of Adam and Eve* (New York: Oxford University Press, 2012).

26. For the passages of the Greek, Georgian, and Slavonic versions of the Life of Adam and Eve, I provide, with certain modifications indicated by italics, the English translation published by Gary A. Anderson and Michael E. Stone, "The Life of Adam and Eve: The Biblical Story in Judaism and Christianity," website of Gary A. Anderson and Michael E. Stone, http://tinyurl.com/SBL066006a, released in 1995.

> And Adam said to Eve: "O Eve, What have you done to us? You have brought great wrath upon us which is death which will rule over our entire race." (GLAE 14.2)

On the other hand, Eve also blames herself:

> And Eve wept and said: "My lord Adam, rise up and give me half of your pain and I will endure it; for it is on my account that this has happened to you, on my account you have these *sufferings*." (GLAE 9.2)

> And Eve wept and said: "Woe is me; if I come to the day of the Resurrection, all those who have sinned will curse me saying: 'Eve has not kept the commandment of God.'" (GLAE 10.2)

In particular, Eve confesses her guilt after Adam asked her shortly before his death to intercede for him:

> And Eve rose up and went outside and fell on the ground and said: "I have sinned, O God, I have sinned, O Father of All, I have sinned against You. I have sinned against your elect angels. I have sinned against the Cherubim, I have sinned against your unshakable Throne. I have sinned, O Lord, I have greatly sinned, I have sinned before You and all sin has begun through my doing in the creation." (32.1–2)

According to these expressions, Eve is responsible for death, for disease, for all sin, and for the future punishment of humankind. This blaming of Eve has been explained differently by various scholars.

Marc Philonenko sees in the construction of the text a sort of symmetry and at the same time an imbalance that would strengthen the responsibility of the woman in the fault. According to Philonenko, this tendentious, even misogynistic version of the biblical account, can be explained by the author's concern to exonerate the man, a glorious being, of the transgression and to lay all the responsibility on the woman, an evil creature.[27]

In his introduction to the textual edition of the GLAE, Daniel A. Bertrand describes Eve as "the only or at least the principal" agent responsible for transgression.[28] The author refers here to verses 7.1; 9.2; 14.2; and 32.2 of the

---

27. André Caquot and Marc Philonenko, "Introduction générale," in *La Bible: Écrits intertestamentaires*, ed. André Dupont-Sommer and Marc Philonenko, BP 337 (Paris: Gallimard, 1987), cxli–cxlii.

28. Daniel A. Bertrand, *La Vie grecque d'Adam et Ève: Introduction, texte, traduction et commentaire* (Paris: Jean Maisonneuve, 1987), 59.

GLAE, which show the guilt of Eve, but he mentions also the only passage that sets forth the guilt of Adam. In the words of Eve:

> After saying these things he [God] commanded his angels to cast us out of paradise: and as we were being driven out amid our loud lamentations, your father Adam besought the angels and said: "Leave me [*a moment*] that I may implore the Lord that he have compassion on me and pity me, for I only have sinned." (27.1–2)

While Bertrand considers both the guilt and innocence of Eve by drawing attention to the responsibility here placed on Adam in the fall, he does not, however, develop this line of thought, but insists constantly on the guilt of Eve. As a matter of fact, the idea of Adam's (exclusive) responsibility would not harmonize with Bertrand's attempt to date the GLAE, as in his view the exaltation of Adam and the corresponding apportioning of blame to Eve link the GLAE to the books of Sirach, Jubilees, and Wisdom of Solomon (while Paul shows a more advanced development).[29] To reach this conclusion Bertrand pointed out already in a contribution published 1985 that the GLAE justifies the final redemption and exaltation of the first man by two arguments: Adam is created in the image of God and the guilt for the fall is attributed to woman.[30] He finds these two motifs bound together in the Wisdom of Solomon too, as it seems to be the likeness of Adam with the creator that allows for the transfer of the responsibility for the fall to "the envy of the devil" (Wis 2:23–24). Likewise, when according to Sir 25:24 Eve sinned first, the result is an exoneration of Adam. In sum, Bertrand's idea of a correspondence between the exaltation of Adam and the condemnation of Eve prevents him from considering the ambiguous role of Eve in the GLAE. Such correspondence is also affirmed by other scholars, particularly those who consider the mortality of humans as one of the fundamental subjects of the GLAE.[31]

---

29. Ibid., 29–31.

30. Daniel A. Bertrand, "Le destin 'post mortem' des protoplastes," in *La littérature intertestamentaire: Colloque de Strasbourg, 17–19 octobre 1983* (Paris: Presses Universitaires de France, 1985), 116. For Adam as the image of God, the author refers to GLAE 10.3; 12.1–2; 33.5; 35.2; see also 37.2. For the attribution of the fall to woman the author refers to GLAE 7.1; 9.2; 14.2; and 32.2.

31. See George W. E. Nickelsburg, *Jewish Literature between the Bible and the Mishnah: A Historical and Literary Introduction* (Minneapolis: Fortress, 1981), 253–57; Nickelsburg, "The Books of Adam and Eve," in *Jewish Writings of the Second Temple Period: Apocrypha, Pseudepigrapha, Qumran Sectarian Writings, Philo, Josephus*, ed. Michael E. Stone (Minneapolis: Fortress, 1981), 112; Natalio Fernández Marcos, "Vida de Adán y Eva (Apocalipsis de Moisés)," in *Apócrifos del Antiguo Testamento*, ed. Alejandro Díez Macho (Madrid: Ed.

In a contribution directly inquiring into the "culpability of Eve," Anderson shows how in early Jewish times two questions were developed from a close reading of Gen 2–3 around the culpability of Adam or Eve.[32] The first concerns the divine commandment to "not eat of the fruit of the tree of knowledge" (Gen 2:17). In the Life of Adam and Eve the command is given both to Adam and Eve (LAE [32] 7.1). The problem pondered in later Jewish exegesis that Adam alone heard the commandment and that he might have transmitted it incorrectly so that Eve could be misled by the devil is not relevant for LAE. The second question concerns Adam's ignorance of what he was doing at the moment when he ate the fruit. For if Eve met the snake/the devil when she was alone (LAE [32–33] 7.3) Adam could have taken the fruit from Eve without suspecting that it came from the forbidden tree. On the basis of these observations Anderson, leaving no room for ambiguities, concludes:

> Eve is a fully responsible moral agent when she meets the snake. According to the *Life of Adam and Eve*, Eve ate the fruit first while physically separated from Adam. She later fed Adam the forbidden fruit while he was completely unaware of what he was doing. This tradition, or one very similar to it, must have been in the mind of the author of 1 Timothy when he ascribed the fall to the person of Eve alone.[33]

3. Eve's Exoneration in the Greek Life of Adam and Eve

3.1. Textual Observations

In opposition to her culpability regarding sin, Eve's innocence—or at least her restricted responsibility—is visible in several passages of the GLAE. On the one hand, she is exonerated by Adam because of her loneliness at the moment of the temptation:

> And the hour drew near for the angels, who were guarding your mother, to go up and worship the Lord, And the enemy gave it to her and she ate from the tree. *He [the enemy] knew* that I was not near her, nor the holy angels. (GLAE 7.2)

Cristiandad, 1983), 2.320–21; M. D. Johnson, "Life of Adam and Eve (First Century A.D.)," *OTP* 2:253–54.

32. Gary A. Anderson, "The Culpability of Eve: From Genesis to Timothy," in *From Prophecy to Testament: The Function of the Old Testament in the New*, ed. Craig A. Evans (Peabody, MA: Hendrickson, 2004), 233–51.

33. Ibid., 246.

On the other hand, she is excused in light of the charge of the opponent in the transgression, sometimes Satan (GLAE 7.2; 15–21; 25.4; 26.1; and 39.2–3), sometimes the serpent:

> And instantly *the snake* hung himself from the *walls* of paradise. And when the angels *of God* ascended to worship, then Satan appeared in the form of an angel, and sang hymns *to God* like the angels. And he [= *Satan*] *leaned* over the wall and I [= *Eve*] saw him, like an angel. (17.1–2a)

> And in that very hour my eyes were opened, and forthwith I knew that I was naked of the righteousness with which I had been clothed (upon), and I wept and said to him [= *the serpent*]: "Why have you done this that you *have alienated* me *from my* glory [*Mss ALC RM with which I was clothed*]?" (20.1–2)

> After he [= *God*] said these things to me, he spoke to the serpent in great wrath saying: "Since you have done this, and become a thankless vessel until you have deceived *those who were weak in their hearts*, be cursed (more than) all beasts." (26.1)

Several scholars have noted this relativization or even lack of culpability in Eve, but to demonstrate it they comment only on her responsibility regarding transgression and then nuance it. As a result, how Eve is presented as a textual figure remains limited. This is why I keep and emphasize the two aspects together, her culpability and her innocence, aspects that, according to my hypothesis, belong together as a contradictory complexity in the narrative of GLAE.

3.2. First Scholarly Differentiations

Marinus de Jonge and Johannes Tromp are the first authors to refute the claim of the exclusive guilt of Eve in the GLAE. They highlight the ambiguity of the rhetoric about the guilt and innocence of Adam and Eve. In other words, the two protoplasts are, at the same time and in the same way, guilty and innocent. About Eve, the two authors point out:

> As a woman, Eve is essentially weak. The devil was able to seduce her, because she was alone, unguarded by either her husband or the angels (7.1–2; 17.1–2; cf. 29.7–13 in manuscripts R and M). The implication of this remark must be that women who are left on their own are especially liable to seduction, probably by nature.[34]

---

34. De Jonge and Tromp, *Life of Adam and Eve*, 53.

While for de Jonge and Tromp, the issue of who is at fault is a minor subject compared with their emphasis on mortality or resurrection, for John R. Levison, the denigration and the exemption of Eve become the central subjects of analysis.[35] Levison stressed the ambivalence of the text on the one hand, about Eve's responsibility, and on the other hand, about her innocence. At first glance, the text would condemn the first woman (GLAE 1–15 and 30–43) at the same time as it excuses her because of her solitude at the time she was seduced (GLAE 15–30). Levison developed these two aspects of the GLAE in two different studies. The first article is taken up in the subsequent work,[36] and this allows me to explain the evolution of his thought on this subject.

Levison offers us the general line of his argument in his first article:

> *GLAE* 15–30, I contended, exhibits several literary characteristics that suggest an effort to exonerate Eve. First, she, rather than Adam, is the testamentary figure who exercises her authority as reliable narrator to provide parenetic information designed to help her children to avoid evil. Second, her dialogue with the serpent evokes sympathy for her. She emphasizes through repetition that Satan could be construed as nothing less than an angel. She proffers, additionally, inside views of her emotions, underscoring several points of resistance before capitulating to this angelic figure. The reader can, then, identify and relate to her internal and protracted struggle against evil in the guise of good. Third, Eve recounts that she promised to give the fruit to her husband before she realized that it was evil; she is bound subsequently by an oath rather than by malicious intent. The solution to this tension between the oath and the realization that the fruit was evil is vitiated by Eve's awareness that she in fact did not speak to Adam but the devil through her (21:3). Eve did not finally actively seduce Adam after being deceived by an allegedly angelic being.[37]

In his second contribution, Levison revises his own position on the basis of a new analysis of the four forms of the Greek text published by Marcel Nagel.[38] The exemption and denigration of Eve should, according to Levison, be corroborated in each of these forms, in order to not fall into simplifications.

35. Ibid., 50–54. Levison, "Exoneration and Denigration of Eve," 252–53.

36. Levison, "Exoneration and Denigration of Eve," 135–50.

37. Ibid., 253–54.

38. In fact, M. Nagel distinguishes three main forms and three groups of manuscripts that bear witness to them: Form I (MSS D, S, V, [K], P, G, B, A, T, L, C), Form II (MSS R, M), and Form III (MSS N, I, [J], K, Q, Z, H, E, W, X, F). See Nagel, *La Vie Grecque d'Adam et Ève*, 1:198. The classification into four text-forms appeared as a consequence of the subdivision of Text I into two subgroups (I: MSS DSV [K] PG B; Ia: MSS ATLC), given the associa-

Regarding the guilt and exemption of Eve, Levison perceives several differences between the four textual forms. While other forms attest in 7.1 that statement, "because of whom [= *Eve*] I die," manuscript M inserts the "plant" (φυτόν) as responsible for death. On the other hand, according to Levison, the additions in form NIK "serve consistently to underscore Eve's culpability and activity not only in her transgression but also with respect to Adam's involvement in the first transgression."[39] In total, Levison recognizes that the phenomenon of exemption and at the same time denigration of Eve is much more widespread in the GLAE than he had suggested a decade earlier.[40]

According to Jan Dochhorn, in his monograph on the Apocalypse of Moses, this combined presence of the guilt and exemption of Eve corresponds to different stages in the drafting of this text and its sources, the strongest indictment of Eve belonging to the last period of redaction.[41] This would imply then that the most positive references to the figure of Eve, contained mainly in the story related by Eve herself (GLAE 15–30), belong to a period prior to GLAE in its present shape, and indeed Dochhorn takes GLAE 15–30 to be (part of) a work originally existing in itself which he labels the "Testament of Eve" and which could have originated sometime after the book of Jubilees.[42]

Unfortunately, I cannot confirm with certainty, as Dochhorn does, this evolution in the representation of Eve in the GLAE, given that his thesis is based on his consideration of some of the relevant passages as later interpolations (GLAE 17.1–2; 7.1–2). The interpolated character of these passages still remains a topic of extensive scholarly discussion. Much as Dochhorn's hypothesis would allow me to understand more clearly the existing dissonances in this text, I feel forced to consider the text as a whole with all its narrative and theological tensions and try to understand the reasons for such ambiguity regarding Eve's figure.

3.3. My Own Hypothesis: Contradictory Complexity

In other words, I must take into account the possibility that the affirmation of Eve's guilt as well as of her exemption belong to the same epoch and that this

---

tion between the second subgroup and the other versions of the LAE. I offer here the sigla of the manuscripts proposed by Bertrand. See Bertrand, *La Vie grecque d'Adam et Ève*, 41.

39. Levison, "Exoneration and Denigration of Eve," 259–60.

40. Ibid., 275.

41. Jan Dochhorn, *Die Apokalypse des Mose: Text, Übersetzung, Kommentar*, TSAJ 106 (Tübingen: Mohr Siebeck, 2005), 135.

42. Ibid., 145.

contradiction could be the result of a complex and sometimes contradictory representation of women in male-stream discourses of these times. I deduce this complexity from an analysis of the specific relationship that the GLAE establishes between Eve and sin. She is not the only agent in transgression, since "the enemy," Satan or the serpent, deceives her. Her nature is described, on the one hand, as inferior to that of Adam and this excuses her because the absence of the angels and Adam means she did not have the protection she would have needed; and on the other hand, she is wrapped with the same divine or glorious attributes as Adam (GLAE 20.1–2). However, her relationship with sin is different from Adam's because she is at the origin of sin by her disobedience to the divine command. Her disobedience implies the emergence of evil as human inclination, against which their offspring will have to fight until the last judgment.

Another reason for not considering the figure of Eve solely in terms of culpability emerges from the analysis of all representations of Eve in the other versions of the Life of Adam and Eve. They too reveal contradictions on this subject. For example, in the Georgian LAE, Adam says to Eve: "How could I raise my hand and cause my own flesh to suffer?" ([3].3).[43] Here it becomes clear that Adam considers himself one with Eve. The Slavonic version seems to go one step further and highlights Eve's nature in a positive way, as according to that version Eve realizes who is trying to deceive her: "And I discerned that he was the devil, and I answered him nothing at all" (38–39 = LAE [9].1–5).[44] This confirms Nagel's opinion that the Slavonic LAE offers a significantly more positive representation of Eve and could potentially be related to the observation of Levison on the Greek manuscripts R and M.[45] However, in contrast to Levison who considers the textual form RM to contain the only positive picture of Eve,[46] I find problematic ambiguities in the representation of the first woman in all textual forms of the Greek version. These ambiguities or incongruities might lead to a text reading less smoothly, but are probably more consistent with the actual composition of GLAE.

---

43. This passage of the Georgian LAE belongs to the narrative of the search of the food, which appears only in Greek MSS RM (29.9), and in the parallel passages of LAE ([3].3). The square brackets indicate its absence in the GLAE.

44. This passage of the Slavonic LAE belongs to the narrative of the second temptation of Eve, which again appears only in Greek MSS RM (29.12), and in the parallel passages of LAE ([9].1–5).

45. Nagel, *La Vie Grecque d'Adam et Ève*, 1:95. See also above n. 20.

46. Levison, "Exoneration and Denigration of Eve," 259–60.

4. The Notion of "Sin of the Flesh" in the Greek Life of Adam and Eve

This incongruity emerges as well regarding the different meanings of sin and the consequences of transgression in the text. I would like to focus now on one of these sins, which is central to the representation of Eve: the "sin of the flesh."

4.1. GLAE 25.1–4 as Exegesis of Gen 3:16

The notion of "sin of the flesh" appears only once in the GLAE and is introduced at the moment when God announces the punishments for Eve. God says to her:

> Since you have hearkened to the serpent, and transgressed my commandment, you *will be in pains and intolerable sufferings*; you shall bear children in *multiple circumstances* and in one hour you shall come to *give* birth, and lose your life, from your sore trouble and anguish. But you shall confess and say: "Lord, Lord, save me, and I will turn no more [ἐπιστρέψω] to the sin of the flesh." And on this account, from your own words I will judge you, by reason of the enmity which the enemy has planted in you. And you shall return [στραφείς] again to your husband and he will rule over you. (GLAE 25.1–4)

The "sin of the flesh" is clearly a sexual transgression, since it refers to the sexual union between Eve and Adam as a necessary requirement for procreation. The authors of the GLAE introduce this concept in a context regarding the suffering of childbirth. Such pains generated by the fall are already present in the biblical book of Genesis (see 3:16).[47] However, consideration of the sexual union as a fault does not appear in Genesis. Rather, this idea seems to be what is expressed by the term "sin of the flesh" and to be the result of a specific exegesis of the biblical account developed by the authors of GLAE.

Genesis 3:16 reads, according to the Masoretic Text:

> To the woman he said, "I will greatly multiply your pains and your pregnancies. In pain you will bring forth children; yet your desire [תשוקתך] will be for your husband, and he will rule over you."

And according to the Septuagint:

47. See also Josephus, *Ant.* 1.49: "Eve He punished by child-birth and its attendant pains, because she had deluded Adam, even as the serpent had beguiled her, and so brought calamity upon him" (Thackeray, LCL).

> And to the woman he said, "I will greatly multiply your pains and your groaning. In pain you will bring forth children, and your return [ἀποστροφή] will be to your husband, and he will rule over you."[48]

Greek Life of Adam and Eve 25.3–4 departs by certain amendments from both texts. The first difference is observed in the expression chosen to indicate the "return" of Eve to her husband (στραφείς) in the GLAE (25.4), which would imply a reference to the term ἀποστροφή of the Septuagint. Already in the Septuagint, ἀποστροφή involves an exegetical differentiation in regard to the corresponding Hebrew term, as explains Monique Alexandre: the Septuagint reads "your return" (תשובתך), instead of "your desire" (תשוקתך) from the Masoretic Text.[49]

Secondly, a doubling of the use of "return" can be noted. This doubling or repetition is due to a specific exegesis of the Hebrew term for desire (תשוקה) in this verse. The Greek word play (ἐπιστρέψω, στραφείς) gives birth to two separate but interrelated ideas: the first phrase ("I will turn no more [ἐπιστρέψω] to the sin of the flesh") seems to allude to both readings in Hebrew ("return" [תשובה] and "desire" [תשוקה]), while the second sentence ("you shall return [στραφείς] again to your husband and he will rule over you") plays with the meaning of "return," in this case return to the husband, which is related to the dominion of the husband over his wife.

4.2. GLAE 25.1–4 and Gen. Rab. 20.7

Likewise, this doubling appears in a later text (probably from the fourth to the sixth century CE), Genesis Rabbah:

> Another interpretation of And thy desire shall be to thy husband: When a woman sits on the birthstool, she declares, "I will henceforth never fulfil my marital duties" whereupon the Holy One, blessed be He, says to her: "Thou wilt return to thy desire, thou wilt return to the desire for thy husband." (Gen. Rab. 20.7)[50]

This paragraph, whose striking similarities with the GLAE have already been noticed by Dochhorn, provides many clues for understanding GLAE 25.3–

48. Both translations are my own.

49. Monique Alexandre, *Le commencement du livre Genèse I–V, La version grecque de la Septante et sa réception* (Paris: Beauchesne, 1988), 318 with reference also to other ancient translations.

50. H. Freedman, trans., *Midrash Rabbah: Genesis Rabbah*, 2 vols. (London: Soncino, 1939), 1:166.

4.[51] It exhibits a similar reduplication of "return" and "desire" ("Thou wilt return to thy desire, thou wilt return to the desire for thy husband"). Where the GLAE has the expression "sin of the flesh," Genesis Rabbah reads, "I will henceforth never fulfil my marital duties" and continues by mentioning "your desire"/"desire for your husband." The sexual union with her husband is in parallel with the desire here, and the two terms are therefore equivalent to the "sin of the flesh" in the GLAE 25.3.

As Dochhorn observes, the midrash has Eve's promise not to "return" followed by a command from God, ordering her to "return" to her desire for her husband. The overall context is God's speech announcing Eve's punishments. The divine order in Gen. Rab. 20.7 finds again its parallel in the GLAE, when God enjoins Eve: "And you shall return [στραφείς] again to your husband."

4.3. GLAE 25.1–4 in the Light of 4Q416 2 iv

The passage of GLAE 25.3–4 contains a notable exegetical development of Gen 3:16, which can further be elucidated through an intertextual reading of that verse with Gen 2:24 by the intermediary of the Qumranic text 4Q416 2 iv, part of the sapiential composition called Musar leMevin (Instruction for an Understanding One). Benjamin G. Wold restores and translates the relevant lines from 4Q416 as follows:

> He has set you in authority over her and [her father]
> He has not set in authority over her, from her mother He has separated her
> and [she will yearn] for you [and she will be]
> to you one flesh, your daughter for another he will separate ....[52]

As the context shows, the male person addressed receives authority (המשיל) over his wife who is considered to be far from her mother and—if Wold's reconstruction is reliable here—the authority of her father. The verb used to designate authority is the same as in Gen 3:16. Wold explains further:

> If the phrase תשוקתה ("her desire") is a reliable reconstruction in the latter part of line 3, then the allusion would be [again] to Genesis 3.16 ("her desire will be to her husband"). 4Q416 2 iv line 4 contains the phrase לך לבשר אחד. The phrase "one flesh" occurs in the Hebrew Bible only in Genesis 2.24 (לבשר אחד) and in the Dead Sea Scrolls there is no occurrence outside of

51. Dochhorn, *Die Apokalypse des Mose*, 407.

52. Benjamin G. Wold, *Women, Men and Angels: The Qumran Wisdom Document Musar leMevin and Its Allusions to Genesis Creation Traditions*, WUNT 2/201 (Tübingen: Mohr Siebeck, 2005), 186.

> *Musar leMevin*. Given the surrounding context there can be little doubt that the phrase 'one flesh' in line 4 is an allusion to Genesis 2.24.[53]

In this text, the notion of "becoming one flesh" (Gen 2:24) is associated with the husband's dominion over his wife and her desire for him (Gen 3:16). Or, as the text has it, the woman's desire for her husband results in becoming one flesh with him.

The intertextual reading of Gen 2:24 and Gen 3:16 is allowed by the idea of sexual union in both passages. Nevertheless, the introduction of this union as a sin in the GLAE, at the given moment of the narrative, implies a substantial modification in the exegesis of Gen 2:24. Sexual union remains in the order controlled by God but belongs to the punishment of Eve. However, this change in the perception of human reproduction should not be understood as a rejection of sexuality, since sexuality as a means of procreation allows for the continuation of the battle against the enemy.

The "enemy" appears in the last verse of this paragraph of the GLAE 25.1–4: "And on this account, from your own words I will judge you, by reason of the enmity which the enemy has planted in you" (25.4). While according to Gen 3:15 enmity is set between Eve's posterity and the serpent, in the GLAE Satan becomes the enemy of humankind.

The punishment of Eve is related to the struggle between her descendants and the enemy. The "sin of the flesh" plays a fundamental role in the fight against the enemy by the perpetuation of humankind, because Eve is forced to renege on her promise of not returning to her husband ("I will turn no more to the sin of the flesh," 25.3), in order to allow her descendants to continue the fight against the enemy, until the last judgment (28.3). As a result, Eve will be found guilty of having not kept her promise—a promise that, due to the enmity that the enemy has put in her, she is forced to disrespect.

The "sin of the flesh" does not correspond to the primary fault of eating of the forbidden fruit, but it would be a consequence of that disobedience of the protoplasts. Given the context in which this motif is introduced (GLAE 25.1–4 as exegesis of Gen 3:16), the "sin of the flesh" appears as a punishment imposed on Eve after her disobedience.

4.4. "Sin of the Flesh" and "Desire" (Gen 3:6)

To elucidate the full connotations of "sin of the flesh" another motif in GLAE

---

53. Ibid., 188.

has to be considered. The serpent asks Eve to confirm by oath that she will give her husband the forbidden fruit. GLAE 19.3 continues:

> And when he [= *serpent/Satan*] had received the oath from me [= *Eve*], he *climbed on the tree* and placed upon the fruit the poison of his wickedness—which is desire [ἐπιθυμία], for it is the beginning of every sin—and he bent the branch on the earth and I took of the fruit and I ate.

The Masoretic Text of Gen 3:6 calls the tree "desirable" (נחמד), a notion that does not occur in the corresponding verse in the Septuagint. However, GLAE connects "desire" (ἐπιθυμία) to the fruit of the forbidden tree and declares it as the cause of every sin.

Precisely, it is desire (תשוקה/נחמד/ἐπιθυμία) that allows the link between the two traditions (as a punishment for the fault, and as the fault itself) existing in the GLAE, since that concept seems, on the one hand, to have inspired the notion of "sin of the flesh," and it appears, on the other hand, at the moment of temptation, to designate the beginning of every sin.

The concept of desire (ἐπιθυμία) introduced in the GLAE 19.3 is crucial in the relationship that it builds with sin. The desire here is the beginning of all sin, because it leads humankind to transgress the divine commandments. This is what Dochhorn establishes when he relates this term with Gen 3:6; Exod 20:17; Deut 5:21; and Rom 7:7.[54] Indeed, desire (ἐπιθυμία) could be associated at this time to other commandments, as can be observed in Rom 7:7; Jas 1:14–15; and in the final paragraph of the Apoc. Ab. 24.5–8.

Finally, in the comprehension of the concept of desire (ἐπιθυμία), we must consider its relationship with sexual desire. This meaning helps to elucidate a singular feature of the GLAE, the complexity regarding the different meanings of sin. On the one hand, since in 19.3 desire keeps a generic sense, it is related to "all sins" (πάσης ἁμαρτίας), and is not restricted to a sexual offense. In this sense, it can be place in a period contemporary to Rom 7:7 and the Apoc. Ab. 24.8.[55] On the other hand, the term desire (ἐπιθυμία) bears the ambiguity of interpretations with a sexual connotation, and this must be taken into account vis-à-vis the readings and innuendos that could be played upon at that time.

---

54. Jan Dochhorn, "Röm 7,7 und das zehnte Gebot: Ein Beitrag zur Schriftauslegung und zur jüdischen Vorgeschichte des Paulus," *ZNW* 100 (2009): 59–77.

55. Nicholas A. Meyer, *Adam's Dust and Adam's Glory in the Hodayot and the Letters of Paul: Rethinking Anthropogony and Theology*, NovTSup 168 (Leiden: Brill, 2016), 204, however, suggests that a sexual reference might also be at play in Rom 7:1–12.

5. Conclusions

The concept of sin in the GLAE must be considered in all its complexity, which includes the simultaneity of contradictory and distinct meanings of "sin"—or aspects of what "sin" could be—in a single text. The notion of "sin of the flesh" would correspond to one of these meanings or aspects, though that notion is still vague and not fully developed, and even mixed with other types of transgressions. This same ambiguity or vagueness is also present with regard to the subject of Eve's guilt and innocence, and constitutes one of the fundamental characteristics of this complex writing. The imprecision reflects the context in which the GLAE originated, where various notions of sin and different ideas concerning the agents of the introduction of evil in the world coexisted concurrently. Such complexity in the concepts and representations of sin reflects a particular period of time, that of the first century CE, as we can see in other writings from this period.

The Greek Life of Adam and Eve, written probably in the first century CE in a Jewish-Palestinian milieu from preexisting oral traditions, was readily accepted within Christianity. This fact contributed, on the one hand, to the establishment of sexual desire as a transgression, comparable in its gravity to disobedience against the law, and, on the other hand, to a progressive acceptance of Eve as the only accountable agent in the transgression, because of her weak and inferior nature, attached to the flesh. The weakness of Eve, which in the GLAE contributed to justify her innocence, will henceforth support the charge that she is to blame in the fall of humanity.

Illicit Male Desire or Illicit Female Seduction? A Comparison of the Ancient Retellings of the Account of the "Sons of God" Mingling with the "Daughters of Men" (Gen 6:14)

Veronika Bachmann
Translated by Richard Ratzlaff

1. Introduction

The mythical theme of sexual union between heavenly beings and earthly beings, especially with humans, is found in many cultures. When these stories involve heterosexual intercourse, it is usually the offspring of such intercourse that are of interest. The narrative function of these stories of sexual union can vary widely. Often the stories are explanations for unusual physical strength, the heroic make up of one or more of the protagonists. The superhuman is explained by its genesis. In the Bible this mythical theme is barely visible.[1] When a text such as Ps 2:7, for example, states of the king that YHWH has begotten him, the focus is not on the sexual intercourse between God and the mother of the king. The image of king as "Son of God" is much better understood as a statement of royal ideology; the significance of these statements become clear when they are compared to similar expressions of the Egyptian, Ancient Near Eastern, or Hellenistic understandings of kingship.[2] Nor is the birth narrative of Jesus, which appears in the New Testament in two versions (Matt 1:18–25; Luke 1:26–38), really a direct parallel to the motif, since the birth narratives are not about Mary's or God's physical desire, but

1. See Martti Nissinen and Risto Uro, eds., *Sacred Marriages: The Divine-Human Sexual Metaphor from Sumer to Early Christianity* (Winona Lake, IN: Eisenbrauns, 2008), which thoroughly examines especially the metaphorical examples.

2. On Ps 2:7, see, for example, Markus Saur, *Die Königspsalmen: Studien zur Entstehung und Theologie*, BZAW 340 (Berlin: de Gruyter, 2004), 32–34.

rather are intended to show that Jesus's conception is a miracle brought about by a divine spirit. The question whether these birth narratives are intended to be counternarratives to the more "physical" conception narratives is a topic to be explored elsewhere.[3]

There is only one text in the Bible, namely, Gen 6:1–4, that explicitly discusses sexual intercourse between divine-human and earthly human beings. This biblical narrative of sexual union contains the following elements: (1) it takes place prior to the flood; (2) it tells of heterosexual intercourse between divine-human men with earthly women, in which both groups are seen exclusively as collectives; (3) the offspring of the union appear to be only masculine, and special characteristics are ascribed to them; (4) the union provokes a response from YHWH.

Apart from Eve, the protagonist in the garden of Eden narrative (Gen 2:4b–3:24), the women described in Gen 6 as the "daughters of men" (בנות האדם) are the only female figures who play a particular role in the first chapters of Genesis.[4] Every exegesis of this text needs to acknowledge the etiological character of these chapters. Like certain Mesopotamian or Greek narratives, these chapters explain facts, realities familiar to the people of the time, by events that took place in earliest times. The Old Babylonian Atrahasis Epic, for example, traces phenomena like infant death or the existence of cultic roles that require women to remain childless, back to the flood (see Atrahasis tablet 3, col. 7).[5] According to this version of the flood story, it was the overpopulation of the world that led the gods to attempt to reverse the creation of humans. Enlil, the chief god, could no longer sleep because of the racket made by humans. Realities newly established after the flood—for example, that there were now barren women or demonic beings who killed infants—had to safeguard the continuing existence of humanity by ensuring that a similar catastrophe does not happen again.[6] The biblical story of the garden of Eden can also be understood as an explanation for social states of affairs (without, however, legitimizing them!), such as the existence of a

3. The motif of the angel who announces the birth of the savior alludes to Judg 13, the birth story of Samson. But the text of the Samson story seems to presume that Manoach, the husband of Samson's mother, is the birth father.

4. Genesis 4:19–24, a genealogical text, is an exception: it refers not only to men but also to the women Adah, Zillah, and Naama.

5. For a German translation, see Wolfram von Soden, trans., "Der altbabylonische Atramchasis-Mythos," *TUAT* 3.3:612–45; for an English translation, see, for example, Benjamin R. Foster, trans., "Atra-Hasis," *COS* 1.130:450–53.

6. For this interpretation, see, among others, von Soden, "Der altbabylonische Atramchasis-Mythos."

patriarchal order or the fact that hard labor is required to obtain the essentials of life.[7]

Today there are many who believe that the purpose of the Eden narrative is above all to explain the origin of sin, although studies of the reception history of the narrative have demonstrated that such an interpretation of the story is not found in the sources until the Roman period.[8] Later interpretations such as these also set the stage for making women wholly responsible for the fall of humanity, thereby legitimating their different moral and legal treatment.[9]

Even before the story about Eve became understood fundamentally as an explanation for human sin, the accounts of sexual union between heavenly and earthly creatures became in Hellenistic and Roman times occasions for reflection on an original (moral) fall of humanity. The texts that develop this notion have not been admitted into the Jewish canon of scripture nor into the biblical canons of most Christian denominations. This does not mean, however, that they were marginal from the beginning. Diverse allusions to these texts in other writings, in the New Testament and in the texts of early Christian and Jewish theologians among others, lead to the conclusion that they were quite well known in Hellenistic-Roman times and even later. In the following the intention is to examine these nonbiblical texts with following questions in mind:

---

7. See, in more detail, Helen Schüngel-Straumann, "Genesis 1–11: The Primordial History," in *Feminist Biblical Interpretation: A Compendium of Critical Commentary on the Books of the Bible and Related Literature*, ed. Luise Schottroff and Marie-Theres Wacker (Grand Rapids: Eerdmans, 2012), 1–14.

8. See Eibert J. C. Tigchelaar, "Eden and Paradise: The Garden Motif in Some Early Jewish Texts (1 Enoch and Other Texts Found at Qumran)," in *Paradise Interpreted: Representations of Biblical Paradise in Judaism and Christianity; Papers Given at a Conference, Groningen, June 1998*, ed. Gerard P. Luttikhuizen, TBN 2 (Leiden: Brill, 1999), 37–62; John J. Collins, "Before the Fall: The Earliest Interpretations of Adam and Eve," in *The Idea of Biblical Interpretation: Essays in Honor of James L. Kugel*, ed. Hindy Najman and Judith H. Newman, JSJSup 83 (Leiden: Brill, 2004), 293–308; Christfried Böttrich, Beate Ego, and Friedmann Eißler, *Adam und Eva in Judentum, Christentum und Islam* (Göttingen: Vandenhoeck & Ruprecht, 2011). Since the Hebrew term for sin (חטאת) appears first in Gen 4, the story of Cain and Abel, it would be much more accurate to speak of the latter story as the story of the origins of human sin.

9. See on this issue the various contributions in Kari E. Børresen and Adriana Valerio, eds., *The High Middle Ages*, BW 6.2 (Atlanta: SBL Press, 2015), and also the contribution of Magdalena Díaz Araujo to the present volume.

1. How much weight does each text give to the motif of sexual union? What literary function does the motif play in the context of the larger literary whole?
2. What characteristics does each text stress in the manner in which it portrays the figures involved, especially the heavenly males and the earthly women? Does the text presume a particular relationship between the "male" and the "female"?

Above all, the second set of questions should make it possible to examine the gender-political tendencies of the texts in a nuanced way and bring to light some possible differences.

My interest in the gender-political profile of source texts is motivated by the insight that feminist exegesis has brought to scholarship: both the biblical as well as the so-called apocryphal texts are, to use the words of Susanne Scholz, "gendered literature with a gendered history of interpretation."[10] For the reception of the union-account in question, a particular text from the New Testament, namely, 1 Cor 11:7–10, became decisive. In this passage Paul argues that women in the Corinthian house churches should wear a head covering and calls upon the men, in contrast, to pray and prophesy without head covering:

> For a man ought not to have his head veiled, since he is the image and reflection of God; but woman is the reflection of man. Indeed, man was not made from woman, but woman from man. Neither was man created for the sake of woman, but woman for the sake of man. For this reason a woman ought to have a symbol of authority on her head, because of the angels. (NRSV)

Many New Testament scholars understand verse 10 as an allusion to the story of the daughters of men in Gen 6:1–4. According to this understanding, the veil worn by the woman would serve to protect the divine beings from being seduced by the beauty of the women. In the scholarly literature there is an ongoing debate on the question whether Paul himself came up with the notion or not.[11] What is clear is that at least some readers of Paul's letter—such as

---

10. Susanne Scholz, *Introducing the Women's Hebrew Bible*, IFTh 13 (London: T&T Clark, 2007), 25.

11. See on this issue already Max Küchler, *Schweigen, Schmuck und Schleier: Drei neutestamentliche Vorschriften zur Verdrängung der Frauen auf dem Hintergrund einer frauenfeindlichen Exegese des Alten Testaments im antiken Judentum*, NTOA 1 (Fribourg: Editions Universitaires, 1986) and most recently on the topic the edited collection Torsten Jantsch, ed., *Frauen, Männer, Engel: Perspektiven zu 1Kor 11,2–16*, BthS 152 (Neukirchen-Vluyn: Neukirchener Verlag, 2014).

Tertullian 150 years later (see *Virg.* 7; *Marc.* 5.8; *Or.* 22)—presume that there is such an allusion.[12] The fact that it is possible to connect the biblical story of sexual union with the thesis that there is a female capacity to seduce that can endanger even heavenly beings raises the question whether already the biblical story and the earliest postbiblical retellings of the story intend to show women as responsible for an incident that is evaluated very negatively.[13] The examination that follows will begin with Gen 6:1–4 and focus primarily on the so-called Book of Watchers (1 En. 1–36).[14] Analysis of two writings from Seleucid times, the so-called Animal Apocalypse (1 En. 85–90) and the book of Jubilees, will demonstrate that while certain versions of the story do indeed strongly ascribe blame, they do not in fact ascribe fault to the women with whom the heavenly beings have intercourse. Finally, on the basis of two texts from Roman times, 2 Baruch and the Testament of Reuben, it will be shown that reinterpretations become important only later.[15]

2. The Biblical Narrative (Gen 6:1–4)

Unlike the nonbiblical versions of the story, the biblical account of the sexual union is curiously short, and more than one feature of the story is puzzling. The text reads as follows:

> And it came to pass, when men [האדם] began to multiply on the face of the earth, and daughters were born unto them, that the sons of God

12. Additional early Christian sources are cited in Jacob Brouwer, "Gott, Christus, Engel, Männer und Frauen: Chronologisch-thematische Bibliographie zu 1 Kor 11,2–16," in Jantsch, *Frauen, Männer, Engel*, 187–235. For medieval examples see Gary Macy, "The Treatment of Women in the Scriptural Commentaries of the Twelfth–Thirteenth Centuries," in Børresen and Valerio, *High Middle Ages*, 37–50.

13. As suggested by, for example, Schüngel-Straumann, "Genesis 1–11," 7.

14. The process gets underway with Gen 6:1–4 as the biblical-canonical version of the story, which should not be taken to imply that these verses are the textual source for every version of the story found in the apocryphal and pseudepigraphic texts, as is suggested by many studies of the topic. Because of the cryptic character of Gen 6:1–4 and the fact that elements of the story are only loosely integrated into the literary context, I favor the thesis that the various elements of the narrative were already widely known before they were integrated into the version found in Genesis. See, for more discussion, Veronika Bachmann, *Die Welt im Ausnahmezustand: Eine Untersuchung zu Aussagegehalt und Theologie des Wächterbuches (1 Hen 1–36)*, BZAW 409 (Berlin: de Gruyter, 2009), 239–40, n. 40.

15. It would be interesting to compare the two texts with gnostic sources. I will not take account of them here, since doing so would be to go beyond the time frame of the volume. For more on the topic, see Claudia Losekam, *Die Sünde der Engel: Die Engelfall-tradition in frühjüdischen und gnostischen Texten*, TANZ 41 (Tübingen: Francke, 2010).

> [בני־האלהים] saw the daughters of men [בנות האדם] that they were fair [טבת]; and they took them wives, whomsoever they chose. And the LORD said: "My spirit shall not abide in man for ever, for that he also is flesh [בשר]; therefore shall his days be a hundred and twenty years." The Nephilim [הנפלים] were in the earth in those days, and also after that, when the sons of God came in unto the daughters of men, and they bore children to them; the same were the mighty men [הגברים] that were of old, the men of renown. (Gen 6:1–4 JPS)

It remains unclear who precisely is meant by these male heavenly beings, the "sons of God." What does it mean that they "took wives" for themselves from the daughters of men? Should we see here accounts of rape or romantic love stories? How might the divine and earthly characters mentioned in the story have perceived their sexual union? What is the meaning of God's statement in verse 3? Verse 4 raises the question of who is meant by the Nephilim, a term that is often translated as "giants"; are they the same as the "mighty men that were of old," who appear to be regarded positively, or not?[16]

Despite the many points of uncertainty, it is possible to determine the literary function of Gen 6:1–4: on the one hand, by examining carefully what the text states clearly; on the other, by paying close attention to the literary context. On the whole it seems that the verses are hardly connected to the immediate context. They follow the genealogical list in Gen 5 and precede the story of Noah and the flood. The parallelism between the opening sentences of Gen 6:1–4 and Gen 6:5–9:19 is an indication that the biblical text postulates no causal connection between the story of sexual union and the flood story.[17] Genesis 6:1–2 tells how heavenly beings took notice of a positive feature of humanity—the beauty of humans and especially the women among them. A story follows that has to do with the theme. In the same way Gen 6:5 begins

---

16. The Septuagint, the Greek translation of the Hebrew Bible, mitigates the question, inasmuch as it uses the same term, namely, γίγαντες, for "giants" (נפלים) and "heroes" (גברים). Some interpreters see in this choice of term a deliberate negative judgment on this class of figures, since it evokes the gigantomachy of Greek myth. For a reading in this vein, see Peter Prestel and Stefan Schorch, "Genesis: Das erste Buch Mose," in *Septuaginta Deutsch: Erläuterungen und Kommentare zum griechischen Alten Testament*, ed. Martin Karrer and Wolfgang Kraus (Stuttgart: Deutsche Bibelgesellschaft, 2011), 1:145–57; 167; and Martin Rösel, "Riesen," in *Wörterbuch alttestamentlicher Motive*, ed. Michael Fieger, Jutta Krispenz, and Jörg Lanckau (Darmstadt: Wissenschaftliche Buchgesellschaft, 2013), 344.

17. See, on this question, the argument made on redaction-historical grounds by Walter Bührer, "Göttersöhne und Menschentöchter: Gen 6,1–4 als innerbiblische Schriftauslegung," *ZAW* 123 (2011): 495–515, esp. 507–9.

with the report that God has taken notice of a negative feature of humanity—human evil. This becomes the impetus for the biblical version of the flood story, whereas in the Babylonian Atrahasis myth the flood is provoked by the need of certain gods for rest.[18]

Genesis 6:3 addresses the theme of human life expectancy. The reflections that are here placed in the mouth of God are reminiscent of the divine concern that is voiced at the end of the Eden narrative, namely, that humans could become immortal and in this way too like God (Gen 3:22). Confronted with the fact of sexual union between heavenly beings and humans, this divine concern appears to surface once more.[19] The reference back to the Eden narrative makes clearer the etiological intent of Gen 6:1–4. The text once more clearly marks the mortality of humans as the feature that decisively distinguishes them from the immortal divine beings. Further, the reference to a concrete life span reduces the tension between the great ages reached by humans before the flood (see the genealogical list in Gen 5) and the more realistic life spans that one encounters in the stories about the time after the flood.[20] Finally, via the reference to offspring, Gen 6:4 connects the biblical etiological message to the view, widely held in surrounding cultures, that heroes were humans who were born of a divine-human sexual union.[21]

It is not only the parallel structure between Gen 6:1–4 and 6:5–9:19 that makes it difficult to see Gen 6:1–4 as a prelude to the flood narrative. Against such an interpretation is also the fact that none of the actors in the story of sexual union are judged negatively. The story establishes neither what the actual misconduct is nor who the guilty parties are. God's intervention is presented less as punishment than as the consequence of divine reflection on

---

18. For other ancient Near Eastern versions of the story, see, for example, Peter Höffken, "Zuversicht und Hoffnung in Verbindung mit babylonischen Fluttraditionen," in *Die Sintflut: Zwischen Keilschrift und Kinderbuch*, ed. Norbert C. Baumgart and Gerhard Ringshausen, LthB 2 (Münster: LIT, 2005), 53–72.

19. This connection is recognized, for example, by Erich Bosshard-Nepustil, *Vor uns die Sintflut: Studien zu Text, Kontexten und Rezeption der Fluterzählung Genesis 6–9*, BWANT 9.5 (Stuttgart: Kohlhammer, 2005), 209–10; John J. Collins, "The Sons of God and the Daughters of Men," in Nissinen and Uro, *Sacred Marriages*, 259–74; 260; and Bührer, "Göttersöhne," 508.

20. See Bührer, "Göttersöhne," 509.

21. According to Andreas Schüle, *Der Prolog der hebräischen Bibel: Der literar- und theologiegeschichtliche Diskurs der Urgeschichte (Gen 1–11)*, ATANT 86 (Zürich: Theologischer Verlag Zürich, 2006), 236, that a piece of Greek mythology is reformulated here under the auspices of Israelite-Judean creation theology ("dass hier ein Stück griechische Mythologie unter dem Vorzeichen israelitisch-jüdischer Schöpfungstheologie reformuliert wird") is to be understood as an intellectual achievement.

human and divine nature.[22] It is probably an indication of the "philosophical" view of the authors and redactors that the sensitivities of the characters involved are of no interest. It is noteworthy that the male activity of the heavenly beings promotes the view that the divine sphere is masculine-immortal. The earth is seen as an environment appropriate for beings of "flesh," which in the given context can be seen as an anthropological statement referring to the mortality of humans. The term suggests this: that two sexes and reproduction by means of sexuality are essential characteristics of the earthly sphere. Earthy men require a female counterpart and vice versa. In Gen 6:1–4 the women are presented as passive, in correspondence to the androcentric perspective both of the chapter in which the text appears as well as the language used.[23] Within a hetero-normative framework, the women appear as attractively formed creatures, who make it possible for humans/אדם to have descendants. Despite the androcentric point of view, however, there is no particular criticism directed at the women, and the difference between the sexes that the text sketches out is focused exclusively on the command to humans in Gen 1 that they multiply. There is also an allusion to the creation story in the use of the Hebrew word טוב, refering to the beauty of the daughters of humans. If one credits the allusion, the beauty of the women is a reminder of how perfectly God created the world.[24]

3. The Book of Watchers (1 En. 1–36)

3.1. Of Angels, Who Have Gone Doubly Astray, and Humans, Who Emulate Them

What Genesis narrates once in four verses is found in much more expansive form in the so-called Book of Watchers, a text that dates to the third century BCE. It is the oldest nonbiblical version that survives of the account of sexual union. The textual fragments from Qumran allow the conclusion that the original language was Aramaic. In time the Book of Watchers became part of a

22. See, contra the widespread interpretation that this is a story of punishment, Horst Seebass, *Genesis 1: Urgeschichte (1,1–11,26)* (Neukirchen-Vluyn: Neukirchener Verlag, 1996), 188–99; Schüle, *Prolog*, 232–35; Collins, "Sons of God," 261; Losekam, *Sünde*, 42–45; Bührer, "Göttersöhne," 506–7.

23. In Biblical Hebrew the expression "to take a wife for oneself" is a terminus technicus for marriage.

24. See Gen 1:31, according to which God saw all that he had made and pronounced it טוב. The customary translation here of טוב as "good" obscures the connection to Gen 6:2.

larger collection of writings, which is today known as 1 Enoch or the Ethiopic book of Enoch.[25] It is a significant book, as it is most likely the first writing to connect the motif of sexual union to narrative material concerning Enoch, a figure who appears in Gen 5 in the list of preflood ancestors.[26] This linking of the materials proved to be very influential in the period that followed. The Book of Watchers presents itself as the words of blessing of Enoch, addressed to a future generation (see the chart for the development of the structure). In the introduction (1 En. 1–5), Enoch announces a great judgment and contrasts the blessed fate of the righteous with the ominous fate of the "blasphemers," those, in other words, who have committed transgressions. In 1 En. 6 the story begins of the union of heavenly male beings with earthly women. In the Book of Watchers the heavenly protagonists are not "sons of God," as in Gen 6, but rather members of a particular group of angels, the so-called watchers.[27] These angels too take earthly wives for themselves but do not become fathers of "heroes" (Gen 6:4) but rather fathers of rapacious giants. Another difference from Gen 6 is that the watchers bring to humans knowledge that they did not previously have. On earth, all of this leads to great upheavals of the worst kind and to great distress. The first continuation (1 En. 9–11) describes the reaction in the heavenly sphere. Four high-ranking angels ask God for advice about what should be done. God's views on the events have been unknown until this time. The Book of Watchers reveals to its readers that God has a clear plan for dealing with the evil-doers: the angels are to be chained and spend the time before the great judgment in a place under the earth's surface. In the second continuation (1 En. 12–36) Enoch appears as a mediator between the watchers and God. Enoch reveals to them that God has rejected their pleas for forgiveness. On the whole this concluding section strengthens the message that God's plans stand fast and that God is supremely capable and willing to punish transgressions that subvert the order of things and cause suffering, even when the perpetrators are heavenly beings.

---

25. For a German translation, see Siegbert Uhlig, *Das äthiopische Henochbuch*, JSHRZ 5.6 (Gütersloh: Mohn, 1984); for an English translation, George W. E. Nickelsburg and James C. VanderKam, *1 Enoch: A New Translation Based on the Hermeneia Commentary* (Minneapolis: Fortress, 2004); for a French, André Caquot, "I Hénoch," in *La Bible: Écrits intertestamentaires*, ed. André Dupont-Sommer and Marc Philonenko, BP 337 (Paris: Gallimard, 1987), 463–625.

26. According to Gen 5:21–24 Enoch is the seventh patriarch after Adam. He stands out on the list of ancestors, since it it said of him that he "walked with God" and that he was taken up to God at the relatively young age of 365 years, which was interpreted to mean that Enoch, like Elijah, did not die but was carried away. On the question why Enoch was especially suitable for the narrative fusion of traditions, see Bachmann, *Welt*, 228–48.

27. For more on the category of watchers, see John J. Collins, "Watchers," *DDD* 893–95.

Table of the Content and Structure of the Book of Watchers

1 Enoch 1–5: Introduction	Introductory rubric announcing that the theme is the blessing of Enoch on a distant generation Announcement of a great future divine judgment at Sinai
1 Enoch 6–8: Account of sexual union ▪ Exposition (6.1–7.2) ▪ Complication (7.3–8.4)	Narrative of how "in the days of Jared" a group of watchers had sexual intercourse with women and brought knowledge to humans; Depiction of the catastrophic consequences of the angel's deeds
1 Enoch 9–11: First continuation ▪ Resolution I (9–11)	The reaction in heaven; God's plan is revealed to the four high-ranking angels, Michael, Sariel, Rafael, and Gabriel
1 Enoch 12–36: Second continuation ▪ Resolution IIa (12.1–13.3) ▪ Hindering factor (13.4–10) ▪ Resolution IIb (14–36)	Enoch mediates between the watchers and God Enoch brings a plea for forgiveness before God God's plan against the watchers and those who have joined forces with them is confirmed*

* Two narratives of Enoch's journeys (1 En. 17–19 and 1 En. 21–36), among other texts, serve to establish this. On the structure of the different dramaturgical parts of the Book of Watchers, see the detailed investigation of Bachmann, *Welt*, 31–46, esp. 32 (table).

The motif of sexual union plays a central role in the Book of Watchers. The text judges the behavior of the heavenly protagonists very severely and presents it as a violation of God's proper order. According to the Book of Watchers the angels are fully aware that they are behaving wrongly. Even before they descend to earth, the leader of the group of angels remarks: "I fear that you will not want to do this deed, and I alone shall be guilty of a great sin."[28] The group swears an oath that all will participate (1 En. 6.3–5). The

28. Translation by Nickelsburg and VanderKam, *1 Enoch*.

Book of Watchers emphasizes quite broadly that appropriate moral conduct consists of accepting the role determined by God for each being and each species. Creatures are, according to this point of view, good or righteous to the extent that they contribute by their behavior to implementing God's perfect order.[29] On the other hand, they are committing a sin when they upset this order. The angels are accused of exactly this, upsetting the divine order, since according to the Book of Watchers, procreation is intended only for mortal earthly beings—"that nothing fail them on the earth" (15.5). It is precisely for this reason that there are no women among the immortal, heavenly spiritual angels. Inasmuch as they have taken wives for themselves and transmitted to them knowledge that God had not intended for humans (see 13.2; 16.3), the angels have illegitimately transgressed the boundary between heaven and earth. The result of such transgression—both the offspring as well as the application of the newly acquired knowledge on the part of humans—can only be harmful.

The story of sexual union has both a paradigmatic and an etiological function within the context of the Book of Watchers. On the one hand, it demonstrates what it means to transgress God's order. On the other, it shows readers that, fundamentally, humans became victims of the actions of angels and that they will have to suffer the consequences until the final judgment.[30] But it also shows that humans run the risk of imitating the sinful behavior of the angels. The paradigmatic and etiological purposes are combined in a peculiar way, therefore, precisely in connection with the illegimately shared knowledge. This is highlighted by means of the terms used for the areas of knowledge that were, according to the Book of Watchers, appropriately withheld from humans. Mantic arts and metallurgical skills for the preparation of weapons and jewelry as well as knowledge of the preparation of cosmetics are mentioned among the kinds of knowledge shared with humans by the angels (see 7.1; 8.1, 3). Theoretical and practical knowledge in all these areas could be viewed positively as achievements of civilization. The Book of Watchers has the opposite view. By describing them in the way it does, the Book of Watchers categorizes these areas of knowledge as among the problematic desires of the angels; they want more than God has intended for them. When the knowledge is shared with humans, it awakens in them also "the desire for more": to know more, to possess more, and to become more beautiful.[31] Humans—and this is

29. In 1 En. 2–5 the heavenly lights and the trees are cited as examples to follow.

30. See Bachmann, *Welt*, 150–70, for a discussion of the complex art by which the Book of Watchers incorporates readers into present, past, and future.

31. See on this point, in more detail, Bachmann, *Welt*, 68–69. Marie-Theres Wacker, "'Rettendes Wissen' im äthiopischen Henochbuch," in *Rettendes Wissen: Studien zum Fort-*

the message on the text-pragmatic level—should not allow themselves to be led astray by these attractions. Rather they should remain modest and live a god-fearing style of life. What exactly such a style of life looks like is taken for granted as obvious and is not further elaborated in the text.

As for ascertaining the gender-political orientation of the Book of Watchers, it is important to recognize that sexual union is, together with the illegitimate transmission of knowledge, one of the two great sins of which the text accuses the angels. The message of the Book of Watchers builts on the implications of both of them. The sexual sin makes it possible to regard humans as victims of the angels' deeds. Even if it remains unclear—as in Gen 6—what is implied for earthly women to be "taken," the text uses unambiguous language for the suffering of humans on earth after the birth of the rapacious giants (1 En. 7.3–6). Moreover, the giants, who end up in their physical existence fighting against each other and are said to have killed each other (1 En. 10.9; 15.8–16.1), live on as evil spirits who will continue to plague humans until the last judgment.[32] The illegitimate sharing of knowledge makes it possible to understand humans as creatures who have the choice whether to follow the example of the angels or not to do so. All, both men and women, have to make a decision.

3.2. A Text That Assigns More Blame to Women than to Men?

In the view of some exegetes the Book of Watchers assigns women much more blame than it does men for these upheavals that it views so negatively. As for the motif of sexual union, Devorah Dimant states that the Book of Watchers—differently from Gen 6:1–2—mentions the beauty of women directly in connection with mention of their birth and uses two adjectives to do so. Both changes, she concludes, serve to underscore the beauty and attractiveness of women, which in turn is a sign of their seductive nature.[33] Indeed, in the Book of Watchers the text runs as follows:

---

gang weisheitlichen Denkens im Frühjudentum und im frühen Christentum, ed. Karl Löning and Martin Fassnacht, AOAT 300 (Münster: Ugarit-Verlag, 2002), 115–54; 127, speaks of death-bringing knowledge.

32. In this way, as well, an etiology for the existence of demons is provided, based on the story of the watchers. In the section 15.8–16.1 it remains unclear whether the death of the physical part of the giants is caused by the self-destructive behavior mentioned in 10.9 or whether the flood is being referred to. On the rather marginal role of the flood story in the Book of Watchers, see Bachmann, *Welt*, 70–73.

33. See Devorah Dimant, "1 Enoch 6–11: A Fragment of a Parabiblical Work," *JJS* 53 (2002): 229.

> When the sons of men had multiplied, in those days, beautiful and comely daughters were born to them. And the watchers, the son of heaven, saw them and desired them. (1 En. 6.1–2)[34]

However, there are several other pieces of evidence that argue against the thesis that this introduction is a way to ascribe to women an active role as seducers. In the first place 1 En. 6, like Gen 6, describes only the heavenly men as active agents, and the stress put on the fact that they know that they are bringing blame upon themselves is a strong sign that the text has placed men and not the women in the center as troublemakers.[35] Second, the way in which the beauty of the women is described is appropriate for the opening chapters of 1 Enoch, in which God, in the context of an announcement of impending judgment, is presented as the creator of a wonderful and perfect universe. From this point of view the description of the women serves to highlight the negative evaluation of the angels. Instead of recognizing the greatness of God in the natural beauty of the women, which would have been the appropriate response, the angels selfishly misinterpret it as an invitation to sex.[36]

From time to time 1 En. 8.1 and 1 En. 19.1–2 are cited as texts that prove that the Book of Watchers does tendentially accuse the earthly women of seduction. First Enoch 8.1 recounts the story of Asael, the second in command of the angels after Shemihasa; Asael is made primarily responsible for the illegitimate sharing of knowledge. The verse describes how Asael instructs the humans in various branches of knowledge. The translation of George W. E. Nickelsburg has it thus:

> Asael taught men to make swords of iron and weapons and shields and breastplates and every instrument of war. He showed them metals of the earth and how they should work gold to fashion it suitably, and concerning

34. Translation by Nickelsburg and VanderKam, *1 Enoch*. In the Aramaic textual witness 4Q202, the second term for "beautiful" has to be restored (the usual restoration is [שפירן ו[טבן). In one of the two Greek versions (that of Georgios Syncellos) the daughters are described only as *ὡραῖαι*, in the second (Codex Petropolitanus) as *ὡραῖαι καὶ καλαί*. The German translation of Uhlig follows the Ethiopic text tradition, which agrees here with the text of Codex Petropolitanus.

35. For this interpretation, see James C. VanderKam, *Enoch: A Man for All Generations* (Columbia: University of South Carolina Press, 1995), 33.

36. That such a connection has only rarely been recognized in the past may be due to the fact that chapters 6–36 are usually treated separately, distinct from the introductory chapters, which are regarded as secondary. For arguments supporting the conclusion that the introductory chapters were already integral parts of a version of the Book of Watchers from the third century BCE, see Bachmann, *Welt*, 20–25.

> silver, to fashion it for bracelets and ornaments for women. And he showed them concerning antimony and eye paint and all manner of precious stones and dyes. And the sons of men made them for themselves and for their daughters, *and they transgressed and led astray the holy ones.* (1 En. 8.1, emphasis added)[37]

The last sentence is found more or less only in this translation, which coheres with Nickelsburg's judgment on the textual witnesses to this passage.[38] He prefers here the excerpt of the Byzantine Chronographer Georgios Synkellos (G^{s}) dating from the ninth century CE rather than the version in other witnesses. Since only G^{s} speaks of someone who "led astray the holy ones," the question arises why Nickelsburg prefers this version.[39] According to Nickelsburg, G^{s} preserves here an old narrative tradition, in which Asael's instructions stood at the beginning. Shemihasa and his colleagues are led astray by the women as a consequence of these instructions.[40] Nickelsburg correctly observes that in other writings from the time of the Second Temple—the Animal Apocalypse and the book of Jubilees, both of which are from the second century BCE—the motif of instruction is separate from the motif of sexual union and is placed before it in the texts.[41] The fact that none of these writings makes the causal connecton between the two motifs that Nickelsburg postulates as original makes it difficult to use this fact as an argument for the thesis that there was an older version of the story in which the causal connection was made.

By alluding to an old tradition, Nickelsburg is attempting to make the case that the text in G^{s} is not simply an accidental textual corruption. It is methodologically problematic, however, that he does not address the question

37. George W. E. Nickelsburg, *1 Enoch 1: A Commentary on the Book of 1 Enoch, Chapters 1–36; 81–108*. Hermeneia (Minneapolis: Fortress, 2001), 188; see the same translation in Nickelsburg and VanderKam, *1 Enoch*.

38. See the translation of 1 En. 8.1 in Uhlig, *Henochbuch*, who has the tendency to follow the Ethiopic textual tradition: "Und Azāz'ēl lehrte die Menschen Schwerter und Messer, Schilde und Brustpanzer herzustellen, und er zeigte ihnen <die Metalle> und ihre Bearbeitung, Armspangen, Schmuck und den Gebrauch der Augenschminken und der Augenverschönerung und das kostbarste und auserlesenste Gestein und allerlei Farbtinkturen. Und die Welt veränderte sich."

39. For a synopsis of the two Greek textual witnesses that reproduces the Greek of Codex Panopolitanus (G^{a}) and G^{s}, as well as the Aramaic textual witness 4Q202, see Kelley C. Bautch, "Decoration, Destruction and Debauchery: Reflections on 1 Enoch 8 in Light of $4QEn^{b}$," *DSD* 15 (2008): 85.

40. See Nickelsburg, *1 Enoch 1*, 196, and already George W. E. Nickelsburg, "Apocalyptic and Myth in 1 Enoch 6–11," *JBL* 96 (1977): 397–98.

41. See Nickelsburg, *1 Enoch 1*, 195. Both texts will be discussed in more detail in the next section.

whether his explanation is the only one possible or whether there are other ways to explain the text. There are many more scholars who find attested in G^s a secondary type of reception of the story in the Book of Watchers that begins over time to stress the female power of seduction.[42] The most recent investigations into the the working methods of the Byzantine Chronists lend support to such a view.[43]

A second passage in the Book of Watchers that is cited in the debate about the theme of women and seduction is 1 En. 19.1–2. The two verses are part of Enoch's first travel narrative (1 En. 17.1–19.3). In this passage Enoch describes how the angels took him away and showed him various parts of the cosmos, among which one region was especially barren and horrifying. One of the angels accompanying him explained that the place was a prison for the stars and the armies of heaven, for those among them who have "transgressed the commandments of God" (28.15). The first two verses of 1 En. 19 reinforce this message.[44]

The text of 19.1–2 reads as follows:

> And Uriel said to me, "There stand the angels who mingled with the women. And their spirits—having assumed many forms—bring destruction on men and lead them astray to sacrifice to demons as to gods until the day of the

42. See already Küchler, *Schweigen*, 263–64, who in his monograph addresses the arguments presented in Nickelsburg, "Apocalyptic," although Nickelsburg has not responded in any of his subsequent work. Among the scholars who come to conclusions similar to those of Küchler are Collins, "Sons of God," 265; Bachmann, *Welt*, 67 n. 12; and Annette Y. Reed, "Gendering Heavenly Secrets? Women, Angels, and the Problem of Misogyny and 'Magic,'" in *Daughters of Hecate: Women and Magic in the Ancient World*, ed. Kimberly B. Stratton with Dayna S. Kalleres (Oxford: Oxford University Press, 2014), 121–22.

43. For more discussion of this question, see Siam Bhayro, "The Use of Jubilees in Medieval Chronicles to Supplement Enoch: The Case for the 'Shorter' Reading," *Hen* 31 (2009): 10–17. To be noted is also the fact mentioned by Bautch, "Decoration," 82 n. 9, namely, that in G^s in particular the expression "holy ones" can refer generally to "the righteous," in which it differs from the Book of Watchers. See the translation of G^s in this sense in William Adler and Paul Tuffin, *The Chronography of George Synkellos: A Byzantine Chronicle of Universal History from the Creation* (Oxford: Oxford University Press, 2002), 17: "And the sons of men did this for themselves and their daughters and they transgressed and led astray the righteous." Finally, this translation makes it clear how difficult it is to determine who G^s has in mind as the subject of the seduction.

44. In adopting this reading I do not follow the transposition of verses proposed by Nickelsburg, *1 Enoch 1*, who bases his view on older textual traditions. For the arguments against, see Bachmann, *Welt*, 39–43.

> great judgment, in which they will be judged with finality. And the wives of the transgressing angels will become sirens."[45]

It is noteworthy that in Uriel's speech at least two features are thematized that otherwise play no role in the Book of Watchers. First, sin is identified with idolatry (v. 1), and second, the fate of the women who have been taken as wives by the angels has suddenly become a topic of interest. These details, and also the fact that the name "Uriel" otherwise appears only in the second travel narrative, which begins in chapter 21, permit the conclusion that the two verses were interpolated at a later time. This was done under the influence of the second travel narrative and was as well due to the expectations of the copyist or translator who added the supplement.[46] The surviving textual witnesses that preserve verse 2—the verse is attested in one Greek manuscript and in the Ethiopic manuscript tradition—permit several translations. Instead of the version above, the following translation by Daniel Olson is also possible:

> And the wives of the angels who went astray will have peace.[47]

Olson bases his understanding of the text, that the women will have peace, on the Ethiopic textual tradition, in which it is literally stated they "would become as peaceful ones." As a rule, the Ethiopic text is explained as a misreading of a Greek *Vorlage*. Instead of εἰς σειρῆνας ("as sirens") the Ethiopian readers are supposed to have read ὡς εἰρηναῖαι ("as peaceful ones") and translated accordingly.[48] Whichever version one prefers, what is implied by the two versions of the text in terms of a judgment on the women remains an interesting question. According to Olson, the text of the Ethiopic version that he prefers is referring to the freeing of the women from the violence of their angel

45. Nickelsburg, *1 Enoch 1*, 276 (= Nickelsburg and VanderKam, *1 Enoch*, 39).

46. See Bachmann, *Welt*, 81–82; Eibert J. C. Tigchelaar, *Prophets of Old and the Day of the End: Zechariah, the Book of Watchers and Apocalyptic*, OTS 35 (Leiden: Brill, 1996), 158.

47. Daniel C. Olson, *Enoch: A New Translation* (North Richland Hills, TX: Bibal, 2004), 55.

48. See Uhlig, *Henochbuch*, 551, with reference to previous editions of the text that defend the older misreading, such as Nickelsburg, *1 Enoch 1*, 277. For a dissenting point of view, see Olson, *Enoch*, 268–69; Bhayro, "Use of Jubilees," 16. Kelley C. Bautch, "What Becomes of the Angels' 'Wives'? A Text-Critical Study of 1 Enoch 19:2," *JBL* 125 (2006): 797 suggests that the Aramaic *Vorlage* read "and the wives of the transgressing angels will be brought to an utter end," which would mean that both versions, the Ethiopic as well as the Greek, should be regarded as secondary.

husbands.[49] Kelley Coblentz Bautch has stressed the fact that such a view of the fate of the women implies that they were innocent or even the victims of the angels. The text announces that there will be an end to their suffering.[50]

The metamorphosis of the women into sirens, as described in the Greek textual witness, Codex Panopolitanus (G[a]) from the fifth or sixth century CE, is more elusive on gender-political grounds, since it remains unclear what exactly is implied by referring to the women as sirens. In Greek literature—one thinks of Homer's *Odyssey*, for example—sirens are beings who might be associated with a form of seduction that results in death. If the text does have such an image of sirens in mind, it could intend to condemn the women as the seducers of the angels.[51] In any case, in ancient Greece sirens also played a role in the context of grave culture, namely, as the beings that lead the laments.[52] Although the women mentioned in 1 En. 19.1–2 are not necessarily branded as seducers, if the image of the women leading a lament is adopted, one can agree with Bautch that in either interpretation of the text the fate of the women is colored negatively.[53] Max Küchler, who associates the sirens much more strongly with lament than with seduction, remarks somewhat sarcastically that the beautiful and attractive women in 1 En. 6.1 do after all find in 1 En. 19 a "narrative fate": "as specters they sit howling on the ruins of the devastation that came out of their own bellies!"[54]

3.3. Magic as Problem?

The remarks above permit the conclusion that, in the context of the motif of sexual union, there are only a few isolated passages that have traces of an accusation against the daughters of humans. In 1 En. 6.1 we saw that the narrative context, especially the introduction to the Book of Watchers (1 En.

---

49. See Olson, *Enoch*, 269.

50. See Bautch, "What Becomes," 772. Bautch, "What Becomes," 769, n. 15 refers to the fact that several Ethiopic manuscripts also speak of the women as seductresses in 1 En. 19.2, inasmuch as they use a verb form that has the women as subjects and the angels as the objects of the seduction. See appropriately on this point the ambiguous German translation of Uhlig, *Henochbuch*, 551 ("ihre Frauen, die die Engel verführten").

51. Such an association is assumed without question by, for example, Nickelsburg, *1 Enoch 1*, 288, and William Loader, *Enoch, Levi, and Jubilees on Sexuality. Attitudes towards Sexuality in the Early Enoch Literature, the Aramaic Levi Document, and the Book of Jubilees* (Grand Rapids: Eerdmans, 2007), 54.

52. For a discussion of the spectrum of intrepretations, see Bachmann, *Welt*, 42, n. 40, and Bautch, "What Becomes."

53. See Bautch, "What Becomes," 772.

54. Küchler, *Schweigen*, 299.

1–5), does not support the reading that the beauty of the women led them to actively seduce. A closer look at 1 En. 8.1 and 19.2 makes clear that whether or not one discerns an accusation against the women in the text depends above all on the choice of textual witness. Also, those passages which can be read to accuse the women play too small a role in the development of the narrative to subvert the main thrust of the narrative of the Book of Watchers. The book clearly judges—as shown in detail above—the behavior of the angels. Anyone who wishes to argue that there is in 1 En. 8.1 an ancient conception that the women are guilty has at least to acknowledge that very little weight was attached to that conception when in the third century BCE the narrative strands of Enoch, Shemihasa, and Asael were woven together.

One can ask, as some exegetes have already done, whether the Book of Watchers values men and women differently in the instruction motif interwoven with the story of sexual union. It is a disputed question whether the Book of Watchers one-sidedly blames women for the spread of magic and thereby focuses on the women in particular to connect it closely with the cosmic origin of evil.[55] Those who hold such a view usually cite 1 En. 7.1:

> These and all the others with them took for themselves wives from among them such as they chose. And they began to go in to them, and to defile themselves through them, and to teach them sorcery and charms, and to reveal to them the cutting of roots and plants.[56]

But according to Annette Yoshiko Reed, in reaching such a judgment one runs the risk of anachronism. She specificially identifies two dangers: on the one hand, a modern understanding of magic can lead one to impose later judgments of legitimate forms of knowledge back onto the past. On the other, it is tempting to denounce complacently premodern misogyny, which leads us to overlook much that is most interesting in earlier discussions about women, fallen angels, earthly power, and heavenly knowledge.[57] As noted above, the Book of Watchers appears to thematise a variety of teachings throughout 1 En. 7–8, which all in their own way have in view the problem of "desire for

55. See Tal Ilan, "Women in the Apocrypha and the Pseudepigrapha," in *A Question of Sex? Gender and Difference in the Hebrew Bible and Beyond*, ed. Deborah W. Rooke, HBM 14 (Sheffield: Sheffield Phoenix, 2007), 133–34; Rebecca Lesses, " 'They Revealed Secrets to Their Wives:' The Transmission of Magical Knowledge in 1 Enoch," in *With Letters of Light: Studies in the Dead Sea Scrolls, Early Jewish Apocalypticism, Magic, and Mysticism in Honor of Rachel Elior*, ed. Daphna V. Arbel and Andrei A. Orlov, Ekstasis 2 (Berlin: de Gruyter, 2011), 196–222.

56. Translation by Nickelsburg and VanderKam, *1 Enoch*.

57. See Reed, "Heavenly Secrets," 110.

more." A more careful examination shows that none of the areas of knowledge named in the text is regarded as better or worse than the others. Also, women as well as men are explicitly named as adressees of the instruction (see 1 En. 8.1 together with 1 En. 7.1). Moreover, texts such as 1 En. 8.2 and 16.3 suggest that both men and women are included among those who seek to imitate the behavior of the angels. Before the explicit targeting of women is interpreted as evidence of misogyny, it seems to me appropriate, therefore, to examine carefully why the text speaks so explicitly of men and women. This means, in turn, that we need to pay attention to the context in which the Book of Watchers originated. From such a point of view, the explicit reference to women can be understood as the means whereby the author sought to address the widest possible audience in the context of Judea in the Ptolemaic period.[58] In that period it was possible especially for Judeans[59] of the upper class, both men and women, to encounter "the wider world" in a new way. Not all were able to do so, but many women and men were able to profit from Ptolemaic influence in cultural life and the economy. In this context the Book of Watchers can be understood as a programmatic writing, intended to stir up the entire Judean population and to provoke it to return to its traditional way of life and traditional values. Through its play with the paradigmatic and etiological potential of the narrative material of the primordial history, the composers or redactors succeeded in smoothly connecting the new perspectives, which were attractive to many, with the ancient transgressions of the watchers.[60]

Despite this context, it must be admitted, on the basis of verses such as 1 En. 7.1, that the book could later—read selectively—serve circles that wanted to connect magic and femaleness in a contemptuous and misogynistic

58. The widely shared view that the Book of Watchers has sectarian origins ("Konventikelliteratur") is not compatible with this interpretation. On the problems with this preconception, see Bachmann, *Welt*, especially chapters 5.4 and 5.5. Among those who presume a broad audience, see already Marie-Theres Wacker, *Weltordnung und Gericht: Studien zu 1 Henoch 22*, FB 45 (Würzburg: Echter Verlag, 1982), 313.

59. Opinions differ on the question whether or in which cases in the context of early Judaism the Greek word Ἰουδαῖοι (like the Hebrew word יהודים) is more appropriately translated as "Jewish" or "Judean." In principle, both translations are possible. For more on the debate, see the contributions to the discussion in Timothy M. Law and Charles Halton, eds., "Jew and Judean: A Forum on Politics and Historiography in the Translation of Ancient Texts," *Marginalia*, 26 August 2014, http://tinyurl.com/SBL066006c. When I speak in this essay of Judeans, I am referrring to the inhabitants of the territory Judea, that is, the population of the Ptolemaic kingdom whose ethnic origins were in this territory.

60. See, with more detail on the historical horizon of understanding, Bachmann, *Welt*, 249–62.

way. But in especially this situation it is essential to distinguish between the intended meaning and the reception of a text.

3.4. Genesis 6 and the Book of Watchers Compared

Although the Book of Watchers addresses men and women and takes both seriously as victims and as actors,[61] on the whole—as in Gen 6—an androcentric and heteronormative perspective dominates. Whereas the angelic beings are described as "holy ones and spirits, living forever" (1 En. 15.4) and, at least when they interact with humans, appear as male beings,[62] of the humans it is said that they received wives from God in order to procreate (1 En. 15.5). If one follows the reading of the Book of Watchers proposed here, there is another allusion to Gen 6 in the fact that there is no special criticism directed at the women, and their beauty is referred to in the context of an image of God as the creator of a wonderful cosmic order. It remains noteworthy, especially if one thinks of later writings, that the Book of Watchers—to some extent still standing within ancient Near Eastern tradition—does not have a negative attitude to human sexuality. Also alien to the book is the notion that human males might have some kind of heavenly nimbus. Just as angels belong to the heavenly spheres, so human males as well as human females clearly belong to the earthly, mortal human species.[63] The fact that Enoch appears as the mediator between heaven and earth also fits within this picture as a whole, since the Book of Watchers presents him as an earthly figure with a particular mission.[64] On one issue, the text admittedly makes more precise—and thereby restricts—what Gen 6 leaves indeterminate. Inasmuch as the feminine is associated exclusively with the earthy, mortal sphere, and this sphere is clearly distinguished from the heavenly sphere, it, the feminine, is de facto excluded from heaven. In the words of Marie-Theres Wacker: "heavenly women are … apparently a *contradictio in adjecto*."[65]

61. See on this issue also Reed, "Heavenly Secrets," 118.

62. See, besides the watchers who have transgressed, also the "good" angels in 1 En. 9–11.

63. That the circle who produced the book intended the work as an allegory, such that the watchers represent a particular group of priests, is not very plausible. See, for a thorough discussion, Bachmann, *Welt*, 131–48. Interpretations that see in the heavenly figures a specific group of human men, Cainites or Sethites, or simply the righteous, are secondary.

64. 1 Enoch 15.2 points to this special role for Enoch, where God, with ironic undertone, tells Enoch to tell the watchers that humans are not the ones who should intercede for angels but rather angels should be interceding for humans.

65. Wacker, "Rettendes Wissen," 149.

4. Narratives from Seleucid Times: The Animal Apocalypse and Jubilees

In the course of the fifth Syrian War (202–198 BCE), the Seleucid ruler Antiochus III conquered Syro-Palestine and thereby ended Ptolemaic rule over Judea. From this Seleucid period, which lasted until 63 BCE, when the region was incorporated into the Roman Empire by Pompey, there are a number of texts that take up the story of sexual union. The influence of the narrative tradition of the watchers is apparent, since apart from the translation of Genesis into Greek for the Egyptian diaspora, the story is now told practically only in versions that mix together various narrative traditions. None of the texts makes the story of sexual union central, as the Book of Watchers does. One exception is the Book of Giants, which focuses on the progeny of the heavenly-earthly union. Probably in reaction to the narrative traditions that had evaluated the progeny in a more positive light,[66] this text has Enoch prophesy clearly and explicitly the unavoidable, ominous fate of the giant offspring. After the Book of Giants, the Animal Apocalypse (1 En. 85–90) and the book of Jubilees give the most space to the story of sexual union. Both writings thematise it in the context of a particular historical summary that recounts the history of the world since creation.

In the case of the Animal Apocalypse, which today like the Book of Watchers is part of 1 Enoch, the story is told within the narrative frame of one of Enoch's visions.[67] Several distinctive features point to the conclusion that the text preserves reflexes of the political events under Antiochus IV and the Maccabean revolt that followed.[68] Just as in the book of Daniel (Dan 7), the present is identified as a time of adversity marked by persecution and oppression. Humans appear throughout this text in the form of animals, hence the scholarly designation "Animal Apocalypse" or "Animal Vision." The various kinds of animals and with differently colored fur represent various groups of humans. This allegorical form makes it possible to portray the oppression described in the story as the result of bestial rule in the full sense of the word (see 1 En. 90). A vision of a kind of new creation is presented, which allows

---

66. See Loren T. Stuckenbruck, *The Book of Giants from Qumran: Text, Translation, and Commentary*, TSAJ 63 (Tübingen: Mohr Siebeck, 1997), 31–40.

67. For a translation of this text, see Uhlig, *Henochbuch* (German) or Nickelsburg and VanderKam, *1 Enoch* (English). A synopsis of the various textual witnesses is found in Patrick A. Tiller, *A Commentary on the Animal Apocalypse of I Enoch*, EJL 4 (Atlanta: Scholars Press, 1993).

68. See Anathea E. Portier-Young, *Apocalypse against Empire: Theologies of Resistance in Early Judaism* (Grand Rapids: Eerdmans, 2010), 349–52, who recapitulates the arguments against other positions.

humans to become white cattle once again, as they were at the beginning of creation.[69] Unlike the Book of Watchers, the Animal Apocalypse begins the history of evil with Cain's murder of his brother (1 En. 85.3–8). The text appears thereby to stress, already before it refers to the appearance of evil brought about by heavenly beings, that it is part of being human to be able to fall into sin and thereby to produce victims and suffering. The narrative material concerning the watchers is woven into the story thereafter (1 En. 86–87). The act of sharing harmful knowledge is ascribed to a star that is the first to fall. There is a description of how his presence brings into confusion the order of things among the cattle, that is, the humans. The other watchers are described as a group of stars that fell from heaven and, in the form of aroused bulls, mounted the cows grazing on earth. The cows bore rapacious elephants, camels, and asses. As mentioned above, no causal connection is made between the sharing of knowledge and the "taking of women."[70] Like the first star, the later stars appear to have mixed with the herd of cattle with a clear purpose. This interpretation is supported, on the one hand, by the passage that follows. Similarly to the Book of Watchers (1 En. 9–11), 1 En. 88 describes the heavenly emergency measures taken against the stars, who are bound as evil-doers for the time being. That the angels are the chief guilty ones is stressed again in the judgment scene in 1 En. 90.20–27. Just as in the Book of Watchers, it is not humans or, more explicitly, women, but the stars who are named and judged as the first great troublemakers.

The book of Jubilees takes up the material of the Book of Watchers but deals with it in a more complex way than does the Animal Apocalypse.[71] References to the story of sexual union, or to the story of the watchers, are found throughout numerous chapters.[72] At times these references are interwoven

69. This is a reference to the characters Adam and Seth, Adam's third son (see Gen 4:25), who are both described as white cattle or bulls (the Ethiopic word can mean both). Whether there is here a kind of gender transformation of humans or whether the focus on male beings is due only to the androcentric perspective of the text is a question that cannot be answered with any confidence.

70. A point stressed as well by Karina M. Hogan, "The Watchers Traditions in the Book of the Watchers and the Animal Apocalypse," in *The Watchers in Jewish and Christian Traditions*, ed. Angela K. Harkins, Kelley C. Bautch, and John C. Endres (Minneapolis: Fortress, 2014), 116.

71. As in the case of 1 Enoch, fragments of this text were found at Qumran, although it is thanks above all to the Ethiopian church that the contents of the book have been preserved. For translations, see Klaus Berger, *Das Buch der Jubiläen*, JSHRZ 2.3 (Gütersloh: Mohn, 1981) (German) or James C. VanderKam, *The Book of Jubilees*, CSCO 511 (Leuven: Peeters, 1989) (English).

72. Jub. 4.15, 22; 5.1–10; 7.20–25; 8.1–4; 10.1–11.

with narrative traditions found neither in Genesis nor in the Book of Watchers. The book is presented as the revelation given by an angel to Moses when he had climbed Mount Sinai in order to receive the commandments. The angel's speech reveals to readers that in the course of time from creation to the present of Moses a structured, manifest pattern can be discerned, in which Israel from the beginning is given a special role. The recital follows closely the order of events as presented in the biblical book of Genesis, but from time to time the text adds its own accents or adverts to extra-biblical narrative traditions, as in the case of the retelling of Gen 6. The heavenly actors in the sexual union are identified, as in the Book of Watchers, as watchers. The first mention of them is in Jub. 4.15. Unlike in the Book of Watchers, their descent to earth is presented positively in Jubilees. Their task—given to them by God—is to instruct humans:

> In his [Jared's] days the angels of the Lord, who were called Watchers, came down to the earth in order to teach the sons of man, and perform judgment and uprightness upon the earth.[73]

Not until Jub. 8.1–4 is it mentioned that the watchers have apparently also brought harmful and false knowledge. They are said to have inscribed this knowledge on rocks so that a grandson of Noah could find it again after the flood, whereby false knowledge and mischief begins to spread once more. This reference to a negatively qualified teaching of the watchers remains unique. The preceding passages put the sexual union of the watchers with the women in the foreground as their real evil act. Enoch functions according to Jub. 4.22 as a witness to the crime of the angels, as they unite and defile themselves with the daughters of men. That "defilement" means the sexual misdeed of the angels and not the behavior of the women is stressed in Jub. 5.1–10 and 7.20–25.[74] Both sections stand out in that they, differently from Gen 6, recount the story of sexual union in connection with the flood story.[75] That fact that Jubilees places the misdeed, "taking wives," in the center, appears to hang together with the understanding of sin that is predominant in Jubilees. Again and again sexual offences are brought to the fore in order to highlight

---

73. Translation of O. S. Wintermute, "Jubilees," *OTP* 2:62.

74. In the Book of Watchers too there is talk of "defilement." For a critical assessment of the view that this is a reference to the cultically impure state of women during menstruation, see Bachmann, *Welt*, 76–77 n. 33.

75. On the rather more marginal meaning of the flood in the Book of Watchers, see Bachmann, *Welt*, 70–73.

moral decadence.[76] Above all, in Jub. 7.20–25 it is clear that the behavior of the angels, which is evaluated as licentious, is regarded as the cause of the flood. Noah explains to his children that in the end the flood came to earth because of licentiousness, impurity, and unrighteousness. The licentiousness of the watchers has resulted in impurity (Jub. 7.21). Jubilees also thereby clearly has heavenly male not earthly female sexual offences as the origin of evil. Human (hetero-)sexuality within the boundaries established by Jubilees continues to be regarded positively.

5. From the Seducing to the Seduced Angels: 2 Baruch and the Testament of Reuben

As noted in the introduction, in Roman times the garden of Eden story becomes more central. In some circles it begins to be seen as evidence that humanity had failed at the very beginning and that therefore the righteous especially are henceforth confronted with the challenge of living among humans who follow a wicked lifestyle. In this period also the idea arises, for the first time, that human mortality is the consequence of the first human couple's disobedience.[77] From this point of view hope for humans is the prospect of a divine judgment, in which all unrighteousness is avenged and the good triumphs. Precisely for the righteous, who had to suffer during their lifetime, this judgment marks the beginning of a peaceful and joyful new existence. Mortality too will be overcome in this period.

Two texts that thoroughly develop such a view of history are 4 Ezra and 2 Baruch.[78] Both are dated to approximately 100 CE, and both can be understood as texts that respond to the collective crisis of identity after the destruction of the temple in Jerusalem by the Roman general Titus in 70 CE and try to counter a fatalistic attitude. Instead of treating the event as evidence for the failure of God and the faith tradition, both texts incorporate it into a larger theology of history or even a supra-historical framework that stresses the ongoing value of the tradition and the sovereignty of God.

One of the differences that becomes apparent when one compares the two texts concerns the motif of the sexual union. In 4 Ezra it is never mentioned,

---

76. For a thorough discussion, see Loader, *Sexuality*, 113–305.

77. It is disputed whether the misogynist passage Sir 25:24, already represents such a concept. For a critical evaluation, see, for example, Collins, "Before the Fall," 296–301.

78. For German translations, see Joseph Schreiner, *Das 4. Buch Esra*, JSHRZ 5.4 (Gütersloh: Mohn, 1981) (4 Ezra) and A. Frederik J. Klijn, *Die syrische Baruch-Apokalypse*, JSHRZ 5.2 (Gütersloh: Mohn, 1976) (2 Baruch); for a recent English translation, see Michael E. Stone and Matthias Henze, *4 Ezra and 2 Baruch* (Minneapolis: Fortress, 2013).

which is not surprising in light of its presentation of history and humanity. According to 4 Ezra, the world order collapsed not because of a misdeed by some heavenly being, but because of the moral fall of the first human. The text ascribes not only the wicked heart of humans but also especially their mortality to Adam's transgression (see 4 Ezra 3.7). Mortality is seen as a symptom of a corrupt world order.[79] Like Adam, the first peoples too ignored the commandments of God, which disobedience led to the flood.[80] Although 2 Baruch does not fundamentally differ from 4 Ezra in terms of its understanding of history or humanity, it incorporates the story of the sexual union in primeval time into its historical overview. In 2 Bar. 56 an angel interprets Baruch's vision of a cloud that twelve times covers the earth with rain, alternating black or light water. The first episode of black water stands, according to the angel, for Adam's disobedience, with the result not only that humans are mortal but also producing evils such as sickness, boasting, and sexual passion (56.6–8). Second Baruch interprets not only mortality therefore but also, connected to it, sexuality as a symptom of a corrupted world. It is here that connection to the story of sexual union arises. The angel describes how the situation became much worse (56.9–15):

> From these black waters again black were born, and very darkness originated. For he who was a danger to himself was also a danger to the angels. For they possessed freedom in that time in which they were created. And some of them came down and mingled themselves with women. At that time they who acted like this were tormented in chains. But the rest of the multitude of angels, who have no number, restrained themselves. And those living on earth perished together through the waters of the flood.[81]

The text of verse 10 is noteworthy: it states that danger for angels originated in humans. Is this a reference to the daughters of men, and does 2 Baruch mean thereby that they have seduced the angels? In fact the text is reticent about explicitly ascribing guilt. Nevertheless, it is clear that the motif of the angels endangered by humans undermines the conventional interpretation of

79. On the question why the text speaks about Adam and not explicitly about Eve, see Karina M. Hogan, *Theologies in Conflict in 4 Ezra: Wisdom Debate and Apocalyptic Solution*, JSJSup 130 (Leiden: Brill, 2008), 113, esp. n. 24.

80. See 4 Ezra 3.10b–11, where Ezra, speaking to God, continues: "As death upon Adam, so the flood upon them [the first peoples]. But you left one of them, Noah with his household, and all the righteous who have descended from him" (translation by B. M. Metzger, "The Fourth Book of Ezra," *OTP* 1:528.

81. Translation by A. F. J. Klijn, "2 (Syriac Apocalypse of) Baruch," *OTP* 1:641.

the point of the story, that it is the angels who are the great evil-doers (see the Book of Watchers, the Animal Apocalypse, and Jubilees).

The so-called Testament of Reuben strikes a note very different from the texts already examined. It is part of a larger text, which presents itself as the collection of the farewell discourses of the twelve sons of Jacob to their descendants.[82] For the circles in which it was written, contact with sexual lust and the relationship between men and women must have been an urgent theme. Genesis 35:22 provides the point of departure for the Testament of Reuben. In Gen 35:22 it is noted that Reuben had slept with Bilhah, one of his father's wives, a deed that is explicitly criticized in Gen 49:4 as an outrage. The Testament of Reuben allows Reuben to explain his deed and admit that he has done something wicked. It allows him to describe his repentence and point to his brother Joseph as an example. Alluding to the story of Potifar's wife, who wanted to take Joseph as her lover (Gen 39), Reuben states (T. Reu. 4.8):

> You heard how Joseph protected himself from a woman and purified his mind from all promiscuity. He found favor before God and men.[83]

Reuben's use of Joseph as an example illustrates the tendency of the text to ascribe to all women more generally the character of Potifar's wife.[84] Reuben continues (T. Reu. 5.1–3) with the following generalized statement:

> For women are evil, my children, and by reason of their lacking authority or power over man, they scheme treacherously how they might entice him to themselves by means of their looks.… Indeed, the angel of the Lord told me and instructed me that women are more easily overcome by the spirits of promiscuity than are men.

---

82. See, in general on the text, Robert A. Kugler, *The Testaments of the Twelve Patriarchs* (Sheffield: Sheffield Academic, 2001); on its misogynistic tendency, see Ishay Rosen-Zvi, "Bilhah the Temptress: The Testament of Reuben and 'The Birth of Sexuality,'" *JQR* 96 (2006): 65–94. For translations, see Jürgen Becker, *Die Testamente der zwölf Patriarchen*, JSHRZ 3.1 (Gütersloh: Mohn, 1980) (German) or Harm W. Hollander and Marinus de Jonge, *The Testaments of the Twelve Patriarchs: A Commentary*, SVTP 8 (Leiden: Brill, 1985) (English).

83. Tranlation here and elsewhere according to H. C. Kee, "Testament of the Twelve Patriarchs," *OTP* 1:775–828.

84. For an investigation of the (late) antique readings of Gen 39, see Joshua Levinson, "An-Other Woman: Joseph and Potiphar's Wife: Staging the Body Politic," *JQR* 87 (1997): 269–301.

He then connects this image of women to the story of the watchers (T. Reu. 5.6–7)

> For it was thus that they charmed the Watchers, who were before the Flood. As they [the Watchers] continued looking at the women, they were filled with desire for them and perpetrated the act in their minds. Then they [the Watchers] were transformed into human males, and while the women were cohabiting with their husbands, they appeared to them. Since the women's minds were filled with lust for these apparitions, they gave birth to giants. For the Watchers were disclosed to them as being as high as the heavens.[85]

In this text therefore the male heavenly beings are clearly no longer evil-doers who function to relieve both God and humans for the entry of a massive evil into the world. The angels themselves are here merely victims, indeed, victims of the women, who have guilefully awakened sexual desire in the angels.[86] This new version of the story of sexual union invites heterosexual men especially to identify themselves with the angels. After all, both are subject to the same danger—being seduced by women. Heaven and earth are now interlinked as it were through the masculine and so there arises a tendency to see the feminine itself as symptom of a disturbed order.[87] Mental or intellectual control over desire and segregation of the sexes now become important themes (see T. Reu. 6.1–3).

6. Conclusion

Observations on Gen 6, the Book of Watchers, the Animal Apocalypse, and Jubilees have confirmed that the story of the sexual union between heavenly males and terrestrial women began to play an important role in the period of the Second Temple. Combined with narrative traditions about Enoch, it became especially important in the context of reflections on the moral downfall of humanity and on the question why the righteous must suffer in this world. Although certain texts reveal a tendency to accuse terrestrial women of seducing the watchers and thereby to blame them for throwing the world

85. The words in square brackets are added.

86. For a discussion of the curious way that the text describes the sexual union, see Rosen-Zvi, "Bilhah," 76.

87. According to Rosen-Zvi (ibid., 86–87), the Testament of Reuben sees women "not just as a danger or temptation but as the enemy in a constant war between the sexes. Since, moreover, the war against πορνεία plays a crucial role in man's choice between God and Beliar, the struggle against women is in fact the ultimate struggle against Beliar and his authority."

order out of joint, the clear thrust of the central narrative of the Book of Watchers is to show the watchers in a negative light. All of the texts from the Hellenistic period in which the story of sexual union is a theme have the same thrust and do not ascribe any special blame to the women. New Testament texts such as Jude (see v. 6) and 2 Peter (see 2:4) can also be seen as witnesses to this tradition of understanding the story.[88] Thus 1 Cor 11 remains a unique text if it does in fact allude to the story of sexual union explored here. Even where the motif of instruction is found in these Hellenistic texts, there is no tendency to see woman as especially responsible for causing the disastrous turn in world history. All of the narrative traditions remain, however, clearly rooted in an androcentric perspective; one might even suspect that women are regarded as too insignificant to be seen as the guilty ones.

I have not yet referred to a deuterocanonical book that can be brought into an intertextual "dialogue," namely, Tobit. Here, too, there is an account of a kind of sexual boundary-crossing, in which it is not an angel that is involved but the demon Asmodeus. Sarah, a young Israelite woman, who lives with her parents in the diaspora, has become the victim of this demon who desires her. Whenever Sarah meets a man she wants to marry, the demon kills him on the wedding night. Thanks to Raphael, one of the mighty angels of God, she is freed from the clutches of Asmodeus. This story too deals with women and men. On a text-pragmatic level the call to a righteous and god-fearing lifestyle is one of the primary concerns of the text, precisely in a context in which other lifestyles appear to be more advantageous. The text is interesting not only because it shares many of its presuppositions with the Hellenistic versions of the story of sexual union—for example, Sarah too is clearly presented as victim of the lecherous male Asmodeus—but also because the theme of magical knowledge is portrayed positively. The story describes how Raphael teaches Tobias various magical practices. This is not a problem, since the angel is after all acting as the agent of God. This example underscores once again how problematic it would be to interpret the Book of Watchers too quickly as a text that combines women and magic and judges both negatively. For the circle that produced the book, neither magical knowledge itself nor the women appear to have been the problem. Rather the problem was the fact that the watchers shared magical knowledge without divine authorization.[89]

88. See Eric F. Mason, "Watchers Traditions in the Catholic Epistles," in *The Watchers in Jewish and Christian Traditions*, ed. Angela K. Harkins, Kelley C. Bautch, and John C. Endres (Minneapolis: Fortress, 2014), 69–79.

89. In Jubilees, for example, Noah receives instructions on how to deal with demonic plagues. He passes on this magical knowledge to his son Shem (Jub. 10.10–14).

Later versions of the story of sexual union attest that there was displacement in the way that the behavior of the woman was perceived. With slight modifications it was possible to present a very different reading of the story. In particular, a different way of perceiving and valuing sexuality and the feminine appears to have come into play here. The consequences were enormous. This essay has shown that later versions, and other narrative traditions impacted by the point of view expressed in these later versions, influenced how the older narrative traditions were read and continue to be influential even today.

“The Princess Did Provide All Things, as Though I Were Her Own” (Exagoge 37–38): Reading Exodus 2 in the Late Second Temple Era

Hanna Tervanotko

1. Introduction

In her essay “Women of Exodus in Biblical Retellings of the Second Temple Period,” Eileen Schuller points out how ancient Jewish literature rarely refers to women as frequently as it does in the first chapters of Exodus.[1] These chapters introduce us to the Hebrew midwives Shiphrah and Puah (Exod 1:15); Moses’s wife Zipporah (Exod 2:21; 4:25–26; 18:2); Amram’s wife Jochebed, the mother of Moses, Aaron, and Miriam (Exod 6:20);[2] Aaron’s wife Elisheba (Exod 6:23); and Miriam (Exod 15:20–21). More women are referred to anonymously: Exod 2 refers to “a Levite woman” (בת לוי, v. 1),[3] the anonymous sister of Moses (vv. 4, 7–8), and the daughter of Pharaoh (vv. 5–10). Given the density of the female figures in these chapters, on the one hand, and their more rare appearance elsewhere in ancient Jewish literature, on the other hand, it is relevant from the point of view of the reception history of women to ask how the early readers of the book of Exodus interpreted these female figures.

My aim in the first part of the paper is to contribute to this discussion by referring to the treatment of Exod 2:1–10 in the rewritings of Exodus from the late Second Temple era.[4] I will compare the different renarrations with

---

I wish to thank John Collins and Ian Werrett for their help in writing this article.

1. Eileen Schuller, “Women of the Exodus in Biblical Retellings of the Second Temple Period,” in *Gender and Difference in Ancient Israel*, ed. Peggy L. Day (Minneapolis: Augsburg Fortress, 1989), 178–94.

2. According to the MT Jochebed bore Aaron and Moses, whereas the LXX refers to her as the mother of Aaron, Moses, and Miriam.

3. The translations of the Hebrew Bible follow the NSRV.

4. Here I understand the Second Temple era broadly as extending to the end of the first century CE and thus including the texts of Philo and Josephus.

each other and will focus especially on the role of Pharaoh's daughter and her involvement in Moses's formation. As this theme appears in particular in the texts that were composed in Greek, in the second part of my paper I will further analyze the portrayal of Pharaoh's daughter within the cultural context of Hellenistic education and argue that in the texts composed in Alexandria she was considered instrumental for providing Moses's necessary Hellenistic training.

Before moving on with my text analysis, a few words concerning my methodological approach to the texts are needed. First, by talking about *renarrations* and *rewritings*, rather than, for example, *parabiblical texts*, my aim is not to differentiate texts regarding their possible status (i.e., were these texts used the same way or did they enjoy similar "authority"), but to treat them all equally. I assume that all of these texts were composed before a "canon" of the Hebrew Bible was decisively established.[5]

Second, regarding my gender approach, while writing about female figures, my guiding principle has been that placing a female figure at the center of the study is already a methodological choice and can thus be interpreted as a feminist method.[6] In this respect the present study participates in the discussion concerning gender and sex in ancient Jewish literature. When working on texts with sparse references to women, I employ what is called a hermeneutics of suspicion, a methodological principle particularly advocated by Elisabeth Schüssler Fiorenza for the study of ancient texts that lack explicit references to women.[7] Schüssler Fiorenza argues that the scholar should not

---

5. I acknowledge that some texts had already gained a foothold before this time, but our textual witnesses, most importantly the Dead Sea Scrolls, suggest that the list of authoritative scriptures was not closed. Moreover, texts that refer to an exact number of canonical books do not agree on the number of these books. See Josephus, *C. Ap.* 1.37–43; 4 Ezra 14:45. For discussion, see Steve Mason, "Josephus and His Twenty-Two Book Canon," in *The Canon Debate: The Origins and Formation of the Bible*, ed. L. M. McDonald and J. A. Sanders (Peabody, MA: Hendrickson, 2002), 110–27.

6. E.g., Cecilia Wassen, *Women in the Damascus Document*, AcBib 21 (Atlanta: Society of Biblical Literature, 2005), 14–15; Bernadette Brooten, "Early Christian Women and Their Cultural Context: Issues of Method in Historical Reconstruction," in *Feminist Perspectives on Biblical Scholarship*, ed. Adela Yarbro Collins, SBLCP 10 (Chico, CA: Scholars Press, 1985), 65–91. Marie-Theres Wacker, "Methods of Feminist Exegesis," in *Feminist Interpretation: The Bible in Women's Perspective*, ed. Luise Schottroff, Silvia Schroer, and Marie-Theres Wacker, trans. Martin Rumscheidt and Barbara Rumscheidt (Minneapolis: Fortress, 1998), 63–82, does not deal with feminist exegesis as a method of its own, but rather as a tool to reveal matters in the text that are relevant for research concerning women.

7. The term *hermeneutics of suspicion* was coined by Paul Ricoeur, *Freud and Philosophy: An Essay on Interpretation*, trans. Denis Savage (New Haven: Yale University Press,

settle with this first impression but ask critically why women are absent from the narrative and if it is nevertheless possible that the text tells something about women, even when they are not mentioned. In my view, the method of hermeneutics of suspicion is particularly well-suited for the study of renarrations. By detecting how literary traditions reflecting women, for example, early interpretations of Exod 2:1–10, varied we discover how different authors interpreted women in different contexts.

2. Exodus 2 Rewritten

2.1. Jubilees

Jubilees is a second century BCE text that renarrates Genesis–Exodus events. The framework of Jubilees is Moses's stay on Mount Sinai for forty days and forty nights during which time an angel reveals to him the history of events from the creation of the world to the present moment.[8]

> 47.1 During the seventh week, in the seventh year, in the forty-seventh jubilee, your father came from the land of Canaan. You were born during the fourth week, in its sixth year, in the forty-eighth jubilee, which was the time of distress for the Israelites. 2. The pharaoh, the king of Egypt, had given orders regarding them that they were to throw their sons—every male who was born—into the river. 3. They continued throwing (them in) for seven months until the time when you were born. Your mother hid you for three months. Then they told about her. 4. She made a box for you, covered it with pitch and asphalt, and put it in the grass at the riverbank. She put you in it for seven days. Your mother would come at night and nurse you, and during the day your sister Miriam would protect you from the birds. 5. At that time Tarmuth, the pharaoh's daughter, went out to bathe in the river and heard you crying. She told her *slaves* to bring you, so they brought you to her. 6. She took you out of the box and pitied you. 7. Then your sister said to her: "Should I go and summon for you one of the Hebrew women who will care for and nurse this infant for you?" [She said to her: "Go."] 8. She went and summoned your mother Jochebed. She gave her wages and she took care of

1970), 28–36. For Schüssler Fiorenza's employment of hermeneutics of suspicion, see, e.g., Elisabeth Schüssler Fiorenza, "The Will to Choose or to Reject: Continuing Our Critical Work," in *From Feminist Interpretation of the Bible*, ed. Letty M. Russell (Philadelphia: Westminster, 1985), 125–36; Schüssler Fiorenza, "Remembering the Past in Creating the Future: Historical-Critical Scholarship and Feminist Biblical Interpretation," in Collins, *Feminist Perspectives*, 55–64.

8. For the date and history, see, e.g., James C. VanderKam, *The Book of Jubilees* (Sheffield: Sheffield Academic, 2001), 17–21.

> you. 9. Afterwards, when you had grown up, you were brought to the pharaoh's daughter and became her child. Your father *Amram* taught you (the art of) writing. After you had completed three weeks [= twenty-one years], he brought you into the royal court.[9]

The first woman to appear in the narrative concerning Moses is his mother, who is said to hide the baby for three months. After that the passage reads "then they told about her" (Jub. 47.3), thus indicating that somehow the hiding was made public or that someone reported about it. Here the Jubilees narrative differs from Exod 2:3, which only mentions that the mother could not hide him any longer (see "When she could hide him no longer she got a papyrus basket for him"). In the following verse (Jub. 47.4) the mother seeks a new asylum for him, places him in a box, puts it on the riverbank, and continues nursing him. The author explains that this happened during the night, perhaps indicating that it happened secretly. While the mother is not with Moses during the day, his sister Miriam is there. Remarkably throughout the passage the mother appears as an anonymous character, and it is only at Jub. 47.8 that the author finally calls her Jochebed. This implies that this name was already connected with the Moses tradition and the Levite family (see Exod 6:20; Num 26:59).[10]

Regarding the sister of Moses of Exod 2:4 the author of Jubilees makes some significant modifications. Most important, whereas in Exodus the sister remains anonymous, in the Jubilees narrative this sister is identified as Miriam (Jub. 47.4). Another change in relation to the Exodus text is Miriam's motive for being around Moses. According to Exod 2:4 the anonymous sister simply wants to know what happens to Moses ("His sister stood at a distance, to see what would happen to him"). In contrast, according to Jub. 47.4 the sister remains close to Moses in order to protect him from birds during the day-

---

9. Translation by James C. VanderKam, *The Book of Jubilees: A Critical Text*, CSCO 510, SAeth 87 (Leuven: Peeters, 1989). For a discussion concerning different witnesses to the passage of Jub. 47.1–8, see VanderKam, *Book of Jubilees*, 305–7.

10. Scholars have pointed out that the writer of Jubilees deals with Jochebed atypically for the general style of the text. Whereas elsewhere the writer spends a great deal of time analyzing the pedigrees of the female figures, strikingly the family lineage of Jochebed is not studied at all! The degree of consanguinity between Moses's parents caused a problem for the writer of Jubilees, who prohibited unions between aunt and nephew. Thus, instead of referring to it, the author avoids it as much as possible. For discussion, see Betsy Halpern-Amaru, *The Empowerment of Women in the Book of Jubilees*, JSJSup 60 (Leiden: Brill, 1999), 123; William Loader, *Enoch, Levi and Jubilees on Sexuality: Attitudes towards Sexuality in the Early Enoch Literature, the Aramaic Levi Document, and the Book of Jubilees* (Grand Rapids: Eerdmans, 2007), 294–95.

time.[11] It is uncertain why the birds were expected to pose a threat to Moses, but for the writer of Jubilees the birds represented some danger; that is, they could be explained as messengers of Mastema, the adversary.[12] In the next verse, the author turns to the daughter of Pharaoh (Jub. 47.5). According to the Jubilees version this woman, whose name is Tarmuth, hears the crying (in contrast to Exod 2:5 where she sees the basket) and asks her slaves to bring it to her.

Next, the sentence "your father Amram taught you the art of writing" (Jub. 47.9) is of interest. As an education-theme does not appear in the Exod 2:1–10 version of Moses's childhood, it should be viewed as a creative addition by the author of Jubilees.[13] The author has an interest in texts and connects Moses's ancestors with them. Jubilees 45.15 attests to Amram's grandfather Levi inheriting his books from Jacob: "He gave all his books and the books of his fathers to his son Levi so that he could preserve them and renew them for his sons until today." Given how rare books and literacy were in antiquity, reference to books should be read as a sign that the author of the text considered Jacob and his son Levi as educated. Moreover, as Jacob *inherited* the books, the narrative implies that they had once belonged to the previous generations. This passage does not reveal *which books* Levi received, that is, with which books the author connected the family.[14] However, as the offspring is asked to *renew* them, the passage implies that their task was not only to keep them but to actively use them.

11. Loader, *Enoch, Levi and Jubilees on Sexuality*, 186, points out Miriam's protective role only during the day, whereas the mother protects Moses in the night.

12. Halpern-Amaru, *Empowerment of Women in the Book of Jubilees*, 123, points out that Jub. 11.11–13, 18–21 mentions birds in relation to Mastema, the term for Satan in the book of Jubilees. Therefore in her view the reference to the birds in 47.4 could likewise be interpreted as a sign of Mastema. See Halpern-Amaru, "Protection from Birds in the Book of Jubilees," in *"Go Out and Study the Land" (Judges 18:2): Archaeological, Historical and Textual Studies in Honor of Hanan Eshel*, ed. Aren M. Maeir, Jodi Magness, and Lawrence H. Schiffman, JSJSup 148 (Leiden: Brill, 2011), 59–68.

13. An emphasis on Amram's presence is noted also by Schuller, "Women of the Exodus," 183–84. For the development of the figure of Amram in the literature of the Second Temple era, see Pieter van der Horst, "Moses' Father Speaks Out," in *Flores Florentino: Dead Sea Scrolls and Other Early Jewish Studies in Honor of Florentino García Martínez*, ed. Anthony Hillhorst, Émile Puech, and Eibert Tigchelaar, JSJSup 122 (Leiden: Brill, 2007), 491–98.

14. Florentino García-Martínez, "Les rapports avec l'écriture des textes araméens trouvés à Qumrân," in *The Old Testament Pseudepigrapha and the Scriptures*, ed. Eibert J. C. Tigchelaar, BETL 270 (Leuven: Peeters, 2014), 19–40, points out that tradition is passed forward through a chain of tradition that goes from Enoch to Levi in Jubilees.

It seems relevant to look for links between Jubilees and other texts that pay particular attention to the members of the Levite family. Notably, the Aramaic Levi Document deals with Levi's interest in books. There Levi summons his children and highlights the importance of books and texts (13.15–16): "And now my sons, reading and writing and the teaching of wi[sdo]m which I lea[rned] I saw … [ ] you will inherit them…."[15] In this fragmentary passage Levi addresses his offspring, perhaps his son Qahat, and his grandson Amram. Levi highlights reading, writing, and teaching of wisdom and seems to suggest that books and education are an integral part of his offspring's inheritance.

I would like to suggest that the author of Jubilees had this broader background of teaching through texts in mind when composing Jub. 47.9. It was important for the author to highlight that Amram, who otherwise is absent in Exod 2:2–10 and also in Jubilees's version of the passage, took heed of his son's education.[16] In a similar way to the other texts that highlight the Levite lineage and where teaching goes from father to son in different generations, the author of Jub. 47.9 specified that Amram taught his son Moses.

2.2. Exagoge

Our second example of rewriting Exod 2 is Exagoge, another text that gives special attention to Moses's birth and childhood.[17]

> And with regard to Moses being exposed by his mother in the marsh, and being taken up and reared by the king's daughter, Ezekiel the tragic poet narrates the events, taking up the story from the beginning, when Jacob and those that were with him came into Egypt to Joseph. Introducing Moses as the speaker, he says: … 12. He [Pharaoh] ordered next the Hebrew race to

15. וכען בני ספר ומוסר ח[כ]מה אלפ[ת]חזית ת..[ ]חו תרתון אנון. The edition and translation follow Jonas C. Greenfield, Michael Stone, and Esther Eshel, *The Aramaic Levi Document: Edition, Translation, Commentary*, SVTP 19 (Leiden: Brill, 2004).

16. For the connection of Jubilees with the testament texts, see, Michael E. Stone, "The Axis of History at Qumran," in *Pseudepigraphic Perspectives: The Apocrypha and Pseudepigrapha in Light of the Dead Sea Scrolls, Proceedings of the International Symposium of the Orion Center, 12–14 January 1997*, ed. Esther G. Chazon and Michael E. Stone, STDJ 31 (Leiden: Brill, 1999), 133–49; Hanna Tervanotko, "A Trilogy of Testaments: The Status of the Testament of Qahat versus Texts Attributed to Levi and Amram," in Tigchelaar, *Old Testament Pseudepigrapha and the Scriptures*, 41–59.

17. The text is often quoted as "Ezekiel the Tragedian," but I prefer referring to it by its title. For studies on Exagoge, consult, e.g., Howard Jacobson, *The Exagoge of Ezekiel* (Cambridge: Cambridge University Press, 1983); R. G. Robertson, "Ezekiel the Tragedian," *OTP* 2:803–19; Pierluigi Lanfranchi, *L'Exagoge d'Ezéchiel le Tragique: Introduction, texte, traduction et commentaire*, SVTP 21 (Leiden: Brill, 2006).

> cast 13. their infant boys into the river deep. 14. At which point, she who bore me from her womb 15. did hide me for three months, as she declared. 16. But when found out, she robed me and exposed 17. me in the marsh hard by the river's edge, 18. and Miriam, my sister, watched close by. 19. The sovereign's daughter, with her maidens, then 20. came down to bathe her limbs, as her wont. 21. And straightaway seeing me, she took me up: 22. she knew that I was of the Hebrew race. 23. My sister, running to the princess, said, 24. Shall I quickly fetch this child a nurse 25. of Hebrew stock? The princess pressed her on: 26. she came and told my mother, who with haste 27. did come herself, and took me in her arms. 28. The sovereign's daughter then said, Woman, nurse 29. this child and I will render you a wage. 30. And she, the princess, named me "Moses" since 31. she took me from the river's soggy shore. 32. And seeing that my infancy had passed, 33. my mother led me to the princess' rooms; 34. but first all things she did declare to me 35. pertaining to my father's God and race. 36. Throughout my boyhood years the princess did 37. for princely rearing and instruction apt, 38. provide all things, as though I were her own.[18]

Regarding the women of this text, one should first consider Moses's mother. Similar to the passage in Jubilees, when the text says that the mother's actions were found out, the author of Exagoge is implying that Moses was hidden (l. 16). After this, the narrative returns to the mother in line 26 when Miriam fetches her to nurse the child and she comes with haste. Finally, the mother appears again in line 33 when the author addresses Moses's education. In these contexts the first person narrator Moses refers explicitly to "my mother."

The figure of Miriam is also outlined in Exagoge. Miriam watches from "close by" what happens to Moses (l. 18). Here the writer of Exagoge employs the Greek verb "to watch closely" or "to observe" (κατοπτεύω).[19] This interpretation was probably not the author's own but came from the LXX translation of the Hebrew Bible where the figure of Miriam and her watching over Moses was given a more intense significance with the verb "to observe" (κατασκοπεύω, Exod 2:4 LXX).[20] The term "near" that appears in the same line emphasizes the physical closeness of Miriam.[21] It has been suggested that this emphasis on Miriam's proximity was made in order to clarify that the sister did not stay as far away as could be concluded from reading Exod 2:4 where

---

18. Trans. Robertson, "Ezekiel the Tragedian," 2:808–819. According to Robertson (808 n. a), the opening statement of the passage goes back to Alexander Polyhistor.

19. LSJ, s.v. "κατοπτεύω." For the Greek text, see Eusebius, *Einleitung, die Bücher I bis X, Werke*, part 1 of *Eusebius Werke: Die Praeparatio Evangelica*, ed. Karl Mras (Berlin: Akademie-Verlag, 1982), 524–26.

20. LSJ, s.v. "κατασκοπεύω."

21. LSJ, s.v. "πέλας."

she stays at a distance.[22] It should be pointed out that in the Exagoge's account of Exod 1–2, Miriam is the only family member whose name is preserved in the text (l. 18). While Moses's mother is referred to several times she is never mentioned by name. Even more striking is that Moses's father is completely absent from the Exagoge's reworking of Exod 2.[23]

The third woman who appears in this narrative is Pharaoh's daughter. Line 19 tells that bathing was her habit, a detail that is not present in the Exodus or Jubilees narratives. According to Exagoge, immediately after seeing Moses, she took him, and the author specifies that she recognized him as a Jewish child (l. 22). Lines 32–38 of Exagoge narrate later events, that is, those that follow Exod 2:10 chronologically but that are not told in the Hebrew Bible. Here the author of Exagoge elaborates on Moses's upbringing. While in Jub. 47.9 it is Amram who is presented as the instructor of his son ("Your father *Amram* taught you [the art of] writing"), in Exagoge remarkably the two women, Moses's mother and Pharaoh's daughter, are entirely responsible for his upbringing, and their educational activities are referred to in various places.

First, the opening lines to Exagoge read: "and with regards to Moses … being taken up and reared by the king's daughter." This sentence implies that according to at least some ancient sources the role of Pharaoh's daughter was not only to rescue Moses from the river but also to rear and educate him. Pharaoh's daughter's educational role is also highlighted in lines 36–37 where the author emphasizes how the princess did everything that was apt for Moses's royal upbringing. "As if I were her own" in line 38 implies that the princess brought up Moses as an adoptive child.[24]

Second, the author does not limit Moses's education to his life in the palace but highlights the contribution of Moses's mother. Lines 34–35 read that before taking Moses to the princess, she first taught him everything

22. Jacobson, *Exagoge of Ezekiel*, 76. See "His sister stood at a distance, to see what would happen to him."

23. The absence of Amram is particularly striking because the LXX assumes his presence in Exod 2:2–3 by referring to both mother and father: "Now when they saw it was handsome, they sheltered it for three months. But when they could hide it no longer." Trans. Larry J. Perkins, "Exodus," in *A New English Translation of the Septuagint and the other Greek Translations Traditionally Included under that Title*, ed. Albert Pietersma and Benjamin G. Wright (New York: Oxford University Press, 2007). Here the LXX runs against the MT, which refers to the mother only: "The woman conceived and bore a son; and when she saw that he was a fine baby, she hid him for three months. When she could hide him no longer."

24. Robertson, "Ezekiel the Tragedian," 809 n. p, for references in Josephus, Philo, and Artapanus to the fact that Moses was legally adopted.

pertaining to "my father's God and race." This statement is interesting when it is compared with Jub. 47.9, which assigns Moses's teaching to Amram. I will return to this topic below.

2.3. *De vita Mosis* 1.9–33

When Philo reworks Exod 2 in *De vita Mosis*, the first woman to appear is Moses's mother.[25] She is referred to in *Mos.* 1.7, where the background of the birth story is given, and Philo describes Moses's parents as ideal spouses to one another: "He had for his father and mother the best of their contemporaries, members of the same tribe, though with them mutual affection was a stronger tie than family connections" (*Mos.* 1.7).[26] Such emphasis on emotions is highly exceptional and suggests that the union between the parents was not merely based on convenience.[27]

Moses's mother appears again in *Mos.*1.9 where Philo explains that the child was kept at home and fed from his mother's breast for three months until *they* could not hide him anymore. Here the author seems to follow the LXX, which talks about the parents in the plural in Exod 2:2–3.[28] The mother appears again more explicitly in section 17, where she is fetched to nurse him. Then the child apparently remains with his mother and nurse until he no longer needs infant's milk and goes to live with Pharaoh's daughter ("as he grew and thrived without break, and was weaned at an earlier date than they had reckoned, his mother and nurse in one brought him to her from whom she had received him, since he had ceased to need an infant's milk," *Mos.* 1.18). In this version of Exod 2, the role of the mother is entirely limited to nursing. The boy's sister appears in *Mos.* 1.12, where Philo relates that she stays there

25. Philo of Alexandria lived ca. 20 BCE–50 CE. Philo's dates can be established rather securely. A known date is his trip to Rome heading a delegation that took place around 40 CE. Philo writes about it in his *Legatio ad Gaium*. Josephus also records this event in *A.J.* 18.257.

26. Quotations from Philo follow the translation of Francis Henry Colson, G. H. Whitaker, and Ralph Marcus, trans. *Philo*, 10 vols. and 2 supplementary vols, LCL (Cambridge: Harvard University Press, 1929–1962).

27. Philo's emphasis on emotions is an interesting detail, as such a motif is unusual in these early Jewish texts. Spouses are described as having obligations towards one another, but only seldom is true companionship referred to in the texts. Michael L. Satlow, *Jewish Marriage in Antiquity* (Princeton: Princeton University Press, 2001), 249, points out that spouses are mostly dealt with from the perspective of a family with its biological ties rather than as two individuals with mutual feelings.

28. See above, n. 23.

because she is moved by her parents' reaction. Philo adds he thinks this was the divine will. Thus, she does not have any autonomy in this.

While the roles of the mother and sister are reduced, Philo's account of the Pharaoh's daughter, whom he calls the "king's daughter," is much more elaborate than in the previously analyzed passages. Philo starts (1.13) by stating that the daughter was an only child, and she was married for a long time. It was her desire to have a child and provide a successor for her father. Philo reports her depression at not having children and explains that usually she would not go out to bathe but on this particular day she went to the river with her maids. Here Philo's narration differs drastically from Exagoge where the bathing is described as her usual habit (1.20). The princess sees the child (*Mos.* 1.14) and approves his beauty (*Mos.* 1.15). Philo mentions the baby's weeping and that the king's daughter felt pity for him, but her decision to take him seems to be influenced, more than anything else, by her desire to become a mother as "her heart was now moved to feel for him as a mother for her own child" (*Mos.* 1.15). Thus, in this passage, Philo emphasizes that Moses's adoption into the royal house happened not least because of emotional reasons: Pharaoh's daughter was longing to become mother and by taking Moses she nourished her own personal desire.

Later Moses is brought to the princess, who takes care of him and brings him up as a prince.[29] Here Philo makes a long excursion on Moses's studies and his talents. Teachers from different parts, for example, Egypt and Greece, come to instruct him (*Mos.* 1.21), and his studies included arithmetic; geometry; the lore of metre, rhythm, and harmony; and also music (*Mos.* 1.23).[30] Apart from these subjects he also studied philosophy and had Greeks to teach him "the rest of the regular school course" (*Mos.* 1.23), which would usually include "grammar, literature, rhetoric, logic, and perhaps astronomy."[31]

Philo's extensive treatment of Moses's studies and his talents (*Mos.* 1.20–31) reveals his interest in this topic. Philo deals with this theme already in his introduction to the birth of Moses in *Mos.* 1.8 where he writes that "he was brought up as a prince, a promotion due to the following cause...." Therefore,

---

29. "Seeing him so advanced beyond his age, she conceived for him an even greater fondness than before, and took him for her son.... So now, he received as his right the nurture and service due to a prince" (*Mos.* 1.19–20).

30. Colson, Whitaker, and Marcus, *Philo*, 6:286–87 n. c, points out that Philo may depend on Plato here, who in *Leg.* 656d, 799a, and 819a refers to mathematics, music, and dancing as "the subjects most stressed by Egyptians" (Plato, *Books 1–6*, vol. 1 of *Laws*, trans. R. G. Bury, LCL 187 [Cambridge: Harvard University Press, 1926]).

31. Colson, Whitaker, and Marcus, *Philo*, 6:288 n. a.

it seems to be important for Philo to explain that not only was Moses an educated man, but that he received the best education available.

Later Philo once refers to Moses's adoptive parents while discussing Moses's attitude toward his families: "Moses ... estimating the claims of his real and his adopted parents like an impartial judge, he requited the former with good feeling and profound affection, the latter with gratitude for their kind treatment of him" (*Mos.* 1.32–33). This passage where the author addresses Moses's two parents raises a question about the presence of the princess's husband in Moses's life. Philo clearly assumes that she was married (see *Mos.* 1.13, 32–33). Despite this, he does not refer to the princess's husband more explicitly, and as a matter of fact he states that Moses's education in the palace was a result of the princess adopting him. As Philo never mentions the husband, he seems to deal with Moses's royal upbringing entirely as the princess's enterprise.

2.4. Liber antiquitatum biblicarum 9.9–16

Liber antiquitatum biblicarum (LAB) is a Jewish composition that was probably originally composed in Hebrew in the first century CE but currently survives only in Latin.[32] This composition contains a version of Moses's birth narrative.

> 9.9. And Amram from the tribe of Levi went out and took a wife from his own tribe. When he had taken her, others followed him and took their own wives. 10. And this man had one son and one daughter; their names were Aaron and Miriam. And the spirit of God came upon Miriam one night, and she saw a dream and told it to her parents in the morning, saying, "I have

32. The text is often quoted as "Pseudo-Philo." For the origin of the title, see Guido Kisch, *Pseudo-Philo's Liber Antiquitatum Biblicarum*, PMS 10 (Notre Dame: The University of Notre Dame, 1949), 3–5. Other fundamental studies on LAB include Leopold Cohn, "An Apocryphal Work Ascribed to Philo of Alexandria," *JQR* 10 (1898): 277–332; Charles Perrot and Pierre-Maurice Bogaert, in collaboration with Daniel J. Harrington, *Les Antiquités Bibliques*, 2 vols., SC 230 (Paris: Cerf, 1976); Frederick J. Murphy, *Pseudo-Philo: Rewriting the Bible* (New York: Oxford University Press, 1993); Howard Jacobson, *A Commentary on Pseudo-Philo's Liber Antiquitatum Biblicarum with Latin Text and English Translation 1–2*, AGJU 31 (Leiden: Brill, 1996); Bruce Norman Fisk, *Do You Not Remember? Scripture, Story and Exegesis in the Rewritten Bible of Pseudo-Philo*, JSPSup 37 (Sheffield: Sheffield Academic, 2001). For the first century date, see, e.g., Perrot and Bogaert, *Les Antiquités Bibliques*, 2:67–70; and Daniel J. Harrington, "Pseudo-Philo," *OTP* 2:299. For proposals regarding a later date, see Jacobson, *Liber Antiquitatum Biblicarum*, 209, who thinks the most plausible date is sometime in the second century CE.

> seen this night, and behold a man in a linen garment stood and said to me, 'Go and say to your parents, Behold he who will be born from you will be cast forth into the water; likewise through him the water will be dried up. And I will work signs through him and save my people, and he will exercise leadership always.'" And when Miriam told of her dream, her parents did not believe her. 11. The strategy of the king of Egypt, however, prevailed against the sons of Israel, and they were humiliated and worn down in making bricks. 12. Now Jochebed conceived from Amram and hid him in her womb for three months. For she could not conceal him any longer, because the king of Egypt appointed local chiefs who, when the Hebrew women gave birth, would immediately throw their male children into the river. And she took her child and made for him an ark from the bark of a pine tree and placed the ark at the bank of the river. 13. Now that child was born in the covenant of God and the covenant of the flesh. 14. And when they had cast him forth, all the elders gathered and quarreled with Amram saying, 'Are not these our words that we spoke, it is better for us to die without having sons than that the fruit of our womb be cast into the waters?' and Amram did not listen to those who were saying these words. 15. Now Pharaoh's daughter came down to bathe in the river, as she had seen in dreams, and her maids saw the ark. And she sent one, and she fetched and opened it. And when she saw the boy and while she was looking upon the covenant (that is, the covenant of the flesh), she said, 'It is one of the Hebrew children.' 16. And she took him and nursed him. And he became her own son, and she called him by the name Moses. But his mother called him Melchiel. And the child was nursed and became glorious above all other men, and through him God freed the sons of Israel as he had said.[33]

With regard to Moses's mother, the author preserves the name of Jochebed in LAB 9.12.[34] This author adds the reason for abandoning Moses: Jochebed cannot keep him because of the local chiefs (LAB 9.12), and she decides to hide him (LAB 9.13). The author explicitly mentions that before Moses's birth Amram and his wife already had two children: Aaron and Miriam (LAB 9.9). In LAB 9.10 the author turns to the figure of Miriam more specifically and narrates her dream vision concerning Moses's birth.[35] In the dream God's

33. Trans. Harrington, "Pseudo-Philo," 2:315–36.

34. It seems that the author was indeed familiar with the union between Amram and Jochebed but purposely avoids discussing their close kinship. I have dealt with the reasons why this motif was excluded from Jubilees above (see n. 10).

35. While often in ancient Jewish literature it can be difficult to distinguish between a dream and a vision, in LAB 9.10 the terminology points to a dream (Lat. *somnium*) that Miriam saw. That may imply that it was a nocturnal experience. Cohn ("Apocryphal Work of Philo of Alexandria," 318) notes that the mention of Miriam's prophecies concerning her younger brother appear in various midrashim: e.g., b. Sotah 12b; Exod. Rab. 2.4.

messenger appears to Miriam and makes an announcement. The text refers to "a man [Lat. vir] in white linen."[36] Apart from announcing Moses's birth, Miriam's dream makes a reference to future events. The content of the dream declares: "likewise through him the water will be dried up." This is clearly an allusion to the events of the crossing of the Sea of Reeds (Exod 14–15).[37] When the author turns to deal with Moses's birth and the following events, that is, Moses's mother hiding the baby, Miriam is not included in the narrative. Her exclusion from the rest of the narrative is somewhat surprising given her importance in the beginning of this LAB passage. Meanwhile, the elders remind Amram about their earlier words, that is, that it is better not to have children than to have them thrown into the river. This seems to refer to LAB 9.2 where the elders ask that no man approach his wife. Thus, the author of the text suggests that the people abstained from sexual relations.

Liber antiquitatum biblicarum 9.15–16 concentrates on Pharaoh's daughter, who, similar to Miriam, has a dream.[38] The context suggests that she did not usually bathe in the river, but because of her dream she did this time. Here the author of LAB shares a similar interpretation of the events with Philo, who likewise describes the princess' bathing as an exceptional event. The mention of the dream that has instructed her emphasizes that it is a part of a divine plan.[39] Her maids see Moses's ark. This follows loosely Exod 2:5 of the MT, where Pharaoh's daughter sees the basket ("She saw the basket among the reeds and sent her maid to bring it"), but it differs from Jub. 47.5, where the princess hears Moses crying. As crying is not emphasized here, the element of pity is also missing.[40]

Liber antiquitatum biblicarum 9.16 continues: "she nursed him. And he became her son." In contrast to Exagoge and *De vita Mosis*, this remark seems to indicate that Pharaoh's daughter nursed Moses and perhaps adopted him

---

36. The following scholars have argued that the man was an angel: Perrot and Bogaert, *Les Antiquités Bibliques*, 2:59–63; Murphy, *Pseudo-Philo*, 59. Jacobson, *Liber Antiquitatum Biblicarum*, 419–21, finds the description of the figure similar to the angel that appears to Joshua at Josh 5:13 and to the divine figure of Dan 8:15. The claim finds the most concrete support in the Jewish Scriptures (e.g., Ezek 9:11; Dan 10:4) where figures dressed in linen garments appear as angels.

37. Fisk, *Do You Not Remember*, 31.

38. Angels announcing births is a pattern in LAB. See Perrot and Bogaert, *Les Antiquités Bibliques* 2:102; Murphy, *Pseudo-Philo*, 59.

39. Murphy, *Pseudo-Philo*, 60.

40. Yet perhaps her decision to keep the child was influenced by pity, because the narrative tells of her seeing his circumcision (i.e., covenant) and recognizing him as one of the Hebrew children. Harrington, "Pseudo-Philo," 316, points out that covenant became a technical term for circumcision in post-biblical Hebrew.

already on the spot, or perhaps the author refers obliquely to his later adoption (see Exod 2:10, "When the child grew up, she brought him to Pharaoh's daughter, and she took him as her son"). Then the passage refers to the mother: "his mother called him Melchiel" (LAB 9.16). Thus, the author implies that Moses's mother continued being present *somehow* in his life.

2.5. Josephus, *Antiquitates judaicae* 2.210–237

Finally, let us turn to Josephus's *Antiquitates judaicae*. Regarding the role of Moses's mother in this passage, Josephus, or the source he paraphrases,[41] reduces her independency considerably. While in the Exodus tradition of the MT the mother appears mostly alone, and in Philo's version of Exod 2 the parents operate together, in *Antiquitates judaicae* it is now the father, Amram, who is the protagonist. The divine dream comes to him, he reveals it to his wife (the name Jocheballe appears in *A.J.* 2.217), and subsequently he makes decisions concerning the future of the child: "For three months they reared the child in secret, and then Amram, fearing that he would be detected and incurring the king's wrath, would perish himself, resolved to commit the salvation and protection of the child to Him" (*A.J.* 2.218–219).[42] The parents hide the child together. All this happens without any despair or even the human feelings described by Philo, but rather with perfect confidence in the divine will. Moses's mother is not mentioned until *A.J.* 2.227 when she is fetched to act as the foster mother. Josephus explains that "by request of the princess, the mother was permanently entrusted with its nurture" (*A.J.* 2.227), highlighting that she continued feeding him, that is, acting only as a caretaker. Josephus does not mention her again.

The role of Miriam is also played down in *Antiquitates judaicae*.[43] First the author attributes the dream vision to Amram,[44] and later he has Miriam

---

41. On Josephus and his sources, see Tal Ilan's essay in this volume.

42. Translations follow Henry St. J. Thackeray et al., trans., *Josephus*, 10 vols, LCL (Cambridge: Harvard University Press, 1926–1965).

43. Many scholars have paid attention to Josephus's treatment of women, concluding that it is not equal to his treatment of men. It reflects a gender bias, and the author seems to mention women only when their presence becomes absolutely necessary for his narration. See, e.g., Louis H. Feldman, "Josephus' Jewish Antiquities and Pseudo-Philo's Biblical Antiquities," in *Josephus, the Bible and History*, ed. Louis H. Feldman and Gohei Hata (Detroit: Wayne State University Press, 1989), 59–80. See further, Schuller, "Women of the Exodus," 187 n. 33 and the literature cited there.

44. This dream has been dealt with by Robert Karl Gnuse, *Dreams and Dream Reports in the Writings of Josephus: A Traditio-Historical Analysis*, AGJU 36 (Leiden: Brill 1996). Gnuse (p. 224) assumes that the shorter and less developed version preserved in LAB is

follow the basket because she was asked to (*A.J.* 2.222), not because of her own initiative. In *A.J.* 2.226 she goes to fetch her mother to nurse the child. Here the narrative states that she is there almost accidentally: "Mariam, who had come upon the scene, apparently without design and from mere curiosity." It is possible that mention of Miriam's "curiosity" aimed at creating a negative reason for her presence in this passage. She does not appear on divine command but because of her own curiosity.

Let us turn to Josephus's portrayal of the king's daughter in this passage. Unlike the other texts that have her bathe, Josephus narrates that she is playing by the river bank when she spots the basket (*A.J.* 2.224). Notably, she is then enchanted by the beauty of the child. According to Josephus the child does not cry, nor do elements of pity or motherly feelings appear here; thus the audience is made to believe that it is due to the child's pleasant appearance that the king's daughter decides to keep him. She seems to be unaware of his Jewish origin, because until Miriam offers to go to search for a Hebrew woman, she invites other women to feed him. In *A.J.* 2.232 Josephus specifies that the king's daughter—who bears the name Thermuthis—adopted Moses as she did not have biological children. Since the author had just described Moses as three years old, it is possible that he thought the adoption took place only at that age and not immediately after the child was found. Finally, Josephus adds that Moses was "educated with the utmost care" (*A.J.* 2.236).

With regard to Thermuthis's presence in Moses's life and her status, it should be noted that Josephus does not preserve any reference to her marriage. In contrast, he emphasizes that she adopted Moses as "her" son.[45] Further, when addressing Thermuthis's plan to make Moses the successor of her father, Josephus appears to deal with the Pharaoh's daughter as the parental figure for Moses and his main educator. He does not mention any other characters to take care of this task.[46]

---

earlier than the version by Josephus. I have argued that already some earlier texts attributed to the figure of Miriam a role as a visionary. See Hanna Tervanotko, "Speaking in Dreams: The Figure of Miriam and Prophecy," in *Prophets Male and Female: Gender and Prophecy in the Hebrew Bible, the Eastern Mediterranean, and the Ancient Near East*, ed. Jonathan Stökl and Corrine L. Carvalho, AIL 15 (Atlanta: Society of Biblical Literature, 2013), 147–68.

45. "Such was the child whom Thermuthis adopted as her son, being blessed with no offspring of her own" (*A.J.* 2.232).

46. Schuller, "Women of the Exodus," 188, writes that "undoubtedly it was Josephus's own pragmatic acknowledgement of the power of influential women (such as Poppaea and Domitia) at the Roman court rather than any feminist sentiments that influenced this portrait of Pharaoh's daughter." Shelly Matthews, "Ladies Aid: Gentile Noblewomen as Saviors and Benefactors in 'Antiquities,'" *HTR* 92 (1999): 199–218, analyzes various noble female

2.6. Intermediary Conclusions

After considering the best preserved renarrations concerning Exod 2, let me now turn to the key finding of the above analysis. While Exod 2:1–10 presents the princess as a plain figure without many attributes, all the renarrations appear to add something to her portrayal, namely, details that concern her reasons to come to the river, her name and status, her initial interest in Moses, her summoning of a nurse (Moses's mother), and Moses's adoption. Moreover, many of the renarrations pay particular attention to the education that Pharaoh's daughter, his adoptive mother, provides him.

This calls for further analysis. Peculiarly, according to Jubilees, it is Amram who teaches Moses to write and Moses is only later (apparently after completing at least some of his education) taken to the palace. In Exagoge the mother appears as Moses's educator while in *De vita Mosis* and *Antiquitates judaicae* Pharaoh's daughter arranges his training. As these renarrations, especially Philo and Josephus, otherwise tend to play down women (as demonstrated above), let me now ask why these authors highlight the daughter of Pharaoh and Moses's mother as his educator.

3. Moses's Mother and Daughter of Pharaoh as Moses's Educators

3.1. Teaching of Mothers

Educational tasks are usually assigned to men in ancient Jewish texts, and only a few women appear to share them. Despite this general observation some texts do hint at women having a role in children's education. For instance, the book of Proverbs refers to the mother's teaching. Proverbs 31 narrates that King Lemuel received certain teachings from his mother: "The words of King Lemuel. An oracle that his mother taught him. No, my son! No, son of my womb! No, son of my vows!" (Prov 31:1–2).[47] The passage contains an instruction on how a king should not drink (vv. 4–7) and continues with the famous praise of the good wife (vv. 10–31). Moreover Prov 1:8 and 6:20 refer to "your mother's teaching" (תורת אמך) that is presented in parallel to a father's instruction (מוסר) and commandment (מצות). These passages contrast wisdom and sinning and warn the addressee, the "son," of the strange woman. Thus, in the context of wisdom literature both mothers and fathers

---

figures that provide help for the Jewish people. She points out (p. 212) that Josephus seemingly prefers Pharaoh's daughter over Moses's mother and sister in his rewriting of Exod 2.

47. For the contents of these teachings, see Prov 31:1–9.

appear as advisors for their children, and the instructions of mothers were appreciated.

In addition to these passages that refer to mothers broadly, some texts portray specific figures in teaching roles. A female figure who clearly instructs her son is Rebecca, whose extensive words of advice to Jacob are preserved in Jubilees (e.g., Jub. 25.1–3). She teaches him about marriage and warns him about marrying foreign women. The style of Rebecca's advice suggests that she acts as Jacob's instructor in this passage. She asks him to listen to her ("And now, my son, heed my voice," Jub. 25.3) and promises that if he follows her advice God will make him prosper.

Another reference to a woman's teaching appears in the book of Tobit, where Tobit himself narrates how his grandmother Deborah instructed him (Tob 1:7–8).[48] In the beginning of chapter 1 he talks about following the laws of Moses and thus, as he was an orphan, he took heed to Deborah's exhortations. Unfortunately, we do not know what Deborah's teachings were. Moreover, another Deborah, that of Judg 4–5, appears as an educator in LAB 33. This passage contains her testament to the people and she instructs them for the future. She calls for their attention in LAB 33:1 ("Listen now, my people ... obey me like your mother") and continues to instruct them in verses 2–5, asking them to direct their hearts to God during their lifetime.[49]

In light of these above quoted passages we can say that the instructive role was not attributed to men alone, and some people were familiar with the idea of women teaching.[50] What these texts share, in my view, is that they do not attest to formal education, but to specific moments where mothers act as instructors for their children.

48. "I would give these to the priests, the sons of Aaron, at the altar; likewise the tenth of the grain, wine, olive oil, pomegranates, figs, and the rest of the fruits to the sons of Levi who ministered at Jerusalem. Also for six years I would save up a second tenth in money and go and distribute it in Jerusalem. A third tenth I would give to the orphans and widows and to the converts who had attached themselves to Israel. I would bring it and give it to them in the third year, and we would eat it according to the ordinance decreed concerning it in the law of Moses and according to the instructions of Deborah, the mother of my father Tobiel, for my father had died and left me an orphan" (Tob 1:7–8).

49. Another woman who instructs her sons is the mother of seven brothers in 2 Macc 7:1–42. For her significance, see Marie-Theres Wacker, "Theologie einer Mutter—Eine Mutter als Theologin: Feministisch-Exegetische Anmerkungen zu 2 Makk 7," in *Gott bin ich kein Mann: Beiträge zur Hermeneutik der biblischen Gottesrede*, ed. Ilona Riedel-Spangenberger and Erich Zenger (Paderborn: Schöningh, 2006), 259–70.

50. For a possible reference to women's teaching preserved in rabbinic literature, see Tal Ilan, *Jewish Women in Greco-Roman Palestine: An Inquiry into Image and Status*, TSAJ 44 (Tübingen: Mohr Siebeck, 1995), 194–95.

3.2. Greek Education

While Jubilees displays a particular interest in Amram's role in Moses's education, those literary traditions that were composed in Greek emphasize the role of the women in his upbringing. In Exagoge, Moses's mother is told to teach him, and in other texts the daughter of Pharaoh appears to facilitate his access to formal education. It is possible that all these texts depend at some level on the LXX translation of Exod 2, but that does not contain remarkable differences vis-à-vis the Hebrew text, at least nothing that would explain this thematic interest. Thus, other factors that may have influenced the interest of these texts in Moses's formation should be considered, and one should inquire into the importance of education as such in the Greek speaking, Hellenistic contexts where these texts were composed.

Greek texts pay particular attention to education beginning in the fifth century BCE when the philosophical schools were established.[51] Philosophers who were permanently a part of the public Athenian culture acted as the specialists of various subjects, including science, philosophy, and rhetoric. Yet schooling also included poetry, music, and physical education, all considered part of the curriculum of a civilized future citizen.[52] Within a short time education was no longer restricted to Athens, and approximately from the third century on inscriptions testify that gymnasia were centers of intellectual and educational activity in Athens and elsewhere in the Greek world, including Egypt.[53]

Education was determined by a family's wealth, because no public, free education was available. As people had to pay for it, it was not accessible for everyone, but only for those who could afford it. Boys would usually start their education at about the age of seven.[54] The length of schooling depended

---

51. Lesley A. Beaumont, *Childhood in Ancient Athens: Iconography and Social History*, RMCS (New York: Routledge, 2012), 134–52.

52. Ibid.

53. Raffaella Cribiore, *Gymnastics of the Mind: Greek Education in Hellenistic and Roman Egypt* (Princeton: Princeton University Press, 2001), 35.

54. For the age to start formal tuition, see Aristotle, *Politics* 1336 (Aristotle, *Politics*, trans. H. Rackham, LCL 264 [Cambridge: Harvard University Press, 1932]): "For children of this age, and up to seven years old, must necessarily be reared at home.… But when the five years from two to seven have passed, the children must now become spectators at the lessons which they will themselves have to learn." Similarly, Plato, *Leg.* 794c (Bury, LCL), who also addresses girls' education: "After the age of six, each sex shall be kept separate, boys spending their time with boys, and likewise girls with girls; and when it is necessary for them to begin lessons, the boys must go to teachers of riding, archery, javelin-throwing and slinging, and the girls also, if they agree to it, must share in the lessons, and especially

on the family's wealth, how long they could absorb the costs.[55] Thus, wealthy families could offer their children the best education.

Whereas the preserved textual evidence mostly refers to the education of boys, many scholars have paid attention to the presence of women in historical material, such as letters and images. At least some women had access to education. Unsurprisingly, the education was most accessible to women of higher social strata, particularly in Athens and Egypt.[56] The many preserved letters written by women in the Hellenistic and Roman eras are the clearest witness to their literacy.[57]

Apart from being educated, that is, literate, there also is some evidence of women who acted as teachers and pedagogues for others. For instance, Raffaella Cribione reports on an Egyptian woman, Apollonous, who writes to her husband who is away on military service in the first century CE. Among other things she tells him that he should not be concerned about affairs at home: "And do not worry about the children; they are in good health and attend classes with a lady *didaskalos* [lady teacher]." This letter is not the only one preserved where a lady teacher is mentioned, yet it is of particular interest since it reveals not only that women could function as teachers but also that while her husband was away, Apollonous arranged and supervised their children's schooling.[58]

Let us consider one more text that points to women's active role in their children's education. In one of his dialogues Plato has Protagoras describe children's education as follows: "They teach and admonish them from earliest childhood till the last day of their lives. As soon as one of them grasps what is said to him, the nurse, the mother, the tutor, and the father himself strive hard that the child may excel, and as each act and word occurs they teach and impress upon him that this is just, and that unjust, one thing noble, another

---

such as relate to the use of arms." For a critical evaluation of these sources and statistics on women's literacy, see William V. Harris, *Ancient Literacy* (Cambridge: Harvard University Press, 1991), 106–8.

55. Beaumont, *Childhood in Ancient Athens*, 135.

56. Sarah Pomeroy, *Women in Hellenistic Egypt: From Alexander to Cleopatra* (Detroit: Wayne State University Press, 1984), 59; Cribiore, *Gymnastics of the Mind*, 75. Polybius reports about "foster siblings" who were brought up with royal children in order to have same education and serve as their companions (Polybius, *Hist.* 15.33.11–12).

57. Roger S. Bagnall and Raffaella Cribiore, *Women's Letters from Ancient Egypt 300 BC–800 AD* (Ann Arbor: University of Michigan Press, 2006). See also Ilan, *Jewish Women in Greco-Roman Palestine*, 192, referring to Jewish women who were probably literate.

58. For further examples of women in the roles of educators see Cribiore, *Gymnastics of the Mind*, 78–83, and for the correspondence between parents and their teachers, see ibid, 102–23.

base, one holy, another unholy, and that he is to do this, and not do that" (Plato, *Prot.* 325d).[59] Significantly, in this passage Plato suggests that before a child is sent to study with a teacher, the mother could educate him or her.[60]

All in all, I think that these references are sufficient to conclude that while men, as the usual breadwinners, may have been in most of the cases responsible for paying for their children's education, it was in the interest of both parents to take care of the formation of their children and provide them the training that they needed as citizens in their societies.[61] It seems logical to think that especially in cases where the father was absent, the mother was responsible for supervising the child's training and keeping an eye on his or her progress.

3.3. Moses's Hellenistic Education

After our excursus on Hellenistic education, we should now return to the renarrations of Exod 2 and evaluate the interest in Moses's education reflected in the Greek texts against this background. Those texts that were composed in contexts where education was important emphasize that Moses was an educated person and a capable citizen in his own environment. Such qualities are present in several other texts that date to the Hellenistic era, for example, in Artapanus's description of Moses. This general observation leads us to some further considerations.

Given that training was not free and was limited to high society and those families who could afford it, Moses's adoption by the daughter of Pharaoh provides him a perfect setting to have access to education. Pharaoh's daughter becomes Moses's adoptive mother and consequently, as his parent, she is responsible for his education. In the absence of a husband, it was logical that the task to supervise his upbringing was ascribed to her. I claimed above that that the idea of women as instructors is not foreign in the Jewish texts. Moreover, in ancient Greece and in Hellenistic and Roman Egypt women appear as students, teachers, and, importantly, parents who are interested in their children's education and follow their training. In a Hellenistic context

59. Plato, *Laches; Protagoras; Meno; Euthydemus*, trans. W. R. M. Lamb, LCL 165 (Cambridge: Harvard University Press, 1924).

60. Similarly, Nicholas Denyer, *Plato's Protagoras* (Cambridge: Cambridge University Press, 2008), 116, who discusses the role of parents (both mother and father) in children's education.

61. For a marriage contract that preserves a clause that a husband was responsible for giving "his children the education proper for free people," see Cribiore, *Gymnastics of the Mind*, 108.

the audience of Exod 2 would have associated Pharaoh's daughter with literary skills and because of her status (and no doubt wealth) she would have been in a position to have the best teachers to educate her son. Therefore the role that the daughter of Pharaoh performs as the primary educator of Moses in the Greek rewritings of Exod 2 is "natural" in the sense that it would have fallen within what was "expected" of her. People would have interpreted it as the regular behavior of an elite woman who wanted to make sure her son got the education to which he was entitled. Moses's Hellenistic curriculum is specified in Philo's list of subjects which Moses studied.[62]

Moses's education seems to contain both informal and formal training. His education is "divided in two" in Exagoge, where first it is his mother who teaches him the traditions ("pertaining to my father's God and race," ll. 34–35) and only after that does he move to the palace to start his proper, official training ("princely rearing," l. 37). The author appears to be aware of different types of formation that a child could have (i.e., informal and formal). In my view, we should see this formation as involving something else than the subjects belonging to the Greek curriculum. The reference is short, and thus anything we say about it remains speculative, but I suggest that the instructions concerning "my father's God and race" should be understood as a reference to his Jewish origins.[63]

It is possible that the author intended to say that just as other female figures taught their children their ancestral traditions, Moses's mother did the same before he was old enough to enroll for a more structured training. The author of Exagoge may have wanted to explain that Moses, while heavily influenced by the Hellenistic educational system, was equally aware of his own roots and the traditions of his people. This idea appears to be present also in Philo's *De vita Mosis*, when he addresses Moses's appreciation of both sets of parents and their presence in his life (ll. 32–33). Thus both Philo and the author of Exagoge are making the claim that Moses's biological and adoptive parents had significance for his education and his life.

62. Note that Philo's description of the Therapeutae in his *De vita contemplativa* is an example of his acceptance of women living a spiritual and intellectual life. For this group, see Joan E. Taylor, *Jewish Women Philosophers of First-Century Alexandria: Philo's 'Therapeutae' Reconsidered* (Oxford: Oxford University Press, 2006) and Taylor's article in this volume.

63. Robertson, "Ezekiel the Tragedian," 809 n., gives the literal translation "my father's race and gifts of God." I think this phrase can be understood as a broad reference to the cultural heritage and not as referring to specific gifts given by God.

6. Conclusions

This presentation has analyzed the female figures in the renarrations of Exod 2:1–10 that were composed during the late Second Temple era. With Schuller, I conclude that some female figures are modified and their roles in the narratives changed. In some cases, those changes diminish women's role in the narratives. Through close and critical reading of the ancient texts I have attempted to shift the focus away from the protagonist of the story, that is, Moses, and instead shed new light on those characters that appear in the margins of the preserved narratives to discover their true relevance for the stories. I argued that some female figures receive more attention in the renarrations. This is the case for the figure of Miriam in LAB or Moses's mother in Exagoge but even more so for the daughter of Pharaoh. I highlighted that those texts that were influenced by Hellenistic ideas and mostly composed in Alexandria are particularly interested in the daughter of Pharaoh; as Moses's adoptive mother she becomes a significant instrument to provide for him the formal education that qualifies him to be a learned and wise man. These texts portray Moses's education differently from Jubilees and other so-called Levitical texts where teaching follows male lineage and goes from father to son. For the authors and audiences of Exagoge, *De vita Mosis*, and *Antiquitates judaicae*, the idea of women supervising their sons' education was equally acceptable to the idea of men serving in this capacity.

Part 3
Writings and Their Historical Context

Flavius Josephus and Biblical Women

Tal Ilan

Flavius Josephus, the great Jewish historian of the first-century of the common era, left four works to posterity: a kind of autobiography (*The Life*) as the conclusion of his literary work; a polemical work in defense of Judaism, *Against Apion*; a comprehensive presentation of and reflection on the first Jewish-Roman War (66–73 CE) and its historical background beginning in the second-century BCE (*Jewish War*); and the *Jewish Antiquities*, a history of the Jewish people in twenty books, which begins with the creation of the world and continues until the beginning of the war in 66 CE.[1] In the first eleven books of *Jewish Antiquities* Josephus orients himself above all on the

---

A few years ago Honora H. Chapman and Zuleika Rogers invited me to collaborate on the Wiley *Companion to Josephus* and to contribute an article on women in the work of Josephus. This reference book has since been published. In my contribution (Tal Ilan, "Josephus on Women," in *A Companion to Josephus*, ed. Honora Howell Chapman and Zuleika Rodgers, BCAW [Oxford: Wiley Blackwell, 2016], 210–21) I deal with all of the female figures mentioned in the work of Josephus and classify them in three groups: (1) biblical women; (2) women from the Hasmonean and Herodian ruling families; and (3) women who were contemporaries of Josephus. The following essay is based on my contribution to the Wiley *Companion* but concentrates on the first part, on biblical women, and expands it with new material. I thank Marie-Theres Wacker, who has helped me a great deal in the preparation of the present essay.

1. For *The Life*, see the new critical edition in the Brill Josephus Project (BJP): Steve Mason, ed., *Life of Josephus*, FJTC 9 (Leiden: Brill, 2001). In addition to the volumes in LCL (Henry St. J. Thackeray et al., trans., *Josephus*, 10 vols., LCL [Cambridge: Harvard University Press, 1926–1965]), a new critical edition of *Against Apion* is in the BJP: John Barclay, ed., *Against Apion*, FJTC 10 (Leiden: Brill, 2007). Editions of the *Jewish War* in the BJP, so far published, are: Steve Mason and Honora Chapman, eds., *Judean War 2*, ed. FJTC 1b (Leiden: Brill, 2008). For editions of the *Jewish Antiquities* in the BJP, the following have already appeared: Louis Feldman, ed., *Judean Antiquities 1–4*, FJTC 3 (Leiden: Brill, 2000); Christopher Begg, ed., *Judean Antiquities 5–7*, FJTC 4 (Leiden: Brill, 2005); Christopher Begg and Paul Spilsbury, eds., *Judean Antiquities 8–10*, FJTC 5 (Leiden: Brill, 2005); Jan Willem van Henten, ed., *Judean Antiquities 15*, FJTC 7b (Leiden: Brill, 2014).

narrative texts of the Bible. He follows very precisely the chronological order of the events narrated and stays close to their essential content. He makes the biblical narratives available in the Greek language for a contemporary public that is not necessarily Jewish. The genre of this part of his work could therefore be accurately described as "rewritten Bible." It is similar to Jubilees or the writing known as Pseudo-Philo (Liber antiquitatum biblicarum).[2] The close literary similarity to these writings, which can be regarded as rewritten Bible, is perhaps the reason why most studies of the first eleven books of the *Jewish Antiquities* are written from a biblical or literary-critical perspective and not by scholars who see themselves first and foremost as historians. Josephus, however, seems to have thought of himself above all as a historian, something that is apparent already in his foreword to the work. It appears that he regarded the biblical stories as reports of events that actually took place.

Because the Bible itself tells the story of numerous women, it comes as no surprise that many of them appear also in Josephus. For this reason, *Jewish Antiquities* offers a rich source for a thorough investigation of Josephus's literary treatment of biblical women.

1. Critique of Past Research

I wish to make my approach clear at the beginning. I take Josephus seriously as a historian who assimilates sources and not simply as a writer who freely creates new literary worlds.

Many studies of Josephus's dealings with the Bible discover great and significant differences, which are used to work out his presuppositions and intentions as well as his roots in the Hellenistic-Roman culture of his time. The alterations that Josephus makes when he departs from the biblical narratives are seen as rooted in his *Sitz im Leben*, and it is believed that they reveal something about the author and his cultural context.

One of the main proponents of this tendency is Louis H. Feldman. In the introduction to his substantial study *Josephus's Interpretation of the* Bible, he lists the numerous authors and genres of Jewish-Hellenistic and pagan literature that might have served for Josephus as a model for his *Jewish Antiquities*.[3] He comes to the conclusion that Josephus did not simply follow any of these models and thereby highlights Josephus's creativity.[4] In opposition to

---

2. Cheryl Anne Brown, *No Longer Be Silent: First Century Jewish Portraits of Biblical Women* (Louisville: Westminster John Knox, 1992), makes this comparison.

3. Louis H. Feldman, *Josephus's Interpretation of the Bible* (Berkeley: University of California Press, 1998).

4. Ibid., 23. On p. 15, where he compares Josephus with Jubilees, he states: "But it

Josephus's assertion that he will faithfully follow the texts of the Bible, Feldman points out many additions and deletions that, in his opinion, undermine Josephus's claim.[5] My argument with this scholarship is aimed not so much at the concept itself but at the extent of the differences these scholars claim they can show. To me it is striking how closely Josephus follows his biblical *Vorlage* and how rarely he departs from it—especially when one bears in mind that most of the variations emphasized in the scholarship are simply omissions. Much of what seem to be additions that Josephus inserts are drawn from other sources besides the Bible. This is true especially where he gives a new twist to the stories about women.

From these considerations my main objection to a major aspect of the work of Betsy Halpern-Amaru becomes clear. Her seminal study from 1988 of the biblical women in Josephus is based on the presumption that Josephus has thoroughly and tendentiously reshaped these characters.[6] He found many of the biblical narratives about women problematic because in his view the women were portrayed as too self-confident and assertive. Where he encounters such character traits, his response takes the following three steps: he (1) "removes the 'problem'"; (2) "creates an unblemished heroine for his Hellenized audience"; and (3) "transforms the 'potential flaw' in the heroine into [a] virtue."[7] Applying this working hypothesis, Halpern-Amaru describes the three matriarchal figures of Genesis as three different role models. Sara is the ideal wife, beautiful, pious, submissive, and chaste. Rebecca is a strong, vigorous heroine who does not, however, misuse her feminine cunning and does not openly display any masculine power. Rachel is "the romantic *ingénue* most beloved by her husband."[8] Josephus counters these role-models, according to Halpern-Amaru, with "scoundrel"-women whose behavior is problematic, presenting them as antiheroines, whose vices are diametrically opposed to the virtues of his heroines.[9] For him the two prime examples of this type are the women of Moab (see Num 25:1–3) and the wife of Potiphar (see Gen 39:6–20). All of the other female characters in the Bible are modeled on these four (or five) types.

---

is only occasionally that the author remains completely faithful to the biblical narrative, whereas Josephus's *Antiquities* often is very faithful."

5. Ibid., 37.

6. Betsy Halpern-Amaru, "Portraits of Biblical Women in Josephus' *Antiquities*," *JJS* 39 (1988): 143–70.

7. Ibid.,144.

8. Ibid., 145, 148, 151.

9. Ibid., 153.

Many other studies have proceeded similarly.[10] Like Halpern-Amaru they begin with the premise that the changed emphases in Josephus's characterization of the biblical women serve to play down these figures and to bring them into conformity with the Hellenistic concepts of his time.[11] The fundamental presupposition of this approach (and of the studies that build on it) is the assumption that the biblical texts contain many details about women that do not fit the Hellenistic dichotomy of the pious, modest "housewife" and/or the oversexed seducer. Inherent in these Hellenistic type-castings, according to this approach, is a high degree of hostility to women. The thesis does not satisfactorily explain, however, what exactly "Hellenism" is and why these female stereotypes are especially "Hellenistic." Nor does the thesis make sufficiently clearly how precisely Josephus deals with the figures of biblical women. I propose to do this in the following pages, and I will divide my discussion into two. First I will show how Josephus stays very loyal to his biblical women, and then I will show that when he deviates from the biblical portrait, this is because he is using sources for his descriptions. He does not invent them.

2. The Example of Deborah

For a first example, let us look at the biblical prophetess Deborah and how Josephus deals with her in *Ant.* 5.200–209. In his 1986 article on Deborah, Louis Feldman underlines the Hellenistic character of the narrative ("Josephus sets the scene for a Greek tragedy") and comes to the conclusion that Josephus, "in his misogyny, both reduced the length of the episode and the

---

10. I should mention here that I know of no German-language monographs dealing with the biblical women in Josephus. Note, however, Bärbel Mayer-Schärtel, *Das Frauenbild des Josephus: Eine sozialgeschichtliche und kulturanthropologische Untersuchung* (Stuttgart: Kohlhammer, 1995); and Regula Grünenfelder, *Frauen an den Krisenherden: Eine rhetorisch-politische Deutung des Bellum Judaicum* (Münster: LIT, 2003). Mayer-Schärtel analyzes thematically Josephus's presentation of women but does not differentiate between biblical and nonbiblical women; Grünenfelder interprets *Jewish War*, in part from a feminist or gender-specific point of view, but she does not discuss the biblical women in Josephus.

11. See Brown, *No Longer Be Silent*; Louis H. Feldman, "Josephus' Portrait of Deborah," in *Hellenica et Judaica: Hommage à Valentin Nikiprowetzky*, ed. André Caquot, Mireille Hadas-Lebel, and Jean Riaud (Leuven-Paris: Peeters, 1989), 115–28; James L. Bailey, "Josephus' Portrayal of the Matriarchs," in *Josephus, Judaism and Christianity*, ed. Louis H. Feldman and Gohei Hata (Detroit: Wayne State University Press, 1987), 257–72; John R. Levison, "Josephus' Version of Ruth," *JSP* 8 (1991): 31–44; Gregory Sterling, "The Invisible Presence: Josephus' Retelling of Ruth," in *Understanding Josephus: Seven Perspectives*, ed. Steve Mason (Sheffield: Sheffield Academic, 1998), 104–71.

importance of Deborah."[12] In a very similar and highly detailed study, several years later, Mark Roncace, however, came to a diametrically opposed conclusion. On the one hand, he determines that "in many respects Josephus' account … is not too different from the biblical narrative" and stresses, on the other hand, that "Josephus' story shows no evidence of misogyny or an effort to reduce the importance of Deborah. Rather she is the most important positively depicted figure in this story."[13] In my opinion, Roncace correctly shows that the concepts and perspectives of Feldman and Halpern-Amaru can readily be turned on their head.

Let us look more closely at a comparison of the opening of the Deborah narrative.[14]

Judg 4:1–10	*Ant.* 5.198–201
1 The Israelites again did what was evil in the sight of YHWH, after Ehud had died. 2 So YHWH sold them into the hand of King Jabin of Canaan, who reigned in Hazor; the commander of his army was Sisera, who lived in Harosheth-ha-goim.	198 Again, however, the Israelites, who had learnt no wisdom from their previous misfortunes, since they neither worshipped God nor obeyed the laws, ere they had enjoyed a brief respite from their servitude to the Moabites, fell under the yoke of Jabin, kin of the Canaanites. 199 For this monarch, issuing from the city of Asor, situated above the lake Semachōntes, maintained an army of 300,000 foot and 10,000 horse, and was owner of 3,000 chariots. Accordingly the general of these forces, Sisares, who held the first rank in the king's favour, so sorely afflicted the Israelites when they joined battle with him, that he forced them to pay tribute.

12. Feldman, "Josephus' Portrait of Deborah," 121, 128.

13. Mark Roncace, "Josephus' (Real) Portraits of Deborah and Gideon: A Reading of *Antiquities* 5.198–232," *JSJ* 31 (2000): 259.

14. The translation of biblical texts throughout follows the NRSV. For the divine name, which is translated in the NRSV as "the Lord," I have used the tetragram YHWH. The translation of *Jewish Antiquities* here and in the rest of the essay is that of Henry St. J. Thackeray et al., *Josephus*.

3 Then the Israelites cried out to YHWH for help for he had nine hundred chariots of iron, and had oppressed the Israelites cruelly twenty years.

200 Twenty years, then, did they pass in this miserable plight, themselves incapable of being schooled in adversity, while God willed to tame their insolence yet more by reason of their ingratitude towards Him, to the end that they might change their ways and thenceforward be wise.

4 At that time Deborah, a prophetess, wife of Lappidoth, was judging Israel.
5 She used to sit under the palm of Deborah between Ramah and Bethel in the hill country of Ephraim; and the Israelites came to her for judgment.

But when they had learned that their calamities were due to their contempt of the laws, they besought a certain prophetess named Dabora—the name in the Hebrew tongue means "bee"—
201 to pray God to take pity on them and not to suffer them to be destroyed by the Canaanites. God thereupon promised them salvation and chose for general Barak of the tribe of Nephtali; *barak* denotes "lightning" in the tongue of the Hebrews.

6 She sent and summoned Barak son of Abinoam from Kedesh in Naphtali, and said to him, "YHWH, the God of Israel, commands you, 'go, take position at Mount Tabor, bringing ten thousand from the tribe of Naphtali and the tribe of Zebulon.
7 I will draw out Sisera, the general of Jabin's army, to meet you at the Wadi Kishon, with his chariot and his troops; and I will give him into your hand.' "
8 Barak said to her, "If you will go with me, I will go; but if you will not go with me, I will not go."
9 And she said, "I will surely go with you; nevertheless, the road on which you are going will not lead to your glory, for YHWH will sell Sisera into the hand of a woman." Then Deborah got up and went with Barak to Kedesh.

202 Dabora then summoned Barak and charged him to select ten thousand of the youth and to march against the foe: that number would, she said, suffice, God having prescribed it and betokened victory.
203 But Barak declared that he would not take command unless she shared it with him; whereto she indignantly replied, "Thou resignest to a woman a rank that God has bestowed on thee! Howbeit I do not decline it."

Then, having mustered ten thousand, they pitched their camp on Mount Itabyrion.

Josephus makes concrete the Deuteronomistic formula of a renewed rebellion of the Israelites against God by specifying their two main sins: worshipping other gods and ignoring the law of God. His account of the threat against Israel from Jabin and his general Sisera is fleshed out with technical military details and the addition of a reproving comment about the intransigence of the Israelites. At this point Deborah enters the story, both in the Bible and in Josephus. In the book of Judges, Deborah's title, "prophetess," is connected to information that she had given judgment (Judg 4:4). Deborah is thereby placed side by side with the other judges, above all with her great successor Samuel. In Josephus she is referred with the title "prophetess" (προφῆτις) and is sought out by the Israelites with the request that she intercede for them with God. Deborah's role is, therefore, that of advocate or intermediary between God and the people. She obtains from God what the people have requested; God promises "salvation" or "deliverance" (σωτηρία). Here already the question can be asked whether the change in the way Deborah is presented has something to do with misogyny. True, in terms of giving judgment, she is no longer compared with her male counterparts, who, as the title of the book in which they feature implies, were "judges." However in place of this she acquires the characteristics of an intermediary between God and the people,—similar to Samuel in *Ant.* 6.24–25. As a woman she is not presented as "more pious," but rather placed side by side with Samuel. The Greek translation here of her name as "bee" does not yet have the negative connotation it will later acquire in the Talmud (see b. Meg. 14b), but rather stands without valuation beside the explanation of the name Barak as "lightning."

There follows the scene that parallels Judg 4:6–8: Deborah summons Barak and commands him to assemble an army and go into battle; Barak does not want to take to the field without her, and she responds with reluctance: "Thou resignest to a woman a rank that God has bestowed on thee! Howbeit I do not decline it" (*Ant.* 5.203).[15] In contrast to the biblical text, which deprives Barak of all glory, the Deborah of Josephus is prepared to share the honor. A few lines later, differently from the biblical text, the fear of the soldiers is stressed, which Deborah counters by referring to God's support of his people (*Ant.* 5.204). Josephus enhances the battle itself. It is obviously important for him to demystify the mythical presentation of the biblical text by replacing the direct intervention of God against Israel's enemies (Judg 4:15) with natural causes—here, a heavy storm that is to the advantage of the Israelites. The gen-

15. Josephus here takes Deborah's comment that God would give victory by the hand of a woman to refer to Deborah herself and not, as do most interpreters, to Jael. I tend to agree with Josephus here.

eral's flight to the tent of Jael (Judg 4:17–21) is reported briefly but follows the relevant details of the biblical text (*Ant.* 5.207–208). In the concluding section Deborah appears once more: "Thus did this victory redound, as Dabora had foretold, to a woman's glory" (*Ant.* 5.209). Deborah is here the prophetess who can see the future. At the same time, there is no hint of Deborah's long song of victory, which she sings together with Barak in the biblical account (Judg 5).

With the omission of the Song of Deborah, the section dealing with this woman is indeed considerably shorter, but must this omission be interpreted as an expression of misogyny? Could it not be due to the need for a more rationalist mode of presentation, like the reinterpretation of the intervention of God in the battle? The picture of Deborah that Josephus paints definitely has "strong" features, albeit with accents different from that of the Hebrew Bible. It is not especially Hellenistic.

3. Jephthah's Daughter

I would like take a second step toward substantiating my position against the *opinio communis* by discussing another episode that, so far as I can see, has been little analyzed. The episode is also not very conclusive if one's goal is to show how much Josephus's version departs from the Bible. I have in mind the episode of Jepthah's daughter, the female counterpart to Isaac. She was sacrificed by her father when he returned victorious from the great battle against the Ammonites. Halpern-Amaru is unsuccessful in incorporating this young woman into one of the principal categories that she had devised for the presentation of biblical women in Josephus. For her, Jephthah's daughter belongs to that group of characters that Josephus does not develop, who are related to a male hero and function to portray him positively, deflecting attention from his weaknesses. She writes: "Jephtah's daughter is not so much the victim of her father's vow as a martyr to 'her father's victory and liberation of her fellow citizens'" (see *Ant.* 5.265).[16] Because the episode is short, I cite it in full with Josephus's version beside it.

Judg 11:29–40	Josephus, *Ant.* 5.263–266
29 Then the spirit of YHWH came upon Jephthah, and he passed through Gilead and Manasseh. He passed on to Mizpah of Gilead, and from Mizpah of Gilead he passed on to the Ammonites.	

16. Halpern-Amaru, "Biblical Women," 169.

30 And Jephthah made a vow to YHWH, and said, "If you will give the Ammonites into my hand,	With these words he dismissed the envoys. Then, after praying for victory and promising to sacrifice,
31 then whoever comes out of the doors of my house to meet me, when I return victorious from the Ammonites, shall be YHWH's, to be offered by me as a burnt offering.	should he return home unscathed, and to offer up the first creature that should meet him,
32 So Jephthah crossed over to the Ammonites to fight against them; and YHWH gave them into his hand.	he closed with the enemy,
33 He inflicted a massive defeat on them from Aroer to the neighborhood of Minnith, twenty towns, and as far as Abel-keramim. So the Ammonites were subdued before the people of Israel.	defeated them outright, and massacring pursued them up to the city of Manniath; then, crossing into Ammanitis, he destroyed many cities, carried off spoil, and delivered his countrymen from a servitude which they had borne for eighteen years.
34 Then Jephthah came to his home in Mizpah; and there was his daughter coming out to meet him with timbrels and with dancing. She was his only child; he had no son or daughter except her.	But on returning he fell foul of a calamity far different from these achievements; for it was his daughter who met him, his only daughter, a virgin yet.
35 When he saw her, he tore his clothes, and said, "Alas, my daughter! You have brought me very low; you have become the cause of great trouble to me. For I have opened my mouth to the YHWH, and I cannot take back my vow.	Wailing in anguish at the greatness of his blow, the father chid his daughter for her haste in meeting him, seeing that he had dedicated her to God.
36 She said to him, "My father, if you have opened your mouth to YHWH, do to me according to what has gone out of your mouth, now that YHWH has given you vengeance against your enemies, the Ammonites."	But she without displeasure learnt her destiny, to wit that that she must die in return for her father's victory and the liberty of her fellow-citizens;
37 And she said to her father, "Let this thing be done for me: Grant me two months, so that I may go and wander	she but asked him to grant her two months wherein to bewail her youth with her fellow-citizens, and thereafter

on the mountains, and bewail my virginity, my companions and I."	he should do in accordance with his vow.
38 "Go," he said, and sent her away for two months. So she departed, she and her companions, and bewailed her virginity on the mountains.	He accorded her the respite aforesaid,
39 At the end of two months, she returned to her father, who did with her according to the vow he had made. She had never slept with a man. So there arose an Israelite custom that	And at its close sacrificed his child as a burnt-offering—a sacrifice neither sanctioned by the law nor well-pleasing to God;
40 for four days every year the daughters of Israel would go out to lament the daughter of Jephthah the Gileadite.	
	for he had not by reflection probed what might befall or in what aspect the deed would appear to them that heard of it.

Clearly, Josephus follows the biblical narrative verse by verse. His version is shorter, not least because he omits two verses. He lacks—in addition to the concluding verse (Judg 11:40), to which I return below—the introduction to the story (Judg 11:29), according to which "the spirit of YHWH came upon Jephthah." Because being equipped with divine power should have made Jephthah's vow superfluous,[17] this could be the reason why Josephus skips over the verse. In so doing Jephthah loses in the eyes of Josephus the favor or grace of God.

Moreover, Josephus appears here to privilege indirect over direct speech. For this reason, as well, his text is shorter than the biblical *Vorlage*. This makes it even more obvious that when he comes to the description of the battle, he becomes more expansive—a true political historian, as we have seen already in the case of the episode of Deborah. His interpretation of the event is noteworthy: Jephthah "delivered his countrymen from a servitude which they had borne for eighteen years." This is a motif that Josephus has used already in the transition from the time of Ehud to the time of Deborah/Barak (*Ant.* 5.198).

17. See Mieke Bal, "Between Altar and Wondering Rock: Toward a Feminist Philology," in *Anti-covenant: Counter-reading Women's Lives in the Hebrew Bible*, ed. Mieke Bal, JSOTSup 81, BLS 22 (Sheffield: Almond Press, 1989), 213.

The beginning of section 264 is formulated in a way that is typical for Josephus: "But on returning he fell foul of a calamity far different from these fair achievements." Here Josephus uses the opportunity to weave in a philosophical reflection that is characteristic of his worldview, namely the idea that fate can also harm the mighty and the successful. He writes something similar about Herod (*Ant.* 16.76):

> In truth, a divine power [δαιμόνιον] had given him a great many instances of good fortune [εὐτυχίαν], even more than he had hoped for, in external affairs, but in his own home it was his fate to meet with the greatest misfortunes [δυστυχεῖν] and such as he had never expected.

After this assessment of Jephthah's situation, Josephus continues following the biblical text and inserts a motif that is not found in the parallel version in the book of Judges, namely, the virginity of the daughter. He has, however, not thereby added anything new to the story, since the biblical text does speak a few verses later about the fact that the girl "had never slept with a man" (Judg 11:39). Josephus has here only relocated the ordering of the theme.

The description of the time that the young woman spends with her friends is on the whole shorter in Josephus. Also, he omits the last verse that describes the ritual that is carried out every year in memory of Jephthah's daughter. It is true that he thereby erases the memory that the Bible seeks to preserve, but this could simply be a result of the fact that at the time that Josephus composed his work the ritual was no longer being observed. On the other hand, the ending, which concludes with a kind of moral sermon, is again typical of Josephus: "a sacrifice neither sanctioned by the law nor well-pleasing to God; for he had not by reflection probed what might befall or in what aspect the deed would appear to them that heard of it."

It could be maintained that Josephus's version is more misogynist than the biblical account because in his retelling Jephthah's daughter remains more in the shadows. However, this is true only in a very restricted sense. Just as in the biblical account, she asks her father for two months to mourn. One could even argue that Josephus values her more highly and puts her father on the sidelines since, as she says, for her too her people's struggle for freedom is important. Moreover, Josephus clearly condemns her father's deed and explicitly expresses his indignation at her sacrifice, whereas the biblical text does so more indirectly.

In conclusion it can be said: Josephus does not repeat the biblical narrative word for word but his paraphrase is most faithful in comparison with the other rewritten biblical narratives and definitely one of the least ideological. By way of comparison, one could refer to an excerpt from Midrash Tanhuma A, according to which Jephthah's daughter goes before the Sanhedrin in order to have her father's vow annulled.[18] Josephus values his claim to report objectively as a historian and sticks to it. Perhaps one can even say that Josephus is not misogynistic, although he is more interested in the male heroes of the biblical narratives since it was these characters, after all, who made history.

4. Esther

Against the background of the observations made in the last two sections, my observations on biblical women about whom Josephus says more (sometimes much more) than the Bible is that he did not freely invent these additions. We should therefore inquire what sources he used and investigate them. A straightforward example with which to begin is Esther. There is no doubt that Josephus knew the so-called Additions to Esther that are found in the Septuagint and made use of them. These additions rework and defuse some of the "problems" that arise in the Hebrew version of the Megillah because of the peculiar and not very pious character of the heroine. Many of the departures from the Hebrew book of Esther that are found in Josephus's retelling (*Ant.* 11.184–296) come from this Greek source. Halpern-Amaru suggests that Esther's words in the presence of the king, for example (*Ant.* 11.240: "as soon as I saw you looking so great and handsome and terrible, my spirit failed me and I was left without life"), can be attributed to Josephus, and that he is thereby aligning his heroine with the type of Rachel.[19] But she failed to notice that the greatly expanded scene of Esther's approach to the king, her fainting, and her flattery are found already in Addition D of the Septuagint version of Esther.

The Septuagint version of the Esther story stresses how god-fearing the protagonist is, as well as her femininity.[20] Josephus it seems that he was interested less in how god-fearing Esther was than in her femininity. Esther's prayer, which is seventeen verses long in the Septuagint and shows Esther to be a reflective theologian and a woman faithful to the law (Esth C, 14–30 LXX), is reduced by Josephus to a few sentences. Esther, a weak woman, prays to God

18. Midrash Tanhuma A is also referred to as Midrash Tanchuma Buber, after its editor: Salomon Buber, ed., *Midrasch Tanchuma* (Vilnius: Romm, 1885). The story of the daughter of Jephthah referred to above is found in the Buber edition of Midrash Tanhuma, Behuqqotai 7.

19. Halpern-Amaru, "Biblical Women," 165.

20. See on this issue Louis H. Feldman, "Hellenization in Josephus' Version of Esther," *TAPA* 101 (1970): 143–70.

for the courage to be able to go before the king and hopes "that the king might be made to feel hatred toward the enemies of the Jews" (*Ant.* 11.233). Nevertheless, Josephus has added a motif to Esther's prayer, which he found in the description of her visit to the king (see Esth D, 1–8 LXX) but not in her prayer: her charming appearance, by which she hoped to win over the king for herself. Whereas in the Septuagint version she herself takes the trouble to ensure that her appearance is as striking as possible, in Josephus she needs God's help to do so. This theme is found in similar form in tractate Megillah of the Babylonian Talmud: before she goes to the king she is clothed with a "holy spirit" (b. Meg. 15a), and when the king sees her she has three ministering angels by her side, who ensure not only that the royal scepter would be extended to her but also stiffen her resolve (literally "her neck") and wrap a ribbon of grace about her. Here too Josephus did not invent the theme but merely gave it new meaning by relocating it.

5. The Moabite or Midianite Women and the Wife of Potiphar

In Josephus, the story of the daughters of Moab, who led Israel astray in the desert, is significantly expanded (*Ant.* 4.126–155). In Numbers this episode encompasses only three verses (Num 25:1–3):

> While Israel was staying at Shittim, the people began to have sexual relations with the women of Moab. These invited the people to the sacrifices of their gods, and the people ate and bowed down to their gods. Thus Israel yoked itself to the Baal of Peor, and YHWH's anger was kindled against Israel.

The episode is only loosely connected—to the preceding narrative about the Aramaean seer Balaam, who was ordered by the king of Moab to curse the people of Israel but instead blessed them (Num 22–24). Josephus, on the other hand, closely connects the two narratives: Balaam was unable to curse Israel yet did give his king advice on how Israel could be defeated.

> Take of your daughters those who are comeliest and most capable of constraining and conquering the chastity of their beholders by reason of their beauty, deck out their charms to add to their comeliness, send them to the neighbourhood of the Hebrews' camp, and charge them to company with their young men when they sue for favours. Then, when they shall see these youths overmastered by their passions, let them quit them and, on their entreating them to stay, let them not consent er ever they have induced their lovers to renounce the laws of their fathers and the God to whom they owe them, and to worship the gods of the Madianites and Moabites. For thus will God be moved to indignation against them. (*Ant* 4.129–130).

The fact that Josephus here speaks of the "gods of the Madianites [= Midianites] and Moabites," and thereby appears to more or less identify the two peoples one with the other, may be connected with the continuation of the story in Num 25. After all, in Num 25:5–18 the story has to do not with a Moabite but with a Midianite woman named Cozbi, who sleeps with an Israelite man. Josephus combines the two themes: the Midianite Cozbi is for him the paradigm of a Midianite/Moabite woman, who leads the Israelite men astray by trickery. The instigator of this trickery is Balaam.

The Midianites/Moabites follow Balaam's advice and the scheme succeeds. The young men of Israel fall in love with the beautiful foreign women and are even ready for marriage. The reaction of the women is given in a long speech:

> "Seeing then," said the maidens, "that ye agree to these conditions and that ye have customs and a mode of life wholly alien to all mankind, insomuch that your food is of a peculiar sort and your drink is distinct from that of other men, it behoves you, if ye would live with us, also to revere our gods; no other proof can there be of that affection which ye declare that ye now have for us and of its continuance in future, save that ye worship the same gods as we. Nor can any man reproach you for venerating the special gods of the country whereto ye are come, above all when our gods are common to all mankind, while yours has no other worshipper." They must therefore (they added) either fall in with the beliefs of all men or look for another world, where they could live alone in accordance with their gods. (*Ant.* 4.137–138)

It is indeed true that Josephus has in this narrative embroidered the art of seduction practiced by the Moabite women and even gives them their own voice, which they do not have in the Bible, but it is clear also that the women act only as instruments of the Moabite king and his men, who want to bring Israel under their control by military means.

I argue that Josephus did not invent this episode, since parts of it are found already in the writings of Philo (*Mos.* 2.292–299).[21] True, in Josephus it is considerably more expansive, and some details can certainly be attributed to Josephus's own creativity, but I assume that both, Josephus and Philo, fall back here on a novel-like Jewish narrative that originated in Hellenistic Egypt and that the original intent of this *Vorlage* was to make comprehensible the somewhat enigmatic notice in Num 31:15–16, where Moses avers that Balaam

---

21. Willem C. van Unnik, "Josephus' Account of the Story of Israel's Sin with Alien Women," in *Travels in the World of the Old Testament: Studies Presented to Professor M. A. Beek*, ed. Matthieu Sybrand Huibert Gerard Heerma van Voss, Philo Hendrik Jan Houwink ten Cate, and N. A. van Uchelen, SSN 16 (Assen: Van Gorcum, 1974), 241–61.

advised the Moabite women to entice the Israelite men. But there is no mention of this in Num 25:1–3, where the story of the Moabite women is told. The postulated *Vorlage*, the Jewish novel that was not preserved, would have combined the two biblical sections into one narrative.

The assumption that there was such a *Vorlage* can be supported by the observation that at least two other such novel-like expansions of stories of women can be found in the works of Josephus. One is concerned with the story of Potiphar's wife and Joseph's resistance to her attempts to seduce him (Gen 39:7–19; *Ant.* 2.41–59). In the biblical account, when the wife is alone in the house with her slave she takes the opportunity to demand that he lie with her (Gen 39:11–12). In Josephus this scene is greatly embellished, turning into a sophisticated plan in which the wife pretends to be sick during a feast given by her husband. She tries to get Joseph to sleep with her, first with flattering words and then violently (*Ant.* 2.45–52). There is a parallel account in the apocryphal Testament of Joseph,[22] half of which in fact deals with the sexual advances that Joseph was subjected to while he was in the house of Potiphar. It is clear that the theme of sexual temptation of chaste Jewish men was a favorite in Second Temple times and was not an invention of Josephus.

6. Tharbis

The other novelistic expansion in Josephus is associated with the deeds of Moses as prince of Egypt and his marriage to an Ethiopian process named Tharbis (*Ant.* 2.238–253). There is a partial parallel to the story of Moses in Ethiopia in the work of the Jewish-Hellenistic writer Artapanus; there is a lively scholarly discussion about the connections between the two texts. Let us look therefore more closely at this example.

I begin where Josephus first mentions Pharaoh's daughter (*Ant.* 2.224; cf. Exod 2:2).[23] Whereas she remains nameless in the Bible, in Josephus she is given the name Thermuthis, as also in Jubilees, which originates in Palestine and of which some fragments were found at Qumran (Jub. 47.5). Although I have found no scholar who claims that Josephus knew Jubilees, it can be assumed that he added this name to the biblical text, using material that he found in other sources—in this case a source used also by Jubilees. As in the story told in the Bible, in Josephus Pharaoh's daughter finds the small, exposed Moses in or near the Nile. Differently from the Bible, she looks for a wet nurse

22. On this, see Martin Braun, *History and Romance in Graeco-Oriental Literature* (Oxford: Blackwell, 1938), 90–104.

23. See Hanna Tervanotko's detailed presentation of the biblical women around Moses in Josephus and in other early Jewish writings in this volume.

for him among the Egyptian women. But Moses declines to suck non-kosher milk and only then is his mother brought to him. The same episode is also found in the Babylonian Talmud in Sotah 12b:

> Why just "of the Hebrew women"?—It teaches that they handed Moses about to all the Egyptian women, but he would not suck. He said: "Shall a mouth which will speak with the *Sechinah* suck what is unclean!? (b. Sot. 12b)[24]

Again Josephus uses here a haggadic source which must have been known in his time, even though it is attested in literary form only in much later Jewish sources.

As in the Bible, Josephus too reports the naming of Moses (Exod 2:10; *Ant.* 2.228). He then inserts another haggadic episode (*Ant.* 2.232–233):

> Now one day she [= Thermuthis, Pharaoh's daughter] brought Moses to her father and showed him to him, and told him how she had been mindful for the succession, were it God's will to grant her no child of her own, by bringing up a boy of divine beauty and generous spirit, and by what a miracle she had received him of a river's bounty, "and methought," she said, "to make him my child and heir to my kingdom." With these words she laid the babe in her father's arms; and he took and clasped him affectionately to his breast and, to please his daughter, placed his diadem upon his head. But Moses tore it off and flung it to the ground, in mere childishness, and trampled it underfoot; and this was taken as an evil omen for the kingdom.[25]

This haggadah also is preserved in a rabbinic version in a late haggadic midrash:

> And Pharaoh's daughter would kiss him and hug him and love him, and would not take him out of the king's palace, because he was so handsome and all wished to see him, and whoever saw him could not walk by, and Pharaoh would hug him and kiss him and [Moses] would take the crown off [Pharaoh's] head and throw it down, as he was destined to do to him. (Tanh. Exod. 8).[26]

---

24. A. Cohen, trans., *Babylonian Talmud: Sotah* (London: Soncino, 1985).

25. In the continuation of the story, the Egyptian sage, who at Moses's birth prophesied the downfall of Egyptian rule, wants to kill Moses as well. Thermuthis and her father, however, prevent him from doing this.

26. Translation by Tal Ilan. In Midrash Exodus Rabbah to Exod 2:10, the same version is found practically word for word, only Moses does not hurl the crown to the ground but places it on his own head. See S. M. Lehrman, trans., *Midrash Rabbah: Exodus Rabbah* (London: Soncino, 1951).

The haggadic patchwork that Josephus stitches together here is continued in what follows and departs completely from any connection to the biblical story. Moses grows and stands out because of his courage and bravery. On one occasion, when the Ethiopians bring the Egyptians into dire military straights, Pharaoh orders Moses to reorganize the Egyptian army and lead it into battle against Ethiopia. The Egyptian sages, who hope for his death, see their opportunity (2.238). But, contrary to all expectations, Moses is successful. The result of his victory, however, is that the hatred against him in the Pharaoh's court increases even more, so that eventually even the Pharaoh is ready to have him killed. Thereupon Moses flees to Midian (2.254–257). A similar story is told by the Hellenistic-Jewish author Artapanus, whose work is transmitted by Alexander Polyhistor, which in turn is excerpted by the church father Eusebius (*Praep. ev.* 9.27). The similarity between the two plots is summarized by Gregory Sterling, who is aware that this is not the whole story, since he continues: "Josephos does know the story told by Artapanos: the structural similarity demands this. The dissimilarities, on the other hand, make it all but certain … that Josephos knew the story in a form other than what Polyhistor preserved of Artapanos."[27] Like me, Sterling favors the hypothesis that there were more narratives circulating in Hellenistic times than are preserved and that one needs to take into consideration that the differences among the various accounts go back to different earlier versions.

This assumption is confirmed by an episode found only in Josephus, inserted in the middle of the flow of the narrative about Moses's campaign to Ethiopia: the episode of the Ethiopian princess Tharbis (*Ant.* 2.252–253).

> Tharbis, the daughter of the king of the Ethiopians, watching Moses bringing his troops close beneath the ramparts and fighting valiantly, marvelled at the ingenuity of his manoeuvres and, understanding that it was to him that the Egyptians, who but now despaired of their independence, owed all their success, and through him that the Ethiopians, so boastful of their feats against them, were reduced to the last straits, fell madly in love with him; and under the master of this passion she sent to him the most trusty of her menials to make him an offer of marriage. He accepted the proposal on condition that she would surrender the town, pledged himself by oath verily to take her to wife and, once master of the town, not to violate the pact, whereupon action outstripped parley. After chastisement of the Ethiopians, Moses rendered thanks to God, celebrated the nuptials, and led the Egyptians back to their own land.

27. Gregory E. Sterling, *Historiography and Self-Definition: Josephus, Luke-Acts and Apologetic Historiography*, NovTSup 64 (Leiden: Brill, 1992), 269, 278.

As numerous studies have confirmed, this episode is very clearly an interpretation of one biblical verse from a different context, Num 12:1, the mention of Moses's Cushite (= Ethiopian) wife.[28] Rabbinic literature usually identifies this woman with his other wife mentioned in the Bible, Zippora.[29] The story in Josephus shows that there were other exegetical interpretations of the enigmatic Num 12:1, in circulation. This short, haggadic, novel-like narrative, which is found only in Josephus, fits well with a widespread exegetical genre found in Hellenistic Alexandria.

Another example of this genre is the early Jewish text, Joseph and Aseneth, an entire novel woven out of a single biblical verse (Gen 41:50).[30] The fact that we have no other evidence in the literature of the period for the story about Tharbis and Moses has to do with the vagaries of the transmission of sources from the time. It can by no means be used as an argument that Josephus himself invented the story.

Tharbis is not an especially interesting or positive role model. If one looks for biblical parallels to this figure, one could most readily compare her to Rahab of Jericho (Josh 2). Rahab protects the two spies sent by Joshua and thereby helps the Israelites conquer the city. Later Jewish interpretations of the story see Rahab in a positive light, even as the wife of Joshua (b. Meg. 11b). These traits reflect the same tendencies found in the story about Tharbis. It is clear that in both cases the stories are told from the perspective of the conquerors, not the conquered or defeated. What would have been regarded as betrayal by the inhabitants of Jericho or Ethiopia is transformed in the eyes of Israel into cunning and strength, to the credit of the two women.[31] One thing is certain: Tharbis is not particularly evil, seductive, or devious, nor is she especially pious. Halpern-Amaru makes no attempt to incorporate this female figure into her schema.[32]

---

28. Tessa Rajak, "Moses in Ethiopia: Legend and Literature," *JJS* 29 (1978): 111–22; Avigdor Shinan, "Moses and the Ethiopian Woman: Sources of a Story in the Chronicles of Moses," *ScrHier* 27 (1978): 66–78; Donna Runnals, "Moses' Ethiopian Campaign," *JSJ* 14 (1983): 135–56; Karen Strand Winslow, *Early Jewish and Christian Memories of Moses' Wives: Exogamic Marriage and Ethnic Identity* (Lewiston, NY: Mellen, 2005), 167–90.

29. The earliest example for this is found in Sifre Num. 99.

30. On Joseph and Aseneth, see the contribution of Angela Standhartinger in this volume.

31. The book of Judith, on the other hand, is told from the perspective of the defeated and the weak. See on this contrast Musa W. Dube, "Jumping the Fire with Judith: Postcolonial Feminist Hermeneutics of Liberation," in *Feminist Interpretation of the Bible and the Hermeneutics of Liberation*, ed. Silvia Schroer and Sophia Bietenhard, JSOTSup 374 (Sheffield: Sheffield Academic, 2003), 60–76.

32. Halpern-Amaru ("Biblical Women," 167) points out that the details of the Tharbis

7. Concluding Observations

Josephus appears to have had access to a large repertoire of stories about Moses and the women around him, as well as about other biblical women such as Esther or the Midianite/Moabite "seducers." Presumably these narrative traditions originated in Hellenistic Egypt. Josephus used them to embroider the biblical stories. Evidence for the claim that he did not invent these episodes is found in the numerous parallels to the traditions that appear in his work, for example, in Jubilees, in the Septuagint, in Philo, in Artapanus, and in rabbinic literature. True, the episode of the Ethiopian princess Tharbis is attested only in Josephus, but it can hardly be regarded as his invention. It is not his style to retell the Bible in a completely new way, as the examples of Deborah and Jephtah's daughter discussed above show.

It is probable that all of the additions, those that I have discussed here as well as other alterations that Josephus made in his characterization of biblical women, are based on Hellenistic models. But one should not thereby conclude that they were inherently more misogynistic than the Bible or that they needed female figures who were more pious or, at the opposite extreme, more seductive sexually, than presented in the Bible. It is much more the case that there was the challenge, with which Josephus too had to contend: the women in the biblical narratives act self-confidently, behave in unconventional ways, and thereby create ethical and religious dilemmas for interpreters hundreds of years later.[33] A variety of methods were developed to meet this challenge and most of them have misogynistic overtones. The novel-like narrative beloved in Hellenistic literature and used as sources by Josephus should be seen more as an exegetical device that Josephus was able to utilize skillfully and less as his own unique response to this challenge.

---

story could have originated among Jews in Alexandria, but she does not draw the obvious conclusion that I have come to, namely, that it is not Josephus who gave the story its specific character but rather that the novel-like story was already circulating.

33. See also my introductory observations in Tal Ilan, *Silencing the Queen: The Literary Histories of Shelamzion and Other Jewish Women*, TS 115 (Tübingen: Mohr Siebeck, 2006), 1–3.

Between Social Context and Individual Ideology: Philo's Changing Views of Women

Maren R. Niehoff

Scholars with a feminist awareness have often been intrigued by Philo of Alexandria, who stands at one of the most important watersheds of Western civilization, namely, at the juncture between Judaism and Hellenism in the first century CE, just before Christianity emerged and adopted many of his ideas. Philo's views of women have regularly been seen as uniformly negative. The only open question has pertained to the origin of his views, whether they derived from Jewish or Greek sources.[1] In this context an important factor has regularly been overlooked, namely, Philo's dramatic intellectual development as a result of his visit to Rome. He was not a monolithic thinker, one who entertained the same views throughout his long and productive life, but rather a versatile and inquisitive mind, confronting the radically changing circumstances of his life. Such changes were prompted by the pogrom in Alexandria in 38 CE and Philo's consequent visit to Rome as the head of the Jewish embassy to Gaius Caligula. Staying in the capital of the empire for at least three years, he was exposed to new, specifically Roman, discourses and engaged many ideas of Roman Stoicism.[2] His identity can thus no longer be understood in light of the supposed dichotomy between Judaism and Hellenism. Other factors also have to be taken into account. Especially prominent is the question whether Rome offered a different approach to women than the one Philo was used to in his home-town of Alexandria and whether this

---

1. See especially Dorothy Sly, *Philo's Perception of Women*, BJS 209 (Atlanta: Scholars Press, 1990); Judith Romney Wegner, "Philo's Portrayal of Women—Hebraic or Hellenic?," in *"Women Like This": New Perspectives on Jewish Women in the Greco-Roman World*, ed. Amy-Jill Levine, EJL 1 (Atlanta: Scholars Press, 1991), 41–66; Sharon Lea Mattila, "Wisdom, Sense Perception, Nature and Philo's Gender Gradient," *HTR* 89 (1996): 103–29.

2. For details, see Maren R. Niehoff, *Philo of Alexandria: An Intellectual Biography* (New Haven: Yale University Press, forthcoming; German translation: Tübingen: Mohr Siebeck, 2017).

had any effect on his attitudes. In other words, we have to investigate how far the social environment influences ideology in his case. To what extent did his physical journey change his worldview and influence his views of women, not necessarily changing them in essence, but perhaps using different categories and intellectual frameworks?

Born in Alexandria around 20 BCE, Philo grew up in a rather peaceful atmosphere, receiving a thorough training in Greek literature, while at the same time being immersed in Bible studies. He began his career as a systematic Bible commentator in the Jewish community of Alexandria, engaging in a lively discussion among experts and offering allegorical interpretations of the book of Genesis. In 38 CE he saw an outburst of ethnic violence in his home-town, which caused many casualties and great damage to Jewish property. These events changed Philo's life. In the autumn of that year he left for Rome as the head of the Jewish embassy to the emperor Gaius Caligula. Philo vividly recalls how his philosophical leisure was abruptly disturbed by the political events:

> There was a time when I could leisurely engage in philosophy and the contemplation of the universe and its contents and enjoyed a truly beloved and blessed state of mind. I constantly associated with Divine subjects and ideas, in which I rejoiced without restraint and insatiate.... But then the most grievous of mischief lay in wait for me, envy the hater of good, who suddenly assailed me and did not cease to drag me down before it had violently pressed me into the ocean of political affairs, in which I am swept away so that I cannot even raise my head above the surface. (*Spec.* 3.1–3)[3]

Philo, who had thus far immersed himself in the minutiae of biblical scholarship within the Jewish community of Alexandria, suddenly became a political figure, addressing broader Roman audiences in order to gain sympathy and understanding for the Jewish cause. Arriving in Rome, he became in an astonishingly quick manner familiar with Roman culture, events, and philosophical discourses, using new genres of writing and appealing to new values. His running commentaries on the biblical text were now replaced by historical and philosophical writings as well as biographies of the patriarchs. He no longer presupposed any knowledge of Judaism but wrote introductory and broad treatises, which would appeal to any sympathetic outsider.[4] Philo's

3. All quotations from Philo are, with adaptations, from Francis Henry Colson, G. H. Whitaker, and Ralph Marcus, trans., *Philo*, 10 vols. and 2 supplementary vols., LCL (Cambridge: Harvard University Press, 1929–1962).

4. On the different audiences of Philo's series of works, see also Ellen Birnbaum, *The Place of Judaism in Philo's Thought: Israel, Jews, and Proselytes*, BJS 290 (Atlanta: Scholars

positions generally became more immanentist, connected to this world, rather than striving for other-worldly spirituality. God, for example, is no longer perceived by him as wholly transcendent Other, but as a providential deity involved not only in the general management of the world, but also in the concrete lives of men and women. Philo himself no longer suppresses his personality behind the format of a commentary but becomes visible in his writings as a tangible author, directly addressing his readers and toying with different literary perspectives.[5]

Both Alexandria and Rome offered women more options than classical Athens. The ideal of a quiet teenage wife, wholly submissive to her much older husband, was in both cities replaced by the reality of mature women acting in the public space. Sarah Pomeroy has convincingly shown that women played a significant part in the government and religious life of Hellenistic Egypt.[6] Women could become queens and act as priestesses. They no longer needed a male representative to handle their legal affairs but could independently transmit their heritage and, according to Demotic law, even divorce their husbands. In Rome women enjoyed a high social standing as mothers and wives, often taking an active part in politics.[7] It is striking that when Philo lived and worked in Alexandria he was oriented inside, towards the higher socioeconomic levels of the Jewish community. He never mentions a queen or priestess and does not seem to have noticed the new opportunities of women in his home-town.[8] Once he even prides himself that Alexandrian Jews held up the traditional ideal of totally secluded women who did not even meet their male relatives (*Flacc.* 89). This ideal obviously pertains to the upper classes who

---

Press, 1996); and James Royse, "The Works of Philo," in *The Cambridge Companion to Philo*, ed. Adam Kamesar (Cambridge: Cambridge University Press, 2009), 32–64.

5. For details, see Niehoff, *Philo of Alexandria*.

6. Sarah B. Pomeroy, *Goddesses, Whores, Wives and Slaves: Women in Classical Antiquity* (New York: Schocken Books, 1975); Pomeroy, *Women in Hellenistic Egypt: From Alexander to Cleopatra* (New York: Schocken Books, 1984).

7. Suzanne Dixon, *The Roman Mother* (London: Routledge, 1988); Dixon, *The Roman Family* (Baltimore: John Hopkins University Press, 1992); Susan Treggiari, *Roman Marriage: Iusti Conjuges from the Time of Cicero to the Time of Ulpian* (Oxford: Clarendon, 1991); Jane Rowlandson, *Women and Society in Greek and Roman Egypt* (Cambridge: Cambridge University Press, 1998).

8. Note that his treatise on the group of Jewish philosophers, the Therapeutae, suggests that they included women and lived near Alexandria; see, especially, Joan Taylor, *Jewish Women Philosophers of First-Century Alexandria: Philo's 'Therapeutae' Reconsidered* (Oxford: Oxford University Press, 2003). This treatise, however, is from the later period of Philo's career and reflects his new Roman orientation; for details, see Niehoff, *Philo of Alexandria*, ch. 4.

could afford separate women's quarters. What is of interest to us, however, is the question of how Philo negotiated his experience of social reality with his philosophical views and, moreover, how his general opening up to the world in Rome affected his attitudes towards women.

Biblical Women in Philo's Early Alexandrian Writings

The dominant philosophical school in Philo's Alexandria was Platonism, which stressed spiritual values and encouraged transcendence of this world. The main aim of ethics was to leave behind the material world and ascend to higher realms. Eudorus, an Alexandrian Platonist of the first century BCE, and a commentator of Plato's *Theaetetus*, whose identity is unknown, spoke about man's ability to resemble god by imitating his virtues.[9] Philo as a young man was thoroughly immersed in Alexandrian Platonism. Like his colleagues, he took a keen interest in Plato's *Theaetetus*. The *Allegorical Commentary* from the beginning of his career shows a clear Platonic orientation and stresses the dichotomy between soul and body, which can be overcome by fleeing the world and imitating God. In this context Philo speaks about the soul's journey to an absolutely transcendent God. His longing for the ultimately Other and totally spiritual realm is often overtly mystical, conceiving of man as a spiritual entity with little, if any connection to the surrounding world.

The nature and status of women are not explicitly addressed in the extant fragments of Alexandrian philosophy. While women assumed a rather visible place in society, they did not become the subject of intellectual inquiry. Following this philosophical trend, Philo never mentions Cleopatra or any other historical woman in his *Allegorical Commentary*. Women only enter the picture as biblical figures, who are interpreted in the course of the running commentary on Gen 2:1–18:2.[10] In this context the matriarchs are consistently

---

9. See Mauro Bonazzi, "Towards Transcendence: Philo and the Revival of Platonism in the Early Imperial Age," in *Philo of Alexandria and Post-Aristotelian Philosophy*, ed. Francesca Allesse, SPhA 5 (Leiden: Brill, 2008), 233–51; David Sedley, "Three Platonist Interpretations of the Theaetetus," in *Form and Argument in Late Plato*, ed. Christopher Gill and Mary Margaret McCabe (Oxford: Clarendon, 1996), 81–101; Sedley, "The Ideal of Godlikeness," in *Plato 2: Ethics, Politics, Religion, and the Soul*, ed. Gail Fine (Oxford: Oxford University Press, 1999), 309–28.

10. Philo probably wrote a no-longer-extant commentary on Gen 1:1–33; see David Sterling, "'Prolific in Expression and Broad in Thought': Internal References to Philo's *Allegorical Commentary* and *Exposition of the Law*," *Euphrosyne* 40 (2012): 55–76; for details, see Niehoff, *Philo of Alexandria*, ch. 9. Philo's commentary on Gen 18:1–2 is not printed in the standard editions of his work, but is preserved in an Armenian fragment, published by Folker Siegert, "The Philonian Fragment *De Deo*," *SPhiloA* 10 (1998): 1–33.

read as allegories of the soul, which have intercourse with God and receive his sperm. They exemplify the process of barren souls receiving divine seed and giving birth to ethereal off-spring.

The biblical reference to Sarah's sterility draws Philo's attention. He stresses the apparent paradox of her being sterile and then giving birth. This must be understood, he explains, in the context of God's role as both a physical and spiritual impregnator, who "opens the womb" (*Migr.* 34, 81; *Congr.* 3–7 [referring to Gen 16:1; 29:31]). On the literal level, God enables even sterile women, long past their menopause, to become pregnant and give birth to significant offspring. On the allegorical level, God convenes with the human soul and impregnates it with ethereal ideas. This spiritual process can only take place when the senses are "barren" and the soul has abandoned feminine features. In Philo's view, Sarah is perfectly prepared for this encounter, because her menopause signifies that she "left behind everything feminine" and has become truly virile. She represents a virtuous soul, which receives divine sperm and gives birth to real wisdom. Sarah moreover illustrates the utter sterility or passivity of the soul, which is filled by God. Rachel, by contrast, who demands children from her husband—"if not, I will die" (Gen 30:1)—fails in Philo's view to understand that the "mind is the cause of nothing, but God who is antecedent to the mind, the only cause."[11] This bold erotic language and the overriding emphasis on divine impregnation distinguish Philo's approach. Integrating mythological language into philosophical discourse, he offers a new version of the idea that human women have intercourse with divine figures.

Gender also plays a significant role in Philo's discussion of Eve, the paradigmatic first woman, about whom he says the following:

> The most proper and exact name for sense-perception is "woman." For just as the man reveals himself in action and the woman in passivity, so the mind proves itself in activity and perception in passivity, namely in the way of women. (*Leg.* 2.38)

Using Aristotelian categories of male activity and female passivity, Philo interprets Eve as a symbol of the senses which introduce the mind to the dangerous passions. She opens the door—or the Pandora's Box—of the irrational realm. Philo associates her even more rigorously than the biblical narrator with the serpent, the symbol of the passions, and contrasts "Eve's serpent" to "Moses's serpent," the latter a symbol of self-mastery. The union of Adam

---

11. *Her.* 249–266; *Cher.* 43–50; *Leg.* 2.46–48; *Fug.* 128; see also Sly, *Philo's Perception of Women*, 145–54.

and Eve, which leads to his "cleaving to his wife," is judged in the most negative terms. Philo fears that she will prompt man to abandon God.[12] Similarly, Mirjam stands for sense-perception, while her brother Aaron represents the Logos, which is not only human rationality, but also the point of contact with God (*Leg.* 3.103).

In the *Allegorical Commentary* from Philo's early career, biblical women thus symbolize mainly passivity, either in the positive sense of a sterile soul receiving divine seed or in the negative sense of sense-perception, which receives impressions from the outside and gives in to seduction. Philo obviously did not critically reflect on the marginalization of women in his particular segment of Alexandrian society, but rather accepted it and used images of segregation for philosophical purposes (e.g., *Leg.* 3.40). Moreover, the dominant philosophical school in his home-town did not advance gender issues in intellectual discourses. Here, too, Philo did not encounter incentives to think about the role of women, but rather socialized with philosophers who took women and especially mid-wifery in an allegorical sense.

Philo's Views of Women in His Later Writings from the Roman Period

Philo's historical writings contain the only reference in his work to a real woman, namely, Augustus's wife Livia. She is praised in the *Embassy* for taking her husband as an "instructor in piety" and receiving a "pure training." This reference to Livia resonates with contemporary Roman discourses. Livia was given "divine honours" by the emperor Claudius "as soon as his power was firmly established." This means that she received special public attention in Rome precisely when Philo was most likely still visiting there (*Legat.* 319–320; Suetonius, *Claud.* 11.1–2).

Roman intellectuals moreover took a lively interest in gender issues and the place of women in society. Livia had provoked numerous reactions. The senate voted to call her "mother of her country" and the emperor Tiberius "son of Livia." The new emperor, however, rejected these honors and generally disliked her continuous influence in Roman politics, even warning her "not to meddle with affairs of importance and unbecoming a woman." Tacitus subsequently criticizes her dominating spirit and provides a rather malicious portrait of her. Philo's late contemporary, the Roman philosopher Seneca,

12. *Leg.* 2.49 (cf. *Opif.* 152); 2.79–81; 3.11; see also *Leg.* 3.184–188; see also Romney-Wegner, "Philo's Portrayal of Women"; contra Verna E. F. Harrison, "Allegorization of Gender: Plato and Philo on Spiritual Child-Bearing," in *Asceticism*, ed. Vincent L. Wimbush and Richard Valantasis (Oxford: Oxford University Press, 1995), 520–34, who attempts to nuance Philo's gender categories.

by contrast, expresses a deep appreciation for Livia. In his *Consolation for Marcia*, his earliest treatise written during Philo's years in Rome, he recommends her to Marcia and his implied readers. While generally assuming that women have a "feminine weakness of mind," Seneca praises the former empress for taking the philosopher Arius Didymus, her husband's friend, as a teacher and thus gaining rational control over her grief after her son's death. Livia is presented to Marcia as a prime role model, who can show her the way to cope with the passions and mourn in a temperate way. She also demonstrates that women, if they make conscious efforts, can be equally brave as men in the struggle for tranquility of mind.[13]

Both Philo and Seneca appreciate Livia as a woman willing to learn and consequently able to develop a philosophical disposition. While Seneca praises her for overcoming her grief, Philo points to her high regard for the Jewish temple, paralleling that of her husband. Both authors assign a crucial role to her education and stress her exceptional status among the women, who, as Philo puts it, are generally "weaker and do not apprehend any mental conception apart from what their senses perceive." Moreover, both Philo and Seneca conceive of Livia as a subordinate wife, who fulfills her husband's expectations at his side. It is through him that she acquires her intellectual training, either directly as his student or indirectly through his philosopher friend. Her public influence and independence of mind, mentioned by Suetonius, are overlooked in this context (Suetonius, *Claud.* 4.1–7).[14] A rather domesticated, yet positive Livia emerges.

Seeing that Philo is exposed to Roman culture and praises Livia in terms very similar to those of Seneca, we have to ask how his experience in the capital has shaped his views of biblical women. To what extent is their image in the *Lives* of the patriarchs, consistent with the portrait of Livia in his historical writings? Can we identify features of Roman philosophy in Philo's sketches of Sarah, Eve, and the women in Moses's family? Vice versa, are there

13. Suetonius, *Tib.* 50.2–3; Tacitus, *Ann.* 5.1.1–5; Seneca, *Marc.* 1.1–5; 4.1; 16.1–5; see also Mercedes Mauch, *Senecas Frauenbild in den philosophischen Schriften* (Frankfurt: Lang, 1997); Mary Rose D'Angelo, "Gender and Geopolitics in the Work of Philo of Alexandria: Jewish Piety and Imperial Family Values," in *Mapping Gender in Ancient Religious Discourse*, ed. Todd Penner and Caroline Vander Stichele, BibInt 84 (Leiden: Brill, 2007), 63–88; J. P. V. D. Balsdon, *Roman Women: Their History and Habits* (London: Bodley Head, 1962), 90–95 (with emphasis on Tacitus's distortion of her image); Anthony A. Barrett, *Livia: First Lady of Imperial Rome* (New Haven: Yale University Press, 2002), 155–58; on the date of Seneca's *Ad Marciam de consolatione*, see Miriam T. Griffin, *Seneca: A Philosopher in Politics* (Oxford: Clarendon, 1976), 366.

14. See also D'Angelo, "Gender and Geopolitics," 67–69, 82–83.

limitations, religious or other, to his effort at integrating the biblical women into wider discourses?

Sarah is the most prominent of the biblical women in Philo's later writings, not least thanks to the fact that her husband's biography has survived. Rebecca, Rachel, and Leah may also have fared well in the *Lives* of Isaac and Jacob, but these are unfortunately no longer extant. Philo praises Sarah as "a wife most excellent with regard to her soul and most beautiful in her body, surpassing all the women of her time" (*Abr.* 93). The matriarch is impressive in the spiritual and the material realm, both of which are appreciated by Philo in the later stage of his career.

Philo uses the short biblical reference to Abraham's mourning over Sarah's death in Gen 23:2 to write a lengthy *encomium*. In his earlier treatises from the Alexandrian period this verse is given no attention, with the exception of *QG* 4.73, where Sarah's death is interpreted allegorically as the demise of wisdom. Philo's new interest in the death of a beloved person and the ways of remembering her is remarkable. His excitement about this topic is so great that he abandons his narrative role as detached biographer and exclaims: "I have many praises to tell about this woman, but will mention one, which will be the clearest proof for the others as well" (*Abr.* 247). Philo identifies to such an extent with the role of the mourner that his description almost reads like an obituary, written as if he has lost his beloved wife and appreciates the opportunity to express his grief. This highly personal interest in the biblical scene of mourning resonates well with contemporary Roman culture, where lengthy inscriptions on tomb stones are fashionable and the remembrance of the deceased has become a subject of philosophical inquiry. Seneca's influential teacher Attalus compares the remembrance of lost relatives and friends to the "agreeably acid taste" of certain fruits, which is recommended no less than "enjoying a meal of cakes and honey" (Seneca, *Ep.* 63.5).[15]

Philo praises Sarah as an exemplary wife and ideal partner, who "is most suitable to his heart and noble in every respect" (ἡ γυνὴ θυμηρεστάτη καὶ τὰ πάντα ἀρίστη; *Abr.* 245). The term "most suitable to his heart" draws attention, because it is absent from the biblical story and suggests a mutual relationship based on feelings and a felicitous matching of personalities. Sarah was in Philo's view dear to her husband and did not only perform marital tasks, which were appreciated for their usefulness. Unlike the biblical narrator, Philo moreover speaks about Sarah's "love for her husband," which she showed in

15. On Attalus, see Mark Morford, *The Roman Philosophers: From the Time of Cato the Censor to the Death of Marcus Aurelius* (New York: Routledge, 2002), 165–66; on the culture of epitaphs in Rome, see Richard Lattimore, *Themes in Greek and Latin Epitaphs* (Urbana: University of Illinois Press, 1942), 275–80.

numerous ways. She was a "real partner in life" (κοινωνὸς ὄντως βίου), "considering it right to share equally good and bad circumstances." In contrast to numerous other women, she did not "run away from misfortunes, lying in wait for pieces of good luck, but accepted her portion in both with utmost readiness as suitable and becoming of a wife" (*Abr.* 246). Philo has invested the biblical marriage with the values of marital partnership and love. This ideal developed in late republican Rome and became highly significant in different public spheres of the early empire. From Cicero and Ovid onwards, love for wives and thankfulness for their partnership became literary topoi. Augustus reinforced this ideal by demanding that every citizen take a "wife who is chaste, domestic, a good house-keeper, a rearer of children … to join you in prosperity and console you in misfortune" (Dio Cassius, *Hist. rom.* 56.3.3). Supporting this policy, Livia dedicated a shrine to *Concordia*. Seneca's loving partnership with his wife Paulina became so famous that Tacitus still spoke about it. The Roman philosopher Musonius asks one generation after Philo, "what is the chief end of marriage"? His emphatic answer is: "community of life" and "perfect companionship and mutual love of husband and wife, both in health and sickness and under all circumstances" (*Diatr.* 13A).[16] Given these distinctly Roman discourses, which have no parallel in Alexandrian sources, it is not surprising that Philo embellishes the biblical story of Sarah and Abraham with new emphasis on their mutual relationship. Sarah is no longer an object, but becomes a self-determined subject, who chooses to be an exemplary wife.

Philo especially praises Sarah's loyalty and steadfastness on the couple's journeys:

> She shared with him the departure from relatives and unhesitatingly migrated from her household, shared continued and successive wanderings on foreign soil and suffered want in famine and joined his war campaigns. (*Abr.* 245)

Philo has considerably expanded the biblical text, which merely says that Abraham "took his wife" from Chaldea to the land of Israel (Gen 12:5). He

16. Translation from Cora Elizabeth Lutz, "Musonius Rufus: 'The Roman Socrates,'" *YCS* 10 (1947): 3–147. Musonius Rufus uses the same keyword as Philo, namely, κοινωνία ("companionship"); see also Seneca, *Ep.* 104.1–5; Tacitus, *Ann.* 15.63; on the Roman ideal of harmonious marriages, see Paul Veyne, "The Roman Empire," in *A History of Private Life*, ed. Paul Veyne (Cambridge: Harvard University Press, 1987), 33–42; Pierre Grimal, *Love in Ancient Rome*, trans. Arthur Train Jr. (Norman, OK: University of Oklahoma Press, 1980), 48–69; Treggiari, *Roman Marriage*, 249–51; Dixon, *Roman Family*, 67–71.

highlights Abraham's journeys and discusses for the first time the contribution of a biblical matriarch. Sarah's cooperation with her husband is no longer taken for granted, as in the biblical story, but acknowledged as a considerable effort and proof of her endurance. Sarah emerges as an independent personality who takes a conscious and noble decision in support of her husband. Philo stresses that she was "unhesitating" in her commitment and "always at his side," promptly taking upon herself all the known hardships of migration (see *Abr.* 246).

This portrait of Sarah as a wife, who courageously shares in her husband's travels, shows unmistakably Roman traces. Seneca praises at about the same time his aunt for sharing her husband's travel. She lost her "dearly beloved husband" in a shipwreck, but "bore up bravely, enduring at the same time both grief and fear, and, overmastering the storm, bore his body safe to land amid the shipwreck." Seneca appreciates her behavior as one of those "outstanding deeds" of women, which regularly go unnoticed. This praise is not an isolated incident, but rather part of a broader discourse. The historian Tacitus records a public debate about the question whether wives should accompany their husbands on their journeys into the provinces. Severus Caecina opposes this idea, arguing that wives have a bad influence on their husbands and will disturb them in their public duties. This position, however, is overruled by a clear majority. Tacitus mentions Valerius Messalinus, who stresses that wives share everything with their husbands and provide the best relaxation after men's return from stressful experiences. Moreover, the prince Drusus is quoted as pointing to Augustus as a model, because he "travelled to West and East in the company of Livia." The emperor thus justifies Drusus's need for his "dearest wife and parent of so many common children." Only in her company, he insists, will he be able to travel with "tranquility of mind" and should therefore not be torn away from her.[17]

One element in Philo's above quoted praise of Sarah is especially remarkable, namely, the motif of her "accompanying [Abraham] on war campaigns." This must be an allusion to Abraham's campaign in the North (Gen 14:13–16). Why does Philo assign such significance to this short biblical story? Moreover, why does he introduce Sarah, who is not at all mentioned in this biblical context? The hermeneutic key is once more provided by Roman culture. The princes Germanicus and Drusus were regularly accompanied by their wives on state and military affairs. Germanicus's wife even gave birth during

17. Seneca, *Helv.* 19.4–5; *Ep.* 57; see also Tacitus, *Ann.* 3.34: *uxor carissima et tot communium liberorum parens* (quoted in Ursula Blank-Sangmeister, *Römische Frauen: Ausgewählte Texte* [Stuttgart: Reclam, 2001], 56).

a campaign in Germany and raised the young Gaius Caligula among the soldiers (Suetonius, *Cal.* 8.3–9.1).[18] Following these precedents, Philo imagines Abraham as a Roman prince who is accompanied by his courageous wife on military campaigns.

Yet Abraham's and Sarah's happiness is disturbed by their lack of children. This well-known problem is easily solved by the biblical narrator in the person of Hagar, Sarah's maid, who gives birth to Abraham's first son (Gen 16:1–2). For Philo, who has stressed the loving partnership between Abraham and Sarah, this is a grave dilemma, which challenges the nature of their marriage. In his retelling of the story, Sarah realizes that her sterility challenges their marriage and offers philosophical reasons for taking an alternative mate, thus justifying a choice which may otherwise appear highly problematic. Indeed, a widower in a funerary inscription from first century BCE Rome, known as the "Praise of Turia," rejects precisely this option in favor of his cherished partnership with his wife. The husband testifies that he was "horrified" by his wife's proposal to take a younger woman and confesses that he "went out of his mind" at the thought of losing his loyal wife.[19]

Philo puts into Sarah's mouth an emphatic appeal to Abraham to take Hagar as an alternative mate who will give birth to an heir:

> For a long time have we lived together, well pleased with each other, but the purpose for which we ourselves have come together and for which Nature has set up the partnership of husband and wife, namely the birth of children, has not been realized and cannot be hoped to come to fulfillment in the future by me, who has grown beyond the age [of procreation]. But do not share my sterility and do not be prevented through goodwill for me from becoming what you yourself can become, a father. Envy for the other woman will not befall me, because you will not come to her out of irrational desire, but in fulfillment of the necessary law of Nature. (*Abr.* 248–249)

Philo's Sarah contrasts the "natural" purpose of marriage with the couple's loving partnership. She describes her marital life thus far in tender and emotional terms

18. See also Donna W. Hurley, *Suetonius: Divus Claudius* (Cambridge: Cambridge University Press, 2001), 181.

19. The text of the Roman funerary inscription with English or German translation is available in Mary R. Lefkowitz and Maureen B. Fant, eds., *Women's Life in Greece and Rome: A Source Book in Translation* (Baltimore: John Hopkins University Press, 1982), 208–11; Blank-Sangmeister, *Römische Frauen*, 92–97; note especially the strong expressions *exhorreo* and *excesserim mente*; see also Teresa Morgan, *Roman Faith and Christian Faith* (Oxford: Oxford University Press, 2015), 128–37, on the conjugal faith expressed in the "Praise of Turia."

as living together "well pleased with each other." Nature, on the other hand, has her "necessary law" and demands procreation, which will be achieved without involving the passions. Neither marital harmony nor procreation is based on sexual desire, but instead on rational cooperation, which leads to good feelings of care and mutual satisfaction. Ideally, partnership and procreation go together, but Sarah stresses that in cases, such as theirs, where they clash, priority has to be given to Nature's demand for procreation.

This appeal to Nature in the context of marriage echoes contemporary Stoic discussions, which were especially prominent in Imperial Rome. Stoic thinkers, in contrast to Platonists, generally advocated family life for the wise man and saw marriage as well as procreation as a commandment of Nature.[20] Arius Didymus, Augustus's philosophical advisor, makes the following emphatic recommendation: a man "will marry and father children, as these are consistent with his nature as a rational being, capable of partnership and fond of fellowship." Augustus legislated in the spirit of such philosophy against celibacy and childlessness within marriage. In Philo's own days Claudius encouraged Roman citizens to marry and beget children, even if his approach was more erratic than that of his admired predecessor. This Roman ideal of children within marriage is also advocated by Musonius, who argues in typically Stoic fashion that "marriage is manifestly in accord with Nature," as humanity was purposely created in two sexes "to be united and live together and to produce and rear children together."[21]

Philo uses these Stoic arguments, popular in Rome, to justify Sarah's suggestion that Abraham should have off-spring from Hagar. Her proposal, which would have horrified Turia's widower, thus appears far more understandable in a Roman context. Under Philo's pen Sarah appreciates her marital partnership with Abraham but gives priority to the demands of Nature, which insists on offspring even at the cost of interrupting a harmonious, monogamous marriage. Sarah thus convinces Abraham on rational grounds to take Hagar. It is remarkable that Philo has attributed this speech on a central Jewish value,

20. See Gretchen Reydams-Schils, *The Roman Stoics: Self, Responsibility, and Affection* (Chicago: University of Chicago Press, 2005), 53–82; Treggiari, *Roman Marriage*, 183–228; Dixon, *Roman Mother*, 71–104.

21. On Arius, see Arius Didymus, *Epitome of Stoic Ethics*, 91, translated in Arius Didymus, *Epitome of Stoic Ethics*, trans. Arthur J. Pomeroy, SBLTT 44, Graeco-Roman 14 (Atlanta: Society of Biblical Literature, 1999) = *SVF* 3:686, who uses the same key terms as Philo: κοινωνικός, φύσις; on Augustus's legislation, see Suetonius, *Aug.* 34.1–2; Dixon, *Roman Mother*, 21–30; on Claudius's policy, see Suetonius, *Claud.* 16.3, on Musonius, see Musonius, *Diatr.* 14.4–5, 9; 12.2–3.

which he will further explain in his treatises *On the Special Laws*, to a woman, who transmits them to her husband.

Sarah's self-effacing love for her husband is prominent also in the story of their journey to Pharaoh, the last example Philo gives of her virtues. While the rabbis critically reacted to the biblical image of Abraham as an inconsiderate husband, who is able to enjoy material benefits in exchange for his wife's sexual services to the Egyptian ruler, Philo interprets the incident with emphasis on the couple's harmony (Gen 12:10–20).[22] He stresses Abraham's helplessness amid "a licentious and cruel-hearted despot" and assigns a highly cooperative role to Sarah. In his story, she prays to God "taking refuge together with that man [i.e. Abraham] to the last remaining alliance" (*Abr.* 95). God's rescue of Sarah in Pharaoh's house thus results from the couple's common appeal. On the one hand, the motif of the couple's partnership in vicious circumstances renders Philo's account more egalitarian than its biblical counterpart, which does not mention Sarah's plight at all. On the other hand, however, Philo confirms traditional hierarchies, assuming the wife's dutiful submission to her husband's interests. Philo obviously does not challenge the patriarchal framework in the modern sense of feminist critique. In his story there is not even a hint, such as we find in later rabbinic literature, that Sarah may have been dissatisfied with her husband. In Philo's view, she is a quiet and ideal wife, proving also in this most challenging incident that she is devoted to her husband and seeks help together with him. Similarly, Philo never allows Sarah to question her husband's authority or to play a dominant role. He omits Sarah's insistence on Isaac as the heir and the consequent expulsion of Ishmael, which is very much against Abraham's will in the biblical story (Gen 21:8–12). As much as Philo does not relate to Livia's independence in politics but portrays her as a dutiful student of her husband, so his Sarah, too, is a highly domesticated partner. She personifies his ideal of a loving and strong, yet obedient wife.

Philo's ideal of a dear wife resurfaces also in his interpretation of two other biblical women: Eve and Moses's mother. As the paradigmatic first woman of the Bible, Eve provides Philo with an opportunity to reflect on the institution of marriage. Eve is introduced as being "glad" about Adam's approach immediately after their creation and "shyly returns his greeting"

22. For details on rabbinic interpretations of Sarah, see Maren Niehoff, "Associative Thinking in Rabbinic Midrash: The Example of Abraham's and Sarah's Journey to Egypt" [Hebrew], *Tarbiz* 62 (1993): 339–61; Noam Zohar, "The Figure of Abraham and the Voice of Sarah in Genesis Rabbah" [Hebrew], in *The Faith of Abraham in the Light of Interpretation throughout the Ages*, ed. Moshe Hallamish, Hannah Kasher, and Yohanan Silman (Ramat Gan: Bar Ilan University Press, 2002), 71–85.

(*Opif.* 152). Self-consciously referring to Plato's creation myth, Philo then praises marital partnership:

> Love supervenes, bringing together as it were the two separate halves of one being, which have been torn apart, and fitting them into one piece. It sets up in each of them a desire for fellowship with the other for the purpose of giving birth to their like. (*Opif.* 152)

This is a sophisticated play on Aristophanes's creation myth in Plato's *Symposium*, where the different kinds of love are explained by reference to the different origins of men. Men who love other men derive from an original all male creature, which has been divided into two halves by Zeus, while men who love women derive from a composite creature, and women who love women from an all female original. In Plato's mind there is little doubt that the (male) homosexual form of love is superior. He stresses that men who require no women are the finest, having "the manliest nature" and "no natural interest in wiving and getting children" (Plato, *Symp.* 189c–192e).[23] Well aware of this Platonic ideal, Philo presents his own and far more Stoic interpretation of marriage. Heterosexual love is the only valid option in his eyes. Adam and Eve's encounter brings the two halves together, implementing the Roman ideal of partnership and procreation. Philo has radically undermined Plato's ideal of male self-sufficiency and replaced it by the image of a harmonious marriage, so popular in contemporary Rome. In this new context Eve is allowed to play a far more positive role than in the *Allegorical Commentary*. Rather than imposing herself on the masculine mind, she now enables Adam to engage in a worthy and productive partnership.

Philo's new interpretation of Eve as a welcome marriage partner anticipates Plutarch, another intellectual from the Greek East who came into intimate contact with Rome. Like Philo, he was deeply immersed in the Platonic tradition and also enriched it with topical Stoic notions. Plutarch opens his *Dialogue on Love* with Protogenes, who expounds the Platonic ideal of homosexual love and male sufficiency. Plato's preference is the starting point of Plutarch's discussion, just as it is for Philo. The rest of the dialogue, however, is geared towards overcoming that position and showing the advantages of heterosexual love. Stoic arguments carry the day. Daphnaeus praises the love between women and men as "normal and natural," conducive to friendship and procreation. Plutarch stresses that the relationship between husband and wife is of much longer duration than that of homosexual couples, who do not

23. See also David T. Runia, *Philo of Alexandria: On the Creation according to Moses, Introduction, Translation and Commentary*, PACS (Leiden: Brill, 2001), 357–58.

enjoy the same sort of commitment, trust, and loyalty. Plutarch's examples of good marital partnerships significantly come from Rome. The successful Roman couples, which populate his dialogue, indicate that he, too, looks to the capital of the Empire rather than to Plato for inspiration regarding marriage. In his *Advice to the Bride and Groom* Plutarch enthusiastically praises the couple's harmony and partnership, recommending that the loving spouses unite both in their souls and bodies, an aim which requires the bride's continuous education. While Plutarch assumes a dominating role for the husband, who makes the principal decisions and sets the tone for the relationship by his own example, he allows some egalitarian features, such as sharing property. Here, too, Plutarch draws on Roman examples and Roman law, self-consciously anchoring his views of marriage not in Platonic philosophy, but in contemporary Roman society. Not surprisingly, Plutarch introduces his treatise *On the Bravery of Women* with a clear rejection of the traditional Greek ideal of a quiet woman at home, embracing instead the Roman custom of publically commemorating the virtues of women.[24]

Moses's mother is the third biblical woman whom Philo interprets as a good marriage partner. While the biblical narrator briefly reports from a male perspective that "a man from the house of Levi went and took to wife a daughter of Levi," Philo presents Moses's parents as partners. Both are introduced as "the best of contemporaries, members of the same tribe." More importantly, they are connected by "mutual concord" (*Mos.* 1.7, cf. Exod 2:1). Philo's attention to the quality of their marital relationship renders his interpretation not only more egalitarian than its biblical counterpart, but also distinctly more Roman.

Philo has thus created three harmonious biblical couples. Biblical women have become Roman ladies, who are beloved by their husbands and trusted for their loyalty. Sarah, the most developed of the matriarchs, also propagates the natural purpose of marriage, namely, procreation, and willingly shares the hardships of her husband's journeys. These flesh-and-blood wives in Philo's later writings significantly differ from their ethereal counterparts in the *Allegorical Commentary* and are clearly modeled on Roman ladies, such as Livia, as well as contemporary Stoic discourses popular in the capital. Philo actively

24. Plutarch, *Amat.* 24 (770c), 4–5 (750c–752a), *Conj. praec.* 13–22 (139–141b), 34–35 (143a), 48 (146a), *Mulier. virt.* pref. (242e–f); see also Sarah Pomeroy, ed., *Plutarch's Advice to the Bride and Groom and A Consolation to His Wife: English Translation, Commentary, Interpretative Essays and Bibliography* (Oxford: Oxford University Press, 1999); Barbara Feichtinger, "Soziologisches und Sozialgeschichtliches zu Erotik, Liebe und Geschlechterverkehr," in *Plutarch, Dialog über die Liebe: Amatorius*, ed. Herwig Görgemanns, 2nd ed., SAPERE 10 (Tübingen: Mohr Siebeck, 2011), 261–66.

engages in cultural discourses which he encounters during his embassy to Gaius. As a Jewish interpreter of the Bible he modernizes Judaism and brings it up to contemporary standards. He is far more systematic in this respect than Josephus, who occasionally adds the motif of romantic love, but refrains from turning all biblical marriages into harmonious partnerships and does not develop the characters of the biblical wives to the same degree as Philo does in the case of Sarah. As an author writing in Greek, Philo moreover translates Roman ideals into Greek terms, significantly anticipating Plutarch. Political, philosophical, and religious factors smoothly combine to furnish Philo with his new images of biblical wives, who are no longer Platonic symbols, but rather flesh-and-blood figures dressed in Roman garb and ready to be received in contemporary salons.

The dramatic development of Philo's position vis-à-vis biblical wives also illuminates early Christian writings, which negotiate the place of women from very diverse perspectives but often show a similar combination of political and religious factors. Most interesting in our context is an author not usually counted among the Second Sophistic but often highly congenial to those Greek writers in the Roman Empire, namely, the author of Luke-Acts. He, too, writes in Greek and regularly looks towards Roman discourses. He mentions three couples, one Roman, one Jewish, and one Christian, who easily travel together and, in the case of Aquila and Priscilla, also share religious responsibilities in the early Christian community. More importantly, when the author of the Gospel of Luke adapts earlier materials from Mark, he adds emphasis to the women, sometimes even adding a scene with female characters, such as the one with Martha and Mary in Jesus's travelogue. Luke also rewrites the story of Jesus's birth with emphasis on the family setting and marital harmony. In his story, it is Mary who receives the message from the angel about Jesus's birth and shares it with her husband. Matthew, by contrast, suggests that Joseph received the announcement about the birth from the Holy Spirit and then suspects his pregnant wife of adultery, even casting her out. Luke avoids marital dissonance and solves the problem by insisting that Mary was not yet pregnant at the time of the angel's announcement (Acts 18:2–3; 24:24; 25:13; Luke 1:26–38).[25] To the author of Luke-Acts, who also addresses broader Greco-Roman audiences, the ideal of marital partnership seems to have been important. Like Philo, he has reinterpreted received traditions and creatively adapted them to current values in Roman culture.

Conclusion

Philo's attitude to women has considerably changed as a result of his stay in Rome. Following his general reorientation towards worldly reality, he appreciates women now as blood-and-flesh figures rather than as allegories of the soul. Sarah, Eve, and Moses's wife emerge as perfect wives who engage in a mutually satisfying relationship with their husbands. To be sure, Philo has not become a modern-day feminist, but he does imagine the biblical matriarchs much more actively and positively than in his earlier days in Alexandria. Moreover, he thinks about the nature and status of women rather than simply taking their supposed material and passive tendency for granted. The main impetus for this change of attitude seems to be Roman Stoicism, which gave attention to gender issues and envisioned a positive role for women in their families.

25. See also Mary Rose D'Angelo, "(Re)Presentations of Women in the Gospel of Matthew and Luke-Acts," in *Women and Christian Origins*, ed. Ross S. Kraemer and Mary Rose D'Angelo (Oxford: Oxford University Press, 1999), 171–98; D'Angelo, "Women in Luke-Acts: A Redactional View," *JBL* 109 (1990): 441–61; Elisabeth Schüssler Fiorenza, "A Feminist Critical Interpretation for Liberation: Martha and Mary: Luke 10:38–42," *RIL* 3 (1986): 21–35. Regarding Luke's dependence on Mark, see Bart D. Ehrman, *The New Testament: A Historical Introduction to the Early Christian Writings* (Oxford: Oxford University Press, 1997), 72–78, 96–99; Helmut Koester, *Ancient Christian Gospels: Their History and Development* (Philadelphia: Trinity Press International, 1990), 332–48; E. P. Sanders and Margaret Davies, *Studying the Synoptic Gospels* (London: SCM; Philadelphia: Trinity Press International, 1989), 51–66, 276–98.

Real Women and Literary Airbrushing: The Women "Therapeutae" of Philo's *De vita contemplativa* and the Identity of the Group

Joan E. Taylor

In *De vita contemplativa* Philo describes a group of contemplative Jewish ascetics who exemplify philosophical ideals. They live outside Alexandria, without possessions, and spend most of their time focusing on God, or rather "Being" (*Contempl.* 2), studying scripture, and composing music in small huts, gathering together only on Sabbath days for communal teaching and a meal. Every seven weeks this extends to an all-night sacred event of dancing and singing, configured in strongly cultic terms.[1] Philo states women's inclusion within his example at the start (*Contempl.* 2), and he then mentions them specifically when they appear with men on the Sabbath days, in a common gathering place for the purposes of teaching, where all participants are portrayed as exhibiting model virtues: thus the women are additionally provided with the feminine virtue of modesty (*Contempl.* 30–33):

> So for six days each of them philosophises solitarily apart by themselves in the aforesaid "solitaria" [μοναστηρίοι], not going beyond the doorway; moreover they do not look from afar. But on the seventh days they come together as into a common congregation [σύλλογος] and sit sequentially according to age with the proper posture, having the hands inside, the right hand between chest and chin, the left one drawn back along the thighs. (*Contempl.* 30)

1. Joan E. Taylor, *Jewish Women Philosophers of First-Century Alexandria: Philo's Therapeutae Reconsidered* (Oxford: Oxford University Press, 2003), 311–40; Celia Deutsch, "The Therapeutae, Text Work, Ritual and Mystical Experience," in *Paradise Now: Essays on Early Jewish and Christian Mysticism*, ed. A. DeConick, SymS 11 (Atlanta: Society of Biblical Literature, 2006), 287–312.

> This common sanctuary [σεμνεῖον] into which they come together on seventh days is a divided enclosure [περίβολος], the one part set aside for the male-area [εἰς ἀνδρῶνα], and the one into the female-area [εἰς γυναικωνῖτιν]. For indeed also women customarily listen together, having the same purpose and the same practice.
>
> The wall between the spaces from the floor to the top is about three or four cubits, constructed in the form of a parapet, with the higher part rising up to the roof left open, for reason of two things: that the proper modesty in the womanly nature be protected and that, in order to have easy reception by their sitting in ear-shot, nothing impedes the voice of the one talking.[2] (*Contempl.* 32–33)

Everything that is said of the group as a whole relates to the women, and they appear specifically mentioned in the sacred event, which is initially divided according to gender at the meal (*Contempl.* 68–69), though this division breaks down when inspired singing and dancing takes place, as people initially are in two choirs but then mingle to form one (*Contempl.* 83–88).

The fact then that here we have a picture of Jewish women learning, studying, composing, singing, dancing, and eating together with men in an environment of philosophical engagement raises all kinds of questions about women's involvement in the heart of Jewish religious life in Alexandria.

1. Meaning of the Term *Therapeutae*

It is common in scholarship to refer to the people described in *De vita contemplativa* by the term *Therapeutae*, a Latin rendering of the Greek word θεραπευταί (*Contempl.* 2, 22, 88, 90), the masculine plural being used as inclusive of the women of the group. The translation of the words θεραπευταί (masc.) and θεραπευτρίδες (fem.) as well as the verb θεραπεύω and the noun θεραπεία can prove troublesome given the multiple meanings in Greek, and Philo enjoys word-plays that make use of these in *Contempl.* 2. However, Philo uses the noun θεραπευταί in his writings in line with the broad contemporary usage defining this word as primarily indicating those who minister or attend to a person or (cultically) to a god,[3] and therefore we may translate the term as "ministers." So in *Contempl.* 2, Philo states that "they are appropriately called 'ministers,' male and female, insofar as either they command a medical

2. Translation my own, from the Greek text of Leopold Cohn and Siegfried Reiter, *Philonis Alexandrini Opera Quae Supersunt*, ed. Leopold Cohn and Paul Wendland (Berlin: Reimer, 1915; repr. Berlin: de Gruyter, 1962), 6:46–71 (editio minor: 6:32–50). The Greek text is also widely available in volume 9 of LCL.

3. See Taylor, *Jewish Women Philosophers*, 56–59.

art better than that of cities—for that ministers to bodies alone, but this one indeed ministers to souls conquered by both difficult and intractable diseases … —or else because they have been schooled from Nature and the sacred laws to minister to Being (God)." That they are "called 'ministers'" would have meant something to people who understood what this word indicates, as a group of devotees of a particular deity, forming a *thiasos*,[4] a religious voluntary association. The fact that both men and women are included in this would not have completely surprised the readers/hearers of the treatise. Celia Deutsch has noted that while *thiasoi* comprised of only one gender were usual in the Greco-Roman world, there were indeed instances of mixed-gender *thiasoi* from Thera (*OGIS* 735) and Miletus (*LSAM* 48).[5] Richard Ascough has recorded that, of the thirty-three members of the *thiasos* of Zeus Hypsistos in Pydna, three were women and that both men and women members were included in the Dionysiac association in Amphipolis as also elsewhere.[6] An association dedicated to Serapis in Opus was established in a woman's house, with administration undertaken by a succession of women (*IG* 10.2.255). In fact, associations dedicated to worshiping Isis and Serapis were invariably mixed sex (*IG* 2.1292). An inscription on Delos testifies to not only a mixed-gender *thiasos* of the Egyptian cult but also to the specific designation θεραπευταί for those who comprise it (*IG* 11.4.1216–1222, third–second century BCE). Overall, then, the people described in *Contemplativa* may be seen as a Jewish voluntary association that has been in some way modeled on patterns known from an Alexandrian milieu, a *thiasos* that is understandable in the context of Alexandrian religious culture, in which men and women were included together.

2. Actuality and Rhetoricity

One of the more significant scholarly debates concerning *Contemplativa* in the past twenty years has been about whether the representation of the group of "ministers" in question could correspond to some historical reality outside the text. This is particularly important for issues of gender, because if

---

4. John Kloppenborg, "Collegia and *Thiasoi*: Issues in Function, Taxonomy and Membership," in *Voluntary Associations in the Graeco-Roman World*, ed. John S. Kloppenborg and S. G. Wilson (London: Routledge, 1996), 18–23; Torry Seland, "Philo and the Clubs and Associations of Alexandria," in John S. Kloppenborg and S. G. Wilson, *Voluntary Associations*, 110–27.

5. Deutsch, "Therapeutae, Text Work," 182.

6. Richard Ascough, *Paul's Macedonian Associations: The Social Context of Philippians and 1 Thessalonians*, WUNT 161 (Tübingen: Mohr Siebeck, 2003), 52, 55–57.

the situation of gender parity, or near parity, that it presents is entirely fictitious then this punctures any claims that there were actual women like those described in the treatise.

2.1. An Imaginary Ideal or Actual People?

This question may be traced to the work of Charles Guignebert. Though accepting that the work was authentic, Guignebert considered Philo's description of the Therapeutae so idealized and stylized that if such people did exist, they were not really as Philo described them.[7] This is actually an appropriate acknowledgement of the rhetoricity of ancient texts. More recently there has been the far more extreme suggestion that Philo means to present a kind of ideal fantasy rather than show actual Jews living their lives in a particular way.[8] Troels Engberg-Pedersen does not wholly dismiss the notion that there was a real group, but they are more dream than reality.[9] There are, however, several reasons why the notion that Philo is dreaming up a fictional utopia seems highly unlikely.

In the first place, Philo wrote at a time of enormous social disruption, and *Contemplativa* is a text that is highly polemical. In Alexandria Jews and Greco-Egyptians were, in Philo's time, on the edge of civil war.[10] We know that Philo's opponents in Alexandria, such as Chaeremon, used the real Egyptian priests to indicate their ideal lifestyle[11] and therefore if Philo created an imaginary group to argue for Jews as representing a philosophical ideal to counter actual examples from the Greco-Egyptian context he would have lost the argument at the very start. It is important that Philo's group be real, even if he has presented and shaped the truth, omitting aspects that were not helpful to him.[12]

---

7. Charles Guignebert, *Des prophètes à Jésus: Le monde juif vers le temps de Jésus* (Paris: La Renaissance du livre, 1935), 320.

8. Troels Engberg-Pedersen, "Philo's *De vita contemplativa* as a Philosopher's Dream," *JSJ* 30 (1999): 40–64; Ross Kraemer, *Unreliable Witnesses: Religion, Gender and History in the Greco-Roman Mediterranean* (Oxford: Oxford University Press, 2011), 66–114, revising Kraemer, "Monastic Jewish Women in Greco-Roman Egypt: Philo Judaeus on the Therapeutrides," *Signs* 14 (1989): 342–70.

9. Engberg Pedersen, "Philosopher's Dream," 48.

10. For primary evidence, see Philo's works *In Flaccum* and *Legatio ad Gaium*; also Josephus, *Ant.* 18.28–30; Claudius, *Letter to the Alexandrians* and the *Acts of the Alexandrian Martyrs*.

11. Chaeremon, "On the Egyptian Priests," in Porphyry, *Abst.* 4.6–8.

12. For this, see Taylor, *Jewish Women Philosophers*, 7–15.

This is not a cool-headed characterization of a perfect philosophical life, but rather a counter-assault, proclaiming that a life of perfect virtue can actually exist within Judaism, in such a way to make it far superior to all those models of excellence presented by Philo's opponents from the spectrum of well-known religious and philosophical groups within the Greco-Roman world, and particularly from within Alexandrian society.

About a third of his treatise is taken up attacking what Maren Niehoff defines as the "Greek Other,"[13] whether current—in the form of cultic devotions—or historical—in the form of Plato's *Symposium*, which informs the current practice of symposia, characterized as opportunities for binge drinking and violence (*Contempl.* 3–11, 40–63). Therefore, an apparently innocuous philosophical question such as "Where does virtue exist?" or "How is the contemplative life most excellently manifested?" masks a deep animosity between Philo and his opponents, opponents whom we know also petitioned the Roman emperors Gaius Caligula and Claudius and incited horrific acts against Jews in the civil strife of 38 to 41 CE.

A depiction of ideal Jews that was a fantasy bearing no relationship to what Jews were actually doing would have been greeted by Philo's readers, both Jewish and non-Jewish, as almost completely worthless, defeating his purpose entirely. Imaginary Jews would have been laughable; the opponents could simply point to their nonexistence to dismiss Philo's entire presentation.

Second, Philo locates the Therapeutae not in a remote place at the ends of the world, unverifiably, but exactly on a low-lying hill near Alexandria, between Lake Mareotis and the Mediterranean Sea (*Contempl.* 23), and thus anyone there could have investigated the truth of his claims. David Winston, an expert on ancient utopia, therefore states: "Having placed the Therapeutae … not far from Alexandria, where he himself lived, it is clear that he could not have invented them. Utopias are usually located at remote distances, safe from any effort at verification."[14] Given that Philo's stated aim is to show a contemplative life, as actually represented by a group of Jews who live in a real place that is in striking distance of the city of Alexandria, his purpose would be totally nullified by any suggestion that his group is not real, when the precise details of the location of the Therapeutae close to the huge metropolis of Alexandria almost invite someone to find them.

Third, Philo makes clear that he has already used an actual example in exploring the "active" philosophical lifestyle. The Essenes, unlike the Thera-

13. Maren Niehoff, "Philo's *Exposition* in a Roman Context," *SPhiloA* 23 (2011): 1–21.

14. David Winston, *Philo of Alexandria: The Contemplative Life, the Giants and Selections*, CWS (New York: Paulist, 1981), 41.

peutae, are widely attested in ancient literature and are described in at least two of Philo's own treatises: *Quod Omnis Probus liber sit* ("Every Good Man is Free," see 75–91) and part of the *Apologia pro Iudaeis* ("Apology for the Jews," as in Eusebius's *Praep. ev.* 8.11, 1–18), a work usually considered part of the *Hypothetica*.[15] It would follow then that if Philo is using an actual group for his presentation of the topic of the active life, he would use an actual group for the presentation of the contemplative life.[16] To use an actual group for one treatise and an invented one for another would be strange.

Fourth, given that Philo provides a single testimony to the existence of a group we call the Therapeutae, it has to be said that if in ancient history we only trusted testimony to actuality if it exists on the basis of multiple attestation in contemporaneous sources, especially in regard to women, then much of our knowledge would be rendered invalid. If anything that contains rhetoricity is rendered inappropriate to use as evidence for actuality, this would rule out the work of ancient historians, since the writing of any given *historia* ("investigation")—from Herodotus onwards—was done within the realm of *rhetorica*, conceptualized as a speech intended to convince an audience, and was designed for rhetorical, argumentative, ends: to prove a thesis.[17] In terms of how we might effectively do the history of women and gender, the strategies of Elisabeth Schüssler Fiorenza[18] remain for me extremely helpful in pointing to a process of recognizing the rhetoricity of a given text, reading it with a hermeneutic of suspicion, and deconstructing the rhetoric so that we can move forward towards some degree of historical reconstruction.

Furthermore, there is in fact clear evidence of the type of people Philo describes elsewhere in his writings. Contemplative ascetics are quite well attested in his work and are by no means an isolated example found only in one treatise. These others will be considered below.

---

15. Joan E. Taylor, *The Essenes, the Scrolls and the Dead Sea* (Oxford: Oxford University Press, 2012), 22–48.

16. See Mary Ann Beavis, "Philo's Therapeutai: Philosopher's Dream or Utopian Construction?," *JSP* 14 (2004): 31; Beavis, *Jesus and Utopia: Looking for the Kingdom of God in the Roman World* (Minneapolis: Fortress, 2006), 59.

17. See Taylor, *Essenes*, 6–20.

18. Elisabeth Schüssler Fiorenza, *In Memory of Her: A Feminist Theological Reconstruction of Christian Origins* (New York: Crossroad, 1983); Schüssler Fiorenza, "The Rhetoricity of Historical Knowledge: Pauline Discourse and its Contextualizations," in *Religious Propaganda and Missionary Competition in the New Testament World: Essays Honoring Dieter Georgi*, ed. Lukas Bornkamm, Kelly del Tredici, and Angela Sandhartinger, NovTSup 74 (Leiden: Brill, 1994), 443–46.

2.2. Genre

We may then consider the fundamental question of genre. Defining the specific genre of the treatise might help us in terms of viewing its rhetorical components and relationship with actuality more accurately. Engberg-Pedersen has suggested that *Contemplativa* conforms to one defined on the basis of Aristotle's usage (*Eth. nic.* 2.2) as a πραγματεία, a scientific treatise, by the internal use of this term in the treatise in *Contempl.* 1.[19] In Engberg-Pedersen's assessment, Philo claims to be writing truth as a ruse to conceal the fiction. However, as Mary-Ann Beavis has noted, this is simply "contrived" and "overly ingenious."[20]

Moreover, in Philo's usage elsewhere the word πραγματεία has no relationship to a literary genre in any place it is found. The term πραγματεία means "subject of a treatise" elsewhere in Philo's work, but in no case in Philo is there any suggestion of a genre of a scientific treatise.[21] The usage of the word in *Contempl.* 1 is completely consistent with Philo's usage elsewhere, and can be read as "subject" or "topic," in this case a reference to the topic of "the contemplative life," a presentation of a philosophical ideal by a description of the lived life of real people. It is, therefore, a *bios*, "life story," in that it illuminates the working of a philosophical life by means of a descriptive presentation of how a real group of people fulfil certain criteria.

Furthermore, Philo intends to describe the Therapeutae accurately (*Contempl.* 2), and we see in his rhetoric that he includes aspects of the group even if they do not fit with his own notions. Philo constructs them by means of a complex mesh of biblical and classical allusions, and by downplaying such features as the junior members whose "active" service of the seniors would muddy his rhetoric in terms of the "contemplative" ideal, since they are actually quite busy, serving seniors during meals (72, 81).[22] In addition, the group appears to follow a solar calendar in which the day begins at dawn: their celebration, on every forty-ninth day, concludes when the sun rises (89; cf. 65),

19. Engberg-Pedersen, "Philosopher's Dream," 41–43.

20. Beavis, "Philo's Therapeutai," 32, and Beavis, *Jesus and Utopia*, 60.

21. In *Sacr.* 120 it is found with this meaning of "matter." In *Gig.* 29, *Deus* 97, and *Abr.* 30 it appears in plural as "occupations" or "labors," but it can also mean a subject or topic under study, such as physics or logic: *Ebr.* 97; *Congr.* 147, 149; *Mut.* 53, 75; *Somn.* 1.102, 120. In *Spec.* 2.65 it refers to the "matter/substance of life," as also in *Spec.* 2.102 and 3.105. In *Hypoth.* 11.6, in plural, it refers to the activities, labors, or occupations in which Essenes work (see 11.5). In *Flacc.* 3, Flaccus became familiar with "Egyptian affairs/matters." In *Praem.* 142, in plural, it means "occupations/industries," as also *Fug.* 33.

22. For further discussion, see Joan E. Taylor, with David M. Hay, *Therapeutae: A Commentary on Philo of Alexandria*, De vita contemplativa, PACS (Leiden: Brill, forthcoming).

when they go back to "work." Most important, the inclusion of women is not required or necessarily positive as an element in the ideal contemplative life, and Philo works hard to ensure that they do not become a negative feature, given the various problematic ways philosophical women could be presented in antiquity.[23] In short, he attempts to define them as modest old virgins who live passionately with Sophia as a life partner (*Contempl.* 32, 68), a curious model in a treatise often read as negative on male homosexuality (*Contempl.* 50–52, 60–62). As Holger Szesnat has pointed out, Philo's "mostly old virgins" in *Contempl.* 68 provide some reason to think that in actuality some of the women were not old, and not virgins, but these are people Philo does not wish us to see.[24] In an artificial fantasy Philo would surely just have said that they are "all old virgins." Philo's "spin" on actuality is also found not only in terms of how he manages such issues of the actual, but also in what he chooses to leave out.[25] A rhetorically-heavy text is still not a "fiction" as such, in terms of genre.

Ancient authors knew their fables from their fact. Quintilian made three genre distinctions: a *fabula* (fable, or myth), an *argumentum* (a narrative story), and a *historia*, "an exposition of actual fact" (*Inst.* 2.4.2). Furthermore, Engberg-Pedersen is right that philosophical writing in antiquity was highly influenced by the principles established in Aristotle's *Rhetorica*, but the genre of *Contemplativa* is best considered by reference to what Aristotle defines regarding how an inductive argument may be built up on the basis of "examples," παραδείγματα (*Rhet.* 1.2.10; 1357b–1358a). In accord with this, the treatise uses the good example of the Therapeutae to contrast with the bad examples used in Greco-Egyptian culture, thus incorporating a rhetorical mode of censure or accusation.

Furthermore, it is critical for philosophers utilizing such examples to be seen to be representing the actual, inasmuch as they assert that their presentations are truthful (so *Contempl.* 2), and inasmuch as they aim to represent philosophical ideals by reference to actual lives.

Clearly, the Therapeutae presented in *Contemplativa* hit the right notes in terms of philosophical ideals, but presuming that any group that reflects preconceived notions of what a philosophical life might be is fictional assumes that the groups in question themselves had no interest in modeling

---

23. See Taylor, *Jewish Women Philosophers*, 171–226.

24. Holger Szesnat, "'Mostly Aged Virgins': Philo and the Presence of the Therapeutrides at Lake Mareotis," *Neot* 32 (1998): 191–201.

25. David M. Hay, "Things Philo Said and Did Not Say about the Therapeutae," in *Society of Biblical Literature 1992 Seminar Papers*, ed. E. Lovering, SBLSP 31 (Atlanta: Scholars Press, 1992), 673–83.

themselves on such lives. Given that examples were known, a certain amount of emulation may well have taken place among actual groups.[26]

What we have then in a work such as *Contemplativa* is an extended *paradeigma* or *deigma*: an actual example presented rhetorically in order to prove a philosophical life of virtue. What is expected of a contemplative life will therefore be the focus, and there will be facets that are included and excluded. Philo uses precisely this genre in his *Life of Moses*.[27]

This treatise then belongs to a genre of literature that defines examples of philosophical lives, a kind of subcategory of the *bioi* ("lives") genre as a whole, here involving a life that is collective rather than just individual. Philo's notion of a philosophical life having both an active and a contemplative side is standard in Greco-Roman philosophy (see Aristotle, *Eth. nic.* 1.5; 10.7–8; Porphyry, *Abst.* 1.53; Diogenes Laertius, *Lives* 7.130), and philosophers could be defined in terms of the lives they exemplified, such as Dichaearchus (active) and Theophrastus (contemplative) (so Cicero, *Fin.* 5.57; Dichaearchus, frags. 29 and 31). Philo thought the active and contemplative lives were both "best lives" (*Decal.* 101), and Moses himself applied himself to the contemplative and practical sides of virtue (*Mos.* 1.48). In *Leg.* 1.52–58 (cf. *Praem.* 11) Philo states that virtue is both contemplative and practical. Ideally, for Philo, all Jews are expected to mix the two together: they should devote six days to the active life of philosophy and one to the contemplative (*Decal.* 100; *Spec.* 2.64). So, using the Essenes as an example of the best active life was a way of demonstrating the best life of Jewish philosophy overall, with the Therapeutae's Sabbath day assemblies and Sabbath-like daily lifestyle of quietness illustrating the contemplative dimension of Jewish life.

Thus a notion of a perfect philosophical life, informed also by concepts of utopia, shaped the form of the presentation, but it does not require us to assume the invention of a group of imaginary Jews bearing no correlation with reality. It is essential to contextualize this treatise within a tumultuous period of history, in which Jewish leaders were being publicly scourged, Jewish property sacked and looted, and synagogues burnt, which culminated in the virtual annihilation of the Jewish community in Alexandria in 117 CE.[28] In

26. For this point, see Doron Mendels, "Hellenistic Utopia and the Essenes," *HTR* 72 (1979): 207–22.

27. Richard A. Burridge, *What Are the Gospels? A Comparison with Graeco-Roman Biography*, 2nd ed. (Grand Rapids: Eerdmans, 2004), 124–49.

28. For this see Joseph Mélèze Modrzejewski, *The Jews of Egypt: From Rameses II to Emperor Hadrian* (Philadelphia: Jewish Publication Society of America, 1995), 207–22; Herbert A. Musurillo, *The Acts of the Pagan Martyrs: Acta Alexandrinum* (Oxford: Clarendon, 1954); Pieter W. Van der Horst, *Philo of Alexandria: Philo's Flaccus, the First Pogrom:*

this environment, Philo successfully argues a case that virtue is indeed found in the verifiable actualities of Judaism in the present time. Notably, Philo does not look for examples from Jewish history—the past that is long gone—but in the world of the Jews now under attack. His examples stretch from Judaea (Syria Palaestina), with the Essenes of the previous treatise illustrating the active philosophical life, to the region around Alexandria, with the so-called Therapeutae illustrating the contemplative life.

3. Identity

This brings us to the question of the identity of the group in question. In my view they appear far less unique and mysterious when one reconfigures them, not as a definable "sect," but as men and women among those of Philo's own allegorical school in Alexandria who have adopted an ascetic and philosophical lifestyle. While they have often been identified with the Essenes,[29] and in fact in some ways the common picture of the Essenes has even been colored by the Therapeutae, they are better understood in line with people Philo refers to quite often in his writings, not always entirely positively.[30] One of the most important differences between the Therapeutae and the Essenes concerns gender. The Essenes are defined as a (largely mature) male group, living communally, who do not bring wives into these communal living arrangements (Philo, *Hypoth.* 11.14–17; Josephus, *J.W.* 2.120–121; Pliny, *Nat. Hist.* 5.15). Some may have had wives who were not included in the community when possessions were shared (Philo, *Hypoth.* 11.14–17; Josephus, *Ant.* 18.21; *J.W.* 2.120–121). Those male Essenes with wives did not live differently to those that were entirely celibate, but only married in order to ensure they had physical offspring (Josephus, *J.W.* 2.160–161). The Essene women were therefore *not* celibate and were expected to be mothers within normal households. However, the Therapeutae community is constituted by men and women living a celibate lifestyle together in one community, and the women are not the wives of the men there, but rather, according to Philo, "mostly old virgins"

Introduction, Translation and Commentary, PACS (Leiden: Brill, 2003); John M. G. Barclay, *Jews in the Mediterranean Diaspora: From Alexander to Trajan (323 BCE–117 CE)* (Berkeley: University of California Press, 1996).

29. See the historical survey by Jean Riaud, "Les Thérapeutes d'Alexandrie dans la tradition et dans la recherche critique jusqu'aux découvertes de Qumran," *ANRW* 2.20.2:1189–1295, and also Geza Vermes, "Essenes and Therapeutai," *RevQ* 3 (1962): 494–504.

30. For further discussion, see Taylor, *Jewish Women Philosophers*, 68–72; Taylor, *Essenes*, 46–47.

(*Contempl.* 2, 32–33, 68–69, 83–88). On his own terms, then, Philo cannot be referring to the Essenes in *Contemplativa.*

The group described in *Contemplativa* is exemplary, according to Philo, and much of what he writes about them accords with his own views, but he also has difficulty in presenting all aspects of their lifestyle, especially the fact that there are both men and women among them. As I have previously explored, the women of the group are a rhetorical problem for Philo, in that he needs to avoid common tropes of "women philosophers" in presenting them as living, learning, eating, singing, and dancing together with men.[31] Elsewhere in his writings he does not by any means consider women, or "femaleness," positively.[32] One senses it would have been easier for Philo not to have them included.

We do get a sense of the Therapeutae being both representative of the excellence of all Jews but distinctive, as is made clear in *Contempl.* 13–20: they have abandoned property and family life to live apart from cities and spiritually dissimilar persons. Their doing so stems from their having received spiritual sight (*Contempl.* 13—evidently an allusion to their seeing or contemplating God, as in *Contempl.* 11–12). This demonstrates their indifference to material possessions and their mastery of human passions, as they undertake a lifestyle that is very austere. Their use of allegorical interpretation links them with the kind of exegetical school of Philo himself, and he greatly approves of their methods and conclusions, so that it would be appropriate to see them as part of Philo's own wider milieu. That they are educated—able to read and write and discourse, even to compose music—would link them with the wealthy sector of society to which Philo also belonged.[33]

We find them referred to elsewhere in Philo's writings in terms of their practice, both in regard to what they do outside the city and what similar people do within the city itself, when elite and philosophically educated people begin to follow the basic premises of this allegorical school, aiming to simplify their lives, giving away their belongings (see *Contempl.* 13–17). In *Spec.* 2.20, for example, Philo mentions that there are wealthy people who drink out of earthen cups. In this report, Philo counts himself also as someone who uses simple artefacts (*Spec.* 2.20). While the food of such people is defined as being

31. See Taylor, *Jewish Women Philosophers*, 173–226.

32. Richard A. Baer, *Philo's Use of the Categories Male and Female*, ALGHJ 3 (Leiden: Brill, 1970); Dorothy Sly, *Philo's Perception of Women*, BJS 209 (Atlanta: Scholars Press, 1990); Taylor, *Jewish Women Philosophers*, 229–36.

33. Joan E. Taylor and Philip R. Davies, "The So-Called Therapeutae of *De vita contemplativa*: Identity and Character," *HTR* 91 (1998): 3–24; Taylor, *Jewish Women Philosophers*, 93–104, 126–36.

spit-baked bread, with olives, cheeses, and green vegetables (when the Therapeutae just eat bread, salt, and hyssop, *Contempl.* 37, 73, 81), their clothing is described as being almost exactly that of *Contemplativa*: "in the summer a belt and a thin *'othonē* (linen wrap) and in winter a thick, tear-proof *chlaina* (mantle)" (see *Contempl.* 38). They sleep on the floor, spurning the inlaid furniture that Philo in *Contemplativa* associates with the bad symposia of his opposition (see *Contempl.* 49). In the *Special Laws* (*Spec.* 2.21) Philo states that such people are not only like this by their nature, but because of the "right education from first youth," and in *Contempl.* 67 the elders of the group are identified as people who "from first youth have put in time and flourished in the contemplative part of philosophy"; in *Contemplativa* Philo assumes a background in which children and young people are properly educated within the city, in the right educational context, before they make a decision to leave the city and join the group outside it, having acquired property, and even sons and daughters (*Contempl.* 13).

In such an example it is important that we consider that Philo may well be referring to men *and* women in his circle, though Philo does not necessarily make this easy to do. In his treatise *On Dreams* (*Somn.* 1.124–126) Philo discusses a pupil (γνώριμος) of the holy Logos as one of the people who have laid down self-control as a foundation and put up with hunger and thirst, heat and cold, not ashamed of a basic *chlaina*, and who sleeps on a soft bit of ground. Their pillows are stones or mounds low-rising above the level (see *Contempl.* 69). "This life the soft-living people call 'very hard,' but those living for goodness name it 'pleasant,' for it suits those who are not just said to be 'men' but really are" (*Somn.* 1.125). Here Philo takes the word "man," ἀνήρ, and its corollary ἀνδρεία, "manliness," "manly virtue," or "courage," as a defining feature of a γνώριμος of the holy Logos, and indeed in *Contemplativa* there is a strong emphasis on the "manliness" exemplified by the Therapeutae (*Contempl.* 60): they are men (*Contempl.* 1, 29, 78), even when they are—rather awkwardly for Philo—women. Philo's Moses is an example, παράδειγμα, of a soul in training, hardening up, and "at war with anything weak and androgynous" (*Somn.* 1.126). Elsewhere in Philo's writings the γνώριμοι of Moses, as they are called in *Contempl.* 63–64, are also those who interpret scripture allegorically (*QG* 3.8; *Her.* 81; *Virt.* 65), a category in which Philo includes himself (*Det.* 86; *Spec.* 1.345).

The other allegorically minded and ascetic people of Alexandria can also be seen from *Gig.* 31, where Philo describes ψυχαὶ ... ἄσαρκοι καὶ ἀσώματοι, "unfleshly and unbodily souls," who spend their days "in the theatre of the All, seeing and hearing divine things." *On the Migration of Abraham* 191 mentions those who close their eyes, stop their ears, restrain the impulses created by senses, and spend their days in solitude and darkness, so that the objects of sense perception will not interfere with "the eye of the soul, which God has given to see noetic (mind) things." This would correspond to the way the Therapeutae spend their days in the inner rooms of huts (*Contempl.* 25) relieved from "the crowd of the senses and objects of sense" (*Contempl.* 27).

Such people are defined as "wise and good" in *On the Change of Names* (*Mut.* 32): they are a *thiasos* (θίασος), a sacred company, who have stripped themselves of external possessions and rejected what is liked by the flesh. However, Philo defines οἱ ἀπο παιδείας, "those from education"—the education provided by God—as ἀθληταί, "athletes": their regimen leaves them pale, faded, and skeletal (ὠχροὶ ... καὶ διερρυηκότες καὶ κατεσκελετευμένοι). Here Philo seems to present, in a slightly less favorable way, the implications that we may rightly draw of the lifestyle of the Therapeutae, largely spent in solitary huts, eating only a very frugal diet (*Contempl.* 34–37, 73). Philo indicates that those who are wise and good—like this—are few in number also (*Mut.* 34). They are people who have "gone to the wild" (ἐξηγριώθησαν) inspired by divine madness, but Philo here advocates instead a tamer type of practicing piety and wisdom within the city, not overlooking human beings, which is to follow Mosaic law regarding family, social, and civic responsibilities (*Mut.* 39–40). This is a quite telling conclusion in terms of Philo's own choices.

The ideal of the release from the body is found also in *Who Is the Heir?* (*Her.* 68–78; cf. 84–85). The soul needs to leave "land"—the body—and "relations"—that is, the senses—to be "like those possessed, even Corybants, Bacchic, and theophoric people, according to a certain prophetic inspiration." This language of divine possession is how he describes what happens to the Therapeutae in their all-night sacred event (*Contempl.* 85). The soul emigrates from the body (*Her.* 71) and "sentences" speech to prolonged speechlessness. "The one who goes out from us and longs to be an attendant of God (ὀπαδος ... θεοῦ) is an heir of the glorious wealth of Nature" (*Her.* 76), and is the one who sees (*Her.* 78). The life of seeing (θεωρία), after all, is the contemplative life (ὁ βίος θεωρετικός).

Still, that Philo can both admire and reject the ascetic choices of those who live the inspired life is found also in *On the Decalogue* (*Decal.* 108–120). Philo writes of people who "having said goodbye to all other matters have put their whole personal life to the ministry of God," but there are others who focus on justice for humanity, and fellowship, the former being lovers of God, the latter lovers of other people. The former do not share the joy and grief of other people regarding the common good, by not engaging in society, and therefore they are like wild animals in nature, especially if they disregard their parents (110). They do not show proper respect for those who brought them into the world, from non-existent to existent (111). In fact, in the crunch Philo states that piety and holiness do not dwell within souls who neglect parents (119; cf. 110), by implication contravening the law of Deut 5:16 and Exod 20:12. While in *Contempl.* 18 Philo defines the Therapeutae as leaving parents and simply passes over this detail, his comments in *On the Decalogue* show that the people he can compliment in one treatise can be criticized in another. Furthermore, it also shows that Philo did wish to present a reasonably truthful account in *Contemplativa,* since he did not omit to mention the leaving of parents—and society—even though he himself did not in fact think this entirely right.

Philo himself opted for a life in society (*Somn.* 1.151; *Her.* 45–46), focusing on the common good, not neglecting his family, and doing his duty. Clearly, he saw those who chose an existence away from the city as providing an admirable and alluring lifestyle in many respects, but it was one which was impossible for himself, and ultimately not even entirely right, in being neglectful of others, particularly parents. The contemplative life could be both extolled and refuted by Philo. This in itself means that it is highly unlikely that Philo simply dreamt up an ideal fantasy: the evidence of his writings indicates that he encountered those who undertook a contemplative, philosophical existence of ascetic self-denial and that he found them at times vexing.

In *On Flight and Finding* (*Fug.* 28–32), for example, Philo justifies keeping money; the challenge is to use it well (*Fug.* 28–29). Fame could be accepted (30) and used well, as could a luxurious dinner (31–32), but one should be modest and moderate. Here too the model of someone who spurns such things is found. In *Fug.* 33 he identifies that there are those who give up their businesses and financial dealings and say they have some contempt for fame and pleasure, but he is not impressed by those who look dirty and sullen (see *Mut.* 32–34). They might say they love order, temperance, and endurance (33–34), but Philo questions a life that rejects community with other people. Philo seems even quite defensive about his own choices, in the face of the lifestyle of ascetic contemplatives: while they ridicule the business of *politeia*, they "do not recognize how useful the matter is" (*Fug.* 35). Ultimately, Philo asserts then that "it is better first to have fought out the active/practical life as a pre-contest to the more perfect contest of the contemplative life," avoiding the charge that anyone has shrunk away from social and business life out of laziness (*Fug.* 36). In other words, using the Levites as a model, they were not supposed to retire until they were fifty (Num 4:3–5) and only after their practical duty was done could they undertake contemplation, delighting in knowledge and principles alone (*Fug.* 37). Virtue should be understood in regard to human interaction before one went away to concentrate on a relationship with God (*Fug.* 38). It is not a good idea to try this lifestyle when young. The life of "ministry to the only God," ἡ θεοῦ μόνου θεραπεία (*Fug.* 40), is tough, and, "we arrive at the court of ministry and turn away from this austere way of living more quickly than we came, for we are not able to bear the sleepless observance, and the unceasing and relentless toil" (*Fug.* 41).

This kind of criticism also serves to sharpen our awareness of how much Philo was crafting his chosen example of the contemplative life for the sake of impressing an audience familiar with certain key features that would obtain in this life, and putting his own personal qualms on one side. It seems that Philo endorsed the lifestyle for those who were mature, but not for those who were young, and his comment that the women of the group were "mostly old virgins" (*Contempl.* 68) also tends to give an impression of the whole group as mature or elderly, which is clearly how Philo would wish it, though he could not insist on this as the reality for all. In such a way he both presents truth and engages in literary air-brushing, to push his readers/hearers into a certain imaginative response. His critiques of those who undertake such a lifestyle ahead of being fifty make it quite likely that there was indeed a greater number of younger people who took up this philosophical and ascetic existence in this group than Philo would have liked and he did not wish to dwell on them. In introducing the juniors of the group, whom his audience would expect to be young, Philo states that they might not *all* have been that young in years (*Contempl.* 67, 72).

We see the personal tension in Philo in *Spec.* 3.1–6, one of the few glimpses we have of Philo's own experience of life, where he admits that he once had time for philosophy, for "contemplation of the universe," companioned by divine words and doctrines. He himself did not care about fame, wealth, or bodily comforts and travelled, inspired, to the heights with the sun and moon, having escaped from "the diseases of mortal life" (1–2), but he was set upon by "envy" (from others) and pulled down into a great sea of troubles, in public life, in which he could barely keep his head above water (3). He can sometimes take a moment and return to the air, but he is stuck in a stormy sea, with matters of civil life and strife that crash down on him on every side (5–6). Here it seems he himself has moved some way towards the contemplative life and been completely stymied by duties to the *politeia.* No wonder, in his frustration, he finds fault at times with those who have just walked away from it all.

It seems, however, that despite any criticisms he may have had of the contemplative, ascetic lifestyle, Philo went along this path for a time and was called back. He yearned for it again. Furthermore, it was while he was so frustrated, in the "great sea of troubles" representing the Jewish community to successive emperors in Rome, that he wrote about the Therapeutae—as ministers of the divine and healers of souls—with such relentless praise.

The Therapeutae are not then made up out of nothing, or very little, and they are not only mentioned in *Contemplativa.* There is plenty of evidence of the kind of people Philo describes in *Contemplativa* in his other writings.

They were a real group of people, and here we find real women. Everything said of men who embrace the austere life would apply also to women who do so.

Philo includes women in his description of the Therapeutae cautiously, with literary airbrushing to make them as good as possible. He certainly did not need them to be there for his purposes of creating a philosophical ideal, since Philo could use as a parallel model the example of the Essenes, who did not include women in their number. Ross Kraemer has suggested that Philo in *Contemplativa* was creating a fantasy on the basis of Exod 15—where the men were led by Moses, singing the Song of the Sea, and the women by Miriam.[34] For Kraemer, the women's inclusion in the group was indeed necessary to create the image of an ecstatic Israel. Clearly, a reception of Exod 15 is signaled by Philo in the singing and dancing of the Therapeutae on their celebrations of the forty-ninth eve, where—after a frugal meal—the men are led by a male choral leader and the women by a female choral leader. Philo writes:

> §83 After the dinner they hold the sacred event all night. The all night event is held in this way. They all stand up together and, firstly, become two choirs in the middle of the *symposion*: the one of men, and the other of women. A leader and chief is chosen for each, one most honoured and musical. §84 Then they sing hymns to God composed of many metres and melodies, in which they sound together, in which there are antiphonal harmonies, clapping hands and tapping feet, and they conjure up now processing choruses, then stationary ones, making both turns and counterturns in choral dancing.
>
> §85 When then each of the choirs has been feasted by itself and by each other, having drunk as in the Bacchic rites the wine-cup of god-loving, they intermingle and become one choir from both, a copy of the one of old established by the Red Sea, on account of the astonishing works there. §86 For by the command of God the sea became a cause of salvation to some, but destruction to others. For when it was split apart and drawn away by violent undercurrents, and from each opposing side it was like solid walls, the space in between widened into a highway road all cleared up and dry, through which the people walked to the opposite shore, conveyed to the higher places. When the people had run over, with the waves both on one side and on the other, and when the sea was poured out into the dried bottom, those of the enemies pursuing them, being submerged, perished. §87 After seeing and experiencing this, which was a work greater than a word, thought or hope, both men and women alike, filled with inspiration, becoming one choir, sang the hymns of thanksgiving to the Saviour God,

34. Kraemer, *Unreliable Witnesses*, 84–107.

> Moses the prophet leading the men and Miriam the prophetess leading the women.
>
> §88 On this, above all, the choir of the ministers (Therapeutae), male and female, is modelled; with re-echoing and antiphonal melodies, the treble of the women mingling with the deep voice of the men, it produces harmonious concord, and it is really music. Lovely are the thoughts, lovely are the words, dignified are the choristers, and also the purpose of the thoughts and the words and the choristers is piety.

As I have previously explored, the initial song sung by the women may well be a Song of Miriam now found in part among the Dead Sea Scrolls (4Q365 6 1–7).[35] While we have an obvious patterning on Exod 15, to suppose this is all Philo's fantasy is, however, to adopt far too sceptical a position. As Pieter van der Horst has noted, contra Kraemer, "If Philo could have patterned his description of the singing of the male and female Therapeutai at the Fiftieth-Day-Festival on his own interpretation of the text of Exod 15, then a contemporary coreligionist of his who was the leader of the 'Therapeutikon' could pattern their celebrations on the same interpretation as well, with the result that the actual (historical) reality was more or less as Philo described it, in spite of all his allegorical twists."[36] Additionally, the women do not just appear in *Contemplativa* in the context of the inspired celebration where Exod 15 is referenced. Philo states women's inclusion within the group at the start (*Contempl.* 2), and he then mentions them specifically when they appear with men on the Sabbath days, in a common gathering place for the purposes of teaching, where all participants are portrayed as exhibiting model virtues: thus the women are, as noted, provided with the womanly virtue of modesty (*Contempl.* 30–33). There is nothing ecstatic here, no women singing and dancing: they are simply there, in the "synagogue" space with men, quietly listening alongside men.

The reception of Exod 15 in *Contemplativa* then is not a case of Philo building up an imaginary world from a text (and there is no other case where he seems to have done such a thing). Rather, Philo bears witness to the scriptural precedent of Miriam being used as a mandate for women's inspired agency within a particular philosophical school of Alexandrian Judaism.

---

35. Taylor, *Jewish Women Philosophers*, 322–34.

36. Pieter W. van der Horst, review of *Unreliable Witnesses: Religion, Gender and History in the Greco-Roman Mediterranean*, by Ross Shepherd Kraemer, *JSJ* 43 (2012): 100.

Conclusions

In terms of identity, the Therapeutae do not constitute an isolated group of "sectarians." Rather, it seems quite clear from Philo's writings that there were men and women in his own social class in Alexandria, educated in the allegorical method, who opted to undertake a lifestyle of austerity for the sake of a philosophical ideal. They could do this by living a very simple life within the city, or else they could completely leave the city and adopt an alternative lifestyle in a place outside. We have therefore a presentation in *Contemplativa* of those who have adopted this alternative noncity lifestyle of withdrawal and detachment. They were not, according to Philo's other comments about them, entirely correct in all ways, unless perhaps they might be older themselves and without parents to look after. However, for *Contemplativa* he lets his criticisms pass.

Philo's comments about contemplatives outside *Contemplativa* do verify the existence of such people. However, such comments also alert us to the rhetorical aims of *Contemplativa*. Philo will pass over anything he does not consider absolutely appropriate and helpful for his case. In terms of the women of the group he has a rhetorical problem, given he would wish to emphasize that the lifestyle of the true disciples of Moses is also very manly. The women are therefore explained and restrained in this text, made particularly modest, virginal, and old. However, at the end of the treatise they are anything but quiet. They are singing and clapping, inspired, following a woman leader of choral song and dance on their forty-ninth eve (a celebration of a special Sabbath every seven weeks), modeled on Miriam.

The women of this group are particularly interesting since, given the foregoing remarks, we should see them as being part of a reasonably elite social milieu in Alexandria that has supported the education of women and girls, so that they too can read and compose music, and also supported their lifestyle choices, so that they can opt to live in such an alternative community.

In Philo's social milieu, there must have been educated women philosophers who also taught, since it was perfectly fine for Philo to use the image of a female teacher of philosophy to further his argument (*Fug.* 55, 58). Philo states that he was bothered by Exod 21:12 in which there is an extra word in the text which did not make sense (*θανάτῳ θανατοῦσι*, "put to death by death"), and he "consulted with a wise woman, by name of Skepsis, in order to seek a solution; she taught me." As Kenneth Atkinson notes, because of the fact the name Skepsis means "consideration" it is common to doubt this is a real person, but Skepsis was a woman's name in antiquity and more likely "it shows that [an] educated woman lectured in the greatest centre of learning in the

Hellenistic world."[37] Furthermore, this wise Jewish woman gave Philo other interpretations, including that "a deathless life is one possessed by love and friendship of God and is to be gained unbodily [ἀσωμάτος κατεσχῆσθαι]" (*Fug.* 58). This is certainly appropriate teaching for one who might be among the wider circle of the group we call the Therapeutae.

37. Kenneth Atkinson, *Salome: Jerusalem's Warrior Monarch of the First Century B.C.E.* (Jefferson, NC: McFarland, 2012), 201. See also Tal Ilan, *Silencing the Queen: The Literary Histories of Shelamzion and Other Jewish Women*, TS 155 (Tübingen: Mohr Siebeck, 2006), 32–34.

The World of Qumran and the Sectarian Dead Sea Scrolls in Gendered Perspective

Maxine L. Grossman

The religious world represented in the sectarian Dead Sea Scrolls is one that assumes distinctive roles for women and men, as well as very particular understandings of acceptable gender dynamics and sexual norms. A feminist critical reading of these texts "against the grain," however, reveals some surprising possibilities for women's presence, participation, and authority in the communities associated with these texts. Such a reading also reveals significant dynamics of contestation around these social roles. Awareness of the apparent power dynamics in the sectarian scrolls suggests that readers must be cautious in making historical claims with regard to the textual evidence. In place of firm historical arguments about women's roles in this ancient Jewish setting, a reading that pays attention to dynamics of religious sectarianism allows us to identify ranges of historical and social possibility in relation to these texts.[1]

1. The Concept of a Sect

To speak of *sectarian* scrolls requires a brief discussion of the term *sect*. Some scholars eschew this term, noting its implied disparagement of others' religious views. For the study of the scrolls, however, it remains a useful point of reference, under a particular set of analytical conditions.

We might note three possible ways of using the term sect. The first, and most general, meaning of sect is simply that of a "small religious group." This loosely correlates with Josephus's use of *haireseis* in reference to the Pharisees, Sadducees, and Essenes: a small politico-religious group whose members share some identifiable views and an understanding of particular social

1. For background on this approach, see Maxine L. Grossman, *Reading for History in the Damascus Document: A Methodological Study*, STDJ 45 (Leiden: Brill, 2002).

boundaries.[2] For much of the history of scrolls scholarship, this use of the term has prevailed.

The last two decades have seen a distinct shift in the treatment of sectarianism, with increased attention to sociological implications and a more nuanced engagement with the concept of sects.[3] The term, from this sociological perspective, refers not only to a small group with defined boundaries, but to a group that separates itself from a larger mainstream.[4] Sectarians share a common heritage with the people around them, but they view their own version of that heritage as the correct one, and they see other perspectives as errors in judgment or as a falling away from the received ideal. Sectarians may introduce novel interpretations and practices—and indeed sectarian groups are often marked by distinctive social structures and attitudes toward family and embodied behaviors—but what makes them sectarian is the fact that they

---

2. On Josephus as a source for ancient Jewish sectarianism, see Honora Howell Chapman and Zuleika Rodgers, eds., *A Companion to Josephus*, BCAW (Oxford: Wiley Blackwell, 2016), especially the article of Albert I. Baumgarten, "Josephus and the Jewish Sects," 261–72.

3. Important foundations for this discussion were laid by Shemaryahu Talmon and Albert I. Baumgarten; see, e.g., Shemaryahu Talmon, "The Community of the Renewed Covenant: Between Judaism and Christianity," in *The Community of the Renewed Covenant: The Notre Dame Symposium on the Dead Sea Scrolls*, ed. Eugene Ulrich and James VanderKam, CJA 10 (Notre Dame: University of Notre Dame Press, 1994), 3–24; Albert I. Baumgarten, *The Flourishing of Jewish Sects in the Maccabean Era: An Interpretation*, JSJSup 55 (Leiden: Brill, 1997). More recently, see the discussion and bibliography in Jutta Jokiranta, "*Serakhim* and Sectarianism," in *Social Identity and Sectarianism in the Qumran Movement*, STDJ 105 (Leiden: Brill, 2013), 17–76; Albert I. Baumgarten, "Karaites, Qumran, the Calendar, and Beyond: At the Beginning of the Twenty-First Century," in *The Dead Sea Scrolls and Contemporary Culture: Proceedings of the International Conference Held at the Israel Museum, Jerusalem (July 6–8, 2008)*, ed. Shani Tzoref, Adolfo D. Roitman, and Lawrence H. Schiffman, STDJ 93 (Leiden: Brill, 2011), 603–19; Jutta Jokiranta, "Sociological Approaches to Qumran Sectarianism," in *The Oxford Handbook of the Dead Sea Scrolls*, ed. Timothy H. Lim and John J. Collins (Oxford: Oxford University Press, 2010), 200–231; David J. Chalcraft, ed., *Sectarianism in Early Judaism: Sociological Advances* (New York: Routledge, 2007); Eyal Regev, *Sectarianism in Qumran: A Cross-Cultural Perspective*, RelSoc 45 (Berlin: de Gruyter, 2007). On sectarian texts in particular, see Devorah Dimant, "Sectarian and Nonsectarian Texts from Qumran: The Pertinence and Use of a Taxonomy," in *History, Ideology and Bible Interpretation in the Dead Sea Scrolls: Collected Studies*, FAT 90 (Tübingen: Mohr Siebeck, 2014), 101–11. Note also the essays in Sacha Stern, *Sects and Sectarianism in Jewish History*, IJSStud 12 (Leiden: Brill, 2011), and on sectarianism at a variety of points in Jewish history, especially the article of Albert I. Baumgarten, "Prologue: How Do We Know When We Are on to Something?," 3–19.

4. See Chalcraft, *Sectarianism in Early Judaism*, especially "Part 1: Max Weber on Sects and Voluntary Associations with Specific Reference to Second Temple Judaism," 26–113.

view their own choices as the authentic understanding of a heritage that other people have simply (and perhaps sinfully) failed to adopt. A natural by-product of sectarianism, according to sociologists like William Sims Bainbridge, is a tendency toward social schism: sectarian groups may split apart repeatedly as a result of religious differences that are obvious and meaningful only to them and to others within their specific religious world.[5]

It is easy to slip from analytically describing a small religious group as divisive and exclusivist to simply disparaging the group in those same terms. It is in this third sense that the term sect can become problematic for a discussion of religion (and especially, one might add, *other* people's religions). But the term itself retains a certain utility especially when it is used to highlight discourses of separation, conflict, and difference between groups.[6] These methodological observations provide a backdrop for a discussion of the scrolls themselves.

2. The Dead Sea Scrolls

The term *Dead Sea Scrolls* refers to a collection of more than nine hundred manuscripts, many of them highly fragmentary, which were discovered in the mid twentieth century, in a series of eleven caves in the Judean Desert, near the Dead Sea.[7] The scrolls date from the last two centuries BCE and the first century CE, corresponding to the late Second Temple period. A significant proportion of the collection, fragments of roughly two hundred manuscripts, represent books later included in the canonical Hebrew Bible; of the canonical biblical books, only Esther is missing. Manuscripts of the books of Enoch and Jubilees appear in numbers significant enough to argue for their centrality within the collection, as well. Another large number of texts reflects attention to biblical themes and characters; these include fragmentary copies of texts familiar from the Apocrypha, such as Ben Sira and Tobit, as well as previously-unknown texts, including the Genesis Apocryphon (an expansive engagement with the literary traditions also preserved in the book of Genesis)

5. William Sims Bainbridge, *The Sociology of Religious Movements* (New York: Routledge, 1997).

6. In contrast, the sociological term *cult* (in the sense of a small, new religion that introduces alien beliefs and practices) has become thoroughly problematic, at least in the United States; see, e.g., James D. Tabor and Eugene V. Gallagher, *Why Waco? Cults and the Battle for Religious Freedom in America* (Berkeley: University of California Press, 1995).

7. For general introductions to the scrolls, see Lim and Collins, *Oxford Handbook of the Dead Sea Scrolls*; James C. VanderKam, *The Dead Sea Scrolls Today*, 2nd ed. (Grand Rapids, MI: Eerdmans, 2010).

and the Temple Scroll (an equally expansive text describing and explaining the legal norms around an idealized temple). Other scrolls in the collection preserve calendars, liturgies and prayers, reworkings of scripture and scriptural themes, horoscopes, and more.[8]

As a collection, the Dead Sea Scrolls reflect some of the diversity of Second Temple period Judaism: evidence for the Masoretic tradition is accompanied by evidence for Septuagintal texts and the Samaritan Pentateuch, as well as unaligned scriptural manuscripts. The sheer number of previously unknown compositions speaks to a vibrancy of religious thought and engagement. But the scrolls probably should not be understood as a representative sample of the Judean or Jewish literature of this period—the distinct absence of explicit contemporary historical accounts, and the lack of interest in history more generally, the lack of explicit philosophical discourses, and many other gaps in the collection indicate that this is a specialized, or at least not fully representative slice of the Jewish cultural production of its day. The large number of manuscripts of texts like Enoch, Jubilees, Daniel, Isaiah, and Psalms similarly points to particular trends within the scrolls.[9]

A distinctive subset of texts within the Dead Sea Scrolls is explicitly *sectarian*. Included among the sectarian scrolls are rule texts, line-by-line scriptural commentaries (pesharim), hymns, and a composition outlining the final war between the sons of light and the sons of darkness. These texts share a cluster of common terminology, although not all scrolls use the same key terms. The sectarian texts include self-referential group designations (*yahad* [יחד], *edah* [עדה], "Doers of Torah," and "Penitents of Israel"), references to group leaders (the Teacher of Righteousness) and leadership roles (*maskil*, *mebaqqer*), and an awareness of opponents and challengers (the Wicked Priest, the Spouter of Lies, the Seekers of Smooth Things [דורשי חלקות], whom scholars often identify with the Pharisees). They make frequent use of scripture, through quotation, citation, and allusion; they also make frequent use of pesher-style interpretation (even in nonpesher texts), to highlight the scriptural meaning of present-day or recent historical experiences.[10]

---

8. On the content of the scrolls manuscripts, see VanderKam, *Dead Sea Scrolls Today*, 47–96. For texts and translations, as well as key bibliography, see Florentino García Martínez and Eibert J. C. Tigchelaar, *The Dead Sea Scrolls Study Edition*, 2 vols. (Leiden: Brill; Grand Rapids: Eerdmans, 1997); a widely available English translation is Geza Vermes, *The Complete Dead Sea Scrolls in English*, 7th ed. (London: Penguin Classics, 2012).

9. See John J. Collins, "Historiography in the Dead Sea Scrolls," in *Scriptures and Sectarianism: Essays on the Dead Sea Scrolls*, WUNT 332 (Tübingen: Mohr Siebeck, 2014), 119–32.

10. On the designation *sectarian* scrolls, see Charlotte Hempel, *The Qumran Rule*

Three sectarian rule texts—the Community Rule (Serek Hayahad), the Damascus Document, and the Rule of the Congregation—provide notable evidence for gender construction among scrolls sectarians.[11] We have multiple witnesses for the first two texts, including two medieval manuscripts of the Damascus Document, which were found in the Cairo Genizah. All three rule texts are composite in form, containing sermons and descriptions of group rituals. The Damascus Document and the Community Rule also contain a variety of lists of rules, and they share a common penal code that also appears in another sectarian text, 4QMiscellaneous Rules (formerly called 4QSerekh Damascus, to indicate its discursive overlap with both major rule texts).[12]

3. The Essene Hypothesis

Early readings of the scrolls, especially those that focused on the well-preserved copy of the Community Rule from Cave 1 (1QS), highlighted resonances between these texts and the ancient Jewish Essenes, a sectarian group

Texts in Context: Collected Studies, TSAJ 154 (Tübingen: Mohr Siebeck, 2013), 2–3, 141, 148–50, and the bibliography found there; Dimant, "Sectarian and Nonsectarian Texts from Qumran"; an important early discussion is Carol Newsom, "'Sectually Explicit' Literature from Qumran," in *The Hebrew Bible and Its Interpreters*, ed. Baruch Halpern and David N. Freedman (Winona Lake, IN: Eisenbrauns, 1990), 167–87.

11. For the Cave 1 manuscript of the Community Rule (1QS), see Elisha Qimron and James H. Charlesworth, "Rule of the Community," in *Rule of the Community and Related Documents*, ed. J. H. Charlesworth, vol. 1 of *The Dead Sea Scrolls: Hebrew, Aramaic, and Greek Texts with English Translations*, PTSDSSP (Louisville: Westminster John Knox Press; Tübingen: Mohr Siebeck, 1994), 7–51; for the Cave 4 manuscripts of the Community Rule (4QS = 4Q255–264), see Philip S. Alexander and Geza Vermes, *Qumran Cave 4:XIX: Serekh Ha-Yahad and Two Related Texts*, DJD XXVI (Oxford: Clarendon, 1998). For the medieval manuscripts of the Damascus Document (CD), see Joseph M. Baumgarten and Daniel Schwartz, "Damascus Document (CD)," in *Damascus Document, War Scroll, and Related Documents*, ed. J. H. Charlesworth with Joseph M. Baumgarten, vol. 2 of *The Dead Sea Scrolls: Hebrew, Aramaic, and Greek Texts with English Translations*, PTSDSSP (Louisville: Westminster John Knox; Tübingen: Mohr Siebeck, 1995), 4–57; for the ancient manuscripts of the Damascus Document (4QD = 4Q266–273), see Joseph M. Baumgarten, *Qumran Cave 4:XIII: The Damascus Document (4Q266–73)*, DJD XVIII (Oxford: Clarendon, 1996). For the Rule of the Congregation, see D. Barthélemy, "28a. Règle de la Congrégation (1QSa)," in *Qumran Cave 1*, ed. D. Barthélemy and J. T. Milik, DJD I (Oxford: Clarendon, 1955), 108–18. I have based my translations on García Martínez and Tigchelaar, *Dead Sea Scrolls Study Edition*, with adaptations in consultation with the above editions and for the sake of clarity and nuance.

12. See further Joseph M. Baumgarten, "Miscellaneous Rules," in *Qumran Cave 4:XXV: Halakhic Texts*, DJD XXXV (Oxford: Clarendon, 1999), 57–78.

described by Philo, Josephus, and Pliny the Elder (among others). Attention to these resonances led to the development of the now-classic Essene hypothesis,[13] whose premises have been critiqued and updated but continue to retain some currency to this day: the Community Rule is to be associated with a habitation site for celibate sectarians at Khirbet Qumran, near the northwest edge of the Dead Sea, while the Damascus Document reflects a group of "marrying Essenes," who live in encampments throughout the land.

This rendering of the evidence makes a certain amount of sense, but it harmonizes the data in sometimes-problematic ways.[14] In turning to a discussion of the sectarian scrolls that pays particular attention to their treatments of gender, sexuality, and norms of group order, it will be useful first to break down this argument and restate some of the evidence underlying it. Seven points of consideration are especially relevant here.

3.1. Celibacy

Philo, Josephus, and Pliny all refer to the Essenes as celibate men, who form small groups and share property in common.[15] Josephus also briefly mentions a subset of marrying Essenes, who have sex only for purposes of procreation.[16]

---

13. Briefly and clearly summarized in Vermes, "Appendix: The Essenes and the Qumran Community," in *Complete Dead Sea Scrolls in English*, 46–48.

14. Virtually every aspect of the Essene hypothesis has been critiqued in recent scrolls scholarship, even as the general outlines of the theory continue to retain relevance. Three important recent reconsiderations of the history and development of the sectarian movement can be found in Hempel, *The Qumran Rule Texts in Context*; John J. Collins, *Beyond the Qumran Community: The Sectarian Movement of the Dead Sea Scrolls* (Grand Rapids: Eerdmans, 2010); and Alison Schofield, *From Qumran to the* Yaḥad*: A New Paradigm of Textual Development for the Community Rule*, STDJ 77 (Leiden: Brill, 2009).

15. For a collection of the classical sources on the Essenes, see Geza Vermes and Martin D. Goodman, eds., *The Essenes according to the Classical Sources* (Sheffield: JSOT Press, 1989). For a discussion of these texts, see Joan E. Taylor, "The Classical Sources on the Essenes and the Scrolls Communities," in Lim and Collins, *Oxford Handbook of the Dead Sea Scrolls*, 173–200.

16. On celibacy and the Qumran scrolls, see most recently Joan E. Taylor, "Women, Children, and Celibate Men in the Serekh Texts," *HTR* 104 (2011): 171–90; Eyal Regev, "Cherchez les femmes: Were the *yaḥad* Celibates?," *DSD* 15 (2008): 253–84; and Cecilia Wassen, *Women in the Damascus Document*, AcBib 21 (Atlanta: Society of Biblical Literature, 2005), and the further bibliography indicated there. An important earlier treatment is Elisha Qimron, "Celibacy in the Dead Sea Scrolls and the Two Kinds of Sectarians," in *The Madrid Qumran Congress: Proceedings of the International Congress on the Dead Sea Scrolls—Madrid 18–21 March, 1991*, ed. Julio Trebolle Barrera and Luis Vegas Montaner, 2 vols., STDJ 11 (Leiden: Brill, 1992), 1:287–94.

3.2. Location

Pliny further places the Essenes in a single specific location, near the Dead Sea and apparently north of Ein Gedi. Philo and Josephus, in contrast, speak of Essenes as living throughout the land, although Philo claims that they avoid big cities, which they consider morally corrupting.[17]

3.3. Individual Sectarian "Volunteers"

The Community Rule refers to a *yahad* community made up of individual "volunteers" (1QS 1:7, 11; 5:1, 6, 8, 10, 21, 22; 6:13); it makes no reference to women, marriage, or families. The androcentric language of the text gives the impression that all the *yahad* sectarians are men, but few if any references in the text treat them as explicitly male persons. The language of the text thus permits that individual women might be counted among the "men" of the group. (This reflects the androcentric erasure of women, but, by extension, the possibility for the presence of "hidden women" within androcentric texts.)[18]

3.4. Marriage and Families in Sectarian Perspective

A passage in the Damascus Document highlights the idea that sectarians might marry and have children, noting that such marrying sectarians will live in "encampments" in the land (CD 7:6–7, 19:2–3). The framing of the statement suggests that marriage was a contested issue, as does the appearance of this passage in two significantly distinct versions.[19]

The Rule of the Congregation (1QSa) assumes a marrying community or congregation of sectarians and seems to have no other possibilities in mind. This composite text incorporates group-identity language (*yahad*, *edah*) that otherwise appears in either the Damascus Document or the Community Rule, but not in both texts.

17. Questions of location are especially addressed in Schofield, *From Qumran to the Yaḥad*.

18. On "invisible" women in these androcentric texts, see Maxine L. Grossman, "Gendered Sectarians: Envisioning Women (and Men) at Qumran," in *Celebrate Her for the Fruit of Her Hands: Essays in Honor of Carol L. Meyers*, ed. Susan Ackerman, Charles E. Carter, and Beth Alpert Nakhai (Winona Lake, IN: Eisenbrauns, 2015), 265–87; and Maxine L. Grossman, "Rethinking Gender in the *Community Rule*: An Experiment in Sociology," in Tzoref, Roitman, and Schiffman, *Dead Sea Scrolls and Contemporary Culture*, 497–512.

19. For a different interpretation of this evidence, see Wassen, *Women in the Damascus Document*, 122–29, and Regev, "Cherchez les femmes," esp. 257–59.

3.5. Correlations: Community Rule and the Classical Sources

Descriptions of sectarian life in the Community Rule line up with Philo and Josephus's treatments of the Essenes in several large ways (small group life; shared property; obedience to the authority of the group; periods of initiation) and also in terms of a number of distinctive and sometimes curious small details from Josephus (avoidance of oaths; punishment for spitting; concern about impurity of oil).[20]

3.6. Connections: The Site and the Caves

Pottery evidence convincingly links Khirbet Qumran to the scrolls caves, and the archaeology of the site supports the interpretation of it as a sectarian habitation (although the site may also have had other uses, in different periods or contemporaneously). Scholarship remains contested about how to understand the primary purpose of the scrolls caves, and especially Cave 4, with its thousands of manuscript fragments. Possibilities include the presence of an active manuscript library, a genizah of "retired" texts, evidence for an emergency effort to protect the scrolls from Roman destruction, or some combination of these explanations.[21]

3.7. The Cemeteries

Interpretations of the Qumran cemetery finds remain similarly contested, although the evidence indicates the presence of a disproportionate number of male burials and very few (some scholars would say no) burials of women and children.[22]

Close consideration of the evidence for gender, sexuality, and embodiment in these texts demonstrates that although the Essene hypothesis provides a reasonable "big picture" sense of sectarian identity, there is a great deal

---

20. Summarized in VanderKam, *Dead Sea Scrolls Today*, 97–125.

21. See Charlotte Hempel, "'Haskalah' at Qumran: The Eclectic Character of Qumran Cave 4," in *The Qumran Rule Texts in Context*, 303–37. On the archaeology of the site and the caves, see Eric M. Meyers, "Khirbet Qumran and Its Environs," in Lim and Collins, *Oxford Handbook of the Dead Sea Scrolls*, 21–45; Katharina Galor and Jean-Baptiste Humbert, eds., *Qumran: The Site of the Dead Sea Scrolls: Archaeological Interpretations and Debates*, STDJ 57 (Leiden: Brill, 2006); Jodi Magness, *Debating Qumran: Collected Essays on Its Archaeology*, ISACR 4 (Leuven: Peeters, 2004); and Jodi Magness, *The Archaeology of Qumran and the Dead Sea Scrolls* (Grand Rapids: Eerdmans, 2003).

22. See Rachel Hachlili, "The Qumran Cemetery Reassessed," in Lim and Collins, *Oxford Handbook of the Dead Sea Scrolls*, 46–78, and the bibliography presented there.

more to say about group formation, social order, and gendered power dynamics in the texts themselves, and consequently in the historical world that we might envision around them.

4. Rethinking the Scrolls Sectarians: Marriage and Social Norms

Perhaps the best source of evidence for sectarian attitudes toward women and gender can be found in the Damascus Document, as Cecilia Wassen demonstrated in an important 2005 monograph.[23] The first section of this rule, the Admonition (CD 1–8, 19–20), begins with a series of sermons that reflect on the founding of the sectarian group (CD 1:1–2:1), God's plan for all eternity (CD 2:2–13), and the history of the people of Israel, understood as one of almost perpetual waywardness and transgression (CD 2:14–3:12). It is interesting to note that the role of women is not particularly highlighted in this third sermon (although mention of the fall of the watchers in CD 2:17–18 would make just such an emphasis possible). Instead the most significant

23. Wassen, *Women in the Damascus Document*. The last decade has seen an explosion in scholarship on women, gender, sexuality, and the scrolls. See, especially, Grossman, "Gendered Sectarians"; Eileen M. Schuller, "Women in the Dead Sea Scrolls: Research in the Past Decade and Future Directions," in Tzoref, Roitman, and Schiffman, *Dead Sea Scrolls and Contemporary Culture*, 571–88; Tal Ilan, "Reading for Women in 1QSa (Serekh Ha-Edah)," in *The Dead Sea Scrolls in Context: Integrating the Dead Sea Scrolls in the Study of Ancient Texts, Languages, and Cultures*, ed. Armin Lange, Emanuel Tov, Matthias Weigold, in association with Bennie H. Reynolds III, VTSup 140 (Leiden: Brill, 2011), 1:61–76; Taylor, "Women, Children, and Celibate Men"; Katharina Galor, "Gender and Qumran," in *Holistic Qumran: Trans-disciplinary Research of Qumran and the Dead Sea Scrolls*, ed. Jan Gunneweg, Annemie Adriaens, and Joris Dik, STDJ 87 (Leiden: Brill, 2010), 29–38; Maxine L. Grossman, "Women and Men in the Rule of the Congregation: A Feminist Critical Assessment," in *Rediscovering the Dead Sea Scrolls: An Assessment of Old and New Methods and Approaches*, ed. Maxine L. Grossman (Grand Rapids: Eerdmans, 2010), 229–45; Tal Ilan, "Women in Qumran and the Dead Sea Scrolls," in Lim and Collins, *Oxford Handbook on the Dead Sea Scrolls*, 123–47; William Loader, *The Dead Sea Scrolls on Sexuality: Attitudes towards Sexuality in Sectarian and Related Literature at Qumran* (Grand Rapids: Eerdmans, 2009); Eileen M. Schuller, "Women in the Dead Sea Scrolls: Some Observations from a Dictionary," *RevQ* 24 (2009): 49–59; Sidnie White Crawford, "Not according to Rule: Women, the Dead Sea Scrolls and Qumran," in *Emanuel: Studies in Hebrew Bible, Septuagint, and Dead Sea Scrolls in Honor of Emanuel Tov*, ed. Shalom M. Paul et al., VTSup 94 (Leiden: Brill, 2003), 127–50; and from an archaeological perspective, Jodi Magness, "Women at Qumran?," in *Debating Qumran*, 113–49. A founding contribution to the discussion is Eileen M. Schuller, "Women in the Dead Sea Scrolls," in *The Dead Sea Scrolls after Fifty Years: A Comprehensive Assessment*, ed. Peter W. Flint and James C. VanderKam, 2 vols. (Leiden: Brill, 1999), 2:117–44.

attention to women appears in the treatments of contemporary controversies over practices of marriage and sexual behavior.

4.1. Sexual Transgressions

The Damascus Document observes that the people of Israel are trapped in various "nets of Belial," or transgressions, which include "taking two wives in their lifetimes" (CD 4:20–21), having sex with menstruants ("a woman who sees a blood discharge" CD 5:7), and marriage between an uncle and his niece (CD 5:9–10). The discursive framing of these transgressions is striking in a number of ways that deserve further attention from a feminist critical perspective. First, the discussion of marriage to multiple wives (whether this means polygyny or remarriage after divorce) has a distinct quality of arising *in medias res*, as if the authors of the text have had this discussion before and are saving time by answering a variety of challenges in one breath. They pile up scriptural references without significant comment, thus stating that the taking of a second wife transgresses "the foundation of creation," which is "male and female he created them" (CD 4:21, referencing Gen 1:27); it goes against the example of the animals in the ark, who appeared "two by two" (CD 5:1); and it ignores the law of the king, who must not "multiply wives for himself" (CD 5:2, citing Deut 17:17). A four-line-long aside then addresses the problem of David, who certainly did "multiply wives for himself," but—as the text explains—did not know about the law against this practice, because it was sealed away in his own day. He is therefore to be held accountable for his acts of violence and treachery ("the blood of Uriah," CD 5:5), but not for his multiple marriages. The disproportionate focus on this example and the use of a series of parallel scriptural references without expanded discussion or explanation suggest that this is but one moment in a larger and rather contested conflict over marital norms, between people who share a common scriptural tradition. Concerns about divorce and remarriage were similarly at issue for early Christians.[24] Sectarian concerns about marriage are thus understandable as part of a larger Second Temple period question about legal

---

24. On relevant themes in the scrolls and the New Testament, see, e.g., Florentino García Martínez, ed., *Echoes from the Caves: Qumran and the New Testament*, STDJ 85 (Leiden: Brill, 2009), especially Lutz Doering, "Marriage and Creation in Mark 10 and CD 4–5," 133–63; Serge Ruzer, "Negotiating the Proper Attitude to Marriage and Divorce," in *Mapping the New Testament: Early Christian Writings as a Witness for Jewish Biblical Exegesis*, JCP 13 (Leiden: Brill, 2007), 131–47; and George J. Brooke, *The Dead Sea Scrolls and the New Testament* (Minneapolis: Fortress, 2005), especially "From Qumran to Corinth: Embroidered Allusions to Women's Authority," 195–214.

practice and gendered social norms, framed in light of scripture but not necessarily as the product of conflicting textual interpretations.

Similarly, the reference to sex with a menstruant (or, technically, with a woman who sees "a blood discharge," possibly including blood outside the normal menstrual cycle) may be understood as part of an ongoing point of legal and social contention. Regrettably, we cannot say more about the specific disagreement here, although it is tempting to read this brief statement as potential evidence for a Second Temple period precursor to the transformations of norms around menstrual practice that developed in later rabbinic contexts.[25]

The third example concerns marriage between uncles and nieces. Although the Levitical laws of near-kin marriage prohibit unions between nephews and aunts, they are silent on relationships between uncles and nieces. The Damascus Document cites the passage from Leviticus (18:13) that forbids men to marry their aunts and then explains that "the law of forbidden unions is written for males, and like them (it applies to) women" (CD 5:9–10). This is an unusually explicit statement about grammar, gender, and textuality within the literature of Second Temple period Judaism.[26]

It is possible to read this statement as evidence for an early pre-history of later Rabbinic discussions of uncle-niece marriage. Scrolls references to "Seekers of Smooth Things" appear to be disparagements of the Pharisees, who themselves are commonly viewed as a precursor to the rabbinic movement. The rabbis, in their turn, ultimately argued in *support* of uncle-niece marriage; classical rabbinic texts also incorporated regular arguments from grammar (which are otherwise unusual within the scrolls corpus). But a genealogical connection is in no way necessary here. Any community that seeks to live by the Levitical marriage laws will need to address the gap in the text around the question of uncle-niece marriage; classical rabbis, medieval Karaites, and others in the history of Judaism have reached their own conclusions about

25. See Aharon Shemesh, "Halakhah between the Dead Sea Scrolls and Rabbinic Literature," in Lim and Collins, *Oxford Handbook of the Dead Sea Scrolls*, 595–616, and bibliography cited there; Steven D. Fraade, Aharon Shemesh, and Ruth A. Clements, eds., *Rabbinic Perspectives: Rabbinic Literature and the Dead Sea Scrolls: Proceedings of the Eighth International Symposium of the Orion Center for the Study of the Dead Sea Scrolls and Associated Literature, 7–9 January 2003*, STDJ 62 (Leiden: Brill, 2006), especially Vered Noam, "Traces of Sectarian Halakhah in the Rabbinic World," 67–85, and Noam, "Divorce in Qumran in Light of Early Halakhah," *JJS* 56 (2005): 206–23.

26. The Temple Scroll, in a series of marriage-related laws, uses scriptural language to designate uncle-niece marriage an "abomination" (תועבה); see 11QT 66:16. It does not address the grammatical gender question treated in the Damascus Document.

such marriages, without necessarily relying upon the conclusions of earlier interpreters. In this case, the appeal to grammar remains interesting indeed.

4.2. Fitness for Marriage

In their treatment of fitness for marriage, the sectarian scrolls address the problem of nonmarital sexual behavior and its implications for women's marriage potential. This discussion also provides a context for new information about women's public roles and the possibilities for women's authority within sectarian norms.

4.2.1. Fitness for Marriage in the Damascus Document

Following a series of statements about civil law, the Cave 4 Damascus Document manuscripts (4QD = 4Q266–273) indicate some norms for proper marriage practice: a father should reveal his daughter's blemishes to a potential husband, lest he otherwise be "leading a blind man astray" (4Q271 3 7–9 and par.; quoting Deut 27:18); a father should not marry his daughter to one who is not "appropriate" for her, since this is a kind of *kilayim*, akin to plowing with an ox and an ass or mixing linen and wool fabrics (3 9–10).[27] In addition, a man is not to marry a woman (that is, "bring her into the holy covenant") if she has been sexually active outside of marriage, whether before marriage ("in her father's house") or after having been widowed (3 10–12).

The treatment of marriage in this passage reflects the standard ancient assumption that it is an economic transaction between father and husband. But the father's authority to choose a husband is limited by the norms of the group, whose larger authority also defines the constraints on acceptable contexts for sexual behavior. A similar sense that sex is absolutely limited to marriage appears in the Rule of the Congregation, with reference to male sectarians: at the age of twenty, a man is eligible for full membership in the sectarian *edah*, or congregation, at which time he may marry and become sexually active (1QSa 1:8–10). Where scriptural law may have room for ambiguity around sexual activity (including awareness of prostitution and nonmarital sexual behavior), these sectarian texts apparently forbid sexual activity outside the limits of legal marriage.

The Damascus Document's discussion of appropriate wives fails to mention the divorcee as a potential (if problematic) marriage partner. Elsewhere

27. Similar themes appear in the discussion of marriage in 4QMMT; see 4Q396 4 4–11 and par.

in the text, the Damascus Document appears to permit divorce, but only with the approval of the *mebaqqer*, or "Guardian," of the group.[28] The absence of the divorcee here might then merely be an oversight, something that can easily be reinterpreted into the text. But it may also support the view that "two wives in their lifetimes" indicates a rejection of marriage after divorce. It may be the case, in other words, that sectarians understood divorce as ending a marriage but not having the power to annul or erase the prior sexual connection.[29]

The Damascus Document passage continues with another important innovation: the evaluation of potential brides, specifically in terms of their worthiness for acceptance into the sacred covenant. As the passage states:

> Every woman who has had a bad reputation while a virgin in her father's house, no man shall marry her except upon the inspection [ראות][30] of trustworthy and knowledgeable women selected by the command of the *mebaqqer* who is over [the Many]. Then he may marry her, and in marrying her, he will act according to the ru[le and will not] speak out about [her]. (4Q271 3 12–15, and par.)

This passage focuses only on the virgin; as in the case of the divorcee considered above, the absence of the widow may reflect a simple shift in focus of the text, or it may indicate that widows of questionable reputation are simply not acceptable for marriage. Here again, final authority lies not with the father or husband, but rather with the group itself, in the person of the *mebaqqer*. Note, finally, that the confirmation of the virgin's status as acceptable for marriage brings with it a constraint upon her husband, who cannot reopen the question of her reputation at a later date. We might read this treatment of the slandered bride as humanistic in intent or as yet another effort to fit marriage and sexual behavior neatly together, without even a hint of complication to the picture.

4.2.2. Evaluation of Fitness for Marriage in the Damascus Document and 4QOrdinances

The evaluation of the potential bride has been the subject of much scholarly attention. Some readers, understanding this evaluation as a medical examina-

---

28. The fragmentary list of laws in CD 13:13–18 appears to indicate that both marriage and divorce require the permission of the Inspector (*mebaqqer*) of the congregation.

29. See Doering, "Marriage and Creation"; Ruzer, "Negotiating the Proper Attitude to Marriage and Divorce"; Noam, "Divorce in Qumran in Light of Early Halakhah"; Aharon Shemesh, "4Q271.3: A Key to Sectarian Matrimonial Law," *JJS* 49 (1998): 244–63.

30. The Hebrew term is fragmentary or reconstructed in two of the manuscript witnesses (4Q269 9 7; 4Q271 3 14) but is present in 4Q270 5 21.

tion, have wondered how a widow can even be evaluated (although, as noted above, the widow is absent from this immediate passage). Scholars also note parallels to a similar text in 4QOrdinances (4Q159), concerning the man who slanders his new bride by saying that she was not a virgin at the time of their marriage (4Q159 2–4 8–10).[31] Scripture solves the problem by having the bride's parents display the evidence of her virginity (thus, Deut 22:13–21). In 4QOrdinances, instead, sectarian authority structures take over: "trustworthy women shall examine her," and the appropriate sanctions then follow (if the husband has lied, he pays a fine and must not divorce her; if he is correct, then she is to be put to death for the crime of fornication).[32]

The language around examination deserves attention here. The knowledgeable women in the Damascus Document are said to "inspect" the virgin in that text, using a form of the verb לראות, "to see." In contrast, the language of 4QOrdinances says they will "examine" her, using the verbal form לבקר (*ləbaqqēr*), which also underlies the role of the *mebaqqer*, or Examiner of the group. The *mebaqqer*, in several passages of the Damascus Document, is said to instruct, have pity on, and otherwise "examine" a sectarian—using the root פקד, "to observe"—to evaluate his knowledge and wisdom, in order to upgrade or downgrade his rank in the group hierarchy (CD 13:7–12). Nowhere in scholarship is the *mebaqqer*'s examination of the sectarian treated as physical; it is an evaluation of spiritual maturity and knowledge. By extension, the examination of the accused wife in 4QOrdinances might possibly be read in a similar fashion: as a verbal evaluation of the woman's actions, a conversation, to sort out precisely what she has or has not done.

The question of how to understand these two evaluations depends on how we read the overlapping terminology. Both texts refer to "trustworthy women" (although the women in the Damascus text are also deemed "knowledgeable"), which may imply the presence of acknowledged experts with common expertise. If their shared expertise is the defining factor, it may follow that both cases are treated in the same way: the expert women evaluate by means of discussion whether the accused's bad reputation is deserved. However, if the defining factor is not the actor but instead the language of action ("looking," as opposed to "evaluating"), the opposite conclusion might indeed be reached. In this case, *evaluation* (by "looking") may indeed refer to some sort

---

31. See "4Q159 (4QOrd[a]) 4QOrdinances[a]," in García Martínez and Tigchelaar, *Dead Sea Scrolls Study Edition*, 308–11; for נאמנות, García Martínez and Tigchelaar read *ne'ĕmānût* (as a reference to her "trustworthiness") rather than *ne'ĕmānôt* (as a reference to trustworthy women).

32. On examination of women and ancient gynecological knowledge, see Wassen, *Women in the Damascus Document*, 83–88.

of gynecological examination (and note that this evaluation is specifically associated with the questionable virgin, the category for whom a gynecological exam might most reasonably be seen as diagnostic).[33] A third possibility is that none of these terms has a technical meaning, in which case, the trustworthy women may be evaluating through speech, gynecological examination, or some combination of the two, in either a systematic or a more ad hoc fashion.

Such ambiguous conclusions are frustrating, but they highlight an important possibility related to the authority of these "trustworthy and knowledgeable women." Power and authority pivot back and forth in our discussion: there is real social impact in the role these women would have played, with significant importance for group stability (given the social power of marriage that seems to be reflected here); at the same time, that social efficacy derives solely from their ability to evaluate other women's bodies and sexual behavior. The possibility of evaluation through conversation is thus important in providing at least a (tiny) shift from focus on women's sexual bodies to acknowledgement of their decisions as actors. If male sectarian group leaders must acknowledge the trustworthy women's conclusions, this too creates a small space for social power in the larger masculinist order. From a feminist critical perspective, this approach acknowledges the ongoing desire to continue "searching for the women," but not at the expense of recognizing the power dynamics and gender constructions through which they are constrained, and, to whatever conclusion, "examined."

4.2.3. The Evidence of the Rule of the Congregation (1QSa)

An important addition to this conversation is found in the Rule of the Congregation, immediately following the reference to a man's ability to marry—and thereby become sexually active—at the age of twenty. The Rule of the Congregation continues from there with the now famous observation that, in the context of their marriage, his wife "shall be received to bear witness about him (concerning) the ordinances of the Torah, and to take a place [להתיצב] in the hearing of the judgments" (1QSa 1:11). Some scholarly readers initially emended the text, assuming that it must have been making reference to *men* as witnesses.[34] But reading this text in parallel to the Damascus Document

33. Ancient medical assumptions differ, of course, from those of modern medicine; standards of medical "reasonableness" cannot be assumed across both contexts. Again, see Wassen, *Women in the Damascus Document*, 83–88.

34. Joseph M. Baumgarten, "On the Testimony of Women in 1QSa," *JBL* 76 (1957): 266–69; see the discussion and bibliography in Grossman, "Women and Men in the Rule of the Congregation."

and 4QOrdinances suggests a different picture: in this context, as well, women are being called upon to witness to proper and improper sexual behavior.

Again, a few clarifications are in order. First, the Rule of the Congregation does not state explicitly that women are witnessing to their husbands' sexual behavior; it refers instead to "ordinances of the Torah." This could apply to any sort of piety, obedience, or transgression. At the same time, our other examples have all reflected women's witnessing to private sexual matters that male sectarian authorities could not otherwise evaluate; thus a reading of this text specifically in terms of a man's sexual behavior may indeed be more appropriate. Note, too, the description of the woman as "taking a place" (להתיצב) in the hearing of judgments; this verbal form is common in the Rule of the Congregation, and in that text it appears to refer to explicitly-sanctioned participatory roles within the group. A sectarian "takes his place" in the group, or among its chiefs, or as the head of a particular clan (1QSa 1:12, 14, 16); each of these roles is publicly acknowledged and visible.

Interpreting women as witnesses in the text of 1QSa requires us to think historically as well as literarily; it requires that we bring a feminist critical reading to the text without allowing that reading to exceed the margins of relevant social possibility. Here the range of possibility is wide, but the possible readings can be framed in very specific terms. Thus, some readers erase women from the account of witnessing altogether. Others see women as witnesses, but only to their husbands' sexuality. A third reading takes seriously the text's claim that women might witness about their husbands' behavior across the range of Torah judgments. A fourth reading, albeit with little supporting outside evidence, might understand the "hearing of judgments" to indicate that women served as actual judges within the sect.

4.2.4. The Evidence of the Qumran Penal Code

The second reading of this passage from 1QSa—that women are legitimate witnesses, but only with respect to sexual behavior—gains support from another passage in the Damascus Document. The Damascus Document's version of the Qumran penal code contains several passages that are absent from the penal code in its other versions. After discussions of a wide variety of transgressions, ranging from insulting one's superiors to disparaging the group as a whole, the Damascus penal code reports that "anyone who approaches to engage in inappropriate sex [זנות] with his wife, not according to rule [אשר לוא כמשפט] shall leave and return no more" (4Q270 7 i 12–13 and par.). The reference to "inappropriate sex" serves as an indication that only certain types of sexual behavior were viewed as acceptable within the sectarian worldview, but we cannot be certain of which sexual behaviors are forbidden here. A fragmentary passage from the Damascus Document states that people are not to have sex "on the day" (4Q270 2 i 18–19), which could mean "during the daytime" or could be a fragmentary reference to "on the Sabbath day."[35] Either of these behaviors, then, may have qualified as *zenut* for the scrolls sectarians. Sex during pregnancy or during a wife's period of menstruation might fall into the category of "inappropriate sex"; the latter is explicitly mentioned in the discussion of *zenut* in the Damascus Document's Admonition (CD 5). Definitions of זנות might have changed over time or varied from sectarian "encampment" to "encampment." It is also possible—though perhaps frustrating from a methodological perspective—that sectarians had a clear, fixed, and stable understanding of the parameters of marital *zenut*, but that this meaning remains opaque to us as outside readers.

The text continues:

> [And whoever complai]ns against the Fathers [shall be sent out] from the congregation and shall not return. But [if] (he complains) against the Mothers, he shall be punished for ten days, for the Mothers have no authoritative status (רוקמה) in the midst of the [congregation] (4Q270 7 i 13–15).

The presence of parallel categories, "Mothers" and "Fathers," is significant as an acknowledgment of women in authoritative public roles on par with those of male leaders in the group. But the text immediately breaks up the balanced pair of terms, by assigning the most dire punishment in the penal code to transgressions against the Fathers and the least significant penalty for transgressions against the Mothers, a mere ten days. Especially interesting is the assertion that the Mothers have no רוקמה, no "authority" in the group.[36] From a rhetorical perspective, the authors' need to say that women have no outward authority in the group almost guarantees that some other members of the group assume the opposite: that these women *do* have precisely this sort of authority, or at minimum that they have a recognized status of some sort. Otherwise, there would be no need to challenge it.

Who were the "Mothers" of the congregation, and how does their role overlap with that of the "trustworthy and knowledgeable women"? In both cases, these terms could simply refer to older or established women within

---

35. See Wassen, *Women in the Damascus Document*, 107–9; Moshe J. Bernstein, "Women and Children in Legal and Liturgical Texts from Qumran," in *Reading and Rereading Scripture at Qumran*, 2 vols., STDJ 107 (Leiden: Brill, 2013), 2:614–34, esp. 623–24 and bibliography cited there.

36. On the possible meanings of רוקמה, see Wassen, *Women in the Damascus Document*, 189–95 and bibliography cited there; Brooke, "From Qumran to Corinth."

the group; they could be informal designations for women with known social agency; or they could be recognized terms for positions with both agency and explicit public authority. The double discounting of authority in the Damascus Document text—implicit in the minimal penalty for showing these women disrespect and explicit in the statement that such respect is not due to them—arguably reflects tensions within the group. Trustworthy women are necessary for social order, which means that at least some women must be given real power and efficacy. But, as the Damascus Document text indicates, this social efficacy is a point of explicit contention.

The parallel penal code in the Community Rule includes no references to marriage, sex, or the Mothers (or, indeed, the Fathers). We might ask whether the earliest versions of the penal code assumed marriage as a typical practice or whether they espoused an avoidance of marriage in more robust terms from an early period. Alternatively, perhaps a general concern to keep sexual behavior where it belonged—one husband, one wife, one set of proper sexual practices, and nothing else, ever, for anyone—might have led to an external perception and perhaps even an eventual reality of the *yahad* as a truly celibate (although originally marrying) sectarian group.

An important point in this context is the literary development of the statement from CD that finds married sectarians "living in encampments" while keeping the laws of the group. As noted already, this passage is preserved in two rather distinct versions. Both begin with the observation that, among those who live "in holy perfection," God's covenant is a guarantee that they will live for a thousand generations (CD 7:4–6). The shorter version then continues,

> and if they dwell in camps, according to the rule of the land, and they take wives and beget children, they shall comport themselves according to the Torah and the judgment of the teachings, according to the rule of the Torah. (7:6–7)

The longer version contains a number of key elements that are not found in the shorter text:

> and if they dwell in camps, according to the rule of the land *as it was from of old*, and they take wives *in accordance with the custom of the Torah* and beget children, they shall comport themselves according to the Torah and the judgment of the teachings, according to the rule of the Torah. (CD 19:2–4)

The italicized text in the longer version sounds something like an addition, or at least a secondary assertion of legitimacy, over against the already assertive claims of the text itself. But what is the social context in which this should be read? Do we take the claims of the longer text at face value, understanding them as reminders to the sectarians that living in various places and having wives and families are ancestral customs that the Torah itself supports? If so, then perhaps some new practice—related to *not* living in encampments, and perhaps *not* having wives and children—might have arisen in the recent memory of the Damascus covenanters. Thus, the voluntaristic collective, without connections to family and procreation, may be the novel element in this picture.

Alternatively, these assertive "extras" may reflect a rather different scenario, in which original sectarian practice included turning away from nuclear family structures and banding together in shared habitations. In that case, the choice of some sectarians to live apart from the group in familial encampments may have put them in a vulnerable position with respect to sectarian ideology—they are in danger of being labeled "backsliders" and returners to the sins of Israel. Such a vulnerable status may thus have led them to reach for more expansive claims to primordial and legal legitimacy. A close and careful reading of the text can support either interpretation.

5. Rethinking the Qumran Sectarians

We began our discussion with two observations that bear repeating here. The first is that the Essene hypothesis might be useful in a most general sense for understanding the scrolls, but that it requires clarification in all of its particulars. The second is that attention to the explicitly sectarian aspects of the rule scrolls may help us to make better sense of their social world and gender formations. In concluding this discussion, a few key observations deserve further attention.

5.1. Snapshots and Moving Pictures

In general for historical studies, and more specifically for the study of sectarian groups, we must remember that our evidence is but a snapshot of a larger moving picture of real events. This is an old and obvious point, but it is especially important for the study of sectarian groups, because these groups are defined, in large measure, by dynamics of differentiation. We should consequently be on the lookout for points of tension and examples of schism in our evidence—and the scrolls certainly provide many examples of this sort—and we must attempt to integrate that fragmentary evidence not into a single comprehensive narrative, but rather into a narrative that acknowledges the complexities and variety in the world behind it, with awareness of change over time, contemporaneous differences among sectarian groups (including differences among groups who valued precisely the same sectarian texts), and conflicts even within groups who considered themselves to be living a coherent life of holy perfection.[37]

5.2. Perceptions of Perfection and More Problematic Realities

The coherence of holy perfection within the sectarian scrolls is an issue that deserves its own separate discussion. Across a diversity of texts and genres, the scrolls demonstrate a comprehensive rejection of messiness and disorder. But the orderly perfection of the scrolls stands counter to a reality that was not so neat. The 364-day calendar so widely represented at Qumran manages to organize days, weeks, months, holidays, and seasons into a perfect balance; its only failure is in managing the actual passage of time. (That is, it just would not have worked in real life, not without regular intercalation at periodic intervals.) The penal code similarly imagines sectarian groups as orderly and harmonious; Charlotte Hempel has wisely observed that this vision of order, too, may have belied a significantly more chaotic social reality.[38] Given this discrepancy between imagination and reality, what shall we make of the very clear sense in the sectarian scrolls that sex should happen only within pair-bonded marriages, between couples who were appropriate for one another and have not (either husband or wife) engaged in intimacy with any other partners? The "disappearance" of divorcees and widows in some of these texts might be understood as a facet of this "perfection complex." The reality, then, may have been more contested, with marriage, divorce, single life, and even nonmarital sexual behavior at stake in the real complexity of an otherwise idealized sectarian life.

5.3. The Significance of Idealized Norms

Complex realities aside, coherent *attitudes* toward sexual behavior can be found in the sectarian texts from Qumran, and those attitudes point to some possible lines of separation between groups. Marriages between uncles and nieces, expansions of rules about menstrual purity, attitudes toward polygyny, divorce, and even nonmarital sexuality were apparently commonplace topics among Second Temple period Jews, and they are topics that would have separated our sectarians from at least some of their neighbors. Disagreements might arise on the nuances of these sexual norms, and sectarians might

37. Again, see Wassen, *Women in the Damascus Document*, 122–29.

38. Hempel, personal communication.

indeed transgress these norms in their daily lives, but the norms themselves would contribute to the terms of the larger social discourse and the articulation of at least conceived social boundaries.

5.4. Reimagining Marriage in Relation to Celibacy

The problem of celibacy is an interesting one in this context. The textual evidence for celibacy remains either secondary (Philo, Josephus, Pliny) or circumstantial (the absence of families in the Community Rule; the apparently "optional" nature of marriage in the Damascus Document). But this secondary and circumstantial evidence suggests that *something* unusual is going on around sexuality in these sectarian groups, and other evidence from the texts—such as the assertion that husbands and wives are capable of committing זנות together, or the fragmentary statement that sex is prohibited on a certain day (or time of day)—suggests that extreme varieties of chastity (if not actual celibacy) may have been the rule for most sectarians much of the time. Rather than thinking in terms of separate categories of marriage and celibacy, we might be better served if we problematize the category of "sectarian marriage" by understanding it in connection with significant sexual restraint.[39]

6. Conclusions

The evidence of the sectarian rule texts does not exhaust the treatments of gender and sexuality in the larger scrolls corpus. Questions remain to be asked about a wide variety of texts that treat these subjects, including, just by way of example: the highly fragmentary papyrus 4Q502, which describes a sectarian ritual including gender-matched age-mate pairs (old men and old women, young men and young women); 4Q184, the so-called Wiles of the Wicked Woman text, which uses wisdom-language to imagine a demonic seductress, perhaps representative of bad theology, who lures righteous men off the path of justice and into the pits of hell; and the Genesis Apocryphon, whose presentation of the Flood and the patriarchal narratives includes sexualized treatments of Bitenosh (2:8–18), the mother of Noah, and Sarah the matriarch (20:2–10).[40] These and other scrolls texts provide further provocations for a feminist critical engagement with Judaism and Jewish textuality in the Second Temple period.

---

39. In imagining marriage as potentially marked by significant sexual constraint, this treatment shows some of the same ambivalence toward sexual behavior that is also expressed by Paul, especially in 1 Cor 5–7.

40. On these texts, see Ilan, "Women in Qumran."

Nevertheless, the sectarian Dead Sea Scrolls do provide important evidence for the complexities of attitudes toward marriage, family, and sexuality in Second Temple period Judaism. They hint at the prehistory of some important disputes that came to be articulated more fully during the classical rabbinic period. They also suggest that our preconceptions about women's social roles and opportunities for public authority in ancient Judaism might require reevaluation. Perhaps most importantly, however, the evidence of the scrolls encourages a reader—especially a feminist critical reader—to pay attention to the uncharted space between textual compositions and lived experience. If a reading of the textual claim that women have no "authoritative status" in a given group ultimately serves to demonstrate that *some* women must have had *some* sort of authoritative roles, this should serve to remind us that textual claims about gender (alongside sexuality, family, social order, authority, and so on) in fact provide evidence not for fixed historical realities but instead for points of tension and conflict within those historical settings.

Bibliography

Ackerman, Susan. “Women and the Religious Culture of the State Temples of the Ancient Levant: Or: Priestesses, Purity, and Parturition.” Pages 259–89 in *Temple Building and Temple Cult: Architecture and Cultic Paraphernalia of Temples in the Levant (2.–1. Mill. B.C.E)*. Edited by Jens Kamlah. ADPV 41. Wiesbaden: Harrassowitz, 2012.

Adamo, David Tuesday. “The African Wife of Joseph, Aseneth (GN 41:45, 41:50, 46:20).” *JSem* 22 (2013): 409–25.

Adams, Sean. *Baruch and the Epistle of Jeremiah: A Commentary Based on the Texts in Codex Vaticanus*. SeptCS. Leiden: Brill, 2014.

Adler, William, and Paul Tuffin. *The Chronography of George Synkellos: A Byzantine Chronicle of Universal History from the Creat*ion. Oxford: Oxford University Press, 2002.

Ahearne-Kroll, Patricia D. “Joseph and Aseneth.” Pages 2525–89 in vol. 3 of *Outside the Bible: Ancient Jewish Writings Related to Scripture*. Edited by Louis H. Feldman, James L. Kugel, and Lawrence H. Schiffman. Philadelphia: Jewish Publication Society of America, 2013.

———. “Joseph and Aseneth and Jewish Identity in Greco-Roman Egypt.” PhD diss., University of Chicago, 2005.

Alexandre, Monique. *Le commencement du livre Genèse I–V, La version grecque de la Septante et sa reception*. Paris: Beauchesne, 1988.

Alexander, Philip S., and Geza Vermes. *Qumran Cave 4:XIX: Serekh Ha-Yahad and Two Related Texts*. DJD XXVI. Oxford: Clarendon, 1998.

Ammann, Sonja. *Götter für die Toren: Die Verbindung von Götterpolemik und Weisheit im Alten Testament*. BZAW 466. Berlin: de Gruyter, 2015.

Andersen, F. I. “2 (Slavonic Apocalypse of) Enoch.” *OTP* 1:91–221.

Anderson, Gary A. “The Culpability of Eve: From Genesis to Timothy.” Pages 233–51 in *From Prophecy to Testament: The Function of the Old Testament in the New*. Edited by Craig A. Evans. Peabody, MA: Hendrickson, 2004.

———. “The Original Form of the *Life of Adam and Eve*: A Proposal.” Pages 215–31 in *Literature on Adam and Eve: Collected Essays*. Edited by Gary A. Anderson, Michael E. Stone, and Johannes Tromp. SVTP 15. Leiden: Brill, 2000.

———. “The Penitence Narrative in the *Life of Adam and Eve*.” Pages 3–42 in *Literature on Adam and Eve: Collected Essays*. Edited by Gary A. Anderson, Michael E. Stone, and Johannes Tromp. SVTP 15. Leiden: Brill, 2000.

Anderson, Gary A., and Michael E. Stone. "The Life of Adam and Eve: The Biblical Story in Judaism and Christianity." Professional Website of Gary A. Anderson and Michael E. Stone. http://tinyurl.com/SBL066006a.

———. *A Synopsis of the Books of Adam and Eve*. 2nd ed. EJL 5. Atlanta: Scholars Press, 1999.

Anderson, Gary A., Michael E. Stone, and Johannes Tromp, eds. *Literature on Adam and Eve: Collected Essays*. SVTP 15. Leiden: Brill, 2000.

Araujo, Magdalena Díaz. "La représentation de la femme et l'invention de la notion du 'péché de la chair' d'après la *Vie grecque d'Adam et Ève*." PhD diss., Université de Paris IV – Sorbonne, 2012.

Arbel, Vita Daphna. *Forming Femininity in Antiquity: Eve, Gender, and Ideologies in the Greek Life of Adam and Eve*. New York: Oxford University Press, 2012.

Arbel, Daphna, J. R. C. Cousland, and Dietmar Neufeld. *And So They Went Out: The Lives of Adam and Eve as Cultural Transformative Story*. London: T&T Clark, 2010.

Aristotle. *Politics*. Translated by H. Rackham. LCL 264. Cambridge: Harvard University Press, 1932.

Arius Didymus. *Epitome of Stoic Ethics*. Translated by Arthur J. Pomeroy. SBLTT 44, Graeco-Roman 14. Atlanta: Society of Biblical Literature, 1999.

Aschkenasy, Nehama. *Woman at the Window: Biblical Tales of Oppression and Escape*. Detroit: Wayne State University Press, 1998.

Ascough, Richard. *Paul's Macedonian Associations: The Social Context of Philippians and 1 Thessalonians*. WUNT 161. Tübingen: Mohr Siebeck, 2003.

Athenaeus Naucratites. *The Deipnosophists: In Seven Volumes*. Edited by Charles B. Gulick. Vol. 5. LCL 274. Cambridge: Harvard University Press, 1980.

Atkinson, Kenneth. *Salome: Jerusalem's Warrior Monarch of the First Century B.C.E.* Jefferson, NC: McFarland, 2012.

Azzoni, Annalisa. *The Private Lives of Women in Persian Egypt*. Winona Lake, IN: Eisenbrauns, 2013.

———. "Women of Elephantine and Women in the Land of Israel." Pages 3–12 in *In the Shadow of Bezalel: Aramaic, Biblical, and Ancient Near Eastern Studies in Honor of Bezalel Porten*. Edited by Alejandro F. Botta. LSTS 64. Leiden: Brill, 2013.

Bachmann, Veronika. *Die Welt im Ausnahmezustand: Eine Untersuchung zu Aussagegehalt und Theologie des Wächterbuches (1 Hen 1–36)*. BZAW 409. Berlin: de Gruyter, 2009.

Baer, Richard A. *Philo's Use of the Categories Male and Female*. ALGHJ 3. Leiden: Brill, 1970.

Bagnall, Roger S., and Raffaella Cribiore. *Women's Letters from Ancient Egypt 300 BC–800 AD*. Ann Arbor: University of Michigan Press, 2006.

Bailey, James L. "Josephus' Portrayal of the Matriarchs." Pages 257–72 in *Josephus, Judaism and Christianity*. Edited by Louis H. Feldman and Gohei Hata. Detroit: Wayne State University Press, 1987.

Bainbridge, William Sims. *The Sociology of Religious Movements*. New York: Routledge, 1997.

Bal, Mieke. "Between Altar and Wondering Rock: Toward a Feminist Philology." Pages 211–31 in *Anti-covenant: Counter-feading Women's Lives in the Hebrew Bible*. Edited by Mieke Bal. JSOTSup 81; BLS 22. Sheffield: Almond Press, 1989.

Balsdon, J. P. V. D. *Roman Women: Their History and Habits*. London: Bodley Head, 1962.

Barclay, John M. G. *Against Apion*. FJTC 10. Leiden: Brill, 2007.

———. *Jews in the Mediterranean Diaspora: From Alexander to Trajan (323 BCE–117 CE)*. Berkeley: University of California Press, 1996.

Barnett, Richard D., Erika Bleibtreu, and Geoffrey Turner. *Sculptures from the Southwest Palace of Sennacherib at Nineveh*. London: British Museum Press, 1998.

Barrett, Anthony A. *Livia: First Lady of Imperial Rome*. New Haven: Yale University Press, 2002.

Barthélemy, D. "28a. Règle de la Congrégation (1QSa)." Pages 108–18 in *Qumran Cave 1*. Edited by D. Barthélemy and J. T. Milik. DJD I. Oxford: Clarendon, 1955.

Baumgarten, Albert I. *The Flourishing of Jewish Sects in the Maccabean Era: An Interpretation*. JSJSup 55. Leiden: Brill, 1997.

———. "Josephus and the Jewish Sects." Pages 261–72 in *A Companion to Josephus*. Edited by Honora Howell Chapman and Zuleika Rodgers. BCAW. Oxford: Wiley Blackwell, 2016.

———. "Karaites, Qumran, the Calendar, and Beyond: At the Beginning of the Twenty-first Century." Pages 603–19 in *The Dead Sea Scrolls and Contemporary Culture: Proceedings of the International Conference Held at the Israel Museum, Jerusalem (July 6–8, 2008)*. Edited by Shani Tzoref, Adolfo D. Roitman, and Lawrence H. Schiffman. STDJ 93. Leiden: Brill, 2011.

———. "Prologue: How Do We Know When We Are on to Something?" Pages 3–19 in *Sects and Sectarianism in Jewish History*. Edited by Sacha Stern. IJSStud 12. Leiden: Brill, 2011.

Baumgarten, Joseph M. "On the Testimony of Women in 1QSa." *JBL* 76 (1957): 266–69.

———. "Miscellaneous Rules." Pages 57–78 in *Qumran Cave 4:XXV: Halakhic Texts*. DJD XXXV. Oxford: Clarendon, 1999.

———. *Qumran Cave 4:XIII: The Damascus Document (4Q266–73)*. DJD XVIII. Oxford: Clarendon, 1996.

Baumgarten, Joseph M., and Daniel Schwartz. "Damascus Document (CD)." Pages 4–57 in *Damascus Document, War Scroll, and Related Documents*. Volume 2 of *The Dead Sea Scrolls: Hebrew, Aramaic, and Greek Texts with English Translations*. Edited by J. H. Charlesworth with Joseph M. Baumgarten. PTSDSSP. Louisville: Westminster John Knox; Tübingen: Mohr Siebeck, 1995.

Bautch, Kelley C. "Decoration, Destruction and Debauchery: Reflections on 1 Enoch 8 in Light of 4QEn^{b}." *DSD* 15 (2008): 79–95.

———. "What Becomes of the Angels' 'Wives'? A Text-Critical Study of 1 Enoch 19:2." *JBL* 125 (2006): 766–80.

Beaumont, Lesley A. *Childhood in Ancient Athens: Iconography and Social History*. RMCS. New York: Routledge, 2012.

Beavis, Mary Ann. *Jesus and Utopia: Looking for the Kingdom of God in the Roman World*. Minneapolis: Fortress, 2006.

———. "Philo's Therapeutai: Philosopher's Dream or Utopian Construction?" *JSP* 14 (2004): 30–42.

Becker, Jürgen. *Die Testamente der zwölf Patriarchen*. JSHRZ 3.1. Gütersloh: Mohn, 1980.

Begg, Christopher. *Judean Antiquities 5–7*. FJTC 4. Leiden: Brill, 2005.

Begg, Christopher, and Paul Spilsbury. *Judean Antiquities 8–10*. FJTC 5. Leiden: Brill, 2005.

Ben-Chorin, Shalom. *Kritik des Estherbuches: Eine theologische Streitschrift*. Jerusalem: Salingre, 1938.

Berger, Klaus. *Das Buch der Jubiläen*. JSHRZ 2.3. Gütersloh: Mohn, 1981.

Berlejung, Angelika. *Die Theologie der Bilder: Herstellung und Einweihung von Kultbildern in Mesopotamien und die alttestamentliche Bilderpolemik*. OBO 162. Fribourg: Universitäts-Verlag, 1998

———. "Washing the Mouth: The Consecration of Divine Images in Mesopotamia." Pages 45–72 in *The Image and the Book: Iconic Cults, Aniconism, and the Rise of the Book Religion in Israel and the Ancient Near East*. Edited by Karel van der Toorn. CBET 21. Leuven: Peeters, 1997.

Bernstein, Moshe J. "Women and Children in Legal and Liturgical Texts from Qumran." Pages 614–34 in vol. 2 of *Reading and Re-reading Scripture at Qumran*. STDJ 107. Leiden: Brill, 2013.

Bertrand, Daniel A. *La Vie grecque d'Adam et Eve: Introduction, texte, traduction et commentaire*. Paris: Jean Maisonneuve, 1987.

———. "Le destin 'post mortem' des protoplastes." Pages 109–18 in *La littérature intertestamentaire: Colloque de Strasbourg, 17–19 octobre 1983*. Paris: Presses Universitaires de France, 1985.

Bhayro, Siam. "The Use of Jubilees in Medieval Chronicles to Supplement Enoch: The Case for the 'Shorter' Reading." *Hen* 31 (2009): 10–17.

Bickerman, Elias J. "The Colophon of the Greek Book of Esther." *JBL* 63 (1944): 339–62.

———. "Notes on the Greek Book of Esther." *PAAJR* 20 (1951): 101–33.

Birnbaum, Ellen. *The Place of Judaism in Philo's Thought: Israel, Jews, and Proselytes*. BJS 290. Atlanta: Scholars Press, 1996.

Blank-Sangmeister, Ursula. *Römische Frauen: Ausgewählte Texte*. Stuttgart: Reclam, 2001.

Bonazzi, Mauro. "Towards Transcendence: Philo and the Revival of Platonism in the Early Imperial Age." Pages 233–51 in *Philo of Alexandria and Post-Aristotelian Philosophy*. Edited by Francesca Allesse. SPhA 5. Leiden: Brill, 2008.

Bons, Eberhard. "Konnte eine Witwe die *naḥalah* ihres verstorbenen Mannes erben? Überlegungen zum Ostrakon 2 aus der Sammlung Moussaïeff." *ZABR* 4 (1998): 197–208.

Börner-Klein, Dagmar. *Gefährdete Braut und schöne Witwe: Hebräische Judit-Geschichten*. Wiesbaden: Marix-Verlag, 2007.

Børresen, Kari E., and Adriana Valerio, eds. *The High Middle Ages*. BW 6.2. Atlanta: SBL Press, 2015.

Bosshard-Nepustil, Erich. *Vor uns die Sintflut: Studien zu Text, Kontexten und Rezeption der Fluterzählung Genesis 6–9*. BWANT 9.5. Stuttgart: Kohlhammer, 2005.

Böttrich, Christfried, Beate Ego, and Friedmann Eißler. *Adam und Eva in Judentum, Christentum und Islam*. Göttingen: Vandenhoeck & Ruprecht, 2011.

Boyd-Taylor, Cameron. "Ioudith." Pages 441–45 in *A New English Translation of the Septuagint and Other Greek Translations Traditionally Included under That Title*. Edited by Albert Pietersma and Benjamin G. Wright. Oxford: Oxford University Press, 2007.

Braun, Martin. *History and Romance in Graeco-Oriental Literature*. Oxford: Blackwell, 1938.

Brenner, Athalya. *A Feminist Companion to Esther, Judith, and Susannah*. FCB 7. Sheffield: Sheffield Academic, 1995; Repr. London: T&T Clark, 2005.

Brine, Kevin R., Elena Ciletti, and Henrike Lähnemann, eds. *The Sword of Judith: Judith Studies across the Disciplines*. Cambridge: OpenBook, 2010.

Brooke, George J. *The Dead Sea Scrolls and the New Testament*. Minneapolis: Fortress, 2005.

Brooten, Bernadette. "Early Christian Women and Their Cultural Context: Issues of Method in Historical Reconstruction." Pages 65–91 in *Feminist Perspectives on Biblical Scholarship*. Edited by Adela Yarbro Collins. SBLCP 10. Chico, CA: Scholars Press, 1985.

Brouwer, Jacob. "Gott, Christus, Engel, Männer und Frauen: Chronologisch-thematische Bibliographie zu 1Kor 11,2–16." Pages 187–235 in *Frauen, Männer, Engel: Perspektiven zu 1Kor 11,2–16*. Edited by Torsten Jantsch. BThS 152. Neukirchen-Vluyn: Neukirchener Verlag, 2014.

Brown, Cheryl Anne. *No Longer Be Silent: First Century Jewish Portraits of Biblical Women*. Louisville: Westminster John Knox, 1992.

Buber, Salomon, ed. *Midrasch Tanchuma*. Vilnius: Romm, 1885.

Budin, Stephanie L. *The Myth of Sacred Prostitution in Antiquity*. Cambridge: Cambridge University Press, 2008.

Bührer, Walter. "Göttersöhne und Menschentöchter: Gen 6,1–4 als innerbiblische Schriftauslegung." *ZAW* 123 (2011): 495–515.

Burchard, Christoph. *Joseph und Aseneth*. JSHRZ 2.4. Gütersloh: Mohn, 1983.

———. *Joseph und Aseneth kritisch herausgegeben von Christoph Burchard mit Unterstützung von Carsten Burfeind und Uta Barbara Fink*. PVTG 5. Leiden: Brill, 2003.

Burns, Joshua Ezra. "The Special Purim and the Reception of the Book of Esther in the Hellenistic and Early Roman Eras." *JSJ* 37 (2006): 1–34.

Burridge, Richard A. *What Are the Gospels? A Comparison with Graeco-Roman Biography*. 2nd ed. Grand Rapids: Eerdmans, 2004.

Camp, Claudia. "Understanding a Patriarchy: Women in Second Century Jerusalem through the Eyes of Ben Sira." Pages 1–39 in *"Women Like This": New Perspectives on Women in the Greco-Roman World*. Edited by Amy-Jill Levine. Atlanta: Scholars Press, 1991.

Caquot, André. "I Hénoch." Pages 463–625 in *La Bible: Écrits intertestamentaires*. Edited by André Dupont-Sommer and Marc Philonenko. BP 337. Paris: Gallimard, 1987.

Caquot, André, and Marc Philonenko. "Introduction générale." Pages xv–cxlix in *La Bible: Écrits intertestamentaires*. BP 337. Paris: Gallimard, 1987.

Carruthers, Jo. *Esther through the Centuries*. Malden, MA: Blackwell, 2008.

Chalcraft, David J., ed. *Sectarianism in Early Judaism: Sociological Advances*. New York: Routledge, 2007.

Chapman, Honora Howell, and Zuleika Rodgers, eds. *A Companion to Josephus*. BCAW. Oxford: Wiley Blackwell, 2016.

Charles, Robert Henry, ed. *The Apocrypha and Pseudepigrapha of the Old Testament in English*. 2 vols. Oxford: Clarendon, 1913.

Charles Perrot, and Pierre-Maurice Bogaert in collaboration with Daniel J. Harrington. *Les Antiquités Bibliques 1–2: Introduction Littéraire, Commentaire et Index*. SC 230. Paris: Cerf, 1976.

Cohen., A., trans. *Babylonian Talmud: Sotah*. London: Soncino, 1985.

Cohen, Shaye J. D. *The Beginnings of Jewishness: Boundaries, Varieties, Uncertainties*. HCS 31. Berkeley: University of California Press, 2000.

Cohn, Leopold. "An Apocryphal Work Ascribed to Philo of Alexandria." *JQR* 10 (1898): 277–332.

Cohn, Leopold, and Reiter, Siegfried. *Philonis Alexandrini Opera Quae Supersunt*. Edited by Leopold Cohn and Paul Wendland. Berlin: Reimer, 1915. Repr., Berlin: de Gruyter, 1962.

Collins, John J. *Between Athens and Jerusalem: Jewish Identity in the Hellenistic Diaspora*. New York: Crossroad, 1983.

———. "Before the Fall: The Earliest Interpretations of Adam and Eve." Pages 293–308 in *The Idea of Biblical Interpretation: Essays in Honor of James L. Kugel*. Edited by Hindy Najman and Judith H. Newman. JSJSup 83. Leiden: Brill, 2004.

———. *Beyond the Qumran Community: The Sectarian Movement of the Dead Sea Scrolls*. Grand Rapids: Eerdmans, 2010.

———. "Historiography in the Dead Sea Scrolls." Pages 119–32 in *Scriptures and Sectarianism: Essays on the Dead Sea Scrolls*. WUNT 332. Tübingen: Mohr Siebeck, 2014.

———. "Sibylline Oracles." *OTP* 1:317–472.

———. "The Sons of God and the Daughters of Men." Page 259–74 in *Sacred Marriages: The Divine-Human Sexual Metaphor from Sumer to Early Christianity*. Edited by Martti Nissinen and Risto Uro. Winona Lake, IN: Eisenbrauns, 2008.

———. "Watchers." *DDD* 893–95.

Colson, Francis Henry, G. H. Whitaker, and Ralph Marcus, trans. *Philo*. 10 vols. and 2 supplementary vols. LCL. Cambridge: Harvard University Press, 1929–1962.

Conway, Colleen. "Gender and Divine Relativity in Philo of Alexandria." *JSJ* 34 (2003): 471–91.

Cook, D. "Joseph and Aseneth." Pages 465–503 in *The Apocryphal Old Testament*. Edited by Hedley F. D. Sparks. Oxford: Clarendon, 1984.

Corley, Jeremy. "Septuagintalisms, Semitic Interference, and the Original Language of the Book of Judith." Pages 65–96 in *Studies in the Greek Bible: Essays in Honour of Francis T. Gignac*. Edited by Jeremy Corley. CBQMS 44. Washington, DC: Catholic Biblical Association, 2008.

Craven, Toni. *Artistry and Faith in the Book of Judith*. SBLDS 70. Chico, CA: Scholars Press, 1983.

Crawford, Sidnie White. "Not according to Rule: Women, the Dead Sea Scrolls and Qumran." Pages 127–50 in *Emanuel: Studies in Hebrew Bible, Septuagint, and Dead Sea Scrolls in Honor of Emanuel Tov*. Edited by Shalom M. Paul, Robert A. Kraft, Lawrence H. Schiffman, and Weston W. Fields. VTSup 94. Leiden: Brill, 2003.

Creech, David. "Now Where's the Fun in That? The Humourless Narrator in the Greek Translation of Esther." *BR* 52 (2007): 17–40.

Crenshaw, Kimberlé. "Demarginalizing the Intersection of Race and Sex: A Black Feminist Critique of Antidiscrimination Doctrine." *UCLF* 139 (1989): 139–67.

Cribiore, Raffaella. *Gymnastics of the Mind: Greek Education in Hellenistic and Roman Egypt*. Princeton: Princeton University Press, 2001.

Crosbie, Christopher James. "Philosophies of Retribution: Kyd, Shakespeare, Webster and the Revenge Tragedy Genre." PhD diss., Rutgers, The State University of New Jersey, 2007.

D'Angelo, Mary Rose. "Gender and Geopolitics in the Work of Philo of Alexandria: Jewish Piety and Imperial Family Values." Pages 63–88 in *Mapping Gender in Ancient Religious Discourse*. Edited by Todd Penner and Caroline Vander Stichele. BibInt 84. Leiden: Brill, 2007.

———. "(Re)Presentations of Women in the Gospel of Matthew and Luke-Acts." Pages 171–98 in *Women and Christian Origins*. Edited by Ross S. Kraemer and Mary Rose D'Angelo. Oxford: Oxford University Press, 1999.

———. "Women in Luke-Acts: A Redactional View." *JBL* 109 (1990): 441–61.

Dalley, Stephanie. *Esther's Revenge at Susa from Sennacherib to Ahasuerus*. Oxford: Oxford University Press, 2007.

Dawson, Lesel. "Revenge and the Family Romance in Tarantino's Kill Bill." *Mosaic* 47 (2014): 121–34.

Day, Linda. *Three Faces of a Queen: Characterization in the Books of Esther*. JSOTSup 186. Sheffield: Sheffield Academic, 1995.

De Troyer, Kristin. *The End of the Alpha-Text of Esther*. SCS 48. Atlanta: Society of Biblical Literature, 2000.

Denis, Albert-Marie. "La vie d'Adam et Ève." Pages 3–58 in vol. 1 of *Introduction à la littérature religieuse judéo-hellénistique*. Turnhout: Brepols, 2000.

Denyer, Nicholas. *Plato's Protagoras*. Cambridge: Cambridge University Press, 2008.

Deutsch, Celia. "The Therapeutae, Text Work, Ritual and Mystical Experience." Pages 287–312 in *Paradise Now: Essays on Early Jewish and Christian Mysticism*. Edited by April DeConick. SymS 11. Atlanta: Society of Biblical Literature, 2006.

Di Lella, Alexander A. "Women in the Wisdom of Ben Sira and the Book of Judith: A Study in Contrasts and Reversals." Pages 39–52 in *Congress Volume: Paris, 1992*. Edited by John A. Emerton. VTSup 61. Leiden: Brill, 1995.

Di Lella, Alexander A., and Patrick W. Skehan. *Wisdom of Ben Sira: A New Translation with Notes*. AB 39. New York: Doubleday, 1987.

Dimant, Devorah. "1 Enoch 6–11: A Fragment of a Parabiblical Work." *JJS* 53 (2002): 223–37.

———. "Sectarian and Nonsectarian Texts from Qumran: The Pertinence and Use of a Taxonomy." Pages 101–11 in *History, Ideology and Bible Interpretation in the Dead Sea Scrolls: Collected Studies*. FAT 90. Tübingen: Mohr Siebeck, 2014.

Dio Cassius. *Roman History*. Translated by Earnest Cary and Herbert B. Foster. 9 vols. LCL. Cambridge: Harvard University Press, 1914–1927.

Diodorus Siculus. *Books 9–12.40*. vol. 4 of *Library of History*. Translated by C. H. Oldfather. LCL 375. Cambridge: Harvard University Press, 1946.

Dixon, Suzanne. *The Roman Family*. Baltimore: John Hopkins University Press, 1992.

———. *The Roman Mother*. London: Routledge, 1988.

Dochhorn, Jan. *Die Apokalypse des Mose: Text, Übersetzung, Kommentar*. TSAJ 106. Tübingen: Mohr Siebeck, 2005.

———. "Röm 7,7 und das zehnte Gebot: Ein Beitrag zur Schriftauslegung und zur jüdischen Vorgeschichte des Paulus." *ZNW* 100 (2009): 59–77.

Doering, Lutz. "Jeremiah and the 'Diaspora Letters' in Ancient Judaism: Epistolary Communication with the Golah as Medium for Dealing with the Present." Pages 43–72 in *Reading the Present in the Qumran Library: The Perception of the Contemporary by Means of Scriptural Interpretation*. Edited by Kristin De Troyer and Armin Lange. Atlanta: Society of Biblical Literature, 2005.

———. "Marriage and Creation in Mark 10 and CD 4–5." Pages 133–63 in *Echoes from the Caves: Qumran and the New Testament*. Edited by Florentino García Martínez. STDJ 85. Leiden: Brill, 2009.

Doty, Susan H. "From Ivory Tower to City of Refuge: The Role and Function of the Protagonist in 'Joseph and Aseneth' and Related Narratives." PhD diss., Iliff School of Theology and University of Denver, 1989.

Dube, Musa W. "Jumping the Fire with Judith: Post-colonial Feminist Hermeneutics of Liberation." Pages 60–76 in *Feminist Interpretation of the Bible and the Hermeneutics of Liberation*. Edited by Silvia Schroer and Sophia Bietenhard. JSOTSup 374. Sheffield: Sheffield Academic, 2003.

Ehrman, Bart D. *The New Testament: A Historical Introduction to the Early Christian Writings*. Oxford: Oxford University Press, 1997.

Eisen, Ute E., Christine Gerber, and Angela Standhartinger. "Doing Gender—Doing Religion: Zur Frage nach der Intersektionalität in den Bibelwissenschaften; Eine Einleitung." Pages 1–33 in *Doing Gender—Doing Religion: Fallstudien zur Intersektionalität im frühen Judentum, Christentum und Islam*. WUNT 302. Tübingen: Mohr Siebeck, 2013.

Eisenbaum, Pamela M. "Sirach." Pages 298–304 in *Women's Bible Commentary*. Edited by Carol A. Newsom and Sharon H. Ringe. Expanded ed. Louisville: Westminster John Knox, 1998.

Elder, Linda Bennett. "Judith." Pages 455–69 in *A Feminist Commentary*. Vol. 2 of *Searching the Scriptures*. Edited by Elisabeth Schüssler-Fiorenza. New York: Crossroad, 1994.

Eldridge, Michael D. *Dying Adam with His Multiethnic Family: Understanding the Greek Life of Adam and Eve*. SVTP 16. Leiden: Brill, 2001.

Emonds, H., and B. Poschmann. "Bußkleid." *RAC* 2:812–14.

Engberg-Pedersen, Troels. "Philo's *De vita contemplativa* as a Philosopher's Dream." *JSJ* 30 (1999): 40–64.

Engel, Helmut. "Das Buch Judit." Pages 362–75 in *Einleitung in das Alte Testament*. Edited by Erich Zenger et al. 8th ed. Stuttgart: Kohlhammer, 2012.

———. "'Der HERR ist ein Gott, der Kriege zerschlägt': Zur Frage der griechischen Originalsprache und der Struktur des Buches Judit." Pages 155–68 in *Goldene Äpfel in silbernen Schalen*. Edited by Klaus-Dietrich Schunck and Matthias Augustin. BEATAJ 20. Frankfurt: Lang, 1992.

———. *Liber Judit*. Vulgata deutsch. Berling: de Gruyter, forthcoming.

———. *Prologus Judit*. Vulgata deutsch. Berling: de Gruyter, forthcoming.

Eusebius. *Einleitung, die Bücher I bis X*. Part 1 of *Eusebius Werke: Die Praeparatio Evangelica*. Edited by Karl Mras. Berlin: Akademie-Verlag, 1982.

Ezkenazi, Tamara Cohn. "The Lives of Women in the Postexilic Era." Pages 11–32 in *The Writings and Later Wisdom Books*. Edited by Christl M. Maier and Nuria Calduch-Benages. BW 1.3. Atlanta: SBL Press, 2014.

Feichtinger, Barbara. "Soziologisches und Sozialgeschichtliches zu Erotik, Liebe und Geschlechterverkehr." Pages 261–66 in *Plutarch, Dialog über die Liebe: Amatorius*. Edited by Herwig Görgemanns. 2nd ed. *SAPERE* 10. Tübingen: Mohr Siebeck, 2011.

Feldman, Louis H. "Hellenization in Josephus' Version of Esther." *TAPA* 101 (1970): 143–70.

———. "Josephus' Jewish Antiquities and Pseudo-Philo's Biblical Antiquities." Pages 59–80 in *Josephus, the Bible and History*. Edited by Louis H. Feldman and Gohei Hata. Detroit: Wayne State University Press, 1989.

———. "Josephus' Portrait of Deborah." Pages 115–28 in *Hellenica et Judaica: Hommage à Valentin Nikiprowetzky*. Edited by André Caquot, Mireille Hadas-Lebel, and Jean Riaud. Leuven-Paris: Peeters, 1986.

———. *Josephus's Interpretation of the Bible*. Berkeley: University of California Press, 1998.

———, ed. *Judean Antiquities 1–4*. FJTC 3. Leiden: Brill, 2000.

Fentress-Williams, Judy. "Esther." Pages 487–94 in *Fortress Commentary on the Bible*. Edited by Gale A. Yee, Hugh R. Page, and Matthew J. M. Coomber. Minneapolis: Fortress, 2014.

Fink, Uta B. *Joseph und Aseneth: Revision des griechischen Textes und Edition der zweiten lateinischen Übersetzung*. FSBP 5. Berlin: de Gruyter, 2008.

Fischer, Irmtraud, Jorunn Økland, Mercedes Navarro Puerto, and Adriana Valerio. "Introduction—Women, Bible and Reception History: An International Project in Theology and Gender Research." Pages 1–30 in *Torah*. Edited by Irmtraud Fischer and Mercedes Navarro Puerto with Andrea Taschl-Erber. BW 1.1. Atlanta: Society of Biblical Literature, 2011.

Fisk, Bruce Norman. *Do You Not Remember? Scripture, Story and Exegesis in the Rewritten Bible of Pseudo-Philo*. JSPSup 37. Sheffield: Sheffield Academic, 2001.

Foster, Benjamin R., trans. "Atra-Hasis." *COS* 1.130:450–53.
Fraade, Steven D., Aharon Shemesh, and Ruth A. Clements, eds. *Rabbinic Perspectives: Rabbinic Literature and the Dead Sea Scrolls; Proceedings of the Eighth International Symposium of the Orion Center for the Study of the Dead Sea Scrolls and Associated Literature, 7–9 January 2003*. STDJ 62. Leiden: Brill, 2006.
Freedman, H., trans. *Midrash Rabbah: Genesis Rabbah*. 2 vols. London: Soncino, 1939.
Frey, Albert, and Frédéric Amsler, eds. *Actes du Colloque International sur la Vie d'Adam et Ève et les traditions adamiques*. Prahins: Éditions du Zèbre, forthcoming.
Frymer-Kensky, Tikva Simone. *Reading the Women of the Bible*. New York: Schocken Books, 2002.
Gäbel, Georg, and Wolfgang Kraus. "Epistole Jeremiu/Epistula Jeremiae/Der Brief des Jeremia." Pages 2842–48 in *Psalmen bis Daniel*. Edited by Martin Karrer and Wolfgang Kraus. SDEK 2. Stuttgart: Deutsche Bibelgesellschaft, 2011.
Galor, Katharina. "Gender and Qumran." Pages 29–38 in *Holistic Qumran: Trans-disciplinary Research of Qumran and the Dead Sea Scrolls*. Edited by Jan Gunneweg, Annemie Adriaens, and Joris Dik. STDJ 87. Leiden: Brill, 2010.
Galor, Katharina, and Jean-Baptiste Humbert, eds. *Qumran: The Site of the Dead Sea Scrolls: Archaeological Interpretations and Debates*. STDJ 57. Leiden: Brill, 2006.
García Martínez, Florentino, ed. *Echoes from the Caves: Qumran and the New Testament*. STDJ 85. Leiden: Brill, 2009.
———. "Les rappots avec l'écriture des texts araméens trouvés à Qumrân." Pages 19–40 in *The Old Testament Pseudepigrapha and the Scriptures*. Edited by Eibert J. C. Tigchelaar. BETL 270. Leuven: Peeters, 2014.
García Martínez, Florentino, and Eibert J. C. Tigchelaar. *The Dead Sea Scrolls Study Edition*. 2 vols. Leiden: Brill; Grand Rapids: Eerdmans, 1997.
Gera, Debora Levine. "The Jewish Textual Traditions." Pages 23–39 in *The Sword of Judith: Judith Studies across the Disciplines*. Edited by Kevin R. Brine, Elena Ciletti, and Henrike Lähnemann. Cambridge: OpenBook, 2010.
———. *Judith*. CEJL. Berlin: de Gruyter, 2014.
———. "Shorter Medieval Hebrew Tales of Judith." Pages 81–95 in *The Sword of Judith: Judith Studies across the Disciplines*. Edited by Kevin R. Brine, Elena Ciletti, and Henrike Lähnemann. Cambridge: OpenBook, 2010.
Gevaryahu, Haim M. "Esther Is a Story of Jewish Defense, Not a Story of Jewish Revenge." *JBQ* 21 (1993): 3–12.
Gnuse, Robert Karl. *Dreams and Dream Reports in the Writings of Josephus: A Traditio-Historical Analysis*. AGJU 36. Leiden: Brill 1996.
Godley, A. D., *Herodotus, with an English Translation*. LCL. Cambridge: Harvard University Press, 1920.
Goldschmidt, Lazarus, ed. *Der Babylonische Talmud*. 12 vols. Darmstadt: Wiss. Buchgesellschaft 2002.
Greatrex, Geoffre, et al., ed. *The Chronicle of Pseudo-Zachariah Rhetor: Church and War in Late Antiquity*. Liverpool: Liverpool University Press, 2011.
Greenfield, Jonas C., Michael Stone, and Esther Eshel. *The Aramaic Levi Document: Edition, Translation, Commentary*. SVTP 19. Leiden: Brill, 2004.

Griffin, Miriam T. *Seneca: A Philosopher in Politics*. Oxford: Clarendon, 1976.

Grimal, Pierre. *Love in Ancient Rome*. Translated by Arthur Train Jr. Norman, OK: University of Oklahoma Press, 1980.

Grossman, Maxine L. "Gendered Sectarians: Envisioning Women (and Men) at Qumran." Pages 265–87 in *Celebrate Her for the Fruit of Her Hands: Essays in Honor of Carol L. Meyers*. Edited by Susan Ackerman, Charles E. Carter, and Beth Alpert Nakhai. Winona Lake, IN: Eisenbrauns, 2015.

———. *Reading for History in the Damascus Document: A Methodological Study*. STDJ 45. Leiden: Brill, 2002.

———. "Rethinking Gender in the *Community Rule*: An Experiment in Sociology." Pages 497–512 in *The Dead Sea Scrolls and Contemporary Culture: Proceedings of the International Conference held at the Israel Museum, Jerusalem (July 6–8, 2008)*. Edited by Shani Tzoref, Adolfo D. Roitman, and Lawrence H. Schiffman. STDJ 93. Leiden: Brill, 2011.

———. "Women and Men in the Rule of the Congregation: A Feminist Critical Assessment." Pages 229–45 in *Rediscovering the Dead Sea Scrolls: An Assessment of Old and New Methods and Approaches*. Edited by Maxine L. Grossman. Grand Rapids: Eerdmans, 2010.

Gruber, Margareta, and Andreas Michel. "Schönheit." Page 503 in *Sozialgeschichtliches Wörterbuch zur Bibel*. Edited by Frank Crüsemann. Gütersloh: Gütersloher Verlagshaus, 2009.

Grünenfelder, Regula. *Frauen an den Krisenherden: Eine rhetorisch-politische Deutung des Bellum Judaicum*. Münster: LIT, 2003.

Guignebert, Charles. *Des prophètes à Jésus: Le monde juif vers le temps de Jésus*. Paris: La Renaissance du livre, 1935.

Günther, Linda-Marie. "Witwen in der griechischen Antike: Zwischen Oikos und Polis." *Historia* 42 (1993): 308–25.

Hachlili, Rachel. "The Qumran Cemetery Reassessed." Pages 46–78 in *The Oxford Handbook of the Dead Sea Scrolls*. Edited by Timothy H. Lim and John J. Collins. Oxford: Oxford University Press, 2010.

Haines-Eitzen, Kim. *The Gendered Palimpsest: Women, Writing, and Representation in Early Christianity*. Oxford: Oxford University Press, 2012.

Halpern-Amaru, Betsy. *The Empowerment of Women in the Book of Jubilees*. JSJSup 60. Leiden: Brill, 1999.

———. "Portraits of Biblical Women in Josephus' *Antiquities*." *JJS* 39 (1988): 143–70.

———. "Protection from Birds in the Book of Jubilees." Pages 59–68 in *"Go Out and Study the Land" (Judges 18:2): Archaeological, Historical and Textual Studies in Honor of Hanan Eshel*. Edited by Aren M. Maeir, Jodi Magness, and Lawrence H. Schiffman. JSJSup 148. Leiden: Brill, 2011.

Hancock, Rebecca S. *Esther and the Politics of Negotiation: Public and Private Spaces and the Figure of the Female Royal Counselor*. Minneapolis: Fortress, 2013.

Hanhart, Robert. *Iudith*. SVTG 8.4. Göttingen: Vandenhoeck & Ruprecht, 1979.

———. *Text und Textgeschichte des Buches Judith*. MSU 14. Göttingen: Vandenhoeck & Ruprecht, 1979.

Harrington, Daniel J. "Pseudo-Philo." *OTP* 2:297–377.

Harris, William V. *Ancient Literacy.* Cambridge: Harvard University Press, 1991.

Harrison, Verna E. F. "Allegorization of Gender: Plato and Philo on Spiritual Child-Bearing." Pages 520–34 in *Asceticism*. Edited by Vincent L. Wimbush and Richard Valantasis. Oxford: Oxford University Press, 1995.

Harvey, Charles D. *Finding Morality in the Diaspora? Moral Ambiguity and Transformed Morality in the Books of Esther*. BZAW 328. Berlin: de Gruyter, 2003.

Hay, David M. "Things Philo Said and Did Not Say about the Therapeutae." Pages 673–83 in *Society of Biblical Literature 1992 Seminar Papers.* Edited by E. Lovering. SBLSP 31. Atlanta: Scholars Press, 1992.

Heath, John. "Women's Work: Female Transmission of Mythical Narrative." *TAPA* 141 (2011): 69–104.

Hempel, Charlotte. *The Qumran Rule Texts in Context: Collected Studies.* TSAJ 154. Tübingen: Mohr Siebeck, 2013.

Hilt [Lange], Lydia. "Dominus contulit splendorem (Idt 10,4): Das Motiv der Schönheit im Buch Iudith." Pages 91–108 in *Kongressakten vom 14. bis 17. November 2013 in Bukarest*, vol. 1 of *Vulgata Studies.* Edited Andreas Beriger, Stefan Maria Bolli, Widu-Wolfgang Ehlers, and Michael Fieger. ATID 8. Bern: Lang, 2014.

Hoek, Annewies van den. "Endowed with Reason or Glued to the Senses: Philo's Thoughts on Adam and Eve." Pages 63–75 in *The Creation of Man and Woman: Interpretations of the Biblical Narratives in Jewish and Christian Traditions.* Edited by Gerard P. Luttikhuizen. TBN 3. Leiden: Brill, 2000.

Höffken, Peter. "Zuversicht und Hoffnung in Verbindung mit babylonischen Fluttraditionen." Pages 53–72 in *Die Sintflut: Zwischen Keilschrift und Kinderbuch.* Edited by Norbert C. Baumgart and Gerhard Ringshausen. LthB 2. Münster: LIT, 2005.

Hogan, Karina M. *Theologies in Conflict in 4 Ezra: Wisdom Debate and Apocalyptic Solution.* JSJSup 130. Leiden: Brill, 2008.

———. "The Watchers Traditions in the Book of the Watchers and the Animal Apocalypse." Pages 107–19 in *The Watchers in Jewish and Christian Traditions.* Edited by Angela K. Harkins, Kelley C. Bautch, and John C. Endres. Minneapolis: Fortress, 2014.

Hogan, Patrick Colm. *Affective Narratology: The Emotional Structure of Stories.* Lincoln: University of Nebraska Press, 2011.

Hollander, Harm W., and Marinus de Jonge. *The Testaments of the Twelve Patriarchs: A Commentary.* SVTP 8. Leiden: Brill, 1985.

Horst, Pieter van der. "Moses' Father Speaks Out." Pages 491–98 in *Flores Florentino: Dead Sea Scrolls and Other Early Jewish Studies in Honor of Florentino García Martínez.* Edited by Anthony Hillhorst, Émile Puech, and Eibert J. C. Tigchelaar. JSJSup 122. Leiden: Brill, 2007.

———. *Philo of Alexandria: Philo's Flaccus, the First Pogrom: Introduction, Translation and Commentary.* PACS. Leiden: Brill, 2003.

———. Review of *Unreliable Witnesses: Religion, Gender and History in the Greco-Roman Mediterranean*, by Ross Shepherd Kraemer. *JSJ* 43 (2012): 100–102.

Hume, C. "The Storie of Asneth: A Fifteenth-Century Commission and the Mystery of Its Epilogue." *AAev* 82 (2013): 44–65.

Humphrey, Edith M. *Joseph and Aseneth*. GAP 8. Sheffield: Sheffield Academic, 2000.

Hurley, Donna W. *Suetonius: Divus Claudius*. Cambridge: Cambridge University Press, 2001.

Ilan, Tal. *Integrating Women into Second Temple History*. TSAJ 76. Tübingen: Mohr Siebeck, 2001.

———. *Jewish Women in Greco-Roman Palestine: An Inquiry into Image and Status*. TSAJ 44. Tübingen: Mohr Siebeck, 1995.

———. "Josephus on Women." Pages 210–21 in *A Companion to Josephus*. Edited by Honora Howell Chapman and Zuleika Rodgers. BCAW. Oxford: Wiley Blackwell, 2016.

———. "Reading for Women in 1QSa (Serekh Ha-Edah)." Pages 1:61–76 in *The Dead Sea Scrolls in Context: Integrating the Dead Sea Scrolls in the Study of Ancient Texts, Languages, and Cultures*. Edited by Armin Lange, Emanuel Tov, and Matthias Weigold, in association with Bennie H. Reynolds III. VTSup 140. Leiden: Brill, 2011.

———. *Silencing the Queen: The Literary Histories of Shelamzion and Other Jewish Women*. TS 115. Tübingen: Mohr Siebeck, 2006.

———. "Women in the Apocrypha and the Pseudepigrapha." Pages 126–44 in *A Question of Sex? Gender and Difference in the Hebrew Bible and Beyond*. Edited by Deborah W. Rooke. HBM 14. Sheffield: Sheffield Phoenix, 2007.

———. "Women in Qumran and the Dead Sea Scrolls." Pages 123–47 in *The Oxford Handbook of the Dead Sea Scrolls*. Edited by Timothy H. Lim and John J. Collins. Oxford: Oxford University Press, 2010.

Inowlocki, Sabrina. *Des idoles mortes et muettes au dieu vivant: Joseph, Aséneth et le fils de Pharaon dans un roman du Judaïsme Hellénisé*. Turnhout: Brepols, 2002.

———. "Le roman d'Aseneth: Un roman feministe?" Pages 111–18 in *La femme dans les civilisations orientales et Miscellanea Aegyptologica: Christiane Desroches Noblecourt in honorem*. Edited by Christian Cannuyer. Louvain-la-Neuve: Centre d'Histoire des Religions, 2001.

Isaac, Ephraim. "1 (Ethiopic Apocalypse of) Enoch." *OTP* 1:5–89.

Jacobs, Friedrich. *Zerstreute Blätter*. Vol. 6 of *Vermischte Schriften*. Leipzig: Dyck'sche Buchhandlung, 1837.

Jacobson, Howard. *A Commentary of Pseudo-Philo's Liber Antiquitatum Biblicarum with Latin Text and English Translation 1–2*. AGJU 31. Leiden: Brill, 1996.

———. *The Exagoge of Ezekiel*. Cambridge: Cambridge University Press, 1983.

Jantsch, Torsten, ed. *Frauen, Männer, Engel: Perspektiven zu 1Kor 11,2–16*. BThSt 152. Neukirchen-Vluyn: Neukirchener Verlag, 2014.

Jerome. *Select Letters of St. Jerome*. Translated by F. A. Wright. LCL. London: Heinemann, 1933.

Jobes, Karen. *The Alpha-Text of Esther*. SBLDS 153. Atlanta: Scholars Press, 1996.

———. "Esther." Pages 424–40 in *A New English Translation of the Septuagint and the Other Greek Translations Traditionally Included under That Title*. Edited by Albert Pietersma and Benjamin G. Wright. 2nd ed. Oxford: Oxford University Press, 2009.

Johnson, M. D. "Life of Adam and Eve (First Century A.D.)." *OTP* 2:249–295.

Johnson, Sara R. "Novelistic Elements in Esther: Persian or Hellenistic, Jewish or Greek?" *CBQ* 67 (2005): 572–89.

Joisten-Pruschke, Anke. *Das religiöse Leben der Juden von Elephantine in der Achämenidenzeit*. GOI 2. Wiesbaden: Harrassowitz, 2008.

Jokiranta, Jutta. "*Serakhim* and Sectarianism." Pages 17–76 in *Social Identity and Sectarianism in the Qumran Movement*. STDJ 105. Leiden: Brill, 2013.

———. "Sociological Approaches to Qumran Sectarianism." Pages 200–231 in *The Oxford Handbook of the Dead Sea Scrolls*. Edited by Timothy H. Lim and John J. Collins. Oxford: Oxford University Press, 2010.

Jonge, Marinus de, and Johannes Tromp. *The Life of Adam and Eve and Related Literature*. Sheffield: Sheffield Academic, 1997.

Joosten, Jan. "The Original Language and Historical Milieu of the Book of Judith." Pages 159–76 in *Meghillot: Studies in the Dead Sea Scrolls V–VI; A Festschrift for Devorah Dimant*. Edited by Moshe Bar-Asher and Emanuel Tov. Jerusalem: Bialik Institute, 2007.

Jovanovic, Ljubica. "Aseneth's Gaze Turns Swords into Dust." *JSP* 21 (2012): 83–97.

Kadari, Tamar. "Asenath: Midrash and Aggadah." In *Jewish Women: A Comprehensive Historical Encyclopedia*. Jewish Women's Archive. http://tinyurl.com/SBL066006b.

Kaestli, Jean-Daniel. "La *Vie d'Adam et Ève*: Un enchaînement d'intrigues épisodiques au service d'une intrigue unifiante." Pages 322–36 in *La Bible en récits 2*. Edited by Camille Focant and André Wénin. BETL 191. Leiden: Peeters, 2005.

Kartzow, Marianne B. *Destabilizing the Margins: An Intersectional Approach to Early Christian Memory*. Eugene, OR: Pickwick, 2012.

Kautzsch, Emil, ed. *Die Apokryphen und Pseudepigraphen des Alten Testaments*. 2 vols. Tübingen: Mohr Siebeck, 1900.

Kee, H. C. "Testament of the Twelve Patriarchs." *OTP* 1:269–301.

Kellermann, Diether. "Apokryphes Obst: Bemerkungen zur Epistula Jeremiae (Baruch Kap. 6), insbesondere zu Vers 42." *ZDMG* 129 (1979): 23–42.

Kim, Lawrence. "Orality, Folktale and the Cross-Cultural Transmission of Narrative." Pages 300–321 in *The Romance between Greece and the East*. Edited by Tim Whitmarsh and Stuart Thomson. Cambridge: Cambridge University Press, 2013.

Kisch, Guido. *Pseudo-Philo's Liber Antiquitatum Biblicarum*. PMS 10. Notre Dame: University of Notre Dame, 1949.

Klijn, A. Frederik J. "2 (Syriac Apocalypse of) Baruch." *OTP* 1:615–52.

———. *Die syrische Baruch-Apokalypse*. JSHRZ 5.2. Gütersloh: Mohn, 1976.

Kloppenborg, John. "Collegia and *Thiasoi*: Issues in Function, Taxonomy and Membership." Pages 18–23 in *Voluntary Associations in the Graeco-Roman World*. Edited by John S. Kloppenborg and S. G. Wilson. London: Routledge, 1996.

Knibb, Michael K. "The Book of Enoch or Books of Enoch? The Textual Evidence for 1 Enoch." Pages 21–40 in *The Early Enoch Literature*. Edited by Gabriele Boccaccini and John J. Collins. JSJSup 121. Leiden: Brill, 2007.

Knittel, Thomas. *Das griechische "Leben Adams und Evas": Studien zu einer narrativen Anthropologie im frühen Judentum*. TSAJ 88. Tübingen: Mohr Siebeck, 2002.

Kobelt-Groch, Marion. *Judith macht Geschichte: Zur Rezeption einer mythischen Gestalt vom 16. bis 19. Jahrhundert*. Munich: Fink, 2005.

Koester, Helmut. *Ancient Christian Gospels: Their History and Development*. Phildelpia: Trinity Press International, 1990.

Koller, Aaron J. *Esther in Ancient Jewish Thought*. Cambridge: Cambridge University Press, 2014.

Kraemer, Ross S. "The Book of Aseneth." Pages 789–816 in *A Feminist Commentary*. Vol. 2 of *Searching the Scriptures*. Edited by Elisabeth Schüssler Fiorenza. New York: Crossroad, 1994.

———. *Her Share of the Blessings: Women's Religions among Pagans, Jews, and Christians in the Greco-Roman World*. New York: Oxford University Press, 1992.

———. "Monastic Jewish Women in Greco-Roman Egypt: Philo Judaeus on the Therapeutrides." *Signs* 14 (1989): 342–70.

———. *Unreliable Witnesses: Religion, Gender and History in the Greco-Roman Mediterranean*. Oxford: Oxford University Press, 2011.

———. *When Aseneth Met Joseph: A Late Antique Tale of the Biblical Patriarch and His Egyptian Wife, Reconsidered*. New York: Oxford University Press, 1998.

———. "Women's Authorship of Jewish and Christian Literature in the Greco-Roman Period." Pages 221–42 in "*Women Like This*": *New Perspectives on Jewish Women in the Greco-Roman World*. Edited by Amy-Jill Levine. EJL 1. Atlanta: Scholars Press, 1991.

Kratz, Reinhard G. "Der Brief des Jeremia." Pages 69–108 in vol. 5 of *ATD Apokryphen*. Edited by Odil H. Steck, Ingo Kottsieper, and Reinhard G. Kratz. Göttingen: Vandenhoeck & Ruprecht, 1998.

———. "Die Rezeption von Jeremia 10 und 29 im pseudepigraphen Brief des Jeremia." *JSJ* 26 (1995): 1–31.

Kraus, Wolfgang, and Georg Gäbel. "Epistole Jeremiu/Der Brief des Jeremia." Pages 1358–61 in *Septuaginta deutsch: Das griechische Alte Testament in deutscher Übersetzung*. Edited by Martin Karrer and Wolfgang Kraus. SDEK 2. Stuttgart: Deutsche Bibelgesellschaft, 2009.

Krause, Jens-Uwe. *Witwen und Waisen im römischen Reich IV: Witwen und Waisen im frühen Christentum*. HABES 19. Stuttgart: Steiner, 1995.

Küchler, Max. *Schweigen, Schmuck und Schleier: Drei neutestamentliche Vorschriften zur Verdrängung der Frauen auf dem Hintergrund einer frauenfeindlichen Exegese des Alten Testaments im antiken Judentum*. NTOA 1. Fribourg: Editions Universitaires, 1986.

Kugler, Robert A. *The Testaments of the Twelve Patriarchs*. GAP. Sheffield: Sheffield Academic, 2001.

Lanfranchi, Pierluigi. *L'Exagoge d'Ezéchiel le Tragique: Introduction, texte, traduction et commentaire*. SVTP 21. Leiden: Brill, 2006.

Lange, Lydia. *Die Juditfigur in der Vulgata: Eine theologische Studie zur lateinischen Bibel*. DCLS 36. Berlin: de Gruyter, 2016.

Langford, Sally O. "On Being a Religious Woman: Women Proselytes in the Greco-Roman World." Pages 61–83 in *Recovering the Role of Women: Power and*

Authority in Rabbinic Jewish Society. Edited by Peter J. Haas. SFSHJ 59. Atlanta: Scholars Press, 1992.

Lattimore, Richmond. *Themes in Greek and Latin Epitaphs*. Urbana: University of Illinois Press, 1942.

Law, Timothy M., and Charles Halton, eds. "Jew and Judean: A Forum on Politics and Historiography in the Translation of Ancient Texts." *Marginalia*, 26 August 2014. http://tinyurl.com/SBL066006c.

Lefkowitz, Mary R. "Did Ancient Women Write Novels?" Pages 199–219 in *"Women Like This": New Perspectives on Jewish Women in the Greco-Roman World*. Edited by Amy-Jill Levine. EJL 1. Atlanta: Scholars Press, 1991.

Lefkowitz, Mary R., and Maureen B. Fant, eds. *Women's Life in Greece and Rome: A Source Book in Translation*. Baltimore: John Hopkins University Press, 1982.

Lehrman, S. M., trans. *Midrash Rabbah: Exodus Rabbah*. London: Soncino, 1951.

Lesses, Rebecca. "'They Revealed Secrets to Their Wives': The Transmission of Magical Knowledge in 1 Enoch." Pages 196–222 in *With Letters of Light: Studies in the Dead Sea Scrolls, Early Jewish Apocalypticism, Magic, and Mysticism in Honor of Rachel Elior*. Edited by Daphna V. Arbel and Andrei A. Orlov. Ekstasis 2. Berlin: de Gruyter, 2011.

Leuenberger, Martin. "'Siehe, das sind deine Götter, Israel, die dich heraufgeführt haben aus dem Land Ägypten' (1 Kön 12,28): Materielle und symbolische Repräsentationen Jhwhs in der offiziell-staatlichen Religion Israels." Pages 288–311 in *Zwischen Zion und Zaphon: Studien in Gedenken an den Theologen Oswald Loretz (14.01.1928–12.04.2014)*. Edited by Ludger Hiepel und Marie-Theres Wacker. AOAT 438. Münster: Ugarit-Verlag, 2016.

Levison, John R. "The Exoneration and Denigration of Eve in the *Greek Life of Adam and Eve*." Pages 251–75 in *Literature on Adam and Eve: Collected Essays*. Edited by Gary A. Anderson, Michael E. Stone, and Johannes Tromp. SVTP 15. Leiden: Brill, 2000.

———. "The Exoneration of Eve in the *Apocalypse of Moses* 15–30." *JSJ* 20 (1989): 135–50.

———. "Is Eve to Blame? A Contextual Analysis of Sirach 25,24." *CBQ* 47 (1985): 617–23.

———. "Josephus' Version of Ruth." *JSP* 8 (1991): 31–44.

———. *Portraits of Adam in Early Judaism*. JSPSup 1. Sheffield: Sheffield Academic, 1988.

Levinson, Joshua. "An-Other Woman: Joseph and Potiphar's Wife; Staging the Body Politic." *JQR* 87 (1997): 269–301.

Lewis, Charlton T., and Charles Short. *A Latin Dictionary*. Oxford: Clarendon, 1966.

Lim, Timothy H., and John J. Collins, eds. *The Oxford Handbook of the Dead Sea Scrolls*. Oxford: Oxford University Press, 2010.

Lipsett, Diane. *Desiring Conversion: Hermas, Thecla, Aseneth*. Oxford: Oxford University Press, 2011.

Lloyd, Genevieve. *The Man of Reason: Male and Female in Western Philosophy*. Minneapolis: Methuen, 1984.

Loader, William. *The Dead Sea Scrolls on Sexuality: Attitudes towards Sexuality in Sectarian and Related Literature at Qumran*. Grand Rapids: Eerdmans, 2009.

———. *Enoch, Levi and Jubilees on Sexuality: Attitudes towards Sexuality in the Early Enoch Literature, the Aramaic Levi Document, and the Book of Jubilees*. Grand Rapids: Eerdmans, 2007.

Losekam, Claudia. *Die Sünde der Engel: Die Engelfalltradition in frühjüdischen und gnostischen Texten*. TANZ 41. Tübingen: Francke, 2010.

Lucian. *On the Syrian Goddess*. Edited by Jane L. Lightfoot. Oxford: Oxford University Press, 2003.

Lutz, Cora Elizabeth, ed. and trans. "Musonius Rufus: 'The Roman Socrates.'" *YCS* 10 (1947): 3–147.

Macy, Gary. "The Treatment of Women in the Scriptural Commentaries of the Twelfth–Thirteenth Centuries." Pages 37–50 in *The High Middle Ages*. Edited by Kari E. Børresen and Adriana Valerio. BW 6.2. Atlanta: SBL Press, 2015.

Maggiorotti, D. "Giuseppe e Aseneth." Pages 423–525 in vol. 4 of *Apocrifi dell'Antico Testamento*. Edited by Paolo Sacchi. Brescia: Paideia, 2000.

Magness, Jodi. *The Archaeology of Qumran and the Dead Sea Scrolls*. Grand Rapids: Eerdmans, 2003.

———. *Debating Qumran: Collected Essays on Its Archaeology*. ISACR 4. Leuven: Peeters, 2004.

Maier, Christl, and Nuria Calduch-Benages, eds. *The Writings and Later Wisdom Books*. BW 1.3. Atlanta: SBL Press, 2014.

Marcos, Natalio Fernández. "Vida de Adán y Eva (Apocalipsis de Moisés)." Pages 320–21 in vol. 2 of *Apócrifos del Antiguo Testamento*. Edited by Alejandro Díez Macho. Madrid: Ed. Cristiandad, 1984.

Mason, Eric F. "Watchers Traditions in the Catholic Epistles." Pages 69–79 in *The Watchers in Jewish and Christian Traditions*. Edited by Angela K. Harkins, Kelley C. Bautch, and John C. Endres. Minneapolis: Fortress, 2014.

Mason, Steve. *Life of Josephus*. FJTC 9. Leiden: Brill, 2001.

———. "Jews, Judaeans, Judaizing, Judaism: Problems of Categorization in Ancient History." *JSJ* 38 (2007): 457–512.

———. "Josephus and His Twenty-Two Book Canon." Pages 110–27 in *The Canon Debate: The Origins and Formation of the Bible*. Edited by L. M. McDonald and J. A. Sanders. Peabody, MA: Hendrickson, 2002.

Mason, Steve, and Honora Chapman, eds. *Judean War 2*. FJTC 1b. Leiden: Brill, 2008.

Matthews, Shelly. "Ladies Aid: Gentile Noblewomen as Saviors and Benefactors in 'Antiquities.'" *HTR* 92 (1999): 199–218.

Mattila, Sharon Lea. "Wisdom, Sense Perception, Nature and Philo's Gender Gradient." *HTR* 89 (1996): 103–29.

Mauch, Mercedes. *Senecas Frauenbild in den philosophischen Schriften*. Frankfurt: Lang, 1997.

Mayer-Maly, Theo. "Vidua." *PW* 2.15:2104.

Mayer-Schärtel, Bärbel. *Das Frauenbild des Josephus: Eine sozialgeschichtliche und kulturanthropologische Untersuchung*. Stuttgart: Kohlhammer, 1995.

Meinhold, Arndt, "Scheidungsrecht bei Frauen im Kontext der jüdischen Militärkolonie von Elephantine im 5. Jh. v. Chr." Pages 247–59 in *"Sieben Augen auf einem Stein" (Sach 3,9): Studien zur Literatur des Zweiten Tempels; Festschrift für Ina Willi-Plein zum 65. Geburtstag*. Edited by Friedhelm Hartenstein and Michael Pietsch. Neukirchen-Vluyn: Neukirchener, 2007.

Mendels, Doron. "Hellenistic Utopia and the Essenes." *HTR* 72 (1979): 207–22.

Merk, Otto, and Martin Meiser. *Das Leben Adams und Evas*. JSHRZ 2.5. Gütersloh: Mohn, 1989.

Metzger, B. M. "The Fourth Book of Ezra." *OTP* 1:517–59.

Meyer, Nicholas. *Adam's Dust and Adam's Glory in the Hodayot and the Letters of Paul: Rethinking Anthropogony and Theology*. NovTSup 168. Leiden: Brill, 2016.

Meyers, Carol. "Archaeology: A Window to the lives of Israelite Women." Pages 61–108 in *Torah*. Edited by Irmtraud Fischer, Mercedes Navarro Puerto, and Andreas Taschl-Erber, BW 1.1. Atlanta: Society of Biblical Literature, 2011.

Meyers, Eric M. "Khirbet Qumran and Its Environs." Pages 21–45 in *The Oxford Handbook of the Dead Sea Scrolls*. Edited by Timothy H. Lim and John J. Collins. Oxford: Oxford University Press, 2010.

Miller, Tricia. *Jews and Anti-Judaism in Esther and the Church*. Cambridge: James Clarke, 2015.

Moatti-Fine, Jacqueline. "Lettre de Jérémie." Pages 287–330 in *Baruch; Lamentations; Lettre de Jérémie*. Edited by Isabelle Assan-Dhôte and Jacqueline Moatti-Fine. BA 25.2. Paris: Cerf, 2005.

Modrzejewski, Joseph Mélèze. *The Jews of Egypt: From Rameses II to Emperor Hadrian*. Philadelphia: Jewish Publication Society of America, 1995.

Moore, Carey A. "Epistle of Jeremiah." Pages 317–58 in *Daniel, Esther and Jeremiah: The Additions*. AB 44. Garden City, NY: Doubleday, 1977.

———. "On the Origins of the LXX Additions to the Book of Esther." *JBL* 92 (1973): 382–93.

Morford, Mark. *The Roman Philosophers: From the Time of Cato the Censor to the Death of Marcus Aurelius*. New York: Routledge, 2002.

Morgan, Teresa. *Roman Faith and Christian Faith*. Oxford: Oxford University Press, 2015.

Murdoch, Brian. *The Apocryphal Adam and Eve in Medieval Europe: Vernacular Translations and Adaptations of the Vita Adae et Evae*. Oxford: Oxford University Press, 2009.

Murphy, Frederick J. *Pseudo-Philo: Rewriting the Bible*. New York: Oxford University Press, 1993.

Musurillo, Herbert A. *The Acts of the Pagan Martyrs: Acta Alexandrinum*. Oxford: Clarendon, 1954.

Nagel, Marcel. "La Vie Grecque d'Adam et Ève: Apocalypse de Moïse." 3 vols. PhD diss., Université de Strasbourg II, 1972.

Nasrallah, Laura, and Elisabeth Schüssler Fiorenza, eds. *Prejudice and Christian Beginnings: Investigating Race, Gender, and Ethnicity in Early Christian Studies*. Minneapolis: Fortress, 2009.

Naumann, Weigand. *Untersuchungen über den apokryphen Jeremiasbrief.* BZAW 25. Gießen: Alfred Töpelmann, 1913.

Newsom, Carol. "'Sectually Explicit' Literature from Qumran." Pages 167–87 in *The Hebrew Bible and Its Interpreters*. Edited by Baruch Halpern and David N. Freedman. Winona Lake, IN: Eisenbrauns, 1990.

Nickelsburg, George W. E. *1 Enoch 1: A Commentary on the Book of 1 Enoch, Chapters 1–36; 81–108*. Hermeneia. Minneapolis: Fortress, 2001.

———. "Adam and Eve, Life of." Pages 17–18 in *Encyclopedia of Religious and Philosophical Writings in Late Antiquity: Pagan, Judaic, Christian*. Edited by Jacob Neusner and Alan J. Avery-Peck. Leiden: Brill, 2007.

———. "Apocalyptic and Myth in 1 Enoch 6–11." *JBL* 96 (1977): 383–405.

———. "The Books of Adam and Eve." Pages 110–17 in *Jewish Writings of the Second Temple Period: Apocrypha, Pseudepigrapha, Qumran Sectarian Writings, Philo, Josephus*. Edited by Michael E. Stone. Minneapolis: Fortress, 1981.

———. *Jewish Literature between the Bible and the Mishnah: A Historical and Literary Introduction*. Minneapolis: Fortress, 1981.

Nickelsburg, George W. E., and James C. VanderKam. *1 Enoch: A New Translation Based on the Hermeneia Commentary*. Minneapolis: Fortress, 2004.

Niehoff, Maren R. "Associative Thinking in Rabbinic Midrash: The Example of Abraham's and Sarah's Journey to Egypt" [Hebrew]. *Tarbiz* 62 (1993): 339–61.

———. "Philo's *Exposition* in a Roman Context." *SPhiloA* 23 (2011): 1–21.

———. *Philo of Alexandria: An Intellectual Biography*. New Haven: Yale University Press, forthcoming; German translation: Tübingen: Mohr Siebeck, forthcoming.

Nir, Rivka. *Joseph and Aseneth: A Christian Book*. HBM 42. Sheffield: Sheffield Phoenix, 2012.

Nisse, Ruth. "'Your Name Will No Longer Be Aseneth.' Apocrypha, Anti-Martyrdom, and Jewish Conversion in Thirteenth-Century England." *Spec* 81 (2006): 734–53.

Nissinen, Martti, and Risto Uro, eds. *Sacred Marriages: The Divine-Human Sexual Metaphor from Sumer to Early Christianity*. Winona Lake, IN: Eisenbrauns, 2008.

Noam, Vered. "Divorce in Qumran in Light of Early Halakhah." *JJS* 56 (2005): 206–23.

———. "Traces of Sectarian Halakhah in the Rabbinic World." Pages 67–85 in *Rabbinic Perspectives: Rabbinic Literature and the Dead Sea Scrolls; Proceedings of the Eighth International Symposium of the Orion Center for the Study of the Dead Sea Scrolls and Associated Literature, 7–9 January 2003*. Edited by Steven D. Fraade, Aharon Shemesh, and Ruth A. Clements. STDJ 62. Leiden: Brill, 2006.

Olson, Daniel C. *Enoch: A New Translation*. North Richland Hills, TX: Bibal, 2004.

Orlov, Andrei A., and Gabriele Boccaccini, eds. *New Perspectives on 2 Enoch: No Longer Slavonic Only.* StudJ 4. Leiden: Brill, 2012.

Perkins, Larry J. "Exodus." Pages 43–81 in *A New English Translation of the Septuagint and the Other Greek Translations Traditionally Included under That Title*. Edited by Albert Pietersma and Benjamin G. Wright. New York: Oxford University Press, 2007.

Perrot, Charles, and Pierre-Maurice Bogaert, in collaboration with Daniel J. Harrington. *Les Antiquités Bibliques.*2 vols. SC 230. Paris: Cerf, 1976.

Pettorelli, Jean-Pierre. "Adam and Eve, Life of." Pages 302–6 in *The Eerdmans Dictionary of Early Judaism*. Edited by John J. Collins and Daniel C. Harlow. Grand Rapids: Eerdmans, 2010.

———. "Deux témoins latins singuliers de la *Vie d'Adam et Ève* Paris, BNF, LAT. 3832 and Milan, B. Ambrosiana, O 35 SUP." *JSJ* 33 (2002): 1–27.

———. "Essai sur la structure primitive de la *Vie d'Adam et Ève*." *Apocrypha* 14 (2003): 237–56.

Pettorelli, Jean-Pierre, Jean-Daniel Kaestli, Albert Frey, and Bernard Outtier. *Vita latina Adae et Evae*. CCSA 18–19. Turnhout: Brepols, 2012–2013.

Philonenko, Marc. *Joseph et Aséneth: Introduction, texte critique, traduction et notes*. StPB 13. Leiden: Brill, 1968.

Plato. *Books 1–6*. Vol. 1 of *Laws*. Translated by R. G. Bury. LCL 187. Cambridge: Harvard University Press, 1926.

———. *Laches; Protagoras; Meno; Euthydemus*. Translated by W. R. M. Lamb. LCL 165. Cambridge: Harvard University Press, 1924.

———. *Lysis; Symposium; Gorgias*. Translated by W. R. M. Lamb. LCL 166. Cambridge: Harvard University Press, 1925.

Pomeroy, Sarah B. *Goddesses, Whores, Wives and Slaves: Women in Classical Antiquity*. New York: Schocken Books, 1975.

———. *Frauenleben im klassischen Altertum*. Translated by Nobert F. Mattheis. Stuttgart: Kröner, 1985.

———, ed. *Plutarch's Advice to the Bride and Groom and A Consolation to His Wife: English Translation, Commentary, Interpretative Essays and Bibliography*. Oxford: Oxford University Press, 1999.

———. *Women in Hellenistic Egypt: From Alexander to Cleopatra*. Detroit: Wayne State University Press, 1984.

Porten, Bezalel, and H. Z. Szubin. "Exchange of Inherited Property at Elephantine." *JAOS* 102 (1982): 651–54.

Portier-Young, Anathea E. *Apocalypse against Empire: Theologies of Resistance in Early Judaism*. Grand Rapids: Eerdmans, 2010.

Prestel, Peter, and Stefan Schorch. "Genesis: Das erste Buch Mose." Pages 145–257 in vol. 1 of *Septuaginta Deutsch: Erläuterungen und Kommentare zum griechischen Alten Testament*. Edited by Martin Karrer and Wolfgang Kraus. Stuttgart: Deutsche Bibelgesellschaft, 2011.

Qimron, Elisha. "Celibacy in the Dead Sea Scrolls and the Two Kinds of Sectarians." Pages 287–94 in vol. 1 of *The Madrid Qumran Congress: Proceedings of the International Congress on the Dead Sea—Madrid 18–21 March, 1991*. Edited by Julio Trebolle Barrera and Luis Vegas Montaner. 2 vols. STDJ 11. Leiden: Brill, 1992.

Qimron, Elisha, and James H. Charlesworth. "Rule of the Community." Pages 7–51 in *Rule of the Community and Related Documents*. Volume 1 of *The Dead Sea Scrolls: Hebrew, Aramaic, and Greek Texts with English Translations*. Edited by J. H. Charlesworth. PTSDSSP. Louisville: Westminster John Knox; Tübingen: Mohr Siebeck, 1994.

Rahlfs, Alfred, and Robert Hanhart, eds. "Epistula Ieremiae." Pages 766–70 in vol. 2 of

Septuaginta: Id est Vetus Testamentum Graece iuxta LXX interpretes; Editio altera. 2 vols. in 1. Stuttgart: Deutsche Bibelgesellschaft, 2006.

Rajak, Tessa. "Moses in Ethiopia: Legend and Literature." *JJS* 29 (1978): 111–22.

Rakel, Claudia. *Judit—Über Schönheit, Macht und Widerstand im Krieg: Eine feministisch-intertextuelle Lektüre.* BZAW 334. Berlin: de Gruyter, 2003.

———. "Judith: About a Beauty Who Is Not What She Pretends to Be." Pages 515–30 in *Feminist Biblical Interpretation: A Compendium of Critical Commentary on the Books of the Bible and Related Literature.* Edited by Luise Schottroff and Marie-Theres Wacker. Grand Rapids: Eerdmans, 2012.

Reed, Annette Y. "Gendering Heavenly Secrets? Women, Angels, and the Problem of Misogyny and 'Magic.'" Pages 108–51 in *Daughters of Hecate: Women and Magic in the Ancient World.* Edited by Kimberly B. Stratton with Dayna S. Kalleres. Oxford: Oxford University Press, 2014.

Regev, Eyal. "Cherchez les femmes: Were the *yaḥad* Celibates?" *DSD* 15 (2008): 253–84.

———. *Sectarianism in Qumran: A Cross-Cultural Perspective.* RelSoc 45. Berlin: de Gruyter, 2007.

Reinhartz, Adele. "Better Homes and Gardens: Women and Domestic Space in the Books of Judith and Susanna." Pages 325–39 in *Text and Artifact in the Religions of Mediterranean Antiquity: Essays in Honour of Peter Richardson.* Edited by Michel Robert Desjardins and Stephen G. Wilson. Waterloo, ON: Wilfrid Laurier University Press, 2000.

Reinmuth, Eckart, ed. *Joseph und Aseneth.* SAPERE 15. Tübingen: Mohr Siebeck, 2009.

Reiss, Moshe, and David J. Zucker. "Co-opting the Secondary Matriarchs: Bilhah, Zilpah, Tamar, and Aseneth." *BibInt* 22 (2014): 307–24.

Reydams-Schils, Gretchen. *The Roman Stoics: Self, Responsibility, and Affection.* Chicago: University of Chicago Press, 2005.

Riaud, Jean. "Les Thérapeutes d'Alexandrie dans la tradition et dans la recherche critique jusqu'aux découvertes de Qumran." *ANRW* 2.20.2:1189–1295.

Ricoeur, Paul. *Freud and Philosophy: An Essay on Interpretation.* Translated by D. Savage. New Haven: Yale University Press, 1970.

Rieder, John. "Race and Revenge Fantasies in Avatar, District 9 and Inglourious Basterds." *SFFT* 4 (2011): 41–56.

Robertson, R. G. "Ezekiel the Tragedian." *OTP* 2:803–19.

Romney Wegner, Judith. "Philo's Portrayal of Women—Hebraic or Hellenic?" Pages 41–66 in *"Women Like This": New Perspectives on Jewish Women in the Greco-Roman World.* Edited by Amy-Jill Levine. EJL 1. Atlanta: Scholars Press, 1991.

Roncace, Mark. "Josephus' (Real) Portraits of Deborah and Gideon: A Reading of *Antiquities* 5.198–232." *JSJ* 31 (2000): 247–74.

Rösel, Martin. "Riesen." Pages 343–46 in *Wörterbuch alttestamentlicher Motive.* Edited by Michael Fieger, Jutta Krispenz, and Jörg Lanckau. Darmstadt: Wissenschaftliche Buchgesellschaft, 2013.

Rosenfeld, Gavriel David. *The World Hitler Never Made: Alternate History and the Memory of Nazism.* Cambridge: Cambridge University Press, 2005.

Rosen-Zvi, Ishay. "Bilhah the Temptress: The Testament of Reuben and 'The Birth of Sexuality.'" *JQR* 96 (2006): 65–94.

Roth, Martha T. "Marriage, Divorce, and the Prostitute in Ancient Mesopotamia." Pages 21–39 in *Prostitutes and Courtesans in the Ancient World*. Edited by Christopher A. Faraone and Laura K. McClure. Madison: University of Wisconsin Press, 2006.

Rowlandson, Jane. *Women and Society in Greek and Roman Egypt*. Cambridge: Cambridge University Press, 1998.

Royse, James. "The Works of Philo." Pages 32–64 in *The Cambridge Companion to Philo*. Edited by Adam Kamesar. Cambridge: Cambridge University Press, 2009.

Runia, David T. *Philo of Alexandria: On the Creation according to Moses; Introduction, Translation and Commentary*. PACS. Leiden: Brill, 2001.

Runnals, Donna. "Moses' Ethiopian Campaign." *JSJ* 14 (1983): 135–56.

Ruzer, Serge. "Negotiating the Proper Attitude to Marriage and Divorce." Pages 131–47 in *Mapping the New Testament: Early Christian Writings as a Witness for Jewish Biblical Exegesis*. JCP 13. Leiden: Brill, 2007.

Saldarini, Anthony J. "The Letter of Jeremiah: Introduction, Commentary, and Reflections." Pages 983–1010 in *Introduction to Prophetic Literature, the Book of Isaiah, the Book of Jeremiah, the Book of Baruch, the Letter of Jeremiah, the Book of Lamentations, the Book of Ezekiel*. Edited by Leander E. Keck. *NIB* 6. Nashville: Abingdon, 2001.

Sanders, E. P., and Margaret Davies. *Studying the Synoptic Gospels*. London: SCM Press; Philadelphia: Trinity Press International, 1989.

Satlow, Michael L. *Jewish Marriage in Antiquity*. Princeton: Princeton University Press, 2001.

Saur, Markus. *Die Königspsalmen: Studien zur Entstehung und Theologie*. BZAW 340. Berlin: de Gruyter, 2004.

Sheer, Tanja S., and Martin Lindner, eds. *Tempelprostitution im Altertum: Fakten und Fiktionen*. Berlin: Verlag Antike e.K, 2009.

Schlipphacke, Heidi. "Inglourious Basterds and the Gender of Revenge." Pages 113–33 in *Quentin Tarantino's Inglourious Basterds: A Manipulation of Metacinema*. Edited by Robert Dassanowsky. New York: Continuum, 2012.

Schmitz, Barbara. "The Function of the Speeches and Prayers in the Book of Judith." Pages 164–74 in *A Feminist Companion to Tobit and Judith*. Edited by Athalya Brenner-Idan and Helen Efthimiades-Keith. London: Bloomsbury T&T Clark, 2015.

———. *Gedeutete Geschichte: Die Funktion der Reden und Gebete im Buch Judit*. HBS 40. Freiburg: Herder, 2004.

———. "Ιουδιθ und *Iudith*: Überlegungen zum Verhältnis der Judit-Erzählung in der LXX und der Vulgata." Pages 359–79 in *Text-Critical and Hermeneutical Studies in the Septuagint*. Edited by Johann Cook and Hermann-Josef Stipp. VTSup 157. Leiden: Brill, 2012.

———. "Judith and Holofernes: An Analysis of the Emotions in the Killing Scene (Jdt 12:10–13:9)." Pages 77–91 in *Ancient Jewish Prayers and Emotions*. Edited by Stefan Reif and Renate Egger-Wenzel. DCLS 26. Berlin: de Gruyter, 2015.

———. "War, Violence and Tyrannicide in the Book of Judith." *DCLY* 2010:103–19.

Schmitz, Barbara, and Helmut Engel. *Judit*. HThKAT. Freiburg: Herder, 2014.

Schofield, Alison. *From Qumran to the* Yaḥad*: A New Paradigm of Textual Development for the Community* Rule. STDJ 77. Leiden: Brill, 2009.

Schökel, Luis Alonso. "Carta de Jeremias." Pages 167–78 in *Daniel; Baruc; Carta de Jeremias; Lamentaciones.* LLS 18. Madrid: Ediciones Cristiandad, 1976.

Scholz, Susanne. *Introducing the Women's Hebrew Bible.* IFTh 13. London: T&T Clark, 2007.

Schreiner, Joseph. *Das 4. Buch Esra.* JSHRZ 5.4. Gütersloh: Mohn, 1981.

Schroer, Silvia. "Der eine Herr und die Männerherrschaft im Buch Jesus Sirach: Frauenbild und Weisheitsbild in einer misogynen Schrift." Pages 96–106 in *Die Weisheit hat ihr Haus gebaut: Studien zur Gestalt der Sophia.* Mainz: Grünewald, 1996.

Schüle, Andreas. *Der Prolog der hebräischen Bibel: Der literar- und theologiegeschichtliche Diskurs der Urgeschichte (Gen 1–11).* ATANT 86. Zürich: Theologischer Verlag Zürich, 2006.

Schuller, Eileen M. "Women of the Exodus in Biblical Retellings of the Second Temple Period." Pages 178–94 in *Gender and Difference in Ancient Israel.* Edited by Peggy L. Day. Minneapolis: Augsburg Fortress, 1989.

———. "Women in the Dead Sea Scrolls." Pages 117–44 in vol. 2 of *The Dead Sea Scrolls after Fifty Years: A Comprehensive Assessment.* Edited by Peter W. Flint and James C. VanderKam. 2 vols. Leiden: Brill, 1999.

———. "Women in the Dead Sea Scrolls: Some Observations from a Dictionary." *RevQ* 24 (2009): 49–59.

———. "Women in the Dead Sea Scrolls: Research in the Past Decade and Future Directions." Pages 571–88 in *The Dead Sea Scrolls and Contemporary Culture: Proceedings of the International Conference held at the Israel Museum, Jerusalem (July 6–8, 2008).* Edited by Shani Tzoref, Adolfo D. Roitman, and Lawrence H. Schiffman. STDJ 93. Leiden: Brill, 2011.

Schüngel-Straumann, Helen. "Genesis 1–11: The Primordial History." Pages 1–14 in *Feminist Biblical Interpretation: A Compendium of Critical Commentary on the Books of the Bible and Related Literature.* Edited by Luise Schottroff and Marie-Theres Wacker. Grand Rapids: Eerdmans, 2012.

Schüssler Fiorenza, Elisabeth. "A Feminist Critical Interpretation for Liberation: Martha and Mary; Luke 10:38–42." *RIL* 3 (1986): 21–35.

———. *In Memory of Her: A Feminist Theological Reconstruction of Christian Origins.* New York: Crossroad, 1983.

———. "Remembering the Past in Creating the Future: Historical-Critical Scholarship and Feminist Biblical Interpretation." Pages 43–64 in *Feminist Perspectives on Biblical Scholarship.* Edited by Adela Yarbro Collins. SBLCP 10. Chico, CA: Scholars Press, 1985.

———. "The Rhetoricity of Historical Knowledge: Pauline Discourse and Its Contextualizations." Pages 443–46 in *Religious Propaganda and Missionary Competition in the New Testament World: Essays Honoring Dieter Georgi.* Edited by Lukas Bornkamm, Kelly del Tredici, and Angela Sandhartinger. NovTSup 74. Leiden: Brill, 1994.

———. "The Will to Choose or to Reject: Continuing Our Critical Work." Pages 125–36 in *From Feminist Interpretation of the Bible*. Edited by Letty M. Russell. Philadelphia: Westminster, 1985.

Sedley, David. "The Ideal of Godlikeness." Pages 309–28 in *Plato 2: Ethics, Politics, Religion, and the Soul*. Edited by Gail Fine. Oxford: Oxford University Press, 1999.

———. "Three Platonist Interpretations of the Theaetetus." Pages 81–101 in *Form and Argument in Late Plato*. Edited by Christopher Gill and Mary Margaret McCabe. Oxford: Clarendon, 1996.

Seebass, Horst. *Genesis 1: Urgeschichte (1,1–11,26)*. Neukirchen-Vluyn: Neukirchener Verlag, 1996.

Seland, Torry. "Philo and the Clubs and Associations of Alexandria." Pages 110–27 in *Voluntary Associations in the Graeco-Roman World*. Edited by John S. Kloppenborg and S. G. Wilson. London: Routledge, 1996.

Seneca. *De Consolatione ad Marciam; De Vita Beata; De Otio; De Tranquillitate Animi; De Brevitate Vitae; De Consolatione at Polybium; De Consolatione ad Helviam*. Vol. 2 of *Moral Essays*. Translated by John W. Basore. LCL 254. Cambridge: Harvard University Press, 1932.

———. *Epistles 1–65*. Vol. 1 of *Epistles*. Translated by Richard M. Gummere. LCL 75. Cambridge: Harvard University Press, 1917.

Shemesh, Aharon. "4Q271.3: A Key to Sectarian Matrimonial Law." *JJS* 49 (1998): 244–63.

———. "Halakhah between the Dead Sea Scrolls and Rabbinic Literature." Pages 595–616 in *The Oxford Handbook of the Dead Sea Scrolls*. Edited by Timothy H. Lim and John J. Collins. Oxford: Oxford University Press, 2010.

Shinan, Avigdor. "Moses and the Ethiopian Woman: Sources of a Story in the Chronicles of Moses." *ScrHier* 27 (1978): 66–78.

Siegert, Folker. "The Philonian Fragment *De Deo*." *SPhiloA* 10 (1998): 1–33.

Siquans, Agnethe. *Die alttestamentlichen Prophetinnen in der patristischen Rezeption: Texte—Kontexte—Hermeneutik*. HBS 65. Freiburg: Herder, 2011.

Sjöberg, Birgitta L. "More than Just Gender: The Classical Oikos as a Site of Intersectionality in Families in the Greco-Roman World." Pages 48–59 in *Families in the Greco-Roman World*. Edited by Ray Laurence and Agneta Strömberg. London: Continuum, 2012.

Sly, Dorothy. *Philo's Perception of Women*. BJS 209. Atlanta: Scholars Press, 1990.

Soden, Wolfram von, trans. "Der altbabylonische Atramchasis-Mythos." *TUAT* 3.3:612–45.

Standhartinger, Angela. *Das Frauenbild im Judentum der hellenistischen Zeit: Ein Beitrag anhand von 'Joseph und Aseneth.'* AGJU 26. Leiden: Brill, 1995.

———. "Humour in *Joseph and Aseneth*." *JSP* 23 (2015): 239–59.

———. "Joseph and Aseneth: Perfect Bride or Heavenly Prophetess." Pages 578–85 in *Feminist Biblical Interpretation: A Compendium of Critical Commentary on the Books of the Bible and Related Literature*. Edited by Luise Schottroff and Marie-Theres Wacker. Grand Rapids: Eerdmans, 2012.

———. "Recent Scholarship on Joseph and Aseneth (1988–2013)." *CurBR* 12 (2014): 353–406.

———. "Zur Wirkungsgeschichte von *Joseph und Aseneth*." Pages 219–34 in *Joseph und Aseneth*. Edited by Eckart Reinmuth. SAPERE 15. Tübingen: Mohr Siebeck, 2009.

Stark, Christine. *"Kultprostitution" im Alten Testament? Die Qedeschen der Hebräischen Bibel und das Motiv der Hurerei*. OBO 221. Göttingen: Vandenhoeck & Ruprecht, 2006.

Steininger, Christine. *Die ideale christliche Frau: Virgo—Vidua—Nupta; Eine Studie zum Bild der idealen christlichen Frau bei Hieronymus und Pelagius*. St. Ottilien: EOS-Verlag, 1997.

Stenström, Hanna. "Masculine or Feminine? Male Virgins in Joseph and Aseneth and the Book of Revelation." Pages 199–222 in *Identity Formation in the New Testament*. Edited by Bengt Holmberg and Mikael Winninge. WUNT 227. Tübingen: Mohr Siebeck, 2008.

Sterling, Gregory E. *Historiography and Self-Definition: Josephus, Luke-Acts and Apologetic Historiography*. NovTSup 64. Leiden: Brill, 1992.

———. "The Invisible Presence: Josephus' Retelling of Ruth." Pages 104–71 in *Understanding Josephus: Seven Perspectives*. Edited by Steve Mason. Sheffield: Sheffield Academic, 1998.

———. "'Prolific in Expression and Broad in Thought': Internal References to Philo's *Allegorical Commentary* and *Exposition of the Law*." *Euphrosyne* 40 (2012): 55–76.

Stern, Sacha. *Sects and Sectarianism in Jewish History*. IJSStud 12. Leiden: Brill, 2011.

Stevens, Anne H. *Literary Theory and Criticism: An Introduction*. Peterborough, ON: Broadview, 2015.

Stocker, Margarita. *Judith: Sexual Warrior; Women and Power in Western Culture*. New Haven: Yale University Press, 1998.

Stone, Michael E. "The Angelic Prediction in the Primary Adam Books." Pages 111–31 in *Literature on Adam and Eve: Collected Essays*. Edited by Gary A. Anderson, Michael E. Stone, and Johannes Tromp. SVTP 15. Leiden: Brill, 2000.

———. "The Axis of History at Qumran." Pages 133–49 in *Pseudepigraphic Perspectives: The Apocrypha and Pseudepigrapha in Light of the Dead Sea Scrolls, Proceedings of the International Symposium of the Orion Center, 12–14 January 1997*. Edited by Esther G. Chazon and Michael E. Stone. STDJ 31. Leiden: Brill, 1999.

———. *A History of the Literature of Adam and Eve*. EJL 3. Atlanta: Scholars Press, 1992.

Stone, Michael E., and Matthias Henze. *4 Ezra and 2 Baruch*. Minneapolis: Fortress, 2013.

Strabo. *Buch XIV–XVII: Text und Übersetzung*. Vol. 4 of *Strabons Geographika*. Edited by Stefan L. Radt. Göttingen: Vandenhoeck & Ruprecht, 2005.

Strotmann, Angelika. "Sirach (Ecclesiasticus): On the Difficult Relation between Divine Wisdom and Real Women in an Androcentric Document." Pages 539–54 in *Feminist Biblical Interpretation: A Compendium of Critical Commentary on the Books of the Bible and Related Literature*. Edited by Luise Schottroff and Marie-Theres Wacker. Grand Rapids: Eerdmans, 2012.

Stuckenbruck, Loren T. *The Book of Giants from Qumran: Text, Translation, and Commentary*. TSAJ 63. Tübingen: Mohr Siebeck, 1997.

Suetonius. *Claudius, Nero, Galba, Otho and Vitellius; Vespasian, Titus, Domitian;*. *Lives of Illustrious Men: Grammarians and Rhetoricians; Poets (Terence. Virgil. Horace. Tibullus. Persiu. Lucan); Lives of Pliny the Elder and Passienus Crispus*. Vol. 2 of *Lives of the Caesars*. Translated by J. C. Rolfe. LCL 38. Cambridge: Harvard University Press, 1914.

Sweet, Anne Marie. "A Religio-historical Study of the *Greek Life of Adam and Eve*." PhD diss., University of Notre Dame, 1992.

Szesnat, Holger. "'Mostly Aged Virgins': Philo and the Presence of the Therapeutrides at Lake Mareotis." *Neot* 32 (1998): 191–201.

Tabor, James D., and Eugene V. Gallagher. *Why Waco? Cults and the Battle for Religious Freedom in America*. Berkeley: University of California Press, 1995.

Tacitus. *The Histories and the Annals*. Translated by Clifford H. Moore and John Jackson. 4 vols. LCL. Cambridge: Harvard University Press, 1931.

Talmon, Shemaryahu. "The Community of the Renewed Covenant: Between Judaism and Christianity." Pages 3–24 in *The Community of the Renewed Covenant: The Notre Dame Symposium on the Dead Sea Scrolls*. Edited by Eugene Ulrich and James VanderKam. CJA 10. Notre Dame: University of Notre Dame Press, 1994.

Taylor, Joan E. "The Classical Sources on the Essenes and the Scrolls Communities." Pages 173–199 in *The Oxford Handbook on the Dead Sea Scrolls*. Edited by Timothy H. Lim and John J. Collins. Oxford: Oxford University Press, 2010.

———. *The Essenes, the Scrolls and the Dead Sea*. Oxford: Oxford University Press, 2012.

———. *Jewish Women Philosophers of First-Century Alexandria: Philo's 'Therapeutae' Reconsidered*. Oxford: Oxford University Press, 2003.

———. "Women, Children, and Celibate Men in the Serekh Texts." *HTR* 104 (2011): 171–90.

Taylor, Joan E., and Davies, Philip R. "The So-Called Therapeutae of *De vita contemplativa*: Identity and Character." *HTR* 91 (1998): 3–24.

Taylor, Joan E., with David M. Hay. *Therapeutae: A Commentary on Philo of Alexandria, De vita contemplativa*. PACS Leiden: Brill, forthcoming.

Tervanotko, Hanna. "Speaking in Dreams: The Figure of Miriam and Prophecy." Pages 147–68 in *Prophets Male and Female: Gender and Prophecy in the Hebrew Bible, the Eastern Mediterranean, and the Ancient Near East*. Edited by Jonathan Stökl and Corrine L. Carvalho. AIL 15. Atlanta: Society of Biblical Literature, 2013.

———. "A Trilogy of Testaments: The Status of the Testament of Qahat versus Texts Attributed to Levi and Amram." Pages 41–59 in *The Old Testament Pseudepigrapha and the Scriptures*. Edited by Eibert J. C. Tigchelaar. BETL 270. Leuven: Peeters, 2014.

Thackeray, Henry St. J., et al., trans. *Josephus*. 10 vols. LCL. Cambridge: Harvard University Press, 1926–1965.

Thielmann, Philipp. *Beiträge zur Textkritik der Vulgata insbesondere des Buches Judit*. Beigabe zum Jahresbericht 1882/1883 der Kgl. Studienanstalt Speier. Speier: Gilardone, 1883.

Thomas, Christine M. *The Acts of Peter, Gospel Literature and the Ancient Novel: Rewriting the Past*. Oxford: Oxford University Press, 2003.

Tigchelaar, Eibert J. C. "Eden and Paradise: The Garden Motif in Some Early Jewish Texts (1 Enoch and Other Texts Found at Qumran)." Pages 37–62 in *Paradise Interpreted: Representations of Biblical Paradise in Judaism and Christianity; Papers Given at a Conference, Groningen, June 1998*. Edited by Gerard P. Luttikhuizen. TBN 2. Leiden: Brill, 1999.

———. *Prophets of Old and the Day of the End: Zechariah, the Book of Watchers and Apocalyptic*. OTS 35. Leiden: Brill, 1996.

Tiller, Patrick A. *A Commentary on the Animal Apocalypse of I Enoch*. EJL 4. Atlanta: Scholars Press, 1993.

Tinklenberg deVega, Jessica Lyn. "'A Man who Fears God': Constructions of Masculinity in Hellenistic Jewish Interpretations of the Story of Joseph." PhD, Florida State University, 2006.

Toorn, Karel van der, Bob Becking, and Pieter W. van der Horst, eds. *Dictionary of Deities and Demons in the Bible*. 2nd rev. ed. Leiden: Brill; Grand Rapids: Eerdmans, 1999.

Torrey, Charles C. *The Apocryphal Literature: A Brief Introduction*. New Haven: Yale University Press 1945.

Tragan, Pius-Ramon. *Josep i Àsenet: Introducció, text grec revisat i notes*. LISup 4. Barcelona: Ed. Alpha, 2005.

Treggiari, Susan. *Roman Marriage: Iusti Conjuges from the Time of Cicero to the Time of Ulpian*. Oxford: Clarendon, 1991.

Trenchard, Warren C. *Ben Sira's View of Women: A Literary Analysis*. BJS 8. Chico, CA: Scholars Press, 1982.

Tromp, Johannes. *The Life of Adam and Eve in Greek: A Critical Edition*. PVTG 6. Leiden: Brill, 2005.

Tull, Patricia K. "The Letter of Jeremiah." Pages 309–10 in *Women's Bible Commentary*. Edited by Carol A. Newsom and Sharon H. Ringe. Expanded ed. Louisville: Westminster John Knox, 1998.

Türck, Ulrike. "Die Stellung der Frau in Elephantine als Ergebnis persisch-babylonischen Rechtseinflusses." *ZAW* 5 (1928): 166–69.

Turdeanu, Émile. *Apocryphes slaves et roumains de l'Ancien Testament*. SVTP 5. Leiden: Brill, 1981.

Uhlig, Siegbert. *Das äthiopische Henochbuch*. JSHRZ 5.6. Gütersloh: Mohn, 1984.

Unnik, Willem C. van. "Josephus' Account of the Story of Israel's Sin with Alien Women." Pages 241–61 in *Travels in the World of the Old Testament: Studies Presented to Professor M. A. Beek*. Edited by Matthieu Sybrand Huibert Gerard Heerma van Voss, Philo Hendrik Jan Houwink ten Cate, and N. A. van Uchelen. SSN 16. Assen: Van Gorcum, 1974.

Van Henten, Jan Willem. *Judean Antiquities 15*. FJTC 7b. Leiden: Brill, 2014.

VanderKam, James C. *The Book of Jubilees*. CSCO 511. Leuven: Peeters, 1989.

———. *The Book of Jubilees*. Sheffield: Sheffield Academic, 2001.

———. *The Book of Jubilees: A Critical Text*. CSCO 510; SAeth 87. Leuven: Peeters, 1989.

———. *The Dead Sea Scrolls Today*. 2nd ed. Grand Rapids: Eerdmans, 2010.

———. *Enoch: A Man for All Generations: Studies on Personalities of the Old Testament.* Columbia: University of South Carolina Press, 1995.

Vermes, Geza. *The Complete Dead Sea Scrolls in English.* 7th ed. London: Penguin Classics, 2012.

———. "Essenes and Therapeutai." *RevQ* 3 (1962): 494–504.

Vermes, Geza, and Martin Goodman. *The Essenes according to the Classical Sources.* Sheffield: JSOT Press, 1989.

Veyne, Paul. "The Roman Empire." Pages 5–233 in *A History of Private Life.* Edited by Paul Veyne. Cambridge: Harvard University Press, 1987.

Vialle, Cathérine. *Une analyse comparée d'Esther TM et LXX: Regard sur deux récits d'une même histoire.* BETL 233. Leuven: Peeters, 2012.

Von Zesen, Philip. *Assenat: Das ist Derselben/ und des Josefs Heilige Stahts- Lieb- und Lebens-geschicht.* Amsterdam: Kristian von Hagen, 1670.

Wacker, Marie-Theres. *The Book of Baruch and the Letter of Jeremiah.* WCS 31. Collegeville, MN: Liturgical Press, 2016.

———. "'Kultprostitution' im Alten Israel? Forschungsmythen, Spuren, Thesen." Pages 55–84 in *Tempelprostitution im Altertum: Fakten und Fiktionen.* Edited by Tanja S. Scheer and Martin Lindner. Berlin: Verlag Antike e.K., 2009.

———. "Methods of Feminist Exegesis." Pages 63–82 in *Feminist Interpretation: The Bible in Women's Perspective.* Edited by Luise Schottroff, Silvia Schroer, and Marie-Theres Wacker. Translated by Martin Rumscheidt and Barbara Rumscheidt. Minneapolis: Fortress, 1998.

———. "Mit Toratreue und Todesmut dem einen Gott anhangen: Zum Esther-Bild der Septuaginta." Pages 312–32 in *Dem Tod nicht glauben: Sozialgeschichte der Bibel; Festschrift für Luise Schottroff zum 70. Gebertstag.* Edited by Frank Crüsemann, Marlene Crüsemann, Claudia Jannsen, Rainer Kessler, and Beate Wehn. Gütersloh: Gütersloher Verlagshaus, 2004.

———. "'Rettendes Wissen' im äthiopischen Henochbuch." Pages 115–54 in *Rettendes Wissen: Studien zum Fortgang weisheitlichen Denkens im Frühjudentum und im frühen Christentum.* Edited by Karl Löning and Martin Fassnacht. AOAT 300. Münster: Ugarit-Verlag, 2002.

———. "Theologie einer Mutter—Eine Mutter als Theologin: Feministisch-Exegetische Anmerkungen zu 2 Makk 7." Pages 259–70 in *Gott bin ich kein Mann: Beiträge zur Hermeneutik der biblischen Gottesrede.* Edited by Ilona Riedel-Spangenberger and Erich Zenger. Paderborn: Schöningh, 2006.

———. *Weltordnung und Gericht: Studien zu 1 Henoch 22.* FB 45. Würzburg: Echter Verlag, 1982.

Walfish, Barry Dov. "Kosher Adultery? The Mordecai-Esther-Ahasuerus Triangle in Midrash and Exegesis." *Proof* 22 (2002): 305–33.

Warren, Meredith. "A Robe Like Lightning: Clothing Changes and Identification in Joseph and Aseneth." Pages 137–54 in *Dressing Judeans and Christians in Antiquity.* Edited by Kristi Upson-Saia, Carly Daniel-Hughes, and Alicia J. Batten. Farnham, Surrey, UK: Ashgate, 2014.

Wassen, Cecilia. *Women in the Damascus Document.* AcBib 21. Atlanta: Society of Biblical Literature, 2005.

Weber, Robert, and Roger Gryson, eds. *Biblia Sacra: Iuxta Vulgatam Versionem*. Editio Quinta. Stuttgart: Deutsche Bibelgesellschaft, 2007.

Willetts, Ronald F. *The Law Code of Gortyn: Edited with Introduction, Translation and a Commentary*. Berlin: de Gruyter, 1967.

Wills, Lawrence M. "The Book of Judith: Introduction, Commentary, and Reflections." Pages 1073–1183 *in Esther, Additions to Esther, Tobit, Judith, 1 and 2 Maccabees, Wisdom of Solomon, Sirach, Introduction to Apocalyptic Literature, Daniel, Additions to D*. Edited by Leander E. Keck. NIB 3. Nashville: Abingdon, 1999.

———. "The Depiction of Slavery in the Ancient Novel." *Semeia* 83/84 (1998): 113–32.

———. *The Jewish Novel in the Ancient World*. Ithaca, NY: Cornell University Press, 1995.

———. "The Marriage and Conversion of Aseneth." Pages 121–62 in *Ancient Jewish Novels*. Oxford: Oxford University Press, 2002.

Winslow, Karen Strand. *Early Jewish and Christian Memories of Moses' Wives: Exogamic Marriage and Ethnic Identity*. Lewiston. NY: Mellen, 2005.

Winston, David. *Philo of Alexandria: The Contemplative Life, the Giants and Selections*. CWS. New York: Paulist, 1981.

Wintermute, O. S. "Jubilees." *OTP* 2:35–142.

Wold, Benjamin G. *Women, Men and Angels: The Qumran Wisdom Document Musar leMevin and Its Allusions to Genesis Creation Traditions*. WUNT 2/201. Tübingen: Mohr Siebeck, 2005.

Wright, Benjamin G. "The Epistle of Jeremiah: Translation or Composition?" Pages 126–41 in *Deuterocanonical Additions of the Old Testament Books: Selected Studies*. Edited by Géza G. Xeravits and József Zsengellér. DCLS 5. Berlin: de Gruyter, 2010.

———. "The Letter of Jeremiah." Pages 942–45 in *A New English Translation of the Septuagint and the Other Greek Translations Traditionally included under That Title*. Edited by Albert Pietersma and Benjamin G. Wright. New York: Oxford University Press, 2007.

Yoder, Christine Roy. *Wisdom as a Woman of Substance: A Socio-economic Reading of Proverbs 1–9 and 31:10–31*. BZAW 304. Berlin: de Gruyter, 2001.

Ziegler, Joseph, ed. "Epistula Ieremiae." Pages 494–504 in *Ieremias; Baruch; Threni; Epistula Ieremiae*. SVTG 15. 4th ed. Göttingen: Vandenhoeck & Ruprecht, 2013.

Zlotnick, Helena. *Dinah's Daughters: Gender and Judaism from the Hebrew Bible to Late Antiquity*. Philadelphia: University of Pennsylvania Press, 2002.

Zohar, Noam. "The Figure of Abraham and the Voice of Sarah in Genesis Rabbah" [Hebrew]. Pages 71–85 in *The Faith of Abraham in the Light of Interpretation throughout the Ages*. Edited by Moshe Hallamish, Hannah Kasher, and Yohanan Silman. Ramat Gan: Bar Ilan University Press, 2002.

Contributors

Editors

Eileen Schuller, osu, is Professor Emerita of Religious Studies at McMaster University, Hamilton, Canada, where she taught since 1990 and held the Senator William McMaster Chair in the Study of Religion. She studied at University of Alberta (BA Hon), University of Toronto (MA), and Harvard University (PhD) and has been a Lady Davis Visiting Professor at Hebrew University, Jerusalem (2013) and recipient of the Alexander von Humboldt Research Prize at Georg-August University, Göttingen (2005–2006). She has been involved with the publication of the Dead Sea Scrolls since 1980, especially manuscripts of prayers and hymns. She edited the Cave 4 Hodayot manuscripts for the Discoveries in the Judean Desert series (DJD XXIX, 1999) and, with Hartmut Stegeman, the re-edition of 1QH^{a} (DJD XL, 2009). She has written extensively on women in the Dead Sea Scrolls, including "Women in the Dead Sea Scrolls: Research in the Past Decade and Future Directions," in *The Dead Sea Scrolls and Contemporary Culture* (Brill, 2010) and "Women at Qumran," in *The Dead Sea Scrolls after Fifty Years: A Critical Assessment* (Brill, 1999). She is an editor of the forthcoming *Paulist Biblical Commentary* and currently Vice-President of the Catholic Biblical Association. She was elected to the Royal Society of Canada in 2015.

Marie-Theres Wacker, Dr. theol. University of Tübingen (1982); Habilitation at Muenster University (1994); Professor of Biblical Studies at Cologne University (1996-1998); since 1998 Professor of Old Testament and Women's/Gender Studies at the Faculty for Catholic Theology, University of Muenster/Germany. She was Visiting Professor in the theological study program at Dormition Abbey, Jerusalem (2001; 2004; 2010), Directeur d'Études invité at the École Pratique des Hautes Études, Paris (spring 2014). Her research fields include biblical prophecy, literature of Hellenistic Judaism, feminist and gender hermeneutics in exegesis and Christian theology, and interreligious dialogue among the monotheistic religions. Her publications include, besides numerous articles on feminist biblical issues, her Habilitationsschrift *Figurationen des Weiblichen im Hosea-Buch* (Herder, 1996); a collection of essays on biblical monotheism and feminist perspectives, *Von Göttinnen, Göttern und dem einzigen Gott* (LIT, 2004); and an eight hundred page, one-volume feminist commentary on the Bible and related literature, coedited with Luise Schottroff, *Kompendium feministische Bibelauslegung* (Gütersloh, 2007), English translation: *Feminist Interpretation: A Compendium* (Eerdmans, 2012). Together with Kristin de Troyer she translated and commented upon the Greek Books of Esther (LXX and Alpha-Text) for the project "Septuaginta deutsch" edited by W. Karrer and W. Kraus (Deutsche Bibelgesellschaft, 2008 and 2011). She is currently working on a commentary on the book of Esther together with Veronika Bachmann for the Herders Theologischer Kommentar Altes Testament series. Her feminist commentary on the book of Baruch and the Letter of Jeremiah appeared in the series "Wisdom Commentaries" (Liturgical Press, 2016).

Contributors

Sonja Ammann is Assistant Professor of Old Testament at the University of Basel (Switzerland). She studied Theology in Lausanne, Buenos Aires, and Heidelberg and received her doctorate in Hebrew Bible Studies at Georg-August-Universität Göttingen. In her dissertation, *Götter für die Toren: Die Verbindung von Götterpolemik und Weisheit im Alten Testament*/"Gods for the Fools: Old Testament Polemics against Heathen Gods and the Wisdom Tradition" (de Gruyter, 2015), she examined polemics against other gods and their worshippers in the Hebrew Bible and the Septuagint. Her current research focuses on historical narratives and constructions of biblical history.

Magdalena Díaz Araujo is Professor of Judaism and Early Christianity at the National University of La Rioja (Argentine), and Professor of Art History at the National University of Cuyo (Argentine). She has been a Visiting Professor at the École Pratique des Hautes Études (2011, 2012, 2014), at Regensburg Universität (2015), and at the Methodist University of Sao Paulo (2016). Her research fields are Second Temple Judaism and early Christianity, Apocrypha and Pseudepigrapha, and gender studies. She obtained her PhD in History of Religions and Religious Anthropology (2012) at the Paris IV-Sorbonne University, with the dissertation "La représentation de la femme et l'invention de la notion du 'péché de la chair' d'après la *Vie grecque d'Adam et Ève*." She is the author of various articles and reviews in international journals and volumes of collected works. Recently, she has published "The Satan's Disguise: The Exoneration of Eve in the *Greek Life of Adam and Eve* 17, 1–2," in *Judaïsme Ancien / Ancient Judaism* 3 (Brepols, forthcoming).

Veronika Bachmann is Lecturer in Old Testament Studies and Bible Didactics at the Religionspädagogische Institut (RPI) at University of Lucerne, Switzerland. She received her doctoral degree from University of Zurich in 2009, and her master degree in Theology, Biblical Studies, and Philosophy from University of Fribourg in 2003. Her research and teaching areas include Old Testament writings in their ancient Near Eastern contexts, iconography, early Jewish literature, contextual readings of biblical texts, as well as gender and religion. She is the author of the book *Die Welt im Ausnahmezustand: Eine Untersuchung zu Aussagegehalt und Theologie des Wächterbuches (1 Hen 1–36)* (de Gruyter, 2009). Among the articles she authored are "More than the Present: Perspectives on World History in 4 Ezra and the Book of the Watchers," in *Interpreting 4 Ezra and 2 Baruch* (Bloomsbury, 2014); "The Early Jewish Origins of Apocalyptic," in *Concilium* 3 (2014); and "The Esther Narratives as Reminders—For Jews and for Christians," in *European Judaism* 47 (2014). She is currently working, together with Marie-Theres Wacker, on an exegetical commentary on the Hebrew and Septuagint version of the book of Esther for the Herders Theologischer Kommentar Altes Testament series.

Maxine L. Grossman is an Associate Professor in the Joseph and Rebecca Meyerhoff Center for Jewish Studies at the University of Maryland, where she also serves as advisor to the undergraduate minor in religious studies. She is a founding coeditor of the *Journal of Ancient Judaism*. Grossman's research interests include the study of ancient Judaism and the Dead Sea Scrolls; methods and theories in the study of religion; gender studies; and conceptions of lived religious experience in contemporary society. Her books include *Reading for History in the Damascus Document: A Methodological Study* (Brill, 2002), and the edited collection, *Rediscovering the Dead Sea Scrolls: An Assessment of Old and New Approaches and Methods* (Eerdmans, 2010). An ongoing scholarly project on the Dead Sea Scrolls in light of gender, embodiment, and postmodern thought has resulted in such articles as "Rethinking Gender in the Community Rule: An Experiment in Sociology," in *The Dead Sea Scrolls and Contemporary Culture* (Brill, 2011); "How Do the Dead Sea Scrolls Help Us to Think about Gender in Ancient Judaism?," in *A Most Reliable Witness: Essays in Honor of Ross Shepard Kraemer* (Brown Judaic Studies, 2015); "Is Ancient Jewish Studies (Still) Postmodern (Yet)?," *Currents in Biblical Research* 13.2

(2015); and "Queerly Sectarian: Jewish Difference in the Dead Sea Scrolls through the Lens of Marital Disciplines," forthcoming in *Journal of Jewish Identities*.

Tal Ilan is Professor of Jewish Studies at the Freie Universität Berlin. She is Israeli born and studied at the Hebrew University Jerusalem where she also received her PhD. She is the author of the four volume *A Lexicon of Jewish Names in Late Antiquity* (Mohr Siebeck, 2002–2012) and current editor of the Feminist Commentary on the Babylonian Talmud (Mohr Siebeck), seven volumes of which have appeared to date. She is currently involved in coediting the updated *Corpus Papyrorum Judaicarum* (Magnes Press, Hebrew University), which collects all the Jewish papyri from Egypt. Tal Ilan is the author of numerous books and articles on Jewish women: *Jewish Women in Greco-Roman Palestine: An Inquiry into Image and Status* (Mohr Siebeck, 1995); *Mine and Yours Are Hers: Retrieving Women's History from Rabbinic Literature* (Brill, 1997); *Integrating Jewish Women into Second Temple History* (Mohr Siebeck, 1999); and *Silencing the Queen: The Literary Histories of Shelamzion and Other Jewish Women* (Mohr Siebeck, 2006). In 2008 she published a feminist commentary on Tractate Ta'anit, and in 2017 her commentary on Tractate Hullin will appear.

Lydia [Hilt] Lange is research associate of Old Testament Studies and Biblical-Oriental Languages at the Faculty of Catholic Theology of the University of Würzburg, where she also received her doctoral degree in theology. Her main areas of research are the book of Judith, narratology, and Septuagint and Vulgate. Her publications include: *Die Juditfigur in der Vulgata: Eine theologische Studie zur lateinischen Bibel* (de Gruyter, 2016); "Die Rezeption des Exodusbuchs in der LXX- und Vg-Fassung der Juditerzählung. Ein Vergleich," in *Exodus: Rezeptionen in deuterokanonischer und frühjüdischer Literatur* (de Gruyter, 2016); "Dominus contulit splendorem (Idt 10,4): Das Motiv der Schönheit im Buch Iudith," in *Kongessakten vom 14. bis 17. November 2013 in Bukarest*, vol. 1 of *Vulgata Studies* (Lang, 2014).

Maren R. Niehoff holds the Max Cooper Chair in Jewish Thought at the Hebrew University and is presently the head of the AMIRIM interdisciplinary honors program in the Humanities. Her research focuses on encounters between Jews, pagans, and Christians in antiquity, with special emphasis on Philo of Alexandria and the rabbinic midrash Genesis Rabbah. Her publications include *Philo of Alexandria: An Intellectual Biography* (Yale University Press, 2017, German and Hebrew translations forthcoming); *Jewish Exegesis* *and Homeric Scholarship in Alexandria* (Cambridge University Press, 2011, awarded the Polonsky Prize in Creativity and Originality in the Humanities 2011); "Mother and Maiden, Sister and Spouse: Sarah in Philonic Midrash," *Harvard Theological Review* 97 (2004); "Jewish Identity and Jewish Mothers: Who Was a Jew according to Philo?," *Studia Philonica Annual* 11 (1999). She also edited the volumes: *Homer and the Bible in the Eyes of Ancient Interpreters* (Brill, 2012) and *Journeys in the Roman East: Imagined and Real* (Mohr Siebeck, 2017).

Adele Reinhartz, PhD (McMaster University, 1983), is Professor in the Department of Classics and Religious Studies at the University of Ottawa, in Canada. She is currently the general editor of the *Journal of Biblical Literature*. Her main areas of research are New Testament, early Jewish-Christian relations, and the Bible and film. She is the author of numerous articles and books, including *Befriending the Beloved Disciple: A Jewish Reading of the Gospel of John* (Continuum, 2001), *Scripture on the Silver Screen* (Westminster John Knox, 2003), *Jesus of Hollywood* (Oxford, 2007), *Caiaphas the High Priest* (University of South Carolina Press, 2011; Fortress, 2012), and *Bible and Cinema: An Introduction* (Routledge, 2013). She was elected to the Royal Society of Canada in 2005 and to the American Academy of Jewish Research in 2014.

Barbara Schmitz holds a theological doctorate from Münster University with a dissertation on the book of Judith and wrote her Habilitationsschrift on narratology in the book of Kings. She holds the Chair of Old Testament and Biblical-Oriental Languages at the Catholic Theological Faculty of Julius-Maximilian University, Würzburg. Her main research areas are in Jewish literature in the Hellenistic-Roman Period, Septuagint studies, and narrative literature of the Old Testament. Her most recent publications include: a commentary on the book of Judith (with Helmut Engel; Herder, 2014); *Geschichte Israels* (Paderborn, 2011, 2014); *Exodus: Rezeptionen in deuterokanonischer und frühjüdischer Literatur* (coedited with Judith Gärtner; de Gruyter, 2016); "Judith and Holofernes: An Analysis of the Emotions in the Killing Scene (Jdt 12:10–13:9)," in *Ancient Jewish Prayers and Emotion* (de Gruyter, 2014).

Angela Standhartinger studied Protestant Theology at Frankfurt am Main, Munich, and Heidelberg and finished her dissertation and habiliation in Frankfurt am Main. She is an ordained Pastor of the Protestant Church of Hessen and Nassau and was a visiting scholar at Union Theological Seminary in New York in 2000. Since 2000 she is Professor for New Testament

Studies at the Philipps-University Marburg, Germany. Her research centers on Pauline letters, the social history of meals and the origin of the Eucharist, Hellenistic Jewish literature, and feminist theology. Recently she published "Recent Scholarship on Joseph and Aseneth (1988–2013)," *Currents in Biblical Research* 12:3 (2014); "Philo im ethnografischen Diskurs: Beobachtungen zum literarischen Kontext von *De Vita Contemplativa*," *Journal for the Study of Judaism* 46 (2015); "Words to Remember—Women and the Origin of the "Words of Institution," *Lectio Difficilior* 1 (2015); and coedited *Doing Gender—Doing Religion: Fallstudien zur Intersektionalität im frühen Judentum, Christentum und Islam* (Mohr Siebeck, 2013) and *Geschlechtergerechtigkeit. Herausforderung der Religionen* (EB-Verl., 2014).

Joan E. Taylor is Professor of Christian Origins and Second Temple Judaism at King's College London. She publishes in the fields of biblical studies, Second Temple Judaism, and early Christianity, with a special focus on women and gender, history, archaeology, and context. In 1995 she won an Irene Levi-Sala Award in Israel's archaeology for the book version of her PhD thesis, *Christians and the Holy Places* (Clarendon, 1993, rev. 2003). In 1996–1997 she was Visiting Lecturer and Research Associate in Women's Studies in New Testament at Harvard Divinity School, a position she held in association with a Fulbright Award. Among other works, she is author of *Jewish Women Philosophers of First-Century Alexandria: Philo's 'Therapeutae' Reconsidered* (Oxford University Press, 2003; paperback edition 2006), a detailed historical analysis of Philo's *De Vita Contemplativa* with a special focus on women and gender. She is also author (with David Hay) of a forthcoming commentary on Philo's *De Vita Contemplativa* (Brill).

Hanna Tervanotko, Th.D., Ph.D. (University of Helsinki and Universität Wien, 2013), is an Academy of Finland funded postdoctoral researcher. She works at the Centre of Excellence "Changes in Sacred Texts and Traditions" at the University of Helsinki and at KU Leuven. She is interested in the portrayal of female figures in ancient Jewish texts. She has published a monograph *Denying Her Voice: The Figure of Miriam in Ancient Jewish Literature* (Vandenhoeck & Ruprecht, 2016) and various articles including "Members of Levite Family and Ideal Marriages in Aramaic Levi Document, Visions of Amram and Jubilees," *Revue de Qumran* 27.2 (2015) and "Unreliability and Gender? Untrusted Female Prophets in Ancient Greek and Jewish Texts," *Journal of Ancient Judaism* (2016).

Index of Ancient Sources

2. Deuterocanonical Works

3. Pseudepigrapha

4. Dead Sea Scrolls

5. New Testament

7. Ancient Greek and Latin Sources

9. Rabbinic and Medieval Jewish Sources

www.ingramcontent.com/pod-product-compliance
Lightning Source LLC
Chambersburg PA
CBHW020608300426
44113CB00007B/558

* 9 7 8 1 6 2 8 3 7 1 8 3 3 *